CORNELL STUDIES IN CIVIL LIBERTY

# Fundamental Liberties of a Free People:

## Religion, Speech, Press, Assembly

BOOKS BY MILTON R. KONVITZ

*On the Nature of Value*
*The Alien and the Asiatic in American Law*
*The Constitution and Civil Rights*
*Civil Rights in Immigration*
*Fundamental Liberties of a Free People*

EDITOR OF

*Freedom and Experience*
(with Sidney Hook)
*Essays in Political Theory*
(with Arthur E. Murphy)
*Law and Social Action*
by Alexander H. Pekelis
*Education for Freedom and Responsibility*
by Edmund Ezra Day
*Bill of Rights Reader: Leading Constitutional Cases*

# Fundamental Liberties of a Free People:

## Religion, Speech, Press, Assembly

## By Milton R. Konvitz

> "The God who gave us life gave us liberty at the same time; the hand of force may destroy but cannot disjoin them."—JEFFERSON

## Cornell University Press

*Ithaca, New York*

CORNELL UNIVERSITY PRESS

*First published 1957*
*Second printing 1962*
*Third printing 1963*

PRINTED IN THE UNITED STATES OF AMERICA

# For Mary

By all means they try to hold me secure
who love me in this world.

But it is otherwise with thy love
which is greater than theirs,
and thou keepest me free.—TAGORE

☆☆☆☆☆

# Preface

CHIEF Justice Warren has said that "each of the 462 words of our Bill of Rights, the most precious part of our legal heritage, will be tested and retested" in the years ahead. Of our Bill of Rights, the forty-five words that comprise the First Amendment are, I think, the most precious of all—certainly they are if one would give equal dignity to the guaranty of the writ of habeas corpus as formulated in Article I of the Constitution. Taken together, the guaranties of the First Amendment freedoms of religion, speech, press, and assembly and the guaranty of the writ of habeas corpus are the bedrock of American freedom.

The First Amendment freedoms have been tested and re-tested so many times that only the specialist can dare to think that he knows the meaning of the forty-five simple yet heavily weighted words; and the specialist, knowing the complexity of the subject, is precisely the one who would hesitate to admit, even to himself, that he possesses firm knowledge. The only contribution he can make, he would say with Virginia Woolf, is a "little pitter-patter of ideas" as his "whiff of shot in the cause of freedom."

But the cause of freedom can be served by scholarship as well as by a "little pitter-patter of ideas"; and in this book the reader will find, I trust, both. The book does not pretend, how-ever, to an exhaustive scholarship. At the end, for the readers who will want them, there are hundreds of notes with numerous references; yet the book is a critical rather than a technical work. What the reader needs today is consolidation and structuring of thought and knowledge—"the figure in the carpet"—rather than a spread of detailed, heavy learning. I am sure, as was Justice Jackson, that "any court which undertakes by its legal processes to enforce civil liberties needs the support of an enlightened and vigorous public opinion which will be intelligent and discriminating as to what cases really are civil liberties cases and what questions really are involved in those cases." And I would add, with Justice Jackson, "I do not think the American public is enlightened on this subject."

Writing to Sir Frederick Pollock in 1919, Justice Holmes complained: "I have had to deal with cases that made my blood boil and yet seemed to create no feeling in the public." The situation has not changed perceptibly. I hasten to add, however, that no words have been written in this book in order to get anyone's blood to boil. I would like to believe that in my writing I was guided by the wisdom of Lord Morley. "Our opinions," he said, "are less important than the spirit and temper with which they possess us, and even good opinions are worth very little unless we hold them in a broad, intelligent, and spacious way."

Yet I would be less than realistic if I pretended to a Jovian distance from the questions that I have undertaken to discuss. The book has been written out of a deep, lifelong concern with civil liberties problems—which to me means, at the same time, a deep, lifelong concern with America. And all that America asks, Sherwood Anderson once told William Faulkner—and I tell the reader—is "to look at it and listen to it and understand it if you can. Only the understanding ain't important either: the important thing is to believe in it even if you don't understand it, and then try to tell it, put it down. It won't ever be quite right, but there's always next time; there's always more ink and paper."

This book was made possible by fellowships granted by the John Simon Guggenheim Foundation and the Fund for the

Republic. It represents, however, the independent work of the author, who is alone responsible for it.

M. R. K.

*Cornell University*
*April 18, 1957*

# Acknowledgments

THE author thanks the following publishers and publications for granting permission to quote from the books and articles listed: Vanguard Press, *Puritanism and Democracy* by Ralph Barton Perry; *Harper's Magazine,* "On Privacy" by William Faulkner; Beacon Press, *McCarthy and the Communists* by James Rorty and Moshe Decter; *Phylon,* "Group Libel and Free Speech" by Joseph Tanenhaus; and *Christianity and Crisis,* "Democracy, Secularism, and Christianity" by Reinhold Niebuhr.

☆☆☆☆☆

# Contents

## *Part III:  Freedom of Speech, Press, and Assembly: The Clear and Present Danger Doctrine*

# Amendment I to the
# Constitution of the United States

Congress shall make no law respecting an establishment of religion, or prohibiting the free exercise thereof; or abridging the freedom of speech, or of the press; or the right of the people peaceably to assemble, and to petition the Government for a redress of grievances.

# Amendment XIV to the
# Constitution of the United States

*Section* 1. . . . No State shall make or enforce any law which shall abridge the privileges or immunities of citizens of the United States; nor shall any State deprive any person of life, liberty, or property, without due process of law; nor deny to any person within its jurisdiction the equal protection of the laws.

# PART I

# Freedom of Religion

# The Roots and the Flower

WHEN the Bolsheviks succeeded in their *coup d'etat* in October 1917, religious freedom became a matter of universal concern, for the Union of Soviet Socialist Republics became the first state in history that made the extermination of all religions an essential part of its program of domestic and international revolution. When the Nazis came into power in 1933, and it became apparent that they were bent on world conquest and on the displacement of all religions with racist ideology and a new pagan cult, concern with religious freedom was felt widely and intensely. In the course of World War II, President Roosevelt found it necessary to proclaim religious freedom as one of the Four Freedoms. We look forward, he said, to a world founded upon four essential human freedoms, among them the "freedom of every person to worship God in his own way—everywhere in the world." As soon as the war was over, however, the U.S.S.R. began to extend its frontiers and to put one country after another behind the Iron Curtain. With every step thus taken by the Communists, religious freedom—and the other essential freedoms as well—suffered a crushing blow. The result was that in the middle of the twentieth century there was less religious freedom in the world than there had been at the beginning of the century. Competent surveys of religious freedom have shown that the "freedom of every person to worship God in his own way" exists in only relatively few places in the world; that there is less religious freedom in the world today than there was in 1941 when Roosevelt delivered his Four Freedoms address.[1]

At the same time, however, the nations of the world have shown an unprecedented readiness to avow a belief in and commitment to religious freedom. This belief and commitment have been expressed in Article 18 of the Universal Declaration of Human Rights, adopted by the General Assembly of the United Nations, as follows:

Everyone has the right to freedom of thought, conscience and religion; that right includes freedom to change his religion and belief, and freedom, either alone or in community with others, and in public or private, to manifest his religion or belief in teaching, practice, worship and observance.[2]

Especially in the United States, where religious freedom signifies more than the definition used by the United Nations and where it is enjoyed in fuller measure than elsewhere in the world, one senses a profound concern over threats to this freedom and an intensified desire to extend and deepen its meaning at home and abroad. Religious freedom has thus become one of the great issues of the twentieth century in the United States and in the world at large.

Which freedom is today considered the most indispensable, the most basic: Is it freedom of religion, or is it freedom of speech and press? It is difficult, and perhaps impossible, to answer this question. With the Nazi and Communist experiences before us, we might say that there have been more eager martyrs for the cause of religious freedom than for freedom of speech and press; that while political freedom (which is dependent upon freedom of speech and press) hath slain its thousands, religious freedom hath slain its ten thousands. Yet this judgment may be due to the fact that religious martyrdom has been more effectively dramatized, and the truth may be that more persons invited the fate of the concentration or slave-labor camps for political than for religious conviction. In any case, today we see that these freedoms stand in intimate relation one with the other, that freedom of conscience and religion implies freedom of thought and freedom of teaching, and that freedom of speech and press is indispensable to religious beliefs which may be laden with unpopular judgments about the conduct of political and economic affairs in the city of man. It is not possible to draw the line between the political and religious freedoms when a minister in the Union of South Africa or South Carolina preaches to his congregation that the Christian conscience must reject all notions of racial inequality, or when a devout Roman Catholic in France or Mexico makes an anticlerical speech, or when an orthodox Jew in Israel writes an article demanding that all business, work, and entertainment be legally prohibited on the Sabbath, or when a Moslem in Saudi Arabia seeks to ban polygamy. If religion is to be free, politics must also be free: the free conscience needs freedom to think, freedom to teach, freedom to preach—freedom of speech and press. Where freedom of religion is denied or seriously restricted, the denial or restriction can be accomplished—as in the U.S.S.R., Yugoslavia, or Spain—by limits or prohibitions on freedom to teach, freedom to preach—by restrictions on freedom of speech and press. Political and religious totalitarianism are two sides of the same coin; neither can be accomplished without the other.[3]

The primacy or even the importance, of religious freedom was not always recognized. Far from being the earliest liberty, "religious liberty was the slowest liberty to develop and flourish." [4] Religious freedom, Luigi Luzzatti has said, "which ought to be first in time, as it is first in importance, generally appears last." [5] Religious freedom is, he said, "the most difficult and slowest of liberties to root itself in private life and in the life of the state, and while it ought to be the very basis of a civil community, generally succeeds in being only its crowning feature." It has been pointed out that in English history Magna Carta, the Petition of Right, the Bill of Rights, and the growth of law and Parliament all came before the achievement of religious freedom.

The United States, itself a latecomer in the history of civilization, seems to be an exception to the rule. Early settlement of the country was in large part due to the search for a haven by persons whose religious beliefs and practices had exposed them to disabilities, or even persecution, in their native lands. Most of these settlers came here with no conviction that it was their duty to found colonies where men of diverse religious beliefs would be free to live in safety and honor; they sought only to establish homogeneous communities, for persons of their own religious persuasion, all of them members of the same congregation. But to these men life offered no greater boon than the freedom to worship God according to the dictates of their own conscience. What they wanted and demanded for themselves, they in time were forced to recognize as a proper value for others. Religious persecution gave way to religious exclusion; exclusion gave way to reluctant toleration; toleration gave way to religious freedom; religious freedom developed into separation of church and state. To this process many forces made their contribution; but at the heart of the process was the conviction that the *summum bonum* in the life of man is the worship of God in conformance with one's own—and only one's own— beliefs, and that even martyrdom may be a more welcome fate than God's judgment of condemnation for disloyalty: though men slay him, yet will he trust in God and argue His ways before them, even as he argued them before God.

This irrepressible need of the American to enjoy the freedom —"in community with others"—"to manifest his religion or belief in teaching, practice, worship and observance," in time compelled, with the co-operation of other irrepressible needs, a reconstruction of all other conditions of private thought and public life to make democracy, with civil liberties as its basis and flower, a living reality. Religious freedom is thus not only the crowning feature but is also the basis of American society. This is even more true today than it was over one hundred and fifty years ago, when the First Amendment—which speaks of freedom of religion, speech, press, and assembly, all in one breath—was adopted.

Religious freedom became rooted in American thought and society, not out of indifference to religion, but precisely for the very opposite reason, out of deference for religion. Matters of conscience were so important that it was considered intolerable to delegate to others the power to dictate with respect to them. To have religion supported by force meant to put expediency in the place of conviction, and pretense in the place of sincerity; it meant the subordination of life's supreme and most sublime value to considerations that were ephemeral and petty. With the passage of time this came to mean that the state had no business to intervene in the relations between man and God, even if the motive for the intervention was to give aid and comfort to the man in those relations; for intervention, even when seemingly friendly, was seen as an impediment, as a compromising of spiritual wholeness and purity. The roots of religious freedom are to be found, therefore, in a soil that was congenial to *both freedom and religion*. Just as the founders of modern science—e.g., Descartes, Boyle, and Newton—were theists who saw no conflict between religion and science, so the founders of our country were religious men who were interested as much in freedom as in religion.[6]

And this is equally true of the American people in the twentieth century. It is doubtful if religion is in a stronger position in Italy, where Roman Catholicism is the state religion, or in England, where the Anglican Church is the established church, than it is in the United States.[7]

When De Tocqueville visited the United States in 1831, he noted that "there is no country in the whole world in which the Christian religion retains a greater influence over the souls of men than in America." The religious aspect of the country was the first thing that struck his attention. He noted especially the intimate relation that existed between freedom and religion, for while religion, he said, does not impart a taste for freedom, "it facilitates the use of free institutions." In France he had always seen "the spirit of religion and the spirit of freedom pursuing courses diametrically opposed to each other; but in America," he wrote, "I found that they were intimately united, and that they reigned in common over the same country."[8] Fifty years later, Lord Bryce noted the same phenomenon. "So far from thinking their commonwealth godless," he said, "the Americans conceive that the religious character of a government consists in nothing but the religious belief of the individual citizens, and the conformity of their conduct to that belief." The influence of Christianity seems to be, he noted, "greater and more widespread in the United States than in any part of western Continental Europe, and I think greater than in England." [9]

While there are many difficulties in an attempt to arrive at accurate statistics relating to religious affiliation, careful students of the subject have asserted that a far larger proportion of the American people are today church members than was the case in the colonial period or in any other period in the history of the American people. While in the middle of the twentieth century one out of every two Americans had a religious affiliation, in colonial New England only one out of every eight persons was identified with a church.[10] It is not to be inferred, however, that the church *as an institution* is in a stronger, more influential position today than it was several hundred years ago; on the contrary, it is perhaps the fact that while at that time the church existed at the center of society, today it exists only at the periphery. This phenomenon can be seen also in related spheres: literacy, too, has spread, yet the influence of scholarship and learning has probably diminished.[11]

No church leader in the United States today questions the wisdom of religious freedom. "We are not asking for general public support of religious schools," Cardinal Spellman wrote in his famous statement released after his visit with Mrs. Franklin D. Roosevelt. The Roman Catholic Church, he said, asked only for the payment of "auxiliary services," involving incidental benefits to parochial school children.[12] So, too, while Protestant and Jewish leaders maintain that there may be a place for religion in the public school—not sectarian teaching, or the teaching of a "common core" of religious doctrines,—that while it may be possible to show the role of religion in our culture without denominational indoctrination, and to discuss religious motivations and influences in courses in literature, history and other subjects without teaching religion as such, they do not question the wisdom of religious freedom or of the separation of church and state.[13] What each group seeks in its own fashion and with its own tools is the accommodation of religious freedom to society in such a way that the influence of religion will tend to move from the periphery to the center of the person's interests and motivation. The Roman Catholic Church holds that it can achieve this result through its own educational institutions, from primary school through college and professional school, and is asking for federal aid for auxiliary services, while Protestant and Jewish leaders, committed to the public school and the state university, seek to develop in these institutions a positive and creatively friendly atmosphere for religion without establishing any direct connection between sectarian or dogmatic beliefs and the person's religious interests and motivation. There is no more reason to doubt the commitment of these religious spokesmen to the basic character of religious freedom than to doubt the religious beliefs of the founders of the Constitution. Several hundred years ago our fathers, seeking religious freedom, put the emphasis where they thought it belonged—i.e., on freedom. Today Americans are not seeking religious freedom—we have it, and enjoy it in fuller measure than any other people in the world; so the emphasis is—on religion. Religious leaders want the church to meet the challenge of hatred, injustice, and war; and they want the American people to live in a moral and spiritual atmosphere which will give them the wisdom and the will not to be satisfied with mere bigness but to seek greatness. The disagreements are over means, not over ends; over the incidents of religious freedom, not over religious freedom itself. The debate necessarily reflects contemporary moral and social conditions.

☆ 2 ☆

# What Is a Church?

WHAT accounts for the fact that religious freedom has become so deeply rooted in the United States and in the character of the American people? We are concerned here with an extremely complex phenomenon. It is not possible to formulate the causes of religious freedom with test-tube exactness; all we can do is indicate in broad strokes certain lines of thought and some events that probably have made their contribution.

Inherent in the position of the Pilgrims who came to Plymouth was separation from the Church of England. Their consciously achieved religious independence implied in the thinking of some of their leaders a recognition that religious diversity is inevitable and that toleration of religious differences is as wise as it is necessary.

As an example of this line of thought we might consider John Robinson. He led the congregation of Separatists who left England and settled in Holland. He intended to join the Pilgrims who went to Plymouth, but died before he could accomplish this purpose. As members of his congregation were getting ready to leave on the "Mayflower," he addressed them in the following memorable words:

Brethren, we are now quickly to part from one another, and whether I may ever live to see your faces on earth any more, the God of heaven only knows; but whether the Lord has appointed that or no, I charge you before God and his blessed angels that you follow me no farther than you have seen me follow the Lord Jesus Christ. If God reveal anything to you by any other instrument of his, be as ready to receive it as ever you were to receive any truth by my ministry: for I am verily persuaded, the Lord has more truth yet to break forth out of his holy word. For my part I cannot sufficiently bewail the condition of the reformed churches, who have come to a period in religion and will go at present no farther than the instruments of their reformation. The Lutherans cannot be drawn to go beyond what Luther saw: whatever part of his will our God has revealed to Calvin, they will die rather than embrace it: and the Calvinists, you see, stick fast where they were left by that great man of God, who yet saw not all things. This is a misery much to be lamented, for though they were burning and shining lights in their times, yet they penetrated not into the whole counsel of God; but were they now living would be as willing to embrace further light as that which they first received. I beseech you to remember it as an article of your church-covenant that you be ready to receive whatever truth shall be made known to you from the written word of God. . . . For it is not possible the Christian world should come so lately out of such thick anti-Christian darkness and that perfection of knowledge should break forth at once.[1]

In this message, full of dignity, Robinson pleads for humbleness in the maintenance of one's religious beliefs. In the first place, he says, only the word of God is important. Luther, or Calvin, or he himself is important only insofar as he serves as a vehicle to make clear to himself and to others what the word of God is, but no further; and God has not said that in the future there will not appear others who will serve as transmitters and interpreters of His word. One must, therefore, ever be a ready student and a sensitive listener; revelation has not ceased for all time, and reformation is an ever present activity and creativity;[2] there is always further light than that which has already been received: "the Lord has more truth yet to break forth out of his holy word."

This approach implies the inevitability of religious diversity. The truth is never completely possessed by any one person—at least, no one can be certain of such possession. Men will see the will of God from many angles of vision. It would be different, of course, if one were to believe that there was a single, divinely ordained authority to interpret and teach the word of God; but this was not the Protestant view. The result, in time, was a proliferation of Protestant denominations in the United States. Americans who do not belong to one of the 325,856 churches of which there is a record,[3] belong, as did Bronson Alcott, to the Church of One Member.

If religion is to be kept pure, argued John Robinson, the state must not invade the realm of faith with establishments and coercive measures; the government has "no power against the laws, doctrine, and religion of Christ." When it comes to religion, good purposes do not justify coercive measures; on the contrary, coercion tends to drive men to atheism or other dangerous extremes.

As no one ought to be coerced into a church, men ought to be left free to form their own churches on a purely voluntary basis. "This we hold and affirm," wrote Robinson in his *Justification of Separation from the Church of England,* published in 1610,

that a company, consisting but of two or three, separated from the world . . . and gathered into the name of Christ by a covenant made to walk in all the ways of God known unto them, is a church, and so hath the whole power of Christ. . . . A company of faithful people thus covenanting together are a church, though they be without any officers among them. . . . This company being a church hath interest in all the holy things of Christ, within and amongst themselves, immediately under him [Christ] the head, without any foreign aid, and assistance.[4]

The consequences of this position were obvious to Robinson and his adherents, and became obvious to many others in the course of time: If a meeting of two or three men in the name of God and for the purpose of serving Him in accordance with their "covenant" is a congregation, a church, then there may be no official body of doctrine or rites prescribed for all churches, and one church can have no authority over another church. This meant necessarily a multiplicity of independent churches, just as the belief in perpetual reform meant necessarily a multiplicity of faiths. A multiplicity of faiths and of independent churches makes impossible the existence of an official faith and church, supported by the coercive arm of the state and enjoying power to define what is orthodox and to punish what the church authorities find to be heresy.[5]

Thus toleration of diversity displaces conformity as a cohesive principle in the community of faiths. Men should seek toleration, said Robinson, not only when they feel themselves threatened by a powerful competition; they should seek a *principled toleration*, issuing from strength instead of weakness, from conviction instead of expediency. Unfortunately, Robinson noted,

men are for the most part minded for, or against toleration of diversity of religions, according to the conformity which they themselves hold, or hold not with the country, or kingdom, where they live. Protestants living in the countries of papists commonly plead for toleration of religions: so do papists that live where Protestants bear sway: though few of either, specially of the clergy, . . . would have the other tolerated, where the world goes on their side.[6]

Such unprincipled toleration is worthy only of contempt; for the true basis of toleration is the belief that "neither God is pleased with unwilling worshippers, nor Christian societies bettered, nor the persons themselves neither," [7] for faith can be found only in a man's conscience and heart, and the key to the conscience and heart is in God's possession—not in St. Peter or his successors, not in an established church, not in any government, but in God's hand alone.

It may well be that John Robinson and other Separatists had no vision of a policy of toleration that would be all-embracing, extended to protect Jews and Roman Catholics, no less than Protestant dissenters from the Anglican Church.[8] John Locke excluded from the policy of toleration Roman Catholics [9] and atheists. Gradually, however, the logic of the argument for the principle of toleration swept aside the exceptions, exclusions, and qualifications, and Americans came to agree with Locke that "the toleration of those that differ from others in matters of religion, is so agreeable to the gospel of Jesus Christ, and to the genuine reason of mankind, that it seems monstrous for men to be so blind, as not to perceive the necessity and advantage of it, in so clear a light." [10]

The views of John Robinson were maintained in the colonies and in the early days of the Republic by Roger Williams, John Clarke, William Penn, Lord Baltimore, Benjamin Franklin, Thomas Paine, Thomas Jefferson, George Mason, and James Madison. The differences among them were differences only in detail or in emphasis; they were variations on a theme. These persons, by their thought, speech, and deeds, taught Americans, step by step, the logic of the argument for toleration, for religious freedom, for separation of church and state, so that in the end

the rejection of theocracy and the separation of church and state in the seventeenth and eighteenth centuries marked the triumph of three ideas: the idea of the autonomy of religion as having both the right and the need to live its own life in the faith and worship of its adherents; the idea of the neutral secular state—the protector of all religions, but the partisan of none; the idea that liberality of outlook and temper is not a mere limitation forced upon all religions by the exigencies of civil order, but an excellence intrinsic to religion itself. [11]

There surely were other forces that influenced the development of religious freedom in the United States. Americans applied to themselves the argument that Leonard Busher in 1614 had addressed to Englishmen; namely, that persecution is bad for trade and commerce. Driving men out of a country impoverishes the country. If toleration were established, said Busher, "great benefit and commodity will redound . . . by the great commerce in trade and traffic, both of Jews and all people which now, for want of liberty of conscience, are forced and driven elsewhere." [12]

In the final reckoning, Puritanism should be put among the forces that contributed to the establishment of religious freedom. Its antidemocratic character cannot be overlooked: Its spirit was authoritarian and unduly rough and rigorous; it frowned upon spontaneity; it sought to confine the human spirit, with its impulses and its hunger for joy and laughter, in a system of rigid legalism; it was theocratic and aristocratic, emphasizing privilege and duty; it was intolerant and misanthropic. Having said all this, one hastens to place on the other side of the scale these considerations: By his stress on the Bible and on the need of every Christian to read and interpret it for himself, the Puritan gave an emphasis to individualism and self-reliance that made Puritanism the parent of the Transcendentalism of Emerson and Thoreau. The compulsion to decide for oneself the elements of spiritual salvation meant necessarily to dignify human nature, human faculties, the soul and the intelligence of every man. To the Puritans, religion became education, the minister became the teacher, the congregation became the school. The emphasis on duties and responsibilities was seen to imply that the human being deserved to be treated with dignity and respect, for he was a *responsible* human being, a person, one who was called upon by God and his neighbors to fulfill his duties; but his primary duty was to find out for himself, by study, prayer, and meditation, what was his station and its duties. So it was that fulfillment of one's duties had an unsuspected twist—self-fulfillment, the living, at whatever cost, in accordance with one's own conscience. Self-reliance became self-fulfillment. One's station became a place of honor and dignity in God's cosmos and in man's world. Since every man had a station, it followed that every man occupied a place of honor and dignity in God's scheme and in man's system. In a significant sense, then, all men were equal.

How are equals to be governed? They govern themselves by making a contract among themselves and instituting a government. In contracting for a government, they contracted for a government of laws and not of men. (At this point, Puritan legalism bore democratic fruit.) Contractualism came to mean constitutionalism and representative government for the state, and congregationalism for the church. Self-reliance expressed itself in contractualism; contractualism came to mean constitutionalism; constitutionalism came to mean that the citizen reserved the right to criticize government and to show that the government has, in a specific instance touching his conscience, violated the terms of the contract by transgressing upon rights reserved unto the people—rights which no man has given up or could give up without giving up, at the same time, his very humanity. Political action is, therefore, subject to moral and religious judgment; conscience must be respected; and in the final contest it is conscience, and not majority vote or public authority, that must be obeyed: "Rebellion to tyrants is obedience to God." [13]

In this intense, striking motto of Thomas Jefferson [14] one can see the Enlightenment fused with Puritanism as a source of democratic ideas and institutions. For the Enlightenment, too, "proclaimed the accessibility of truth, even basic truths of religion, to the faculty of reason." [15] In both Puritanism and the Enlightenment "man was originally endowed with the faculties requisite for his salvation, and by which he might be trusted to govern himself." [16] Ralph Barton Perry justly offers Locke as the most significant symbol of the kinship between Puritanism and the Enlightenment; for Locke came of Puritan stock, he was brought up and educated in a Calvinistic environment. If he "was the father of modern democracy, he was nonetheless a descendant of Calvin." [17] This could be said with equal truth of Grotius, John Milton, Algernon Sidney, and Burlamaqui. One may say with Reinhold Niebuhr that,

as a matter of history, both Christian and secular forces were involved in establishing the political institutions of democracy; and the cultural resources of modern free societies are jointly furnished by both Christianity and modern secularism. . . . Free societies are the fortunate products of the confluence of Christian and secular forces. . . . As a matter of history, the later Calvinism and the Christian sects of the 17th century and the rationalism of the 18th century equally contributed to the challenge of religiously sanctified political authority. In our own nation, the equal contributions which were made to our political thought by New England Calvinism and Jeffersonian deism are symbolic of this confluence of Christianity and secularism in our democracy.[18]

# ☆ 3 ☆

# Before 1776

IT TOOK less than two centuries—a short time as history is reckoned—for the Enlightenment and the democratic implications of Puritanism to become effective and institutionalized in church-state relations. The development from theocracy to democracy was so peaceful and gradual that the progressive steps were hardly noted at the times they were taken.

The Old World tradition contemplated a close relation between church and state. The church taught civil obedience, and the state enforced church decisions. Persons convicted of heresy by the spiritual courts were burned at the stake by the civil authorities. Religious belief and worship were community, not individual, concerns. The state did not claim to be omnipotent; it was assumed that its powers were limited by divine and natural law. The Protestant Reformation, as projected by Calvin, Luther, and Knox, did not change the conception of religion as a community concern; and co-operation between church and state survived the Reformation. The Reformers abandoned Rome only to create a church and a state more nearly Christian from their own points of view. And in England the King took the place of the Pope as "Supreme Head of the Church and Clergy of England," and by an act of Parliament was given the right to "correct, restrain, and amend" all "heresies, abuses, offences, contempts and enormities." The Book of Common Prayer was authorized by an act of Parliament, and as recently as 1927 and 1928 the House of Commons dramatically illustrated the legal right of Parliament to control the worship of the Anglican Church by rejecting revisions of the 1662 Book of Common Prayer.

The Anglicans who settled at Jamestown, Virginia, in 1607 contemplated no changes in the relations between their church and their government. The Puritans who settled at Massachusetts Bay in 1630 sought to effect a reformation within the Anglican Church, but looked for no essential change in church-state relations. The Pilgrims who came to Plymouth in 1620, however, were Separatists as far as the Anglican Church was concerned; they formed their own, independent church. By 1692 the Puritans of Massachusetts Bay had also become Separatists, and it became possible for the two colonies to unite under a single charter. The united Puritans of Massachusetts now had a church that was independent of the Church of England; it became, in fact, the Church of Massachusetts, displacing the church of the mother country as the established church, protected and supported by the government. Neither the Anglicans of Virginia nor the Puritans of Massachusetts objected to the use of the power of the government on behalf of religion if it was on behalf of *their* kind of religion: all agreed that their own brand of orthodoxy must be supported by the state. Thus the Virginia colony banished Puritan clergymen, Quakers, and Catholic priests. The Puritans at Plymouth gave the suffrage only to orthodox believers and legislated against Quakers. At Massachusetts Bay the voting privilege was given only to church members (there was only one church); the church and clergymen were supported by taxes, and church attendance was compulsory. The Puritans at New Haven conformed to this theocratic pattern.

In New Netherland, through Dutch tolerance or indifference, diverse religious elements were permitted to settle: Calvinists, Jews, Quakers, Mennonites, Lutherans, Catholics—a motley population. New Netherland was the first settlement to manifest the existence of religious and cultural pluralism. The intention of the authorities, however, was to make the Dutch Reformed Church the state church. Toleration was practiced, and Stuyvesant, a bigoted governor, was ordered by the Dutch West India Company not to persecute Jews and to shut his eyes to the influx of Quakers. When the English took over the settlement and changed its name to New York, they established the Church of England, but there were by then too many non-Anglicans to make the establishment effective.

Roger Williams went further than the Dutch. He was a Separatist in a double sense—he believed not only in separation from the Church of England but also in the separation of church and state. His doctrine of the two tables (of the Decalogue) was that offenses against the first table, which governed man's relations with God, ought not to be punished by the state, and that the civil authorities ought to enforce only the laws of the second table, which governed the relations between man and man. To Williams religion was a purely personal matter, and a church was a voluntary association of like-minded persons; and he drew no line concerning Jews and Catholics. He was a profoundly religious man, and more of a seeker than a dogmatist. Although he seems to have had no use for Quakers, he opposed the enactment of penal statutes against them. The Rhode Island colony that he founded in 1636 at Providence consistently maintained religious freedom in the seventeenth century, but later an effort was made to bar non-Protestants from citizenship and public office. In his *Queries of Highest Consideration,* Williams argued for the complete separation of church and state, and in the *Bloudy Tenent of Persecution for Cause of Conscience Discussed,* published in 1644, he anticipated John Locke by some fifty years and went even further as a protagonist of religious freedom by refusing to exclude Catholics and atheists from its enjoyment.

In the proprietary colonies of East and West Jersey the desire to attract buyers and tenants of land was in part responsible for a substantial measure of religious toleration. There was no established church in these colonies. Pennsylvania also had no established church, but a belief in God was required. Settlers could attend any religious service, but only Christians enjoyed political privileges—a Christian society without enforced conformity. Catholics, however, were excluded from public office.

Maryland insisted on Christian belief—a person who denied the existence of the Trinity was subject to the death penalty (there is no evidence that this law was ever enforced). Lord Baltimore, a Catholic, established the mutual toleration of Catholics and Protestants; before long, however, Anglicans gained control of the colony, and then liberty was denied to Catholics and non-Anglican Protestants. In the Carolinas, although the Church of England was established there, the authorities did not generally molest non-Anglicans; but atheists were excluded.

In short, religious freedom existed only in Rhode Island. Toleration in varying degrees was to be found in New Netherland under Dutch rule, and in the proprietary colonies. There was no religious freedom, and not even toleration, in the Anglican and Puritan colonies.

# ☆ 4 ☆

# The Virginia Experiment

BY 1776 the established churches, found in a majority of the colonies, had lost their aggressive spirit and were on the defensive. Rhode Island, Pennsylvania, Maryland, New York, and the New Jersey colonies, prosperous under freedom or toleration, constituted dangerous examples. Virginia became the laboratory where the most significant experiments were tried.

Virginia, as we have seen, had an Anglican establishment. Presbyterians had won toleration, but Baptists were considered too radical and were sent to prison. By the time of the Revolution, however, the Anglicans had lost much ground; they constituted now only about one-fourth of the population. A declaration of revolt against England made disestablishment a political necessity. The state convention of 1776 formally severed political relations with England and adopted a Declaration of Rights, which included the following provision, drafted mainly by George Mason:

That religion, or the duty which we owe our Creator, and the manner of discharging it, can be directed only by reason and conviction, not by force or violence, and therefore all men are equally entitled to the free exercise of religion, according to the dictates of conscience; and that it is the mutual duty of all to practice Christian forbearance, love, and charity towards each other.

It is significant to note that, as originally drafted by Mason, the provision used this language: "that all men should enjoy the

21

fullest toleration in the exercise of religion." Upon the urging of James Madison, "fullest toleration" became "the free exercise of religion."

Shortly thereafter the Virginia Assembly convened under the new constitution and passed an act, drafted under the guidance of Mason, which repealed all oppressive criminal laws respecting religion and exempted non-Anglicans from supporting by any part of their taxes the Anglican Church. The act stated that a great variety of opinions had arisen as to the propriety of a general assessment "or whether every religious society should be left to voluntary contributions for the support and maintenance of the several ministers and teachers of the gospel who are of different persuasions and denominations," and since the differences of opinion could not then "be well accommodated," the matter was left for discussion and final determination at a future session.[1]

From 1776 to 1785 there was agitation for a general assessment bill, which provided for support of Christianity and the division of taxes among Christian churches. Christianity would have a preferred position, and all Christian churches would, in effect, constitute the establishment. Madison led the fight against this proposal. Patrick Henry's arguments in support of the proposal recall contentions being made today; namely, that the decay of religion led to the decay of the nation; that the low state of religion in Virginia, due to disestablishment, led to a decline of morals.

Madison argued that the legislature had no power to enact the bill, for religion was not within the purview of civil authority. Further, he contended that religion flourishes when it is *not* supported by the state (e.g., in primitive Christianity, the Reformation, and the time when dissenters from the Anglican Church were under legal disabilities). As to the low state of morals, this was caused, said Madison, by wars and bad laws, and not by disestablishment. Better education, an improved administration of justice, and personal example will improve morals. Furthermore, he wanted to know who was going to define "Christianity." The true question, said Madison, is not,

"Is religion necessary?" but "Are religious establishments necessary for religion?"

The assembly voted to refer the question to a committee, headed by Patrick Henry, charged with the duty to frame a proper bill. Madison and Jefferson, considering Henry the most formidable threat to their own position, looked for a way to get him out of the assembly. They contrived to have him elected governor. Then supporters of the general assessment proposal attempted to camouflage the measure as an educational bill, calling it "a bill establishing a provision for teachers of the Christian religion." They said that the purpose of the bill was merely to provide for the instruction of citizens in Christian knowledge. The assembly stalled. Then Madison drew up his famous "Memorial and Remonstrance against Religious Assessments." [2] This protest was signed by many citizens. The result of Madison's efforts was that the assembly finally refused to consider the general assessment bill.

The extent of church support that could be purchased by the levy in question was trifling. Had there been an absolute guaranty that the proponents of general assessment would never seek to go further—such guaranty can never be given or accepted, of course—Madison might have been induced to put aside his objections on the basis of the maxim *de minimis non curat lex*. He felt, however, as the Supreme Court often feels when it is faced with this maxim, that the bill was representative of other measures that were sure to come if it were enacted, the total incidence of which might well have become far-reaching.[3] Madison looked beyond the immediate levy and "saw its ultimate consequence in the denial of liberty and [the] imposition of clerical control upon the state." It is proper, he wrote in the "Memorial and Remonstrance," "to take alarm at the first experiment on our liberties. We hold this prudent jealousy to be the first duty of citizens, and one of [the] noblest characteristics of the late Revolution." We should not wait, Madison said to his fellow citizens, until usurpation had "strengthened itself by exercise, and entangled the question in precedents. They [opponents of assessment] saw all the consequences in the principle, and they avoided the consequences by denying the principle."

In view of the fact that the Virginia Constitution at that time provided for religious freedom, and that since 1779 there had been no established church, this argument in the "Memorial and Remonstrance" is especially significant. The relevance of the argument to the situation today warrants our spending on it a little time. For Madison was not afraid that public support of all Christian denominations, or of all churches without distinction or preference—co-operation between church and state displacing separation [4]—would lead to the establishment of one religion as the state religion. What he did fear was that the removal of some stones from the new wall of separation of church and state in Virginia might lead to the collapse of the wall and to state support of religion in general; and he was as opposed to the establishment of Protestantism, or of Christianity, or of all religion as to the establishment of any one denomination.

There is always the question of drawing a line. Madison knew this just as well as did Mr. Justice Holmes.[5] He also knew that "the interpretation of constitutional principles must not be too literal. We must remember that the machinery of government would not work if it were not allowed a little play in its joints." [6] But when he considered the general assessment plan, he saw not merely a small departure from principle by persons who *accepted* the principle. Such a departure might have been tolerated on the argument that, when the Declaration of Rights and the religious freedom acts of 1776–1779 were adopted, the "traditions and habits of centuries were not intended to be overthrown," and that "structural habits count for as much as logic in drawing the line." [7] Madison saw, instead, an attack on the principle of separation by its *opponents,* a covert declaration of war, a subtle attempt to ensnare the fighters for religious freedom, a case of Foxy-woxy saying to Hennypenny and her friends: "I know the proper way. Shall I show it to you?"

Throughout our discussion, in later chapters as well as in this chapter, the position taken by Madison with respect to the assessment plan will need to be kept in mind; for time and again it will be necessary for us to think: "Here is a question of degree. 'When you realize that you are dealing with a matter of degree you must realize that reasonable men may differ widely as to the place where the line should fall.' [8] But the measure is not part of a strategy to undermine the principle; it is merely an instance of the truth that 'constitutional rights like others are matters of degree,' and 'must be allowed a certain latitude in the minor adjustments of life.' " [9] Or we shall need to think: "Here it is not a question of degree; it is an attempt to undermine the principle. This measure is an instance of tyranny rather than liberty, though so small as to be almost palatable; but we must resist it; for 'it is from petty tyrannies that large ones take root and grow. This fact can be no more plain than when they are imposed on the most basic rights of all. Seedlings planted in that soil grow great and, growing, break down the foundations of liberty.' " [10] Reasonable minds will differ as to when either of these positions should be taken. The business of the mind, however, is to make the choice, to take a stand, employing in the process all the wisdom that it possesses.

Following the adoption in 1776 of the Virginia Declaration of Rights, Jefferson framed a bill to implement the guaranty of religious freedom. It was not, however, until 1785, following Madison's victory with his "Memorial and Remonstrance," that Jefferson's Bill for Establishing Religious Freedom [11] came before the legislature for effective action. It became law in 1786.[12] Jefferson regarded this law, the Declaration of Independence, and the founding of the University of Virginia his three most significant accomplishments—more important even than the Presidency of the United States for two terms. The act recited that the "Almighty God hath created the mind free"; that "to compel a man to furnish contributions of money for the propagation of opinions which he disbelieves is sinful and tyrannical"; and that "even the forcing him to support this or that teacher of his own religious persuasion" is wrong. Then follow phrases which have become part of the American heritage:

that to suffer the civil magistrate to intrude his powers into the field of opinion, and to restrain the profession or propagation of principles on supposition of their ill tendency, is a dangerous fallacy, which at once destroys all religious liberty, because he being of course judge of that tendency will make his opinions the rule of judgment, and approve or condemn the sentiments of others only as they shall square with or differ from his own; that it is time enough for the rightful purposes of civil government, for its officers to interfere when principles break out into overt acts against peace and good order; and finally, that truth is great and will prevail if left to herself, that she is the proper and sufficient antagonist to error, and has nothing to fear from the conflict, unless by human interposition disarmed of her natural weapons, free argument and debate, errors ceasing to be dangerous when it is permitted freely to contradict them.

The act, following the enacting clause, provided

that no man shall be compelled to frequent or support any religious worship, place or ministry whatsoever, nor shall be enforced, restrained, molested, or burthened in his body or goods, nor shall otherwise suffer on account of his religious opinions or belief; but that all men shall be free to profess, and by argument to maintain, their opinion in matters of religion, and that the same shall in no wise diminish, enlarge or affect their civil capacities.

The legislature concluded the act with the statement that a repeal of the act, or a narrowing of its operation, will be "an infringement of natural right."

This was probably the first statutory enactment of complete religious freedom and equality in the world. Its influence was felt in Europe as well as in the rest of the United States.[13] In effect, when Virginia won religious freedom for herself, it won it also for the rest of the country. Jefferson and Madison, together with Roger Williams, Lord Baltimore, and William Penn, stand out in the front rank of fighters for religious freedom in American and in world history.

It is from Jefferson that we have received the phrase, which has been given constitutional sanction, "a wall of separation between Church and State." In a letter written as President of the United States, Jefferson said:

Believing with you that religion is a matter which lies solely between man and his God; that he owes account to none other for his faith or his worship; that the legislative powers of the government reach actions only, and not opinions, I contemplate with sovereign reverence that act of the whole American people which declared that their Legislature should "make no law respecting an establishment of religion, or prohibiting the free exercise thereof," thus building *a wall of separation between Church and State.*[14]

And it is from Madison that we get a summary of the most forceful arguments for the "wall of separation between Church and State." Writing in 1823, Madison tried to explain how it was that the Virginia state university, supported at the common expense, failed to provide "a religious tuition." A summary of his reasons is as follows:

(1) Religion is essentially distinct from government and "exempt from its cognizance."

(2) A "connection" between religion and state is injurious to both.

(3) Rival sects, with equal rights, watch over each other in the interests of good morals.

(4) If sects with absurd notions arise, the proper remedies are time, forbearance, and example.

(5) The establishment of religion without toleration is unthinkable.

(6) The establishment of religion with toleration would be a source of discord and animosity.

(7) The experience of the states that had no established church, like Pennsylvania and New Jersey, shows that separation is as safe in practice as it is sound in theory.

(8) The experience of the states that had no established church, and of Virginia before and after disestablishment, shows that religion flourishes much more without legal patronage than with it. Not only is the law not necessary to the support of religion; such support is even a hindrance to it.[15]

By 1789, when the Constitution of the United States was adopted, Virginia and Rhode Island were states in which complete religious freedom was enjoyed. Remnants of establishment or intolerance lingered in the other eleven states. Tax support of religion was found in Massachusetts (Congregational churches), New Hampshire (Protestant churches), Connecticut (Christian churches), South Carolina (Protestant churches), and Maryland (Christian churches). In New York, Catholics were excluded from citizenship. In New Jersey and North Carolina only Protestants, and in Delaware only Christians, could hold public office. In Georgia, only Protestants could be members of the legislature. Pennsylvania required a belief in God, and only Christians could vote and hold public office.[16] Despite all the restrictions, however, there was a "live-and-let-live" atmosphere, a latitudinarianism that pointed to complete religious freedom as the final development in a historical movement. Protestantism, Paul Tillich has pointed out,

in spite of its emphasis on the individual conscience, was established as a strictly authoritarian and conformist system, similar to that of its adversary, the Roman Church of the Counter-Reformation. There was no individualism in either of the great confessional groups. And there was only hidden individualism outside them, since they had drawn the individualistic trends of the Renaissance into themselves and adapted them to their ecclesiastic conformity.[17]

In the United States, the situation described by Tillich lasted from 1607, when Virginia was first settled, to 1786, when the Bill for Establishing Religious Freedom was enacted in Virginia, a period of about one hundred and eighty years—a remarkably short stretch of time when one considers how deep were the roots of religious conformism and intolerance.

When the Constitutional Convention met in 1787 it was generally assumed that the new Constitution would give Congress no control over the status of religion in the states. As we have seen, the people of each state had their own idea as to the relations between church and state; and they did not want to put into the Constitution any provision that might disturb those relations. When the Constitution was submitted to the states for ratification, it contained, therefore, no provision regarding religion, except what was stated in Article VI; namely, "No religious test shall ever be required as a qualification to any office or public trust under the United States." In its context in the Constitution, this provision means that while all the legislative, executive, and judicial officers of the United States are bound by oath or affirmation to support the Constitution, they may not be required to pass a religious test as a qualification for office. Thus, although, in New Jersey only Protestants, and in Pennsylvania only Christians, could hold public office under the constitutions of those states, any one could hold a federal office without regard to his religious beliefs. Only North Carolina, which limited public offices to Protestants, voted against the adoption of this clause. The temper of the times may in part by gauged by the fact that when Charles Pinckney offered the test oath clause, quoted above, Roger Sherman "thought it unnecessary, the prevailing liberality being a sufficient security against such tests." [18]

## ☆ 5 ☆

# The First Amendment

LITTLE was said at the Constitutional Convention regarding religious freedom or a bill of rights. Elbridge Gerry and George Mason proposed a committee to prepare a bill of rights, but the motion was lost.[1] Apparently there were three reasons why the delegates decided against a bill of rights: (1) the matter could be left to the states, some of which, like Virginia, had gone far to guaranty religious freedom and equality; and (2) a provision for religious freedom in a bill of rights would be strongly opposed by states that had established churches, so "it seemed best to make haste slowly." (3) There was the conviction on the part of Madison, James Wilson, and others that, as Madison said, "there is not a shadow of right in the general government to intermeddle with religion. Its least interference with it would be a most flagrant usurpation." [2] This argument was also made by Hamilton in *The Federalist*. A bill of rights, he contended, is not only unnecessary, but would even be dangerous; for a bill of rights would contain "various exceptions to powers not granted; and, on this very account, could afford a colorable pretext to claim more than were granted. For why declare that things shall not be done which there is no power to do?" [3]

These arguments, however, failed to end the agitation in the states for a bill of rights, but the agitation was insufficient to thwart ratification of the Constitution. The first session of

Congress began on March 4, 1789. On April 30, 1789, Washington was inaugurated as the first President. On May 4, Madison told the House of Representatives, to which he had been elected, that he would soon bring in some amendments for consideration. He kept his promise. In the autumn of that year Congress approved the Bill of Rights. The required number of state ratifications was met by December 15, 1791.

The preamble to the joint resolution which contained the amendments recited that in a number of states the conventions which ratified the Constitution had "expressed a desire, in order to prevent misconstruction or abuse of its powers, that further declaratory and restrictive clauses should be added."

Since Madison was, more than any other American, responsible for the drafting of the amendments and their adoption by Congress, it is well to note the reasons which motivated him in his actions, especially in view of his opinion that a bill of rights was really unnecessary. His statements have much relevance and force in interpreting the amendments.

In a significant letter to Jefferson, dated October 17, 1788, Madison wrote:

My own opinion has always been in favor of a bill of rights, provided it be so framed as not to imply powers not meant to be included in the enumeration. At the same time, I have never thought the omission a material defect, nor been anxious to supply it even by *subsequent* amendment, for any other reason than that it is anxiously desired by others. I have favored it because I supposed it might be of use, and if properly executed could not be of disservice. . . . There is great reason to fear that positive declaration of some of the most essential rights could not be obtained in the requisite latitude. I am sure that the rights of conscience in particular, if submitted to public definition would be narrowed much more than they are likely ever to be by an assumed power. One of the objections in New England was that the Constitution by prohibiting religious tests, opened a door for Jews [,] Turks & infidels. . . . In Virginia I have seen the [state] bill of rights violated in every instance where it has been opposed to a popular current. Notwithstanding the explicit provisions contained in that instrument for the rights of Conscience, it is well known that a religious establishment would have taken place in that State, if the Legislative majority

had found, as they expected, a majority of the people in favor of
the measure; and I am persuaded that if a majority of the people
were now of one sect, the measure would still take place, and on
narrower grounds than it was then proposed, notwithstanding the
additional obstacle which the law has since created. Wherever the
real power in a government lies, there is the danger of oppression.[4]

Madison's view was that the strongest guaranty of religious
freedom was to be found in a "multiplicity of sects"; such
multiplicity may be, indeed, "the best and only security." [5] A
bill of rights, if its provisions have the "requisite latitude," may,
however, be of some use, especially if its inclusion in the Constitution meets with popular approval.

Jefferson, writing to Madison on December 20, 1787, said:

I will now add what I do not like; first, the omission of a bill of
rights, providing clearly, and without the aid of sophisms, for freedom of religion, freedom of the press. . . . Let me add that a bill
of rights is what the people are entitled to against every government
on earth . . . and what no government should refuse.[6]

Madison proposed two provisions regarding religion; namely,

(1) The civil rights of none shall be abridged on account of religious belief or worship, nor shall any national religion be established, nor shall the full and equal rights of conscience be in
any manner, or on any pretext, infringed.
(2) No state shall violate the equal rights of conscience, or the freedom of the press, or the trial by jury in criminal cases.

As adopted by the House of Representatives, these proposed
amendments read as follows:

(1) Congress shall make no law establishing religion, or to prevent
the free exercise thereof, or to infringe the rights of conscience.
(2) The equal rights of conscience, the freedom of speech or of the
press, and the right of trial by jury in criminal cases, shall not
be infringed by any state.

The Senate, however, failed to approve the second of these
proposed amendments. Had this amendment been adopted by
the Senate and ratified by the states, important guaranties im-

plied in the Fourteenth Amendment would have been anticipated by about eighty years.

The Senate, in the course of the debate over what became the First Amendment, at various times considered proposed texts that would have prohibited the establishment of a single denomination but would have permitted multiple establishments, i.e., would have permitted support of all denominations on a basis of equality. The text of one of these proposals was as follows: "Congress shall make no law establishing one Religious Sect or Society in preference to others, or prohibiting the free exercise thereof, nor shall the rights of conscience be infringed." Another text was as follows: "Congress shall make no law establishing any particular denomination of religion in preference to another, or prohibiting the free exercise thereof, nor shall the rights of conscience be infringed." [7] These proposals were rejected by the Senate. In the light of the argument made in the middle of the twentieth century that the First Amendment prohibits only the establishment of a single national church but does not prohibit multiple establishments or co-operation between church and state,[8] this action of the Senate shows "that Congress was not satisfied with a proposal which merely prevented an advantage to any one denomination over others as far as Church-State separation was concerned. It wished to go further." [9]

The Senate and the House of Representatives each appointed members to a conference committee to eliminate differences between the two bodies. Madison was a member of this committee, and the final version of the amendment, as approved by the conference committee and which became the text of the First Amendment, was his accomplishment.[10]

# The Fourteenth Amendment

AS WE have seen, Madison wanted an amendment that would have prohibited the states, as well as Congress, from infringing the rights of conscience and freedom of speech and the press; but he had to bow to expediency, for some of the states were not yet ready to disestablish their churches, and some states still questioned the propriety of treating Jews, Moslems, or Roman Catholics on a basis of civil equality with Protestants. By its very terms the First Amendment is a limitation on Congress only; and until the adoption of the Fourteenth Amendment in 1868, the states were free to do as they saw fit respecting religious practices and beliefs: [1] the religious establishments and the measures restricting religious freedom in the states were left unaffected by the First Amendment. Thus, it was not until 1816 that Connecticut repealed the act making church attendance compulsory, and it was not until 1818 that it disestablished the Congregational Church. The Congregational Church in Massachusetts was not disestablished until 1833.

The Fourteenth Amendment contains two provisions which seem to make it possible for the Supreme Court to hold that a state may not infringe religious freedom; namely, (1) that no state "shall make or enforce any law which shall abridge the privileges or immunities of citizens of the United States"; and (2) that no state shall "deprive any person of life, liberty, or property, without due process of law."

Is religious freedom a privilege or immunity of citizens of the United States which is protected against abridgment by a state? It has been only a minority of dissenting Justices of the Supreme Court who have taken a broad view of the Privileges and Immunities Clause of the Fourteenth Amendment. The majority have consistently rebuffed the effort to include among the privileges and immunities of American citizens the fundamental or broad rights and freedoms, such as those enumerated in the Bill of Rights.[2]

Is a person protected in his religious freedom against state abridgment by the Due Process Clause of the Fourteenth Amendment? The word "liberty" in this clause has been interpreted and applied broadly. Early proponents of a liberal interpretation were Justices Harlan and Brandeis. In 1925 in the *Gitlow* case the Supreme Court said that it assumed that freedom of speech and of the press were among the "fundamental personal rights and liberties" protected by the Due Process Clause of the Fourteenth Amendment against abridgment by any state.[3] In 1940 the Supreme Court squarely held that religious freedom is included in the concept of "liberty," as the term is used in the Due Process Clause.[4] Since that decision the proposition has not been questioned by the Court.

Are all the freedoms and rights enumerated in the Bill of Rights incorporated into the Due Process Clause of the Fourteenth Amendment and protected thereunder against infringement by the states? There are two schools of thought in the Supreme Court with regard to this matter. In 1937 Justice Cardozo, in *Palko v. Connecticut,* distinguished fundamental liberties from those of inferior significance.[5] The Bill of Rights, he maintained, includes both types. As instances of fundamental liberties, absorbed into the Fourteenth Amendment, Cardozo mentioned the following: freedom of speech, freedom of the press, "the free exercise of religion," "the right of peaceable assembly," and "the right of one accused of crime to the benefit of counsel." These, he said, are "implicit in the concept of ordered liberty"; if they were sacrificed, "neither liberty nor justice would exist." On the other hand, the requirement of trial by jury and the provision that no person may be compelled in any criminal case to be a witness against himself are not of "the very essence of a scheme of ordered liberty." Their abolition by a state would not violate "a principle of justice so rooted in the traditions and conscience of our people as to be ranked as fundamental."

A majority of the Court, with Justice Frankfurter as their chief spokesman, have adopted the views of Justice Cardozo with respect to this matter. Justices Murphy, Rutledge, Black, and Douglas have opposed this position and have maintained that the Due Process Clause of the Fourteenth Amendment incorporates all of the rights guarantied by the Bill of Rights.[6] The rationale of the latter position, as formulated by Justice Black, is as follows:

I fear to see the consequences of the court's practice of substituting its concept of decency and fundamental justice for the language of the Bill of Rights as its point of departure in interpreting and enforcing that Bill of Rights. If the choice must be between the selective process . . . applying some of the Bill of Rights to the States, or the . . . rule applying none, I would choose the . . . selective process. But rather than accept either of these choices, I would follow what I believe was the original purpose of the Fourteenth Amendment—to extend to all people of the nation the complete protection of the Bill of Rights. To hold that this Court can determine what, if any, provisions of the Bill of Rights will be enforced, and if so, to what degree, is to frustrate the great design of a written constitution.[7]

As we have indicated, the difference between the majority and minority approaches is not significant when the case before the Court involves any one of the First Amendment freedoms, for all the Justices agree that these freedoms are embodied in the concept of "liberty," as the term is used in the Due Process Clause of the Fourteenth Amendment; so that, as a practical matter, the First Amendment freedoms are guaranteed against state no less than against federal action. The difference between the majority and the minority may be seen, however, when other guaranties of the Bill of Rights are before the Court in cases that come up from state courts. Thus, e.g., the majority have held that the denial of counsel to an accused in a state trial is not necessarily against the command of the Sixth Amendment, though it would be in a federal trial, and that in a state trial the judge may admit evidence obtained as a result of a search and seizure that would be illegal in a federal court under the Fourth Amendment.[8] The question in such cases, according to the majority, is not whether a state has acted contrary to the express provision of a specific amendment, but whether the state has outraged the demands of "civilized decency" or of "fundamental liberty and justice," or has violated a right that is "implicit in the concept of ordered liberty," in violation of the Due Process Clause of the Fourteenth Amendment.

Justice Black has argued that at the time of the adoption of the Fourteenth Amendment, specific individual liberties enumerated in the Bill of Rights were considered "essential supplements to the First Amendment";[9] that is to say, it was thought that without the specific guaranties against arbitrary court action in the imposition of criminal punishments the First Amendment freedoms could be rather easily suppressed or restricted. Study of the historical events that culminated in the Fourteenth Amendment, said Justice Black,

and the expressions of those who sponsored and favored, as well as those who opposed its submission and passage, persuades me that one of the chief objects that the provisions of the Amendment's first section, separately, and as a whole, were intended to accomplish was to make the Bill of Rights applicable to the states.

This historical judgment is, I believe, strongly supported by the evidence.[10]

Achievements of our civilization, Justice Frankfurter has said,

as precious as they were hard won [,] were summarized by Mr. Justice Brandeis when he wrote that "in the development of our liberty insistence upon procedural regularity has been a large factor." . . . It is noteworthy that procedural safeguards constitute the major portion of our Bill of Rights.[11]

If substantive rights—such as those guaranteed by the First Amendment—are not safe unless they are supported by procedural rights—such as those enumerated in many of the Bill of Rights amendments—why, then, should the latter be excluded from necessary implication in the concept of "liberty" or the meaning of "due process" as these terms are used in the Fourteenth Amendment?

It may be admitted that "due process" "is not a technical conception with a fixed content unrelated to time, place and circumstances," that it "cannot be imprisoned within the treacherous limits of any formula." [12] It does not follow from this that "due process" does not mean, *as a minimum,* the procedural guaranties formulated in the original amendments. It could be taken to mean these specific guaranties and any others disclosed by the process that is "compounded of history, reason, the past course of decisions, and stout confidence in the strength of the democratic faith which we profess." [13]

The basic conflict between the two schools of thought in the Supreme Court is not, one suspects, over the question as to what the framers of the Fourteenth Amendment intended to accomplish by the use of the terms "liberty" and "due process." The basic conflict is over the question of the value of the guaranties of the Bill of Rights outside of those embodied in the First Amendment. The majority feel that these guaranties, if taken literally, may stand in the way of experimentation by states with different approaches to the concept of "ordered liberty." They seem to think that such free experimentation is in itself a good thing, that it is, on the whole, preferable to the absolute restrictions which the Bill of Rights imposes on the Federal Government.

The answer to this has been supplied by Justice Rutledge, who said that he knew of no better substitutes for the guaranties in question. "A few may be inconvenient. But restrictions upon authority for securing personal liberty, as well as fairness in trial to deprive one of it, are always inconvenient—to the authority so restricted." [14] And the answer has been given, too, by Justice Black, when he said that he could not consider the Bill of Rights to be an outworn eighteenth-century "strait jacket"— the term once used by the Court.[15] Its provisions, said Justice Black, may be thought outdated abstractions by some. And it is true that they were designed to meet ancient evils. But they are the same kind of human evils that have emerged from century to century wherever excessive power is sought by the few at the expense of the many. In my judgment the people of no nation can lose their liberty as long as a Bill of Rights like ours survives and its basic purposes are conscientiously interpreted, enforced and respected so as to afford continuous protection against old, as well as new, devices and practices which might thwart those purposes. I fear to see the consequences of the Court's practice of substituting its own concepts of decency and fundamental justice for the language of the Bill of Rights as its point of departure in interpreting and enforcing that Bill of Rights.[16]

# Is Freedom of Religion
# an Absolute?

RELIGIOUS freedom, as it has come to be understood in the United States, operates within the bounds of two broad limiting concepts; namely, (1) separation of church and state, and (2) reasonable exercise of the police power. The former is negative in its import; it signifies a prohibition upon government. The latter is permissive; it signifies the power of government to prohibit or regulate conduct, though such conduct may have a religious significance to certain persons. In actual operation, often only a thin line seems to mark the boundary between the two conceptions. If the state is permitted to interfere with certain conduct, we say that the state's action is a constitutional exercise of the police power.[1] If the state is prohibited from interfering with certain conduct, we say that the attempted interference is an infringement of the principle of religious freedom or of separation of church and state. One principle is a label for the exclusive dominion of the state, the other for the exclusive dominion of the person. In Biblical terms, we have been speaking of the two realms: the things that are God's and the things that are Caesar's.[2]

But at once the question arises, What things *are* God's and what things *are* Caesar's? When the Roman conqueror of Palestine installed the image of the Emperor in the Temple, he was certain that he was acting within the jurisdiction of Caesar, while the Jews were equally certain that the realm of God had been invaded. When the board of education of West Virginia ordered that all pupils participate in a flag salute ceremony in the public schools, they were certain that their action was a reasonable exercise of the state's police power, while Jehovah's Witnesses were just as certain that the requirement was a breach in the wall of separation of church and state. The point, in brief, is that things, actions, events do not come bearing the label "God's" or "Caesar's," except insofar as human beings affix one label or the other; and human beings may differ sharply as to which label should be affixed.

It should not be assumed that "secularists" will attempt to broaden Caesar's jurisdiction, while church members will naturally tend to look out for God's jurisdiction. The process of distribution and definition does not by any means work in such a simple fashion. A person may be a "secularist" when it comes to the flag salute issue—he may argue that the flag salute requirement is a reasonable assertion of the police power. He may be equally a "secularist" when it comes to the state paying the bus fares of children riding to and from parochial schools. On the other hand, he may be a church man when the question is Bible reading in the public schools—this, he may contend, is an invasion of the realm of God. Is a Sunday statute an exercise of the police power or a breach in the wall of separation? The same person may be found to favor a Sunday statute and Bible reading in schools and to oppose the released time plan of religious education and the payment of bus fares of parochial school pupils. The argument over these issues is not advanced by the use of epithets, such as "secularism" or "theocracy."

In addition to religious freedom issues that are of a consequential character and that may be resolved ultimately by Supreme Court decision, there are several types of situations that have only a theoretical interest.

(1) *Actions that have only a symbolic or ceremonial significance.* Since 1864 some of our coins have had on them the motto: "In God we trust." [3] In April 1954 a stamp with a religious sentiment was introduced: the eight-cent stamp carried

the inscription "In God we trust" arched over the Statue of Liberty. The stamp was introduced with elaborate religious and patriotic ceremonies. Practically no defenders of separation as an absolute principle have publicly urged action to change the Government's policy with respect to the coins or stamps.[4] In his opinion for the majority of the Court in *Zorach v. Clauson,* Justice Douglas assumed that the following acts do not violate constitutional principles:

Prayers in our legislative halls; the appeals to the Almighty in the messages of the Chief Executive; the proclamations making Thanksgiving Day a holiday; "so help me God" in our courtroom oaths— these and all other references to the Almighty that run through our laws, our public rituals, our ceremonies.[5]

Such actions by the Government do not violate the First Amendment, said Douglas, although "the constitutional standard is the separation of Church and State." In a time of crisis such actions are likely to increase, but there is no limit on them outside of public sentiment or a standard of good taste.

(2) *Actions that the citizen cannot get litigated.* Each House of Congress has its own chaplain, who opens meetings with a prayer. In 1789 Congress established chaplaincies, and they have existed ever since.[6] In 1953 a prayer room was established in the Capitol. Now, just as the members of Congress may establish, by law or appropriation, cafeterias and restaurants, barbershops, chauffeurs, and other services for their own use or comfort, so, too, they establish chaplaincies and a prayer room if they believe that such facilities will help Congress in its deliberations and work. President Eisenhower opened meetings of his Cabinet with prayer; and preceding his own inaugural address in January 1953, he read a prayer which he had written. It is difficult to see how the courts could undertake to review actions of this kind by a co-ordinate branch of the government.[7]

(3) *Actions that have persisted for a long time.* Church property, for example, has been generally exempt from local taxation, and this practice is an old one.[8] The Constitution, Justice Reed has said, should not be stretched to forbid "national customs" or "accepted habits of our people." With re-

spect to them, he said, history takes precedence over a study of the constitutional text. Established practices and customs show, he said, that the Constitution does not bar "every friendly gesture between church and state." The First Amendment is "not an absolute prohibition against every conceivable situation where the two [church and state] may work together." [9]

With regard to such well-established customs, it may be wise to take seriously the observation of Justice Holmes that "tradition and the habits of the community count for more than logic." [10]

In the area under examination it may be well generally to bear in mind the following statement by Justice Holmes:

Many laws which it would be vain to ask the Court to overthrow could be shown, easily enough, to transgress a scholastic interpretation of one or another of the great guaranties in the Bill of Rights. They more or less limit the liberty of the individual or they diminish property to a certain extent. We have few scientifically certain criteria of legislation. . . . With regard to the police power, as elsewhere in the law, lines are pricked out by the gradual approach and contact of decisions on the opposing sides.[11]

In brief: While religious freedom, like other constitutional freedoms, tends to declare itself an absolute—total separation of church and state—it is in fact limited by the principle of the police power and by practices that have become deeply rooted as symbols or in tradition, or that are beyond effective legal challenge.[12] The Constitution, Justice Frankfurter has said,

commands neither logical symmetry nor exhaustion of a principle. "The problems of government are practical ones and may justify, if they do not require, rough accommodations—illogical, it may be, and unscientific." [McKenna] . . . In adjudication as in legislation the Constitution does not forbid "cautious advance, step by step, and the distrust of generalities" [Holmes].[13]

## ☆ 8 ☆

# The Police Power

IN THE judicial interpretation of the First Amendment, the limits on religious freedom imposed by the police power were asserted in the only case to come before the Supreme Court in the nineteenth century in which a conflict between an act of Congress and the guaranty of religious freedom was tested. The case was *Reynolds v. United States,* decided in 1878.[1]

Before Utah became a state, Congress passed an act making bigamy in the territory a federal offense. The defendant, when charged with this crime, showed that at the time of his second marriage he was a member of the Mormon Church; that it was a doctrine of this church that polygamy was a duty; that it was a practice, moreover, that was directly enjoined by God upon man in a revelation to Joseph Smith; and that the church taught that failure to practice polygamy will lead to eternal damnation. Here, then, was a direct conflict between religious belief and practice and a criminal statute. The Supreme Court held that the act of Congress did not violate the First Amendment. By this amendment, the Court said, "Congress was deprived of all legislative power over mere opinion, but was left free to reach actions which were in violation of social duties or subversive of good order." In this connection the Court quoted from the Virginia Bill for Establishing Religious Freedom, drafted by Jefferson, "that it is time enough for the rightful purposes of civil government for its officers to interfere when principles break out into overt acts against peace and good order." Human sacrifices, or the suicide of a wife committed on her husband's funeral pyre, although the acting out of religious beliefs, may nonetheless be prohibited. The Court marshalled evidence to show that polygamy "has always been odious among the Northern and Western Nations of Europe" and among the people who have settled the United States. "In the face of all this evidence," said the Court, "it is impossible to believe that the constitutional guaranty of religious freedom was intended to prohibit legislation in respect to this most important feature of social life." Religious belief is no excuse for the commission of a crime. The Court said:

Laws are made for the government of actions, and while they cannot interfere with mere religious belief and opinions, they may with practices. . . . Can a man excuse his practices . . . [when they violate laws] because of his religious belief? To permit this would be to make the professed doctrines of religious belief superior to the law of the land, and in effect to permit every citizen to become a law unto himself. Government could exist only in name under such circumstances.

This decision has been cited repeatedly for the proposition, now firmly settled, that religious belief cannot be accepted as justification or excuse of an overt act that has been made criminal by the legislature.

There are, however, instances of the law taking into consideration religious beliefs and making these beliefs a justification of an overt act that has been made criminal by statute. Thus, under the draft law men are exempt from normal military service if they can show that they are conscientiously opposed to participation in all war and that they are so opposed "by reason of religious training and belief." [2] In World War I the statute provided exemption only from combatant service; there was no exemption for those who had conscientious scruples against noncombatant as well as against combatant military service; the 1940 act, however, allowed persons who were opposed to noncombatant service to be assigned to "work of national importance under civilian direction."

Christian Scientists have also been given exemptions from certain laws; thus, in some states, employees who adhere to the faith or teachings of a church which has as a tenet the healing by prayer or spiritual means are exempt from compulsory disability insurance. In several states parents are liable to fine or imprisonment if medical attention is not given an ailing child, but the law exempts parents who afford their children healing in accordance with their religious tenets; and in some states the children of Christian Scientists are, by law, excused from attendance at health and hygiene courses in public schools.[3]

An analogous situation is found in some states with respect to their Sunday laws. In these states the laws provide that persons who, for religious reasons, choose to observe Saturday as their day of rest, shall not be liable to penalties for working or transacting business on Sunday.

In these instances legislation expressly permits a person who has religious scruples against complying with the law "to become a law unto himself." The exemption in these instances is the result of legislative discretion and not of constitutional guaranties, for conscientious objection to military service is not a right protected by the First Amendment; [4] Christian Scientists have resorted to legislative measures rather than court action, and it is doubtful if they could win exemption on constitutional grounds; [5] and Sunday laws which do not provide for the exemption of seventh-day sabbatarians have been upheld as constitutional.[6] It is, however, a constitutional right to substitute attendance at a private or a parochial school for attendance at a public school.[7]

Some of these matters will be considered more closely at a later point. Here it is important only to recognize the principle that generally when Congress or a state legislature, in the exercise of some constitutional power, enacts a statute which requires or prohibits some action, and makes the violation a criminal offense, there is no requirement inherent in the First Amendment that religious beliefs shall constitute a sufficient excuse or justification for noncomplicance with the terms of the statute. The legislature may, however, in the exercise of its discretion, give special consideration to religious scruples—as in the case of pacifists or Christian Scientists; but the failure to exercise legislative discretion in favor of religious scruples does not violate the Constitution.

When the interest sought to be protected by the legislature is considered a vital one, it is hardly likely that exceptions will be made. A Tennessee statute which makes it unlawful to handle poisonous snakes in such a manner as to endanger the life or health of any person does not exempt from its terms the members of a religious sect which practices snake handling as a form of evangelism; and a conviction of a member of a sect for violation of the act violates no constitutional provision.[8] No human authority, the Tennessee constitution provides, "can, in any case whatever, control or interfere with the rights of conscience." This language seems to be even more sweeping and emphatic than the language of the First Amendment, yet it did not have the effect of making the statute invalid. It is even likely that the act was adopted by the Tennessee legislature with an eye specifically on the snake-handling practices of a sect, for who but members of a sect would invite or seek such experiences? Yet this would not condemn the act.[9]

How can one tell whether a statute is to be condemned as an infringement of religious freedom or as a valid assertion of legislative power? Generally, the test is whether the statute is reasonable under all the circumstances.[10] How is reasonableness determined? This is done by comparing the relative importance of the competing interests—e.g., religious freedom and the state's interest in protecting the monogamous family or the life of its citizens. To what extent are the competing interests in conflict? Perhaps the interests may be reconciled, as, e.g., by having a compulsory school attendance law but allowing parents to send their children to a public or a private school. If the interests can be thus reconciled, a statute which avoids reconciliation and compels a clash of the conflicting interests may be unconstitutional.[11]

One cannot, however, be altogether certain of the sweep of this proposition. Allowing conscientious objectors to substitute noncombatant for combatant service, or work of national importance under civilian direction for noncombatant service, seems to reconcile the conflict of interests in the case of all pacifists except certain absolutists.[12] The pattern provided by the Selective Training and Service Act of 1940 seems, on the whole, to protect conscience, while utilizing the manpower resources of pacifists to advance the national interest in case of war. Suppose, however, that Congress were to disregard entirely the scruples of the pacifists—as in World War I it disregarded the scruples of the men who objected to noncombatant service, and as in World War II it disregarded the scruples of certain absolutists. Such congressional action would not be, I believe, unconstitutional; for conscientious objection is not supported by the Constitution; it hangs on a thread of congressional discretion or grace. The capacity of the legislature to reconcile the conflict of interests is not the constitutional test, but it may serve as one of the factors in the court's reasoning respecting the reasonableness of the legislation.

Even when the interests competing with religious freedom seem at first glance to be approximately on the same level, the courts may not treat them in the same way. Reconciliation of conflict is possible with respect to Sunday laws, for the law could permit a seventh-day sabbatarian to substitute Saturday for Sunday as his day of rest and to work on Sunday without causing noise or any other form of annoyance or offense; in this way an undue economic burden on the seventh-day sabbatarians would be avoided. Yet the courts have refused to hold that this form or any other form of reconciliation is constitutionally imperative with respect to Sunday laws. Why is reconciliation of conflict required with respect to compulsory school attendance but not with respect to Sunday rest laws? The answer may be that the educational prerogatives of parents deserve greater protection than the economic rights of persons who observe the seventh day of the week as their sabbath.

In the latter case, it may be observed, the seventh-day sabbatarian is not compelled by the law (though he may by economic considerations) to work or do business on Saturday; he may freely observe that day as his sabbath if he is willing to pay for the privilege by suffering some economic loss. Can we say that the test of reasonableness (or constitutionality) is whether the statute imposes a compulsion upon the conscience directly by forcing or prohibiting the doing of an act which violates a person's religious conscience? This does not appear to be the test; for the snake-handling cultist is prohibited from handling poisonous snakes; and the believer in polygamy is compelled to limit himself to a single wife; and the member of a spiritual healing sect may be compelled to subject his child to vaccination or to a blood transfusion in order to save the child's life.[13]

Religious freedom is constitutionally protected; but what is to one man religion is to another man primitive superstition, or immorality, or even criminality. The questions we have considered demonstrate the impossibility of a judicial definition of "religion"—a definition which would make what is excluded from its terms constitutionally unprotected.[14]

Apart from "narrow exceptions," the Supreme Court has said, "it is no business of courts to say that what is a religious practice or activity for one group is not religion under the protection of the First Amendment." [15] What are the "narrow exceptions"? The court failed to say, except to cite two cases that involved polygamy. Its failure to go beyond that is, I think, quite justified.

"The law knows no heresy," Justice Miller said for the Supreme Court in 1871,[16] and in 1944 Justice Douglas reaffirmed this view when he said that freedom of religion, under the Constitution,

embraces the right to maintain theories of life and of death and of the hereafter which are rank heresy to followers of the orthodox faiths. Heresy trials are foreign to our Constitution. Men may believe what they cannot prove. They may not be put to the proof of their religious doctrines or beliefs. Religious experiences which are as real as life to some may be incomprehensible to others. . . . Man's relation to his God was made no concern of the state. He was granted the right to worship as he pleased and to answer to no man for the verity of his religious views.[17]

And Justice Jackson has restated this view in language no less emphatic:

If there is any fixed star in our constitutional constellation, it is that no official, high or petty, can prescribe what shall be orthodox in politics, nationalism, religion, or other matters of opinion or force citizens to confess by word or act their faith therein.[18]

The broad significance and intent of these pronouncements are beyond attack or even question, but one cannot press some of the propositions without running into trouble. Is it true that Americans are granted the right to worship as they please? We have seen that when extreme cases are met—like snake-handling —the proposition shows cracks.

Justice Frankfurter has chosen to state the scope of the First Amendment in negative terms. "The constitutional protection of religious freedom," he has said, "terminated disabilities, it did not create new privileges. It gave religious equality, not civil immunity. Its essence is freedom from conformity to religious dogma, not freedom from conformity to law because of religious dogma." [19] This formulation accounts for the cases in which religious belief was held to be no excuse or justification for the violation of a police measure; but by its terms it fails to comprehend the cases in which the police power was required to accommodate itself to the First Amendment guaranty of religious freedom—a parent does, e.g., have constitutional freedom from conformity to law because of religious dogma when he chooses to send his child to a parochial school.

In the *Barnette* case Justice Jackson seemed to project the clear and present danger test in cases in which an attempt is made to restrict religious freedom.[20] Freedoms "of speech and of press, of assembly, and of worship," he said, may not be infringed on the "slender grounds" of the "rational basis" test. These freedoms, he said, "are susceptible of restriction only to prevent grave and immediate danger to interests which the state may lawfully protect." It is doubtful if the use of this test is more likely to rationalize the cases than the use of the balance-of-interests test. For example: When Congress declares war, the country faces a grave and an immediate danger, and so the religious scruples of conscientious objectors may constitutionally be disregarded by the draft laws. But suppose we have peacetime conscription to prepare for a danger that may never become grave and immediate? It would not matter: the exemption of pacifists is always a matter of legislative grace and not of constitutional right.[21] While the clear and present danger may rationally explain the prohibition upon snake handling, it fails to rationalize all the cases in which compulsion upon conscience has been sustained.

The freedoms of the First Amendment remain "majestic generalities." [22] "General propositions do not decide concrete cases," Justice Holmes said. "The decision will depend on a judgment or intuition more subtle than any articulate major premise." [23] To a considerable degree, insofar as it allows or prohibits legislative restrictions on conduct, the constitutional guaranty of religious freedom is and will remain "a brooding omnipresence in the sky." [24]

# ☆ 9 ☆

# The Principle of Separation
# of Church and State

WE have discussed the principles or doctrines which, as applied in specific instances, limit the claims of religious freedom. Now we shall discuss the extent or sweep of the guaranty of religious freedom at the point where its claims appear to be very broad.

The *Reynolds* case of 1878, which formulated the limits on the guaranty by stating the principle that religious belief cannot justify an overt act (in that case polygamy) that has been made criminal by the legislature, also, for the first time in the Supreme Court, spoke of Jefferson's "wall of separation between Church and State." [1]

Chief Justice Waite, in his opinion for the Court, said that the First Amendment expressly forbids legislation which restricts the free exercise of religion. But what is "religion"?— "what is the religious freedom which has been guarantied?" For his answer, Waite turned to the history of the time when the First Amendment was adopted, and after quoting from Jefferson's famous letter to the Danbury Baptist Association, he said: "Coming as this does from an acknowledged leader of the advocates of the measure, it may be accepted almost as an authoritative declaration of the scope and effect of the amendment thus secured."

The Supreme Court sixty-eight years later unanimously

adopted Chief Justice Waite's line of reasoning and confirmed
—this time without the qualification of "almost"—as authoritative Jefferson's phrase as descriptive or definitive of the scope
and effect of the religious freedom clause of the First Amendment. "In the words of Jefferson," said Justice Black in the
*Everson* case in 1946, "the clause against establishment of religion by law was intended to erect 'a wall of separation between
Church and State.' *Reynolds v. United States.*" [2] This interpretation of the religious freedom clause was adopted by the Court
in the light of the history of the clause and, said Justice Black,
"the evils it was designed forever to suppress." The Court
adopted this interpretation with full awareness that it meant
giving the religious freedom clause a "broad" meaning.

Now, what does the separation of church and state involve?
This is the Court's answer, in the language of Justice Black:

Neither a state nor the Federal Government can set up a church.
Neither can pass laws which aid one religion, aid all religions, or
prefer one religion over another. Neither can force nor influence
a person to go to or to remain away from church against his will
or force him to profess a belief or disbelief in any religion. No person can be punished for entertaining or professing religious beliefs
or disbeliefs, for church attendance or non-attendance. No tax in
any amount, large or small, can be levied to support any religious
activities or institutions, whatever they may be called, or whatever
form they may adopt to teach or practice religion. Neither a state
nor the Federal Government can, openly or secretly, participate in
the affairs of any religious organizations or groups and vice versa.

Justice Rutledge's opinion in the *Everson* case went more
extensively and profoundly into the historical background of
the First Amendment and confirmed Justice Black's interpretation that the religious freedom clause meant separation of
church and state: "a complete and permanent separation," said
Rutledge, "of the spheres of religious activity and civil authority," such as would forbid "comprehensively" "every form
of public aid or support for religion"; and the word "religion,"
as used in the Constitution, "connotes the broadest content."
(The prohibition of the First Amendment "broadly forbids state
support, financial or other, of religion in any guise, form or

degree." The meaning and scope of the First Amendment, said Rutledge, are such as were intended by Madison and Jefferson (especially the former); for

all the great instruments of the Virginia struggle for religious liberty thus became warp and woof of our constitutional tradition, not simply by the course of history, but by the common unifying force of Madison's life, thought and sponsorship. He epitomized the whole of that tradition in the Amendment's compact, but nonetheless comprehensive, phrasing. . . . With Jefferson, Madison believed that to tolerate any fragment of establishment would be by so much to perpetuate restraint upon that freedom. Hence he sought to tear out the institution not partially but root and branch, and to bar its return forever. . . . Our constitutional policy . . . does not deny the value or the necessity for religious training, teaching or observance. Rather it secures their free exercise. But to that end it does deny that the state can undertake or sustain them in any form or degree. For this reason the sphere of religious activity, as distinguished from the secular intellectual liberties, has been given the twofold protection and, as the state cannot forbid, neither can it perform or aid in performing the religious function. The dual prohibition makes that function altogether private. It cannot be made a public one by legislative act. This was the very heart of Madison's Remonstrance, as it is of the Amendment itself. . . . The realm of religious training and belief remains, as the Amendment made it, the kingdom of the individual man and his God. It should be kept inviolately private.

Two years after the *Everson* decision the Supreme Court was asked to declare the quoted passages from Justice Black's opinion to have been mere *obiter dicta* and to repudiate them. It was contended that the First Amendment forbids only government preference of one religion over another and not impartial assistance of all religions; furthermore, that the Fourteenth Amendment does not incorporate the "establishment of religion" clause of the First Amendment. In the *McCollum* case in 1948, the Court, again in an opinion by Justice Black, rejected these contentions.[3] The opinion for the Court again quoted the "wall of separation" passage from Jefferson's letter and stated that in the *Everson* case the full Court had agreed "that the First Amendment's language, properly interpreted, had erected a wall of separation between church and state." This wall, the Court added, "must be kept high and impregnable."

Again, in 1952, in *Zorach v. Clauson* the Supreme Court, in an opinion by Justice Douglas, stated:

There cannot be the slightest doubt that the First Amendment reflects the philosophy that church and state should be separated. And so far as interference with the "free exercise" of religion and an "establishment" of religion are concerned, the separation must be complete and unequivocal. The First Amendment within the scope of its coverage permits no exception; the prohibition is absolute.[4]

The principle of separation, however, Justice Douglas went on to say, does not make church and state enemies one to the other; there may be some give and take between them. This is how Justice Douglas put the matter:

The First Amendment, however, does not say that in every and all respects there shall be a separation of church and state. Rather, it studiously defines the manner, the specific ways, in which there shall be no concert or union or dependency one on the other. That is the common sense of the matter. Otherwise, the state and religion would be aliens to each other—hostile, suspicious, and even unfriendly. Churches could not be required to pay even property taxes. Municipalities would not be permitted to render police or fire protection to religious groups. Policemen who helped parishioners into their places of worship would violate the Constitution. Prayers in our legislative halls; the appeals to the Almighty in the messages of the Chief Executive, the proclamations making Thanksgiving Day a holiday; "so help me God" in our courtroom oaths—these and all other references to the Almighty that run through our laws, our public rituals, our ceremonies would be flouting the First Amendment. A fastidious atheist or agnostic could even object to the supplication with which the Court opens each session: "God save the United States and this Honorable Court."

In these passages from his opinion for the Court, Justice Douglas confirms the view we have previously stated; namely, that while the principle of separation of church and state tends to declare itself as an absolute, it is in fact limited by the police power and other constitutional powers (e.g., the war power), and by practices that have become widely accepted as national symbols or traditions, as well as by practices that appear to be beyond effective legal challenge. Justice Douglas attempted to summarize this extremely complex situation by saying: "The constitutional standard is the separation of church and state. The problem, like many problems in constitutional law, is one of degree."

The debate over religious freedom has thus far resulted in the projection of three leading points of view as to the essential meaning of the First Amendment provision guarantying the free exercise of religion and prohibiting an establishment of religion. We shall now consider them.

## A. THE PRINCIPLE REJECTED

At one extreme is the view of the Roman Catholic hierarchy that rejects the principle of separation and would substitute for it the principle of co-operation.[5] Jefferson's metaphor, according to this view, signified nothing except that there should be no established church, no national religion, no official church that would be the recipient from the government of special favors, benefits extended to one church and withheld from all other churches; the prohibition upon the establishment of religion meant only that the government may not extend preferential treatment to one religion as against another; it did not mean governmental indifference to religion and the exclusion of co-operation between government and religion. In the place of "separation" should be the concept "distinction."

Distinction and cooperation are correlatives; they must exist together. They necessarily mean peace. . . . Distinction and cooperation. These are the instruments the Catholic Church offers with which to work out in the concrete the eternal dilemma of the claims of the temporal and the eternal, a dilemma that faces every believer.[6]

This theory requires the state to have a friendly interest in the end which the churches seek to achieve and to assist them in attaining those ends; but governmental aid is to be extended to all churches or religions equally. According to this view, equal treatment of all religions is of the essence of the First Amendment's prohibition upon an establishment of religion— "prohibition of a preferred position to any one religion, to the disadvantage of the others; and equality of all religions before the state." [7]

This position involves a negative and a positive proposition; namely, (a) the government is prohibited from setting up any one church in a preferred, let alone monopolistic, position, and (b) the government has the positive duty to co-operate with all churches or religions.

This view was formulated as a reaction to the decisions of the Supreme Court in the *Everson* and *McCollum* cases, which were characterized as "an entirely novel and ominously extensive interpretation" of the establishment of religion clause of the First Amendment.[8]

### B. THE PRINCIPLE AS AN ABSOLUTE

At the other extreme is the separation doctrine, as stated in the *Everson* and *McCollum* cases, and affirmed in the *Zorach* opinion by Justice Douglas. While it is the official doctrine of the Supreme Court, from which no member of the Court has expressly dissented, it may be said that the supporters of the doctrine in its extreme formulation have been Justices Black, Frankfurter, Jackson, and Rutledge. To make clear their position one needs to consider the dissenting opinions in the *Everson* and *Zorach* cases.

In the *Everson* case the Court had before it the following facts: A New Jersey statute authorized local boards of education to provide for the transportation of children "to and from school other than a public school," except a school operated for profit, over established public school routes, or by other means when the child lives "remote from any school." Acting under the authority given to it by this statute, the school board of Ewing Township provided by resolution for the transportation of pupils of the township to certain public schools "and Catholic schools by way of public carrier." The practice under this resolution was for parents to pay for the transportation of their children to public or parochial schools, and for the school board to reimburse them semiannually. The highest court in New Jersey upheld these arrangements as consistent with the state constitution and with the United States Constitution. The United States Supreme Court, by a five-to-four vote, affirmed the decision.

The dissenting Justices contended that while the majority advocated "complete and uncompromising separation of church from state," their decision in fact violated this principle; for here money raised by taxation was used to support a transgression of the principle of separation insofar as the money was used to pay parents the costs of transportation of their children on their way to and from schools in which religion was a prominent feature of the educational program. "I should be surprised," said Justice Jackson,

if any Catholic would deny that the parochial school is a vital, if not the most vital, part of the Roman Catholic Church. . . . Catholic education is the rock on which the whole structure rests, and to render tax aid to its Church school is indistinguishable to me from rendering the same aid to the Church itself.

Religious worship or instruction or attendance at religious institutions of any character can never be made public business. The Constitution, the dissenters argued, has the effect to take every form of propagation of religion out of the realm of things which could "directly or indirectly" be made public business and thus win public support "in whole or in part." Religious freedom is guarantied "in absolute terms, and its strength is its rigidity."

The guaranty of religious freedom works in two ways; namely, it keeps the state's hands off religion, and it keeps religion's hands off the state. The Supreme Court has zealously protected religion whenever the state attempted, however indirectly, to touch it, even if protection of religion under the circumstances meant a sacrifice of the state's interest in the maintenance of public order, or the privacy of the home, or taxation. "But we cannot have it both ways." If religion cannot be made to suffer restrictions imposed on it by the state, it cannot seek benefits from the state.

If these principles seem harsh in prohibiting aid to Catholic education, it must not be forgotten that it is the same Constitution that alone assures Catholics the right to maintain these schools at all when predominant local sentiment would forbid them. . . . If the state may aid these religious schools, it may therefore regulate them.

The Constitution prohibits every form of interference with the free exercise of religion, so it prohibits "every form of public aid or support for religion." Said Justice Rutledge:

The prohibition broadly forbids state support, financial or other, of religion in any guise, form or degree. It outlaws all use of public funds for religious purposes. . . . Does New Jersey's action furnish support for religion by use of the taxing power? Certainly it does, if the test remains undiluted as Jefferson and Madison made it, that money taken by taxation from one is not to be used or given to support another's religious training or belief, or indeed one's own; . . . and the prohibition is absolute.

It is clear from Justice Rutledge's dissenting opinion, with which the three other dissenting Justices concurred, that this prohibition on state aid would rule out, not only the cost of transportation, but also "the cost of textbooks, of school lunches, of athletic equipment, of writing and other materials"; indeed, whatever aids, contributes to, promotes, or sustains the propagation of beliefs.

The dissenting Justices considered the majority's decision to be perhaps the second breach in the wall of separation, the *Cochran* decision in 1930 being the first.[9] In that case the Court upheld as constitutional legislation which authorized the state to purchase nonreligious textbooks for both public and parochial school pupils. Justice Rutledge pointed out that the religious freedom clause of the First Amendment was not presented as an issue by the briefs in that case; furthermore, he doubted if in a parochial school the division of education into secular and religious could be justified. It is clear, I think, that if the issue of textbooks had been presented in the *Everson* case, the four dissenting Justices would have held that free textbooks for parochial schools was unconstitutional. How the other Justices would have voted on this issue in 1946, it is hazardous to say.

In the First Amendment the dissenting Justices saw an absolute bar. There is no room for the question of degrees of trespass upon the Amendment. A measure that is "at the very threshold of departure from the principle" should be declared unconstitutional, otherwise the question of principle may become "entangled in corrosive precedents."

The majority contended that the payment of bus fares was comparable as a safety measure (by protecting the lives and safety of the pupils) to police and fire protection made available to church schools. This analogy was rejected by the minority, who argued that police and fire protection are "matters of common right, part of the general need for safety"; for a fire department cannot stand idly by while a church burns.

The *Zorach* case in 1952 settled the constitutional issue involved in the released time plan of religious education by a six-to-three decision that the plan as it was set up in New York City did not violate the guaranty of religious freedom. The dissenting Justices here found an occasion to affirm their adherence to the principle of separation as a fairly absolute constitutional injunction. In order to comprehend their position as it is stated within the context of the facts in the case, it is necessary first to examine briefly the Court's decision in the *McCollum* case of 1948, which also involved the released time plan of religious education.

The board of education of a school district in Champaign County, Illinois, permitted the giving of religious instruction by clergymen in the schools. Pupils whose parents signed "request cards" were permitted to attend the denominational classes, which were held weekly for either thirty or forty-five minutes. Classes were conducted in the regular classrooms of the school building. Students who did not choose to take the religious instruction left their classrooms and went to some other part of the school for a continuation of their secular studies. Students who chose religious instruction attended classes conducted by Catholic priests or by Protestant teachers (at one time a rabbi conducted a class in Judaism). The denominational teachers were not paid by the school authorities. These teachers reported to the secular teachers on the attendance or absence of the pupils.

These facts, the Court held, showed the use of public property for religious instruction "and the close cooperation between the school authorities and the religious council [sponsor of the plan] in promoting religious education." The state's compulsory education system assisted and was integrated with a program of religious instruction, and pupils were released in part from their legal duty if they agreed to attend religious classes. "This," Justice Black said in his opinion for eight Justices, "is beyond all question a utilization of the tax-established and tax-supported public school system to aid religious groups to spread their faith." The Champaign plan, the Court held, fell "squarely under the ban of the First Amendment (made applicable to the states by the Fourteenth)."

In a concurring opinion Justice Frankfurter stated that

separation is a requirement to abstain from fusing functions of government and of religious sects, not merely to treat them all equally. That a child is offered an alternative may reduce the constraint; it does not eliminate the operation of influence by the school in matters sacred to conscience and outside the school's domain. The law of imitation operates, and non-conformity is not an outstanding characteristic of children. The result is an obvious pressure upon children to attend. . . . We renew our conviction that "we have staked the very existence of our country on the faith that complete separation between the state and religion is best for the state and best for religion." . . . If nowhere else, in the relation between church and state, "good fences make good neighbors."

The case, said Justice Frankfurter, did not involve merely the question of enabling children to obtain religious instruction for thirty or forty-five minutes; for if that were all, Saturday or Sunday could be utilized for this purpose, or the authorities could adopt the dismissed time or French plan, whereby one school day is shortened and *all* children are dismissed and allowed to go wherever they please, "leaving those who so desire to go to a religious school." But the people in Champaign County interested in religious instruction were not satisfied merely to find or make time for such instruction:

The momentum of the whole school atmosphere and school planning is presumably put behind religious instruction, as given in Champaign, precisely in order to secure for the religious instruction such momentum and planning. To speak of "released time" as being only half or three quarters of an hour is to draw a thread from a fabric.

In the *Zorach* case the Court was called upon to consider the released time plan as it was set up in New York City. There the pupils who were released on the written request of their parents left the school property and went to church centers, and those not released remained in the classrooms. The churches made weekly reports to the schools on attendance. One hour a week was allowed for this program. No announcement was made in the public schools relative to the program, and the public schools assumed no responsibility for attendance at the religious schools. A majority of six Justices held that

this "released time" program involves neither religious instruction in public school classrooms nor the expenditure of public funds. All costs, including the application blanks, are paid by the religious organizations. The case is therefore unlike *Illinois ex rel. McCollum v. Board of Education.* . . . In the *McCollum* case the classrooms were used for religious instruction and the force of the public school was used to promote that instruction. Here . . . the public schools do no more than accommodate their schedules to a program of outside religious instruction. We follow the *McCollum* case. But we cannot expand it to cover the present released time program.

In dissenting, Justice Black said that the only difference between the Champaign and New York City programs was that in the latter the school buildings were not used; but in both programs the public schools aided the churches by providing pupils for the religious classes, through releasing some of the children from regular class work, manipulating "the compelled classroom hours of its compulsory school machinery so as to channel children into sectarian classes." New York has used its compulsory education laws

to help religious sects get attendants presumably too unenthusiastic to go unless moved to do so by the pressure of this state machinery. . . . Any use of such coercive power by the state to help or hinder some religious sects or to prefer all religious sects over nonbelievers or vice versa is just what I think the First Amendment forbids.

To Justice Black there was no question of degree: "In considering whether a state has entered this forbidden field the question is not whether it has entered too far but whether it has entered at all."

Justice Frankfurter again pointed out that the churches and the school authorities could easily resort to a constitutional method to achieve the furtherance of religious education; namely, by instituting a dismissed time program, whereby all pupils would leave school, some to study music, some to receive ethical instruction, some to receive sectarian instruction—every one being free to make use of his leisure time as he saw fit. But it was obvious that the churches lacked confidence in the appeal of their educational offerings, so they sought to make use of the public schools as the instrument for securing attendance at denominational classes. When the school authorities fulfill this sectarian objective—as they do in New York City—they violate the Constitution.

Justice Jackson agreed with this view of the New York City program, which contemplates the school "as a temporary jail for a pupil who will not go to church." It is compulsion when, by indirection or forthrightly, Caesar is used to collect what should be rendered to God. The distinction attempted to be drawn by the majority between the Champaign and the New York City programs is "trivial, almost to the point of cynicism, magnifying . . . nonessential details." The wall of separation has become "warped" and "twisted."

It should be made clear that the proponents of the principle of separation as an absolute prohibition upon co-operation between church and state are not motivated by any antireligious feeling; on the contrary, they believe in separation because only under this condition can the sphere of religion be kept inviolate. As they see the situation, *state aid to religion* must in time become *injury to religion*. Only aid may be intended, but unintended injury will be the consequence. For the state's power is almost always coercive in its effects; only rarely—e.g., when it aids the victims of a flood—is the state's action organized benevolence untainted by coercion (although even here the funds distributed by the state have been raised by taxation, which is always coercive with respect to the taxpayer).

Thus, in the New York City released time program it appeared that the school authorities were merely lending a friendly hand to the churches in the interest of a religious education program that had been organized on a voluntary basis by the denominational groups themselves; but this way of looking at the facts disregards the bedrock upon which the entire scheme had been built; namely, the state's compulsory education laws. When the released time hour comes, the pupil must choose between two alternatives: he may leave school and go to his church school, or he may remain in public school. If he chooses the former alternative, his attendance at the church school will be a compliance with the state's compulsory education laws. True, he has the choice of not going to the church school; but he is limited in his choice between alternatives each of which fulfills a requirement imposed by the state. It is this point that is stressed—and rightly so—by Justice Frankfurter. If advocates of religious education were willing to forego state aid, they would, Justice Frankfurter contended, substitute the dismissed time for the released time program. The controversy would promptly end, he said, if the advocates of religious instruction

were content to have the school "close its doors or suspend its operations"—that is, dismiss classes in their entirety, without discrimination—instead of seeking to use the public schools as the instrument for securing attendance at denominational classes. The unwillingness of the promoters of this movement to dispense with such use of the public schools betrays a surprising want of confidence in the inherent power of the various faiths to draw children to outside sectarian classes—an attitude that hardly reflects the faith of the greatest religious spirits.

The dismissed time program would avoid the constitutional issue and represent an accommodation or reconciliation of the spheres of church and state to one another without either institution aiding or hindering the other. The persistent failure or refusal of the church groups to seek dismissed time in the place of released time is proof that they prefer released time for the advantages it offers—advantages which have their source in the state's power to coerce the will of the public school pupils, advantages which do more than merely encourage religious instruction or co-operate with religious authorities. Under dismissed time children would go to religious instruction not because the law compelled them to choose between such instruction and remaining in the public school, but because, being free from the coercion imposed by the compulsory school attendance laws, they would freely choose religious instruction. Their choice would then be as free "as the choice of those who answered the call to worship moved only by the music of the old Sunday morning church bells." [10] There is coercion, not freedom, Justice Jackson said, when the public school is made to serve as a temporary jail for the pupil who will not go to a church school; and we start down a rough road, he added, "when we begin to mix compulsory public education with compulsory godliness." [11]

In brief, while dismissed time would reconcile the interests of church and state, released time utilizes the state on behalf of the church. The purpose of the First Amendment is to prohibit both the immediate advantages to church or state that may result from their commingling or their co-operation, howsoever small these advantages may be, and the long-run injury to both church and state that is bound to follow when the principle of co-operation is substituted for the principle of separation. This is why the question is not whether the state has entered the field of religion *too far,* but whether it has entered *at all.*

## C. THE PRINCIPLE AS A RULE OF REASON, OR CO-OPERATIVE SEPARATION

### (1) *The Zorach Released Time Case*

While the principle of separation has been affirmed unanimously by the Supreme Court, only a minority of Justices, as we have seen, interpret the principle in absolute terms and apply it as a bar to any form of state aid to religion. A majority of Justices have, however, in fact whittled down the principle to the point where it has become a rule of reason. Theoretically, they adhere to the principle of separation; practically, they tend in the direction of the principle of co-operation. They try to steer a middle course, but a middle course between separation and co-operation can mean only—co-operation. There is, however, a significant difference between the all-out co-operation urged by some churchmen and the restrained co-operation approved by these Justices of the Supreme Court. The latter position may be spoken of as "co-operative separation."

The first formulation of this position in the Supreme Court was by Justice Reed. In his dissenting opinion in the *McCollum* case he directed attention "to the many instances of close association of church and state in American society" and recalled that "many of these relations are so much a part of our tradition and culture" that they are accepted without dispute. The First Amendment, he said, is "not an absolute prohibition against every conceivable situation" where church and state may work together; it does not bar "every friendly gesture between church and state." The sweep of the First Amendment is limited by "precedents, customs and practices," by "practices embedded in our society by many years of experience," by "national customs," "accepted habits of our people," "the history of past practices," and by "those incidental advantages that religious bodies . . . obtain as a by-product of organized society." To Justice Reed the following were among "well-recognized and long-established practices" that were constitutional: "recognition of the interest of our nation in religion, through granting, to qualified representatives of the principal faiths, of opportunity to present religion as an optional extracurricular subject during released school time in public school buildings"; also, the transportation of children to church schools, as in the *Everson* case; free textbooks to the pupils of church schools, as in the *Cochran* case; lunch for children in all tax-exempt schools, under the terms of the National School Lunch Act; [12] a contribution by the Federal Government to a hospital owned and operated by the Roman Catholic Church for the building of an addition; [13] chaplains in Congress, in the armed forces, and in the naval and military academies; training for the ministry by eligible veterans at government expense; [14] and the opening exercises in the schools of the District of Columbia, which include a reading from the Bible without comment and the Lord's Prayer.

What this comes to is a flexible interpretation of the First Amendment to spare some practices which have the advantage of relative antiquity, and other practices which are the subject of sharp attack.

It is in the majority opinion of the Court in the *Zorach* case, however, that the absoluteness of the principle of separation is reduced to relativity, without at the same time expressly approving as constitutional all practices that have the support of history. The problem, said the Court, is "one of degree." The opinion of Justice Douglas for the Court projects a distinction between *aid to a denomination,* which is prohibited, and *encouragement of and co-operation with religion in general*—undifferentiated, noninstitutional religion,—which is permitted. From now on the Court will need to consider, in specific cases as they arise, whether the facts spell out aid or only comfort to religion; and if the comfort (encouragement and co-operation) is for religion in general, or for institutionalized, organized denominations.

The Supreme Court, in a case decided in 1892, stated that "this is a religious people," that "this is a religious nation," and that "this is a Christian nation." [15] Then in 1930 the Court again said: "We are a Christian people." [16] Justice Douglas, without reference to precedents, and without reference to Christianity, said: "We are a religious people whose institutions presuppose a Supreme Being." [17] From this followed the proposition that when the state encourages religious instruction or cooperates with religious authorities by adjusting the schedule of public events to sectarian needs, it follows the best of our traditions. For it then respects the religious nature of our people and accommodates the public service to their spiritual needs. To hold that it may not would be to find in the Constitution a requirement that the government show a callous indifference to religious groups. That would be preferring those who believe in no religion over those who do believe . . . we find no constitutional requirement which makes it necessary for government to be hostile to religion and to throw its weight against efforts to widen the effective scope of religious influence.

This view does not mean, Justice Douglas indicated, that the bars between church and state are down. He gave examples of the types of activities that remain prohibited: a released time program such as the facts in the *McCollum* case disclosed; the thrusting of any sect on any person; making a religious observance compulsory; coercing anyone to attend church, or to observe a religious holiday, or to take religious instruction; also:

government may not finance religious groups nor undertake religious instruction nor blend secular and sectarian education nor use secular institutions to force one or some religion on any person. . . . The government must be neutral when it comes to competition between sects.

The position taken by the Court in this case is, I believe, quite different from the position it took in the *McCollum* case. In the *McCollum* case the Court found no difficulty in adherence to a doctrine of neutrality as defining the relations between church and state; but in the *Zorach* case the Court seems to say that neutrality is impossible; that neutrality would mean "hostility," or "callous indifference," which in turn would mean "preferring those who believe in no religion over those who do believe." The government must be "neutral when it comes to competition between sects," but may not be neutral toward religion.

"Now I protest," said Abraham Lincoln in his speech on the *Dred Scott* decision, "against the counterfeit logic which concludes that, because I do not want a black woman for a slave I must necessarily want her for a wife. I need not have her for either. I can just leave her alone." [18] The state may not enslave the church, nor may it marry her; it must leave her alone; but—adds the Supreme Court—it must be nice to her. For apparently the church is a rather vain lady; and a man ought not to leave a lady alone to the point where she may judge his "neutrality" to be "callous indifference"; he must leave her alone—and yet not leave her alone. The state may not—at least not directly and brazenly—spend money on the church; it may not start on the road toward making her a "kept" church; but it may give ample evidence of its awareness of the existence of the church and of her significance, appeal, worth, and desirability.[19]

In the opinion of Justice Douglas we see an attempt at the commingling of the currents of thought, each in its own way representing an extreme position; namely, (1) complete, absolute separation of church and state, and (2) not separation, but "distinction and cooperation." These two streams are not yet altogether fused, to make up an organically and functionally adequate "third force" in constitutional doctrine. It will take some time before such an achievement will be altogether apparent and clear. At the present, the two streams pass through each other without commingling. But if the *Zorach* decision foreshadows future developments, more emphasis will be placed on co-operation than on separation.

### (2) *The Doremus Bible-Reading Case*

Although Justice Jackson dissented in the *Zorach* case, and on the whole, as we have seen, belongs with the absolute separatists, one can see from his concurring opinion in the *McCollum* case that his absolutism will be mitigated on occasion.

While he made it clear that he objected to the Champaign plan of released time, and that he would prohibit "teaching of creed," "catechism," "ceremonial," and "forthright proselyting" in the public schools, he added that "it remains to be demonstrated whether it is possible, even if desirable," to cast out of the public school "all that some people may reasonably regard as religious instruction." He would find it extremely difficult, he said, to decide when "instruction turns to proselyting and imparting knowledge becomes evangelism," except in the "crudest cases." Apart from such cases, we must, he said, "leave some flexibility to meet local conditions, some chance to progress by trial and error." The Court, he thought, should not lay down "a sweeping constitutional doctrine," or decree "a uniform, rigid and, if we are consistent, an unchanging standard for countless school boards," and thereby force the Court to act as a "super board of education for every school district in the nation." The Constitution, he maintained, does not contain "one word" to help judges decide "where the secular ends and the sectarian begins in education."

Under these given conditions, he thought that the Court should not review cases brought by persons who are dissatisfied "with the way schools are dealing with the problem" but who fail to demonstrate that they have suffered a penalty or are making a tax contribution to the church. The Court, in other words, should not review cases which allege a violation of the First Amendment unless it is shown that "a person is required to submit to some religious rite or instruction"—e.g., to salute the flag when such an act is against his conscience,[20]—or unless it is shown that tax money is being used "directly or indirectly to support a religious establishment." [21]

When the Bible-reading case came before the Court in 1952, Justice Jackson was afforded an opportunity to express these views in a majority opinion. To a consideration of this case we now turn.

A New Jersey statute provided that at least five verses of the Old Testament shall be read, without comment, in each classroom at the beginning of each school day or at the school assembly. There was also a prohibitory statute which provided that no religious service or exercise, "except the reading of the Bible and the repeating of the Lord's Prayer," shall be held in any public school. Implementing these provisions, the board of education of the borough of Hawthorne issued a directive that "any student may be excused during the reading of the Bible upon request." An action was brought by two persons to have the statutes declared unconstitutional. One of them showed that he was a citizen and a taxpayer; the other plaintiff was a citizen, a taxpayer, and also the mother of a pupil. They contended that the reading of the Bible and the reciting of the Lord's Prayer in the public schools were religious services, religious exercises, and religious instruction, in violation of the First and Fourteenth Amendments.

The Supreme Court of New Jersey, considering the case on its merits, upheld the constitutionality of the statutes. The United States Supreme Court, by a six-to-three decision, dismissed the appeal.[22] There was no showing, said Justice Jackson, that the mother and daughter were injured or offended by the school practice, or even that the daughter had been compelled to listen. The other plaintiff's action was not "a good-faith pocketbook action." His grievance was "not a direct dollars-and-cents injury" but a "religious difference." It is not, said Jackson, "a question of motivation but of possession of the requisite financial interest that is, or [that] is threatened to be, injured by the unconstitutional conduct. We find no such direct and particular financial interest here." [23]

This decision seems to be clearly a vindication of the position taken by Justice Jackson in the *McCollum* case. The effect of this decision will be to reduce greatly the number and types of cases that may be brought to the Supreme Court involving the religious freedom guaranty of the First Amendment. The decision of the Supreme Court is especially significant in view of the fact that the New Jersey court expressly refused to dispose of the case on technical grounds and decided the case on its merits.

The United States Supreme Court has not approved of the state court's decision on its merits, nor has it disapproved of it; but since it is doubtful if in the foreseeable future the Supreme Court will again permit a Bible-reading case to come before it, the opinion of the New Jersey Supreme Court regarding the constitutional question deserves consideration.

In his opinion for the New Jersey Supreme Court, Justice Case put the following question: "Was it the intent of the First Amendment that the existence of a Supreme Being should be negated and that the governmental recognition of God should be suppressed?" He answered: "Not that, surely." He went on to say that the Constitution itself assumes as an unquestioned fact the existence and authority of God and that preceding, contemporaneously with and after the adoption of the constitutional amendment all branches of the government followed a course of official conduct which openly accepts the existence of God as Creator and Ruler of the Universe; a course of conduct that has been accepted as not in conflict with the constitutional mandate. . . . The confederated colonies and, later, the states organized as a constitutional nation, acknowledged the existence of and bowed before the Supreme Being.

The court pointed out that there were in 1950 twelve states that required the reading of the Bible in public school classes; [24] that the statutes of five other states made its use permissive; [25] that the state court decisions that sustained the constitutionality of such acts outnumbered the cases in which Bible reading had been declared illegal; that the board of education of the District of Columbia required the reading of the Bible and the Lord's Prayer; and that the Bible was read in the schools of many states where the statutes were silent on the subject.

The court held that the Old Testament, "because of its antiquity, its content, and its wide acceptance," is not a sectarian book when read without comment. The Old Testament, said Justice Case, "is accepted by three great religions, the Jewish, the Roman Catholic and the Protestant. . . . The adherents of those religions constitute the great bulk of our population." While the atheist or the person who belongs to a small religious sect "has all the protection of the Constitution," still "he lives in a country where theism is in the warp and woof of the social and the governmental fabric and he has no authority to eradicate from governmental activities every vestige of the existence of God."

As to the permissive reading of the Lord's Prayer, Justice Case said:

That short supplication to the Divinity was given its name because it was enjoined by Christ as an appropriate form of prayer. It is used by Roman Catholics and Protestants with slight variations. But nothing therein is called to our attention as not proper to come from the lips of any believer in God, His fatherhood, and His su-

preme power. . . . It is, in our opinion, in the same position as is the Bible reading.

The New Jersey court, like the United States Supreme Court, said in effect that the doctrine of separation must be maintained, but—"While it is necessary that there be a separation between church and state," said Justice Case,

it is not necessary that the state should be stripped of religious sentiment. . . . The American people are and always have been theistic. It may be of highest importance to the nation that the people remain theistic, not that one or another sect or denomination may survive, but that belief in God shall abide. It was, we are led to believe, to that end that the statute was enacted; so that at the beginning of the day the children should pause or hear a few words from the wisdom of the ages and to bow the head in humility before the Supreme Power. No rites, no ceremony, no doctrinal teaching; just a brief moment with eternity.

The court also assimilated the statutes in question to our national struggle against the Communist threat: "Organized atheistic society is making a determined drive for supremacy by conquest as well as by infiltration." [26]

The opinion of the New Jersey Supreme Court can scarcely be said to emanate from and to reflect a commitment to the doctrine of separation of church and state. The opinion speaks of "the strict wording of the First Amendment" and states that the Constitution does not prohibit government "from recognizing the existence and sovereignty of God." This is, indeed, a far cry from the meaning of the First Amendment as formulated in the opinions of Justice Rutledge in the *Everson* case and of Justice Black in the *McCollum* case, but it is not alien to the position taken by the Court in the *Zorach* case. In any event, the United States Supreme Court, in denying the appeal from the judgment of the New Jersey court, has given to that judgment a strength and dignity that make it fairly impregnable.

While Bible reading in the public school has been upheld as constitutional, the distribution of copies of the Bible to public school pupils has been denied constitutional approval by the same courts.

The Gideons International, a Protestant organization, has for years distributed the Bible in hotels and hospitals, and recently it began to distribute copies of the "Gideons Bible"—consisting of the New Testament, the Book of Psalms, and the Book of Proverbs—to public school pupils. Both Roman Catholics and Jews have objected to the distribution of this book to public school pupils. The board of education of Rutherford, New Jersey, authorized distribution to pupils who had written permission from their parents; copies were given out to such pupils at the close of the school day, when only the pupils who were to receive copies were to remain in the classroom.

The New Jersey Supreme Court, in an opinion by Chief Justice Vanderbilt, held that the action of the Rutherford school officials violated the state and federal constitutions, and the United States Supreme Court refused to review this decision.[27] Chief Justice Vanderbilt said that the distribution of the "Gideons Bible" to public school pupils was a sectarian act by which the Protestant religion was preferred to Judaism, contrary to the "neutrality" that the state must maintain. Whether or not there is a wall of separation between church and state, certainly it is clear, said Chief Justice Vanderbilt, that "the state or any instrumentality thereof cannot under any circumstances show a preference for one religion over another. Such favoritism cannot be tolerated and must be disapproved." The distribution of the King James version or of the "Gideons Bible," the court held, constituted "a preference of one religion over the Hebrew faith," and "the King James version of the Bible is as unacceptable to Catholics as the Douay version is to Protestants."

The court distinguished the earlier Bible-reading case by again affirming that "the Old Testament and the Lord's Prayer, pronounced without comment, are not sectarian" and that their brief use did not constitute "sectarian instruction or sectarian worship."

It was argued that no one was forced to take a copy of the "Gideons Bible"; that the pattern established in Rutherford was merely an "accommodation" of religion, which the Constitution permits. Chief Justice Vanderbilt said that making a religious act voluntary, by excusing dissenters from its exercise or performance, did not save the act from being sectarian; nor is an "accommodation" of religion constitutional (as in the *Zorach* case) if the facilities of the public school are actively used to give a preferential status to one religion over another.

When one reads and co-ordinates the opinions of Douglas in the *Zorach* case and of Case and Vanderbilt in the New Jersey cases, one ends up with the feeling that the courts are not likely to condemn as unconstitutional actions which seem to favor religion in general, but which do not offer strong offense to any one of the three major faiths and which fall short of direct indoctrination. This position is hardly consistent with the view that the Constitution has erected a high and impregnable wall of separation. The position falls somewhere between the doctrine of separation and the competing doctrine of distinction-with-co-operation. There is thus a zone in which conflict is to be anticipated—an area of constitutional law in which one will find nice distinctions, numerous qualifications, resulting in decisions on the facts of the cases. They will be hard cases, making for hard law, and tending to be expressions of common sense rather than of high principles.

### (3) *Sunday Rest Laws*

One may now, in fact, wonder whether the judgment in the Bible-reading case is not more impregnable than the wall of separation. And the wonder grows as one considers the position of the Supreme Court with respect to Sunday rest laws.

In some of the American colonies Sunday church attendance was compulsory. As an aid to the enforcement of church attendance laws, work and business on Sunday were prohibited. Sunday rest laws also preserved the Christian Sabbath from desecration.[28] These were "the twin religious purposes" of the so-called blue laws: "to prevent desecration of the Christian Sabbath and to remove temptations from the path of potential churchgoers." [29] These statutes became a permanent feature of the American scene; apparently Nevada is the only state that has no laws regulating conduct on Sunday.[30] The rationale of these statutes has, however, changed, largely because of the influence of Stephen J. Field.

In 1857 Field was elected to the California Supreme Court. In the following year there came before this court *Ex parte Newman*,[31] in which the constitutionality of the state's "Act for the better observance of the Sabbath" was challenged. A majority of the court held that the statute violated the state constitution. The court found that the act was not intended by the legislature as a civil rule requiring a man to rest on one day out of seven, but as a religious institution, to enforce the observance of a day held sacred by the followers of one faith. Rest on Sunday, said the court, was not required by the act as a civil duty,

necessary for the repression of any existing evil, but in furtherance of the interests, and in aid of the devotions of those who profess the Christian religion. . . . Now, does our Constitution, when it forbids discrimination or preference in religion, mean merely to guaranty toleration? . . . In a community composed of persons of various religious denominations, having different days of worship, each considering his own as sacred from secular employment, all being equally considered and protected under the Constitution, a law is passed which in effect recognizes the sacred character of one of these days, by compelling all others to abstain from secular employment, which is precisely one of the modes in which its observance is manifested and required by the creed of that sect to which it belongs as a Sabbath. Is not this a discrimination in favor of the one? Does it require more than an appeal to one's common sense to decide that this is a preference? . . . The truth is, however much it may be disguised, that this one day of rest is a purely religious idea . . . [The act is unconstitutional] because it was intended as, and [is] in effect, a discrimination in favor of one religious profession, and gives it a preference over all others.

Field dissented, and in his dissenting opinion he charted the reasoning which has since then been adopted by all courts, including the United States Supreme Court. In fixing a day of rest, said Field, the legislature established only a rule of civil conduct. The statute merely prohibits a person from keeping open his place of business on "the Christian Sabbath, or Sunday"; it limits its command to secular pursuits, "it necessarily leaves religious profession and worship free." The prohibition on the sale of merchandise does not interfere with religion or worship. The act establishes, "as a civil regulation a day of rest from secular pursuits, and that is its only scope and purpose." The term "Christian Sabbath" is used "simply to designate the day selected by the legislature." Since the power of selection is in the legislature, "there is no valid reason why Sunday should not be designated as well as any other day." A civil regulation, said Field,

can not be converted into a religious institution because it is enforced on a day which a particular religious sect regards as sacred. . . . The law against homicide is not the less wise and necessary because the Divine command is, "thou shalt do no murder." . . . The establishment by law of Sunday as a day of rest from labor, is none the less a beneficent and humane regulation, because it accords with the Divine precept that upon that day "thou shalt do no manner of work."

The motives which influenced the legislators, said Field, were not relevant to the question of power. Perhaps they were influenced by religious considerations; but "Christianity is the prevailing faith of our people; it is the basis of our civilization."

Three years later [32] the same court repudiated its earlier decision, and the latter remains the only case that has invalidated a Sunday statute. [33]

Years later, when he was a Justice of the United States Supreme Court, Field had an opportunity to say for a unanimous Court: "Laws setting aside Sunday as a day of rest are upheld, not from any right of the Government to legislate for the promotion of religious observance, but from its right to protect all persons from the physical and moral debasement which comes from uninterrupted labor." [34]

The extremes to which some courts have gone in order to uphold the validity of Sunday statutes will be illustrated by a New York case, *People v. Moses*. [35] In this case the defendant was found guilty of fishing on Sunday in a pond that was the *private property of a club of which he was a member*. The statute prohibited "all shooting, hunting, fishing, playing, horse racing, gaming, or other public sport, exercises, or shows upon the first day of the week, and all noise disturbing the peace of the day." The court held that the act prohibited fishing *anywhere* in the state on Sunday, regardless of circumstances.

The Sunday rest laws of the State of New York have been felt burdensome by many persons living in that state who observe the seventh day as their holy time—orthodox Jews and Seventh Day Baptists and Adventists. When two Kosher butchers, who kept their shops closed from sunset on Friday to sunset on Saturday, were convicted in 1949 for keeping their shops open on Sunday, persons and organizations interested in religious freedom and civil liberties undertook to support their cases through the courts. The Court of Appeals upheld the conviction and held that the Sunday law is a valid police regulation, and that it is neither an establishment of religion nor an interference with the free exercise thereof. "The power of the Legislature to regulate the observance of Sunday as a civil and political institution is well settled." The United States Supreme Court dismissed the appeal.[36]

The case presented an opportunity to the Supreme Court to consider the question whether a state has the right, under the Constitution, to enact legislation which patently protects the Christian Sabbath and which makes "Sabbath breaking" a crime, and which, as construed by the state's highest court, in effect aids or prefers one religion over others. The refusal of the Supreme Court to consider the appeal can hardly serve to sustain the wall of separation.

The New York laws make a distinction between *working* and *doing business* on Sunday. A person must rest from work or labor on Sunday unless he uniformly keeps another day as holy time, but he may not engage in selling any property[37] unless his activity falls within one of the exceptions enumerated in the law.

The decision of the Supreme Court led to the formation in New York of a Joint Committee for a Fair Sabbath Law, made up by leading Jewish organizations and supported by the Protestant Council of New York and the State Federation of [Protestant] Churches. Due to the efforts of this committee,

Governor Thomas E. Dewey, in his annual message to the legislature in 1952, urged re-examination of the Sunday laws. In
response to the governor's request, the legislature appointed a
special committee to make a study of the subject and to submit
recommendations. The Joint Legislative Committee on the
Sabbath Law rejected the proposal that the statute be amended
so that persons who observe a day other than Sunday as their holy
time may be permitted by local law to conduct their businesses
on Sunday if their activity would not interfere with the rest
and repose of the remainder of the community. The Joint Legislative Committee said that the proposed change would be "im-
practical of regulation, virtually impossible of effective enforcement and lead to uncontrollable abuses." These reasons are
absurd when one considers the fact that the present Sunday law
is as often honored in the breach as in the observance. At the
trial of the two butchers, evidence was offered to prove that for
many years sixty-eight chain cigar stores operating in New York
County have consistently and openly violated the law by selling
items on Sunday included in the statutory ban. When a drug-
store is open on Sunday in New York, does it confine its sales
strictly to "drugs, medicines and surgical instruments," and the
few other items which the Penal Law exempts from the ban? Is
there any official concern that the present law in fact is "imprac-
tical of regulation, virtually impossible of effective enforcement" and leads to "uncontrollable abuses"? The factual and
legal situation has been well summarized in the following statement:

The New York Sunday law is a mass of inconsistencies and self-
contradiction. What reason can lie behind a law which permits
the sale of bread, milk and eggs on Sunday, but not meat or fish?
Why should it be legal (as it is) to sell gasoline, oil and tires, but
not anti-freeze or tire jacks? Beer may be sold on Sunday, but not
butter. No law is violated by engaging in a professional hockey
game, but polo and bicycle racing are prohibited. The American
Legion can hardly be blamed for finding it difficult to understand
why its planned circus for disabled soldiers should be unlawful
while the law specifically allows professional baseball, football, bas-
ketball and hockey.

Not only is the law as it is written on the books devoid of rational plan, but its enforcement likewise lacks semblance of consistency or justice. The American Legion could not hold its circus for charitable purposes on Sunday, but a commercial circus is allowed to perform Sundays at Madison Square Garden unmolested. Only recently the State Attorney General ruled that performance of the roller skate derby would violate the Sunday law, but the derby was performed the following Sunday in New York City without interference by the police or District Attorney. It is unlawful to open a motion picture theatre before 2 P.M. on Sunday, but there is hardly a theatre on Broadway which is not open by noon. No one, as far as is known, has ever been prosecuted for violating the law.

Consistent enforcement of the Sunday law would completely alter the social and economic habits of our community. It would, for instance, put an end to radio and television broadcasting on Sunday. It would halt publication (though not sale) of newspapers and publications on the first day of the week. The law provides that goods unlawfully exhibited for sale on the Sabbath shall be forfeited. Imagine, if you can, what would happen if this provision were enforced against all chain drug and cigar stores which, in effect, operate miniature department stores on Sunday.[38]

The statutes of several states exempt seventh-day religious observers from the Sunday laws.[39] There is no evidence that religious observance has suffered in those states because of the statutory sensitivity to denominational differences.

In view of the fact that the Supreme Court has refused to reconsider the problem of Sunday laws, it has been suggested that a program for state legislative action should have the following phases:

First, repeal of all statutes prohibiting or regulating business, labor or other activity on Sunday. Second, enactment of a statute providing that in every week each person must receive at least one day of rest and that each business must close at least one day, except in emergencies. . . . Third, enactment of a statute prohibiting any wilful disturbance of a religious meeting whenever held. In addition, conscientious and effective enforcement of existing peace statutes is essential to protect the community right to quiet and repose.[40]

These proposals, it is contended, "would eliminate the religious overtones of Sunday statutes while accomplishing their legitimate civil objectives." [41]

It is doubtful, however, if in the foreseeable future any significant changes will be effected in our Sunday laws. In Great Britain, too, blue laws that date from 1625, 1677, and 1780 are still on the books, presenting "a hodge-podge of cans and can'ts," so that

an Englishman can play cricket or golf on Sunday, but he cannot go to the dogs, or watch a football game in the stadium. He can go to the cinema, a concert, the zoo, or a museum, but he can't see a play. It is a crime to kill game, but rabbits are okay. Fishing is allowed,—but only for salmon with a rod and line.[42]

When a private member introduced a bill to repeal almost all of the Sunday observance laws, Parliament, in January 1953, defeated the measure. In Great Britain, however, there is no constitutional principle of separation of church and state. In the United States, as has been manifested in the attitude of the Supreme Court with respect to Sunday laws, and in its treatment of the New Jersey Bible-reading case, and in the *Zorach* decision, separation often means co-operative, not absolute, separation. The most (and the least) that can be expected is that the law, while preserving Sunday as the Sabbath, will provide relief for those who observe the seventh day as their Sabbath, by permitting them to engage in their vocation or business on Sunday, provided they conduct themselves "in such manner as not to interrupt or disturb other persons in observing the first day of the week as holy time." [43]

# ☆ 10 ☆

# The Liberty of
# Private Schools

IN TOTALITARIAN ideology and practice, the state has a monopoly on the education of children. This is necessary if the party or leader in control of the machinery of state is to continue in power and if ideological *Gleichschaltung* is to be assured. This monopoly is achieved in part by a prohibition upon the establishment of private schools as substitutes for government schools, rigid control of the school curriculum, and by laws which practically make it impossible for parents to supplement, by private instruction at home or elsewhere, the public school education compulsorily imposed upon their children.

Such educational monopoly is impossible under the United States Constitution. Several decisions of the Supreme Court are important in this connection.

1. Pupils in American schools originally were taught in English or in some foreign language congenial to the parents. Some states required that English be taught as one of the subjects. Some states required that some foreign language, specified in the statute, be taught. Between the Civil War and World War I, however, many states prescribed English as the basic language in elementary schools. In World War I some states, spurred by hatred of the enemy or by nationalist zeal, went further and forbade the teaching of all foreign languages or of German in

particular. Some states or communities permitted the teaching of German in high schools only.[1]

In 1923 the Supreme Court had an opportunity to consider the constitutionality of these prohibiting statutes.[2] A Nebraska law of 1919 provided that no foreign language shall be taught to a pupil before he has completed the eighth grade. Robert Mayer, an instructor in a parochial school, was convicted for having taught German to a pupil in violation of the statute.

In support of the statute before the Supreme Court, the state contended that until children "had grown into" English and "until it had become a part of them," they should not be taught any other language in the schools. The legislative purpose was to make English the mother tongue of all children. The state argued that the schools hours are necessarily limited; a child's "daily capacity for work is comparatively small"; a selection of subjects from among many that may be taught is obviously necessary; the state has the right to make that selection, and may express its will by imposing a prohibition upon the teaching of specific subjects.

The Supreme Court was not impressed with these arguments. In an opinion by Justice McReynolds, the Court held the act a violation of the Due Process Clause of the Fourteenth Amendment: the legislature had attempted "materially to interfere with the calling of modern language teachers, with the opportunities of pupils to acquire knowledge, and with the power of parents to control the education of their own [children]."

The state, said Justice McReynolds, "may do much, go very far" to improve the quality of its citizens, physically, mentally, and morally; but to achieve these ends, the state must use means which show that it respects the fundamental rights of the individual. The legality of the end sought does not necessarily validate every means used; it may be proper for the state to seek to give to all its citizens a ready understanding of English, but this objective may not be sought by the coercive method provided by the Nebraska statute.

Plato's *Republic*, said Justice McReynolds, suggested the wisdom of communalizing all children, and Sparta took all male children away from the custody and control of their parents;

but no state could impose such restrictions without doing violence to both the letter and the spirit of the Constitution. "The desire of the legislature," said the Court,

to foster a homogeneous people with American ideals, prepared readily to understand current discussions of civic matters, is easy to appreciate. . . . But the means adopted, we think, exceed the limitations upon the power of the state. . . . The power of the state to compel attendance at some school and to make reasonable regulations for all schools, including a requirement that they shall give instructions in English, is not questioned. Nor has challenge been made of the state's power to prescribe a curriculum for institutions which it supports. . . . No emergency has arisen which renders knowledge by a child of some language other than English so clearly harmful as to justify its inhibition, with the consequent infringement of rights long freely enjoyed.

2. In some states efforts have been made to compel, by law, all children to attend public schools only. In 1922 Oregon enacted such a law by popular referendum supported by rabidly anti-Catholic forces.[3] The law was challenged in the Supreme Court in cases involving a Catholic school and a military academy.[4] The law provided that children between eight and sixteen years of age shall attend a public school until they have completed the eighth grade; failure of a parent to send his child to a public school was a misdemeanor.

In his opinion for a unanimous Court, Justice McReynolds said that no question was raised concerning the following powers of the state: (1) reasonably to regulate all schools; (2) to inspect, supervise, and examine all schools, their teachers, and their pupils; (3) to require that all children of proper age attend some school; (4) to require that teachers shall be of good moral character and patriotic disposition; (5) to require that "certain studies plainly essential to good citizenship" shall be taught; and (6) to require that nothing be taught which is manifestly inimical to the public welfare.

As to the Oregon statute, the Court held (1) that enforcement of the law would destroy the business and property of the parochial and private schools, though they were engaged in undertakings "not inherently harmful, but long regarded as useful and meritorious"; and (2) that the law "unreasonably interferes with the liberty of parents and guardians to direct the upbringing and education of children under their control." With respect to the latter point, the Court made the following extremely significant statement:

The fundamental theory of liberty upon which all governments in this Union repose excludes any general power of the state to standardize its children by forcing them to accept instruction from public teachers only. The child is not the mere creature of the state; those who nurture him and direct his destiny have the right, coupled with the high duty, to recognize and prepare him for additional obligations.

3. Hawaii at various times attempted to regulate the study of foreign languages because of the Japanese, Chinese, and Korean elements in its population. An act of the Hawaiian legislature, adopted in 1920 and amended in 1923 and 1925, was challenged in the Supreme Court. In the 1920's there were 163 foreign language schools in the territory, operated entirely by private funds. The challenged act provided that no foreign language school shall be conducted unless it received a permit from the department of public instruction; the fee for the permit was one dollar per pupil; each school was to file with the department a list of its pupils; persons teaching or exercising administrative powers in the schools were required to apply for permits, and these were not to be granted unless the department was satisfied that the applicant was possessed of the ideals of democracy, had knowledge of American history and institutions, and knew how to read, write, and speak the English language. Foreign language schools were not to be conducted during the hours while the public schools were in session; pupils were not to attend foreign language schools for more than one hour each day, or more than six hours a week, or more than thirty-six weeks in any school year. The department had the power to prescribe the subjects and courses of study of all foreign language schools, including their textbooks, entrance, and other

requirements. The declared object of the act was to regulate the foreign language schools in order that the "Americanism" of the pupils may be promoted.

The Supreme Court unanimously declared the act unconstitutional.[5] The opinion by Justice McReynolds made it clear that the act offended constitutional guaranties by going "far beyond mere regulation of privately supported schools where children obtain instruction deemed valuable by their parents and which is not obviously in conflict with any public interest." The state may not give "affirmative direction concerning the intimate and essential details of such schools, intrust their control to public officers, and deny both owners and patrons reasonable choice and discretion in respect of teachers, curriculum and textbooks." The act, in brief, seriously interfered with the fair opportunity that parents should have to procure for their children instruction which they think important and which the Court could not say was harmful; the "Japanese parent [in Hawaii] has the right to direct the education of his own child without unreasonable restrictions; the Constitution protects him as well as those who speak another tongue."

This right of parents to send their children to private or parochial schools is, I believe, one of the most important rights under our Constitution. The following passages from a statement made in 1955 by the Roman Catholic bishops of the United States are in accord with the facts and the law, and are founded in sentiments that Americans can express with just pride:

> Historically and actually our nation has been blessed with educational freedom. Her school system is not a closed, unitary creation of the state, a servile instrument of governmental monopoly, but one which embraces, together with the state-supported schools, a whole enormous cluster of private and church-related schools, including many of the most honored names in the entire educational world, and devoted to the education of many millions of the nation's youth. . . .
>
> But if the unparalleled growth of the schools supported by public funds is a mighty tribute to America's zeal for learning and her ambition to build an intelligent democratic society, no less astonishing has been the growth and accomplishment of the private and

church-related schools during the same relative period. In candor, it deserves to be said that their record affords an even more impressive example of the American spirit at work, for it has been brought about not by the advantage of public funds nor by the spur of legislative mandate, but by the free co-operation of those convinced of their importance and necessity. . . .

Let this be fully understood: Private and church-related schools in America exist not by sufferance but by right. The right is implicit in the whole concept of American freedom and immunity from totalitarian oppression and in the constitutional framework of our Federal Government and of the several States. . . .

Thus far, happily, the right of the parent to educate the child has not been successfully challenged in any American court. The country agrees that this right is basic to the definition of freedom. Be that education provided by the state-supported school, the private school or the church-affiliated school, the choice of the parent is decisive. If the state has a concurrent right to decree a minimal education for its citizens, as a vital necessity in a modern democratic society, that right does not extend to an arbitrary designation of the school or the educational agency.

It is, rather, a general right, limited by the primary right of the parent to exercise his choice according to his best wisdom and his conscience. Indeed, it is worth remarking that while the state may usefully engage in the business of education, as demonstrated in our national experience, it has no authority either to monopolize the field or to arrogate to itself exclusive privileges and powers. The state, by definition, is not itself primarily an educative agency.[6]

In the case of schools, constitutional principles have accommodated themselves one to the other—the right of the state to conduct public schools and to enact compulsory attendance laws, and the right of parents to select private schools for their children. This principle of accommodation should be extended to a substitution of dismissed time for released time, and to a relaxation of rest laws to allow a seventh-day sabbatarian to substitute Saturday for Sunday as his day of rest without suffering undue economic sacrifices. If the extension will not come from the Court, it should come from the legislatures. In this way both public need and private conscience will be served and respected.

# The Liberty of Churches

THE churches in the United States, as other institutions, have felt and have reacted to the great social and political problems and movements of domestic or world scope. Though concerned with metaphysical truths and religious values, the churches are organizations of human beings who have loyalties to institutions that seek to win the support of religious associations or seek at least to neutralize them when the ends of churches and of other institutions seem to touch one another at some point. There may be separation of church and state; but the doctrine of separation does not keep the church from feeling the social and political earthquakes or tremors.[1] Devoted as most of them are to what may appear to be enduring human values, the churches have found ways to survive earth-shaking events that have made rubble of other institutions;[2] but they have not been spared threats, attacks, and crises.[3]

The most deeply felt domestic events in the history of the American people have been the Civil War and—though one can say this with much less certainty—the fight against the Communist danger. The emotional responses of Americans to these events were often more profound than those caused by world wars with external enemies. Like conflicts between members of a family, the struggle between two Americans was full of barely suppressed hatred, and was conducted in an atmosphere of suspicion and hysteria, in which each combatant looked upon his opponent as Cain with his arm raised ready to strike and kill.

Both these events touched the churches; they led to sectarian splits and conflicts, which found their way to the highest state courts and the United States Supreme Court. Factional struggles within the churches led to legal struggles for the possession of church property, and these struggles afforded the courts an opportunity to attempt an accommodation of freedom of religion and of the doctrine of separation of church and state to questions of ownership of church property as they arise out of doctrinal or factional disputes. In this connection we shall examine two significant Supreme Court cases, one that arose out of the slavery issue, and the other that arose out of the struggle against Communist domination or influence.

*Watson v. Jones*[4] arose out of a schism in the Presbyterian Church in Kentucky as a result of the Civil War. From the beginning of the war to its close, the General Assembly of the Presbyterian Church in the United States of America took the position that it was the obligation of every citizen to support the Federal Government in the war; and after the Emancipation Proclamation in 1862, the General Assembly openly opposed slavery. Instructions were issued that no person shall be engaged as a missionary or admitted as a member or minister of a Presbyterian church unless there shall first be an inquiry into his loyalty to the Federal Government and into his sentiments on the subject of slavery. Persons who had voluntarily aided the Confederate States, or who believed that slavery was a "divine institution" which the church should conserve, were required to repent and forsake these sins before they could be accepted.

Southern Presbyterians who supported the Confederate cause and slavery organized in 1861 the Presbyterian Church in the Confederate States. This organization changed its name in 1865 to the Presbyterian Church in the United States.[5] But Presbyterians in the Southern States did not solidly affiliate with this organization; there were splits within the state synods and local presbyteries: loyalties, divided loyalties, revolts, and secessions were the order of the day.

The case of *Watson v. Jones* arose out of a split in the Walnut Street Presbyterian Church in Louisville, Kentucky. The members and officers of this church divided into two distinct and bitterly opposing groups, and each group claimed to be the true Walnut Street Presbyterian Church and sought to deny to the other the right to any such claim and to use of the church property. It was the dispute over property rights that brought the factional controversy before the courts.

In his opinion for the Supreme Court, Justice Miller distinguished three possible situations, as follows: (1) when church property is devoted by the deed or the will of the donor to the teaching or support of some specific form of religious doctrine or belief; (2) when property is held by a congregation that is completely independent of other congregations and that in its church government owes no obligation to any higher authority; and (3) when property is held by a congregation that is a subordinate body of a church organization in which there are superior ecclesiastical tribunals that have ultimate power of control.

In the first type of situation it is the duty of the courts to see to it that the dedicated property is not diverted from the trust attached to its use. As long as there are persons with an interest in the execution of the trust, the diversion of the property or fund to different uses will be prevented. In such a case, even a majority of the congregation will not be allowed to use the property to support a conflicting doctrine. The principle is the same when the organization to which the property is donated under a trust agreement is of the second or congregational type. In a proper case it may be necessary for the courts to go into the question whether the party accused of violating the trust is "holding or teaching a different doctrine, or using a form of worship which is so far variant as to defeat the declared object of the trust."

When a church of the independent or congregational type holds property with no specific trust attached to it other than that it is to be used by the congregation as a religious body, and a schism leads to a separation of the members into conflicting bodies, in that case if the principle of government has been majority rule, then the majority of the members will control the right to the use of the property. If in the government of that congregation the officers are vested with final authority, then they will determine the property right. The dissenters may withdraw, but they will take with them no rights to the use of the church property. In this type of situation it will not be necessary for the courts to conduct an inquiry into the religious beliefs or practices of the contending factions; for even if it is the minority who remain the only faithful supporters of the religious dogmas of the founders of the congregation, they will not get judicial relief.

In the third type of situation, where the local church is part of a larger organization with which it is connected by religious views and ecclesiastical government, as was the case of the Louisville church in *Watson v. Jones,* the questions of faith, discipline, church rule or law are left for ultimate decision to the hierarchy of church judicatories. Their decisions are final and will be taken by the courts as binding and as final dispositions.

In this country, said Justice Miller in a memorable passage,[6]

the full and free right to entertain any religious belief, to practice any religious principle, and to teach any religious doctrine which does not violate the laws of morality and property, and which does not infringe personal rights, is conceded to all. The law knows no heresy, and is committed to the support of no dogma, the establishment of no sect. The right to organize voluntary religious associations to assist in the expression and dissemination of any religious doctrine, and to create tribunals for the decision of controverted questions of faith within the association, and for the ecclesiastical government of all the individual members, congregations and officers within the general association, is unquestioned. All who unite themselves to such a body do so with an implied consent to this government, and are bound to submit to it. But it would be a vain consent and would lead to the total subversion of such religious bodies, if any one aggrieved by one of their decisions could appeal to the secular courts and have them reversed. It is of the essence of these religious unions, and of their right to establish tribunals for the decision of questions arising among themselves, that those decisions should be binding in all cases of ecclesiastical cognizance, subject only to such appeals as the organism itself provides for.

If the matter concerns theological controversy, church discipline, ecclesiastical government, or the conformity of church members to the standard of morals required of them, the tribunals of the church organization have final authority to dispose of the matter, and the courts will not intervene on the plea that the church authorities have exceeded the power vested in them, or that they have used procedures not authorized by the laws of the church. If the rule were otherwise, said Justice Miller, it would mean that the civil courts, where the question of church property is involved, would need to go into questions of church doctrine and the validity of church decrees would be determined in the civil courts.

In 1952 the Supreme Court had an opportunity to reconsider the principles formulated in *Watson v. Jones,* and it found that those principles, although formulated some eighty years before, when it had not yet been held that the religious freedom guaranty of the First Amendment was a limitation on state as well as on federal action, radiated "a spirit of freedom for religious organizations, an independence from secular control or manipulation, in short, power to decide for themselves, free from state interference, matters of church government as well as those of faith and doctrine."

In the case decided in 1952—the *St. Nicholas Cathedral* case [7] —the Court had before it a factional dispute which involved the question who was entitled to use St. Nicholas Cathedral in New York, the archiepiscopal see of the Russian Orthodox Church in North America. The two factions were the following: (1) a group led by Archbishop Leonty, who was elected Metropolitan of all America and Canada and Archbishop of New York by convention of the American churches, and (2) a group led by Archbishop Benjamin, who was appointed Archbishop of the Archdiocese of North America and the Aleutian Islands by the Supreme Church Authority of the Russian Orthodox Church, i.e., the Patriarch of Moscow and all Russia and its Holy Synod.

Until 1924 there was no question but that the Russian Church in America (also known as the Eastern Orthodox or Greek Catholic Church) was subject to the jurisdiction of the Most

Sacred Governing Synod or the Patriarchate in Moscow. In that year the Russian Orthodox Greek Catholic Church of North America was formed at a convention (*sobor*) held at Detroit, which was declared to be an administratively autonomous North American church. This convention was held at a time when the Patriarch of Moscow was in prison charged with counter-revolutionary activity and when an attempt was made by the Russian government to displace the Orthodox Church with a so-called Living Church. The Detroit *sobor* decided that temporarily the church in the United States shall be governed by an archbishop elected by the American church, but that the question of the relationship between the American church and Moscow be left to a future "true sobor of the Russian Orthodox Church" when conditions of political freedom will obtain. But in the same or next year the Patriarch was released from prison, and in 1933 Benjamin was appointed Archbishop by one of the three bishops who succeeded to the patriarchal throne. Gradually the Russian government and the church in Russia accommodated themselves to each other's existence, and in 1945 a new Patriarch was elected at a *sobor* which both American factions recognized as a true *sobor* held in accordance with church canons. The new Patriarch issued a ukase in 1945 requiring the American church to convene a *sobor*, at which should be expressed the decision of American members to reunite with the Russian Mother Church and the resolution of the American church to abstain "from political activities against the U.S.S.R." At this American *sobor* the delegates were to elect a Metropolitan, subject to confirmation by the Patriarch. Such a *sobor* was held in Cleveland in 1946, but the delegates refused to observe the instructions from Moscow and instead resolved "that any administrative recognition of the Synod of the Russian Orthodox Church Abroad is hereby terminated, retaining, however, our spiritual and brotherly relations with all parts of the Russian Orthodox Church abroad."

The New York legislature in 1945 concluded "that the Moscow Patriarchate was no longer capable of functioning as a true religious body, but had become a tool of the Soviet Government primarily designed to implement its foreign policy." [8] Desiring to free the American church from the influence or domination of an atheistic and antireligious government, it enacted a statute,[9] the purpose of which was to bring all the New York churches which were formerly subject to the Moscow Synod or Patriarch into an administratively autonomous metropolitan district, which would take in all of North America. The act provided that all the churches should in the future be governed by the ecclesiastical body and hierarchy of the Russian Church in America. The statute added that "in all other respects" the churches shall "conform to, maintain and follow the faith, doctrine, ritual, communion, discipline, canon law, traditions and usages of the Eastern Confession (Eastern Orthodox or Greek Catholic Church)."

St. Nicholas Cathedral was in the possession of Archbishop Benjamin, appointed by Moscow. An action to eject him was brought by the faction that supported Archbishop Leonty, who was elected by an American *sobor*. The New York Court of Appeals held in favor of the latter on the basis of the New York statute. The United States Supreme Court reversed the judgment, holding that the statute prohibited the free exercise of religion in violation of the Constitution.

In an opinion by Justice Reed, the Court held that while a legislature may punish subversive action, and that a clergyman's robe or pulpit is no defense in an action for subversion, a church has the constitutionally guarantied freedom to select its clergy without any interference from the state. Who effectively selected the Archbishop of the Russian Church in America? The Russian Church is a hierarchical organization, with ultimate authority in the Sacred Synod or the Patriarch. Neither the Synod nor the Patriarch ever relinquished authority over the American church or ever recognized its autonomy. When churches in the United States are governed by a central authority, a statute may not transfer their control to another church organization against the wishes of the highest authority in the hierarchy of the church. Said Justice Reed:

Such a law violates the Fourteenth Amendment prohibiting in this country the free exercise of religion. Legislation that regulates church administration, the operation of the churches, the appointment of clergy, by requiring conformity to church statutes . . . prohibits the free exercise of religion. Although this statute requires the New York churches to "in all other respects conform to, maintain and follow the faith, doctrine, ritual, communion, discipline, canon law, traditions and usages of the Eastern Confession . . . ," their conformity is by legislative will. Should the state assert power to change the statute requiring conformity to ancient faith and doctrine to one establishing a different doctrine, the invalidity would be unmistakable.

The legislature of the State of New York cannot undertake to minimize the political use of church pulpits by transferring control over churches from one group of persons to another. Such statutory transfer, said the Court, "violates our rule of separation between church and state." In the case of a hierarchical church—like the Walnut Street Presbyterian Church in Louisville or St. Nicholas Cathedral in New York—where a split in the congregation occurs over the issue of slavery or Communist influence or what-not, ultimate resolution rests with the ecclesiastical, and not civil, court of last resort. "Freedom to select the clergy," said the Court, "where no improper methods of choice are proven, we think, must now be said to have federal constitutional protection as a part of the free exercise of religion against state interference." Even in cases where property rights follow as an incident from decision on an ecclesiastical issue, the church rule controls. "This under our Constitution necessarily follows in order that there may be free exercise of religion." In brief, religious freedom under the Constitution requires that when rival factions come to court for a determination of their secular or religious rights, the court will decide the issue according to the laws of their church, and a legislature is not free to act differently. If the church belongs to a hierarchical order, rule within that church will not be determined by a counting of heads; nor may a state protect itself or church members from "submission by the mother church in Moscow to political authority." [10] There are churches throughout the United States, Justice Frankfurter pointed out, that have ties to various countries, but no state has the right to assess the extent of the entanglements of a religious body in a foreign political order, and to dispose of church authority and property in accordance with that assessment. "Bismarck sought to detach German Catholics from Rome by a series of laws not too different in purport" from the New York statute; but no American government has the right "to reinforce the loyalty of . . . citizens by deciding who is the true exponent of their religion."

In his dissenting opinion, Justice Jackson argued that a state has the right to make its own property law, and apply it to churches without regard to canon law. "To me," he said, "whatever the canon law is found to be and whoever is the rightful head of the Moscow patriarchate, I do not think New York law must yield to the authority of a foreign and unfriendly state masquerading as a spiritual institution." But the answer to this argument is given by Justice Frankfurter: Here is no dispute over the mere title or use of property, for "St. Nicholas Cathedral is not just a piece of real estate. . . . A cathedral is the seat and center of ecclesiastical authority. . . . What is at stake here is the power to exercise religious authority. That is the essence of this controversy." The cathedral was merely "the outward symbol of a religious faith." This would be equally true, as we know from *Watson v. Jones*, were the case one involving only a neighborhood church.[11]

Our discussion should point up the fact that often it is not possible or desirable to draw a sharp line between the things that are God's and the things that are Caesar's. In the interest of maintaining the wall of separation, it becomes necessary at times to assimilate to the church or God things that ordinarily seem to belong to the state or Caesar; for human beings find that it is indispensable for their religious faith to have outward symbols like churches, cathedrals, cemeteries, and other tangible goods, which become consecrated vessels for spiritual use. "Where two or three are gathered together in My Name, there am I in the midst of them." [12] But when two or three are gathered together, they form a congregation, and they seek a meeting place for their gathering, and then the Name is appropriated for both the gathering and the meeting place, and all three—congregation, church, and Name—become inextricably merged in one religious faith. To treat a church as if it were mere real estate, as Justice Jackson would have it, would often mean pulling the thread that would undo the whole fabric. Men believe that in a church—as in the churches involved in the litigation before the Supreme Court—the choir of heaven comes down to use the furniture of earth, so that what was profane becomes sacred, what was property becomes consecrated ground, what was an object of merchandise becomes an object of reverence.[13] Church and state are separate; but to keep them separate it becomes necessary, at times, to treat them *as if* they were not separate, and the state says to the church: "Thy will be my will." [14]

# The Law Knows No Heresy

JUST as the government is not permitted, through legislation or judicial proceedings, to upset or even interfere with the processes and decisions of ecclesiastical bodies, even when they affect property or contractual rights, so, too, the government is not permitted to inquire into the truth or falsity of religious beliefs, even when persons attempt to acquire money or property by an appeal to religious beliefs that most people would consider patently and shockingly untrue.

The *"I Am"* or *Ballard* case [1] will serve to illustrate the latter principle. The Ballard family organized the "I Am" movement by claiming miraculous power to communicate with the spirit world and to heal the sick. They were indicted for using the mail to perpetrate fraud. They were charged with knowingly making false representations, among them that the late Guy W. Ballard had been designated as Saint Germain, through whom would be transmitted divine messages to mankind under the teachings of the "I Am" movement; that Edna and Donald Ballard, by reason of their high spiritual attainments, have been selected as divine messengers; that the Ballards possessed the power to heal persons afflicted with any diseases or injuries, curable or incurable, and that they had in fact cured hundreds of persons. The indictment charged that the Ballards knew that their representations were false, and that they were made for the purpose of defrauding persons of money and property. In brief, the Ballards were accused of being religious fakers; that is, that they made claims of possessing supernatural powers for the purpose of exploiting the gullibility of innocent and ignorant persons, and that the Ballards knew that in fact they did not possess such powers. The Federal Government proceeded against them on the theory that it had a duty to punish the defendants for using the mail to accomplish their fraudulent scheme.

At the trial in the United States district court the judge instructed the jury that the truth or falsity of the religious beliefs of the defendants was not the government's concern. The only question that the jury could consider was whether or not the defendants honestly and in good faith believed what they claimed. If, e.g., the defendants in fact believed that Jesus had appeared to them and had dictated some of the works published by them, they were to be acquitted, even though the jury might consider the claim an outrageous one; but if the jury should find that the defendants lacked an honest belief in the claims they made, then they were to convict them of fraudulent use of the mail. The jury found the defendants guilty. The court of appeals reversed the judgment of conviction on the ground that the government should have proved that some of the representations made by the defendants were in fact false.

In the Supreme Court five Justices agreed with the trial judge and held that the government may not concern itself with the question of the objective truth or falsity of any person's religious beliefs or concepts. There may be no trial as to the truth of claimed spiritual events or the possession of supernatural powers. The Constitution safeguards the free exercise of the religion chosen by any person.[2] Said Justice Douglas for the Court: "Freedom of thought, which includes freedom of religious belief, is basic in a society of free men." This freedom, he said,

embraces the right to maintain theories of life and of death and of the hereafter which are rank heresy to followers of the orthodox faiths. Heresy trials are foreign to our Constitution. Men may believe what they cannot prove. They may not be put to the proof of their religious doctrines or beliefs. Religious experiences which are as real as life to some may be incomprehensible to others. Yet the fact that they may be beyond the ken of mortals does not mean that they can be made suspect before the law. . . . [The Fathers of the Constitution] fashioned a charter of government which envisaged the widest possible toleration of conflicting views. Man's relation to his God was made no concern of the state. He was granted the right to worship as he pleased and to answer to no man for the verity of his religious views.

Justice Jackson, in a notable dissenting opinion, urged the Court to go further and to hold that the government may not raise any question relating to the sincerity or honesty of a person's belief; in other words, the Constitution, according to Jackson, prohibits the state from looking into (1) the question of the objective truth or falsity of a person's religious beliefs, and (2) the question as to whether or not the person really believed what he professed to believe. The two questions are, said Jackson, intimately related; in fact, one would not raise the question of subjective honesty or sincerity in the profession of beliefs unless one first concluded that the substance of the belief was demonstrably false; the honest or dishonest belief in the making of a representation can become a question only if the representation were in fact false. That one knowingly falsified is best proved when it is shown that what he said happened never did happen. "How can the government prove these persons knew something to be false which it cannot prove to be false?"

The decision of the Court in the *Ballard* case is certainly a gain for religious freedom in the United States. In the teachings of the Ballards there was probably "nothing but humbug, untainted by any trace of truth," but if the government were permitted to prosecute and punish for the perpetration of a religious hoax, it would mean an end of religious freedom; for religious faith is "the substance of things hoped for, the evidence of things not seen. . . . Blessed are they that have not seen, and yet have believed." [3] Could St. Paul have proved the verity of the experience that converted Saul of Tarsus into Paul the Apostle? And St. Augustine, who also was converted by mystical experiences, found it necessary to say: "What is faith save to believe what you do not see?" [4] The Court's position leaves the door open for the perpetration of gross frauds; but to millions of men, other men's religions are always gross frauds.

But the Court did not go far enough. It is not possible to measure a person's honesty or sincerity when it comes to religious beliefs. No fundamentalist reads *everything* in the Bible as the literal truth; no "liberal" reader of the Bible reads *everything* in it as metaphor, parable, or allegory. The human mind plays with subtleties, shadings of meanings, nuances, refinements of thoughts, ideas and shadows of ideas, myths, metaphors, parables, paradoxes, hyperboles, anthropomorphisms, circumlocutions, and a thousand and one other devices, which often make the mind a captive of snares which the mind itself has made. "The heart is deceitful above all things" and only God "knoweth the secrets of the heart" [5]—these are religious as well as psychological truths. How sincere in his religious beliefs is a person who, while professing belief in the immortality of his soul and in rewards and punishments in the next world, seemingly spends his time doing practically nothing but accumulating the things that you can't take with you, or a preacher who in the same breath will say that God is love and that sinners are in the hands of an angry God? Who can weigh and measure the quantity and quality of honesty in professions of religious faith? If heresy trials are foreign to our Constitution, then trials for hypocrisy should be equally foreign.

Furthermore, Justice Jackson rightly emphasized the point that we cannot try religious sincerity apart from religious verity. Said Jackson:

If we try religious sincerity severed from religious verity, we isolate the dispute from the very considerations which in common experience provide its most reliable answer. . . . When does less than full belief in a professed credo become actionable fraud if one is soliciting gifts or legacies? Such inquiries may discomfort orthodox as well as unconventional religious teachers, for even the most regular of them are sometimes accused of taking their orthodoxy with a grain of salt.

# ☆ 13 ☆

# The Right to Seek Converts

WE HAVE seen that the Constitution prohibits government from concerning itself in any way with the question of the truth or falsity of any religious dogmas, beliefs, or doctrines, no matter how outrageously false, foolish, or evil they may appear to public officials or to the overwhelming majority of the people. Essentially this is a negative or protective freedom which the Constitution has thrown about religious belief. What of the positive or aggressive freedom to teach or preach religious doctrine in an effort to win converts—the right to proselytize or evangelize, especially on behalf of an unpopular sect? While this freedom is obviously an aspect of freedom of speech, press, and assembly, it is of sufficient significance to merit consideration, although briefly, as a phase of religious freedom.

The fact is that while in some parts of the world, although the constitutions and laws may offer a measure of protection to the exercise of freedom of speech, press, and assembly, the line is drawn at efforts by an unpopular religious sect to distribute literature, to preach openly, or to engage in any other form of sectarian propaganda or missionary work. To cite several examples: In Spain, a Protestant chapel may not bear any outward sign as a place of worship; Protestant clergymen may not hold outdoor meetings; they may not proselytize in any way; they may not distribute religious tracts. A front-page editorial in the newspaper which speaks for the Roman Catholic Church in

Catalonia and for the Archbishop of Barcelona put the rationale of these restrictions in the following language:

> We do not hesitate to affirm that we should prefer to see 10,000,000 Communists in Spain to 1,000,000 Protestants. The worst that could happen to our country would be a religious split. Communism will pass from the world, but a religious rift in Spain would be permanent and would give rise to the most bloody civil struggles. We Spaniards have filled history with fratricidal struggles on political questions, yet if spiritual reasons for discussion appeared on the horizon our survival as a nation would be impossible.[1]

Variations on this theme may be found in Italy: the Archbishop of Milan explained in 1952 that Italy was a Roman Catholic nation and "for superior reasons of a religious and political order, there should be a check on the liberty, particularly of ministers of other faiths, to split the unity of Italy by building on our territory seventh columns under the command of foreign (ecclesiastical) hierarchies." [2]

In the United States, however, religious splits, instead of being viewed as a calamity, are viewed as a necessary condition— as well as a consequence—of religious freedom. Is uniformity of opinion desirable? "No more than of face and stature," answered Jefferson. Differences of opinion are advantageous in religion, he added. For the different sects "perform the office of *censor morum* over each other." He pointed out that in states where the church had been disestablished, religious freedom did not lead to "the most bloody civil struggles" (to quote the Archbishop of Barcelona); on the contrary, said Jefferson, "their harmony is unparalleled." [3] Today, with several hundred denominations in the field, Jefferson's judgment stands confirmed; the "experiment" for which he pleaded has proved itself a success.

"How shall they call on him in whom they have not believed?" asked Paul; "and how shall they believe in him of whom they have not heard? and how shall they hear without a preacher? and how shall they preach except they be sent?" [4] In this statement one finds the religious motivation of church missions, to whom proselytization is a religious act and duty.

This duty has been taken in its most compelling and literal sense by Jehovah's Witnessess, who hear themselves personally addressed by Jesus: "Ye shall be witnesses unto me both in Jerusalem, and in all Judea, and in Samaria, and unto the uttermost part of the earth." [5] Acting as "witnesses," they have often aroused as much antagonism against themselves and their message as have Protestants in Spain or Italy, or Christians in India, Afghanistan, or Russia; but their constitutional right to be "witnesses" to the truth as they see it has been repeatedly vindicated in the Supreme Court. In notable cases, they have tested and have had confirmed their right to conduct open-air meetings and parades, and to distribute or sell their tracts on the streets or from door to door. No sect in the United States needs to hide its light under a bushel, or fear to show its wares in the open market. No one is compelled to listen, no one is compelled to buy; and no one is prohibited from making extravagant claims for his own brand of salvation, or from making a fool of himself. The rule is: *caveat emptor*. There are sharp differences in the realms of religious and political faiths; what is dogma to one man is heresy to another; and to persuade others

a person often resorts to exaggeration, to vilification of men who have been, or are, prominent in church or state, and even to false statement. But the people of this nation have ordained in the light of history, that, in spite of the probability of excesses and abuses, these liberties are, in the long view, essential to enlightened opinion and right conduct on the part of the citizens of a democracy. . . . The essential characteristic of these liberties is, that under their shield many types of life, character, opinion and belief can develop unmolested and unobstructed.[6]

The driving force, we find again and again, is recognition of a commitment to pluralism: we start with a diversity of races, creeds, opinions; each man finds himself compelled to be a "witness" to the truth as he sees it; exercise of the right to be a "witness," and to be a "witness" who may be different from all others, leads to a multiplication of different creeds and opinions; pluralism is then seen as both a necessity and a virtue; and the First Amendment guaranty of freedom is seen, paradoxically, as the basis of both American unity and American diversity—without it there would be no *e pluribus unum*. In this diversity some "witnesses" are rich in worldly possessions: they have cathedrals, churches, or synagogues; they have cardinals, bishops, ministers, or rabbis; they do not feel themselves impelled to seek converts on the highways and byways of the country; they have their established seats of power, jurisdiction, and influence in the congregation, parish, and diocese, and they wait for those who will respond to their call, "Come unto me. . . ." But there are also the itinerant evangelists, those who cannot pay their own way, men who do not wait for the unredeemed to come unto them but who go out to seek the souls that need saving, missionaries who use ancient or unconventional methods for the propagation of their faith—handbills and tracts, street-corner sermons, park meetings, doorbell ringing, playing of phonograph records on the sidewalk. Such persons, given their evangelistic zeal, and the human propensity to exaggerate one's own truth and to enlarge the next man's error and blindness, naturally create, or find themselves in, situations in which the police authorities claim the right to have something to say and do: prevent interference with traffic on the streets, protect the householder from fraudulent or annoying peddlers, prevent possible public disorder, keep vagrants off the streets, keep the parks as places of refuge for those who seek quiet and relaxation, keep public places from becoming littered with papers and pamphlets. Given these conditions, Jehovah's Witnesses became perfect guinea pigs for the testing of the limits of the First Amendment freedoms. They were charged with "excesses and abuses." Beginning with 1938, they provided the Supreme Court with a long series of cases in which various phases of these freedoms were subject to careful examination. The result, on the whole, has been the establishment of precedents which have strengthened the foundations and reaches of freedom of religion and, no less, of freedom of speech, press, and assembly.

These decisions may be briefly summarized by saying that unconventional evangelical methods are forms of "religious ac-

tivity" that occupy "the same high estate under the First Amendment as do worship in the churches and preaching from the
pulpit"; they have "the same claim to protection as the more
orthodox and conventional exercises of religion"; for "freedom
of speech, freedom of the press, freedom of religion are available to all, not merely to those who can pay their own way." [7]
In these notable cases Jehovah's Witnesses have brought home
the truth of Woodrow Wilson's statement that the "history of
liberty is a history of resistance." [8] The law is not interested
either in the content—the truth or falsity—of sermons, or in
the manner in which they are delivered, or whether they are
preached by ministers of popular or of unpopular sects. In
England there is an Established Church, and all other Protestant
churches are known as Free Churches. In the United States,
every church is a Free Church.

# PART II

# Freedom of Speech, Press, and Assembly

# ☆ 14 ☆

# The Freedom Not to Speak

"GOD has given you one face," says Shakespeare in *Hamlet,* "and you make yourself another." Can the state coerce a man to show still another face? Can the state coerce a man to make public avowal of beliefs or sentiments—even such as he believes, let alone beliefs or sentiments he does not believe— under threat of a criminal penalty for his refusal to do so? We are not concerned here with the problem of loyalty oaths, upon the taking of which may depend the getting or retaining a job or some other privilege at the disposal of the government, or with compulsory testimony before courts or legislative committees. At this point we are interested only in the question whether the state may say to a person: "You must stand up and repeat the words which we require you to utter, or you will go to jail!"

Only once in our history was an effort made to compel persons to make public expression of loyalty, under threat of criminal penalties for an obstinate refusal to comply. The event involved a religious sect which found compliance with the law to be inconsistent with their religious convictions; but the principles involved transcended religious freedom and touched the very heart of all the First Amendment freedoms. The unique attempt to coerce religious conscience by compulsory expression was part of an epidemic of attacks on Jehovah's Witnesses at the end of the 1930's and in the first several years of the following decade.

The sect known since 1931 as Jehovah's Witnesses was previously known as the International Bible Students Association. They have no churches and are opposed to all organized religion. They spread the Christian Gospel by word of mouth, phonograph records, and printed tracts and periodicals published by the Watch Tower Bible and Tract Society. They do not keep a membership roll, but in 1952 they had about 133,000 missionary ministers and a world total of about a half million.[1]

A document filed with the Department of Justice by the American Civil Liberties Union in the fall of 1940 showed that in a period of about six months 1,488 persons were the victims of mob violence in 335 communities in 44 states. Nothing similar to such extensive mob violence had taken place since the Ku Klux Klan riots in the 1920's, and no religious sect in the United States had suffered such persecution since the days when the Mormons were attacked. "Nothing in the record of attacks against Communists, strikers or Negroes is comparable."[2] These attacks were brought on by the refusal of school children who were Jehovah's Witnesses to salute the flag during school exercises, the zeal of members of the sect in distributing their literature on the streets and from house to house, and playing their phonograph records for members of the public who consented to listen. Fortunately for the development of civil liberties, the leaders of the sect followed an aggressive policy in the legal protection of the rights of Jehovah's Witnesses in the courts. We owe to their vigilance and constitutional militancy some of our most valuable legal precedents on the meaning and force of the First Amendment. It is to them that we owe credit for the decision of the Supreme Court that an expression of belief or sentiment may not be coerced.

The attitude of Jehovah's Witnesses to the flag salute has been stated by them in the following language:

First: To salute the flag would be a violation of the divine commandment ". . . Thou shalt have no other gods before me. . . . Thou shalt not make unto thee any graven image. . . . Thou shalt not bow down thyself to them nor serve them. . . ."

Second: The salute to the flag means in effect that the person saluting the flag ascribes salvation to it, whereas salvation is of Jehovah God.

Third: Flag saluting is part of a creed of a sect of so-called patriots, teaching a ritual of patriotism, and from such all true Christians are commanded to turn aside.[3]

　　In 1907 Kansas adopted the first flag salute act; by 1939 there were seventeen such state statutes; in other states flag salute was required by school board regulation.[4] These statutes and regulations were sponsored by the same "defenders of patriotisms" who also sought enactment of teachers' loyalty oaths. Pupils who refused to salute the flag were suspended, and then their parents were subjected to prosecution for violation of the compulsory school attendance laws. In Massachusetts, New York, and New Jersey the laws were upheld as constitutional, while in California and Georgia the courts ordered the children reinstated in school.[5] Where such laws were upheld, it was not always without a strong dissent. In the case before the New York Court of Appeals, Judge Irving Lehman in a dissenting opinion said that "the flag is dishonored by a salute by a child in reluctant and terrified obedience to a command of secular authority which clashes with the dictates of conscience." [6] As we shall see, Judge Lehman's view ultimately became the view of the United States Supreme Court. To achieve this result two cases had to be considered by the Court: the *Gobitis* case [7] in 1940 and the *Barnette* case [8] in 1943. These cases are of considerable importance and need to be considered in some detail.
　　In the *Gobitis* case several children who were Jehovah's Witnesses had been expelled from the public schools of Minersville, Pennsylvania, for refusing to salute the flag as part of a daily school exercise required by the local board of education. The father of the children sought an injunction against the school authorities. The Supreme Court, by a vote of eight to one, upheld the school officials. In his opinion for the Court, Justice Frankfurter held that the requirement of the flag salute ceremony did not infringe the constitutional guaranty of freedom of religion.

Justice Frankfurter stated the issue as one involving the reconciliation of two conflicting rights in order to prevent either from destroying the other. These rights are, on the one hand, freedom of religion, and, on the other hand, "the felt necessities of society," or promotion of the secular interests of society. In attempting this reconciliation, "because in safeguarding conscience we are dealing with interests so subtle and so dear, every possible leeway should be given to the claims of religious faith." [9]

Citing polygamy and military draft cases, Justice Frankfurter said that general laws, not aimed at the promotion or restriction of religious beliefs, have been sustained against those who refused obedience from religious conviction, when the laws were manifestations "of specific powers of government deemed by the legislature essential to secure and maintain that orderly, tranquil, and free society without which religious toleration itself is unattainable." In view of this general principle, must the Gobitis children be excused "from conduct required of all the other children in the promotion of national cohesion"? The Court's answer was, "No." In a contest between religious freedom and a means chosen by the legislature to attain national unity, which is the basis of "national security," religious freedom must give way.

In a sense, the case for the exertion of the power of the state is stronger here than in the situations involving the compulsory draft in the interests of the common defense, or the prohibition of polygamy in the interests of the family; for these interests presuppose the existence of an organized political society, to the maintenance of which the flag salute requirement is intended as a means. Said Justice Frankfurter:

The ultimate foundation of a free society is the binding tie of cohesive sentiment. Such a sentiment is fostered by all those agencies of the mind and spirit which may serve to gather up the traditions of a people, transmit them from generation to generation, and thereby create that continuity of a treasured common life which constitutes a civilization. . . . The flag is the symbol of our national unity, transcending all internal differences, however large, within the framework of the Constitution.

The Court had no authority, said Frankfurter, to bar public school officials "from determining the appropriateness of various means to evoke that unifying sentiment without which there can ultimately be no liberties, civil or religious." The end is legitimate; the means chosen may seem to the courts harsh or foolish; but the prevalent belief in the efficacy of the flag salute puts it within the pale of legislative power, so that the question of its wisdom is not for the courts to decide: "the courtroom is not the arena for debating issues of educational policy." To hold otherwise would mean making the Court "the school board for the country." The Court, said Frankfurter, cannot give to dissidents an exceptional immunity without introducing elements of difficulty into the school discipline, "which might cast doubts in the minds of the other children which would themselves weaken the effect of the [flag salute] exercise."

From this opinion Justice Stone was the lone dissenter. He argued that the decision sustained a law that was unique in the history of Anglo-American legislation, for by the Minersville school regulation the government sought to *coerce* the Gobitis children to express a sentiment which they did not entertain and which violated their deepest religious convictions. It is one thing to suppress religious practices that are dangerous to morals, public safety, health, or good order, or to compel military service notwithstanding conscientious objection, and a totally different thing for the government, "as a supposed educational measure and as a means of disciplining the young," to compel public affirmations which violate the children's religious conscience. When there is a conflict of interests between a freedom guaranteed by the Bill of Rights and a governmental power, there must, when that is possible, "be reasonable accommodation between them so as to preserve the essentials of both." It is the function of the courts to determine whether such accommodation is reasonably possible. There are other ways to teach loyalty and patriotism than by compelling a pupil to affirm what he does not believe and by commanding a form of affirmance which violates his religious convictions.

The very essence of the liberty which the First Amendment

guaranties is "the freedom of the individual from compulsion as to what he shall think and what he shall say, at least where the compulsion is to bear false witness to his religion . . . whatever may be the legislative view of the desirability of such compulsion." Nor could it be pretended, said Justice Stone, that the compulsory expression of loyalty by children in violation of their religious convictions plays so important a part in our national unity that a school board is free to exact it despite the constitutional guaranty of freedom of religion.

It is no answer to say, Justice Stone contended, that the legislative judgment must be left intact "as long as the remedial channels of the democratic process remain open and unobstructed," for this would mean a surrender of "politically helpless minorities" to the popular will. "We have," said Justice Stone,

previously pointed to the importance of a searching judicial inquiry into the legislative judgment in situations where prejudice against discrete and insular minorities may tend to curtail the operation of those political processes ordinarily to be relied on to protect minorities. . . . And until now we have not hesitated similarly to scrutinize legislation restricting the civil liberty of racial and religious minorities although no political process was affected. . . . Here we have such a small minority entertaining in good faith a religious belief, which is such a departure from the usual course of human conduct, that most persons are disposed to regard it with little toleration or concern. In such circumstances careful scrutiny of legislative efforts to secure conformity of belief and opinion by a compulsory affirmation of the desired belief, is especially needful if civil rights are to receive any protection. . . . The Constitution expresses more than the conviction of the people that democratic processes must be preserved at all costs. It is also an expression of faith and a command that freedom of mind and spirit must be preserved, which government must obey, if it is to adhere to that justice and moderation without which no free government can exist.

The opinion of Justice Stone, at first "a still, small voice," won the support of the Bill of Rights Committee of the American Bar Association, as well as of most law review commentators, and soon became a voice "rotund, sweeping, and final." Chief

Justice Hughes and Justice McReynolds retired; Jackson and Rutledge joined the Court, and Justice Stone became Chief Justice. In 1943 the Court decided the *Barnette* case and in this decision overruled the *Gobitis* case. This time Justice Frankfurter wrote the dissenting opinion, in which he was joined by Justices Roberts and Reed.

Following the decision in the *Gobitis* case, West Virginia adopted an act, under which the state board of education passed a resolution requiring flag salute exercises in the public schools and providing that refusal to participate shall be dealt with as an act of "insubordination," leading to expulsion, treatment of the child as a delinquent, and prosecution of the parents. A federal district court of three judges enjoined enforcement of the act and the school board resolution, notwithstanding the decision of the Supreme Court in the *Gobitis* case. On appeal by the state board of education, the district court judgment was affirmed.

In his opinion for the Court, Justice Jackson pointed out that the case is not one in which a citizen asserts a freedom which brings him into conflict with a right asserted by some other person; the refusal by Jehovah's Witnesses to salute the flag does not impair the right of others to engage in the flag salute ceremony; the sole conflict here was between authority and the rights of the individual; "we are dealing," said Jackson, "with a compulsion of students to declare a belief." The flag salute is a form of utterance. West Virginia required the individual to communicate his acceptance of the political ideas the flag bespeaks. The Bill of Rights protects the individual against coerced communication and against affirmation of a belief and an attitude of mind. Expression may be censored or suppressed constitutionally only when the expression creates a clear and present danger of action of a kind that the state is empowered to prevent and punish; involuntary expression can be coerced only "on even more immediate and urgent grounds than silence." West Virginia did not even allege that a failure to salute the flag would create any such danger. The Court contrasted the law of West Virginia with a joint resolution of Congress which makes the flag observance voluntary and makes provision for the nonconformist. Because boards of education are educating the young for citizenship is reason for their scrupulous protection of the constitutional freedoms of individuals; but unfortunately there are "village tyrants as well as village Hampdens," and the courts must protect individuals from the former if the Bill of Rights is to be preserved. The question whether the means of effecting political change are left free has nothing to do with the constitutional issue, for the freedoms of the Bill of Rights are beyond the reach of political majorities: "One's right to life, liberty, and property, to free speech, a free press, freedom of worship and assembly, and other fundamental rights," said Justice Jackson, "may not be submitted to vote; they depend on the outcome of no elections."

National unity may be fostered, said the Court, by persuasion and example, but not by compulsion. "Those who begin coercive elimination of dissent soon find themselves exterminating dissenters. Compulsory unification of opinion achieves only the unanimity of the graveyard." The Constitution was designed "to avoid these ends by avoiding these beginnings." Authority in the United States "is to be controlled by public opinion, not public opinion by authority." Constitutional limitations are to be applied

with no fear that freedom to be intellectually and spiritually diverse or even contrary will disintegrate the social organization. . . . We can have intellectual individualism and the rich cultural diversities that we owe to exceptional minds only at the price of occasional eccentricity and abnormal attitudes. When they are so harmless to others or to the state as those we deal with here, the price is not too great. But freedom to differ is not limited to things that do not matter much. That would be a mere shadow of freedom. The best of its substance is the right to differ as to things that touch the heart of the existing order.

If there is any fixed star in our constitutional constellation, it is that no official, high or petty, can prescribe what shall be orthodox in politics, nationalism, religion, or other matters of opinion or force citizens to confess by word or act their faith therein.

This brief and forceful summary of the American philosophy of cultural pluralism, of the rationale of the Bill of Rights, and of the belief in inherent and inalienable individual rights,[10] belongs with the classic statements of American ideals.[11]

In his dissenting opinion, Justice Frankfurter took an extremely narrow view of judicial review of legislation, saying that the only opinion of the Court that is material when it looks in the direction of the wisdom or evil of a statute is the opinion "whether legislators could in reason have enacted such a law." If "reasonable legislators" could have taken the action being reviewed by the Court, the action must be considered constitutional; if the legislature of West Virginia could reasonably conclude that the flag salute was a means to the promotion of good citizenship, the flag salute requirement was constitutional. This approach contrasts sharply with that of the majority of the Court, who took the position that in the face of conscientious objection to an act made compulsory by legislation, the question is as follows: Is there a rational connection between a refusal to perform the act and peril to the public welfare? The majority found that the Jehovah's Witnesses in the public school who refused to comply with the law did not create by their refusal a clear and present danger of peril to the national welfare (security, health, morals).

There is a sharp and deep gap between these two approaches. If Frankfurter's view were sustained, the Bill of Rights would be greatly emasculated in the interests of the broad legislative principle of majority rule; [12] for it is practically impossible to prove the negative proposition that the legislators could *not* in reason have enacted a specific law, that the statute is *not at all* justified in reason; for a show of some "reason" on behalf of a statute is almost always possible.[13] The doctrine of presumptive constitutionality could become in fact legislative absolutism. But Justice Frankfurter saw no difference between the civil "liberty" of the Fourteenth Amendment that protects freedom of speech, press, and religion, and the economic "liberty" which protects a person when, e.g., he wants to operate an ice house or engage in the slaughtering business; nor would Justice Frankfurter admit any difference between a law which requires the flag salute of pupils who are compelled to attend school and one which requires military training of college students who are not compelled to attend college: in no case may the Court sit as a "super-legislature," he said; *judicial self-restraint* is necessary whenever legislative power is challenged. But this view is contradicted by the view implicit in the majority opinion that *legislative self-restraint* is made necessary by the Bill of Rights. By implication, Frankfurter himself contradicted his position when he maintained that legislation deserves the mark of constitutionality as long as there remain "open and unobstructed" "the remedial channels of the democratic process." This seems to concede that certain freedoms at least—e.g., freedom of speech, freedom of the press, freedom of assembly, freedom of suffrage—enjoy a status of priority.

Justice Frankfurter contended that the children who were Jehovah's Witnesses could go to a private school, to which the flag salute law would not apply. He argued that the state could not compel the flag salute ceremony in private schools, for such schools could not be placed "under a strict governmental control," the state could not direct such schools with respect to "intimate and essential details." But certainly the state may require private schools to give courses in certain subjects, such as American history, mathematics, or the English language. If the flag salute requirement may be reasonably made for public school pupils, why may it not be made a requirement for the pupils of private schools as well? "Only if there be no doubt that *any* reasonable mind could entertain can we deny to the states," said Frankfurter, "the right to resolve doubts their way and not ours." [14] Judged by this broad test of legislative immunity from constitutional limitations, almost any law could easily withstand a constitutional attack.

In his dissenting opinion Justice Frankfurter counselled *judicial* humility. But humility practiced by judges on the wrong occasion may be judicial abdication. Where was the *legislative* humility when the officials in West Virginia refused to avoid an unnecessary clash with the dictates of conscience? The flag salute may be thought necessary for the inculcation of patriotism, but, as Justice Stone pointed out in his *Gobitis* dissent, instruction in the guaranties of civil liberty may also tend to inspire patriotism and love of country.

# ☆ 15 ☆

# The Freedom Not to Listen

THE freedom *not* to speak, *not* to profess beliefs, may be more important than the freedom *to* speak, since the *profession* of beliefs that one does not maintain may do more violence to the conscience than the *failure* to express the beliefs that one does maintain. Between the freedom not to speak and the freedom to speak may be put the freedom not to listen, for compulsory listening to speeches which shock the conscience may be almost as unsettling, psychologically and spiritually, as forced confession of beliefs in politics or religion that are contrary to one's convictions.

## A. COMPULSORY LEARNING

In our colonial period it was not considered wrong to force a person to become a member of a captive audience; attendance on public worship was compulsory: a Virginia statute of 1610 provided that "every man and woman shall repair in the morning to the divine service and sermon preached upon the Sabbath day." [1] For the first absence the penalty was loss of a week's provision and allowance; for the second offense, whipping; for the third offense, the offender was to suffer the penalty of death. This act was modeled after Elizabeth's Act of Uniformity, 1559, which provided that every inhabitant of the realm "shall diligently and faithfully" attend his parish church every Sunday or holy day, "and then and there to abide orderly and soberly during the time of common prayer, preachings, or other service of God." [2]

Compulsory listening has been made the issue in several situations in recent years. First we shall consider cases in several states which challenged the compulsory school attendance laws as imposing compulsory listening on children in violation of their constitutional rights.

In Pennsylvania, members of the Old Order Amish Church have contended that their religious beliefs prevent them from sending their children to school after they have attained the age of fourteen and have completed the eighth grade of the public schools. They take their stand on the Dortricht Creed, a confession of faith adopted at Dort, Holland, in 1632, by followers of Menno Simons, founder of the Mennonite Church, from which the Amish derive their creed. The relevant statement in their creed is as follows:

And since it is a known fact that a lack of faithful ministers, and the erring of the sheep because of the lack of good doctrine, arise principally from the unworthiness of the people; therefore, the people of God, needing this, should not turn to such as have been educated in universities, according to the wisdom of man, that they may talk and dispute, and seek to sell their purchased gift for temporal gain; and who according to the custom of the world do not truly follow Christ in the humility of regeneration.

Basing themselves on this pronouncement, the heads of the church adopted a statement of principles which provided that children should be trained "to read, to write, and to cipher"; that children "have attained sufficient schooling" when they have passed the eighth grade; that thereafter their children's home and church training and their religious beliefs and faith can best be safeguarded "by keeping them at home under the influence of their parents."

The Superior Court of Pennsylvania held that the state law which compels school attendance up to the age of seventeen should be enforced notwithstanding these objections.[3] Children, said the court, "may be educated in the public schools, in private or denominational schools, or by approved tutors; but educated they must be within the age limits and in the subjects prescribed by law." The enlightened intelligence of the citizens is necessary for the preservation and enhancement of the democratic way of life, said the court, and these objectives are paramount. The court saw no conflict between these objectives and religious freedom or civil liberty, for religious freedom cannot survive unless democracy lives. A person may forbear doing that which is against his conscience, but only if his refusal to act "is not prejudicial to the public weal."

An even more extreme position than that taken by the Amish was taken by some ultraorthodox Jews, who sent their children to Jewish religious schools which did not comply with the requirement of the New York education law that all schools must give instruction in at least the following subjects: arithmetic, spelling, English, geography, United States history, civics, hygiene, physical training, New York State history, patriotism, and citizenship. The parents contended that their religious beliefs would be violated by permitting instruction of their children in secular subjects—the religious school which the children attended limited its instruction to religious subjects, and English was not the language of instruction. In finding the parents guilty of violation of the compulsory school attendance law, the court said that the religious convictions of the parents must yield to "the total public interest. . . . Religious convictions of parents cannot interfere with the responsibility of the State to protect the welfare of children." [4]

These and similar decisions [5] stand for the proposition that the state may compel children to receive instruction in certain subjects, up to an age fixed by law, and in an approved public or private school or from a qualified tutor. The principle on which this proposition is based is that the state may protect its people "from the consequences of an ignorant and incompetent citizenship." [6]

But this principle is much too broad; for if one were to accept it in all its sweep, it would follow that the state would have a right to ban newspapers that feed and breed "an ignorant and incompetent citizenship"; that the state could rigidly censor all media of communication in the interest of what the legislature considers the fulfillment of its duty "to diffuse knowledge and learning through the community." [7] It is only a totalitarian state that can make such claims on the minds of the people. In a free, democratic society the government may not claim that only the truth has rights, and that error must be suppressed. In an open society, the human mind —not the truth—has rights; and while the mind may have the duty to seek for and cling to the truth, the mind has the right to be wrong. If it has the duty to search for the truth, it must be left free to search for it in its own way, and even to pick up many errors in the process.

The state has the duty to encourage education, and to provide schools as a means of education. The state may compel parents to send their child to a public or private school where he would acquire the basic means with which to search for the truth *in his own way*. From this point of view, it would follow that the state may prescribe only the minimum number of subjects, study of which would be compulsory, such as English, spelling, arithmetic, American history and geography, and hygiene. The state should permit the parents to be substituted for the school if they can demonstrate their competence as teachers.[8] The state should not make *secondary* education compulsory as against the claims of religious objectors; [9] for I do not see that a free, pluralistic society stands to lose in the long run if some people know their holy books thoroughly but are ignorant of Faulkner and Hemingway or even of Shakespeare, as long as they have acquired the basic tools for the pursuit of secular knowledge and there is a public library in their community to which they can go for books.

The state, it seems to me, must not exaggerate its role as educator if we are not to lose sight of the constitutional principle that the state does not have the power to standardize children, and that the child, as Justice McReynolds said in *Pierce v. Society of Sisters*,[10] "is not the mere creature of the State; those who nurture him and direct his destiny have the right, coupled with the high duty, to recognize and prepare him for additional obligations"—that is, for a life that goes beyond the confines of citizenship.

There are those, I know, who would preclude private instruction, and even instruction in parochial schools; they maintain that the attributes of citizenship can be acquired only in the public school. From their point of view, the parochial or private school is "divisive"; and private instruction deprives the child of "experiences in group activities and in social outlook." [11] If the parochial school is "divisive," this means only that a pluralistic society must allow room for the "divisive" as well as for the "additive," lest the state be given a monopoly on education or occupy the position of *parens patriae* and subject all children to a *Gleichschaltung* suggestive of a totalitarian society. And if private instruction outside of a school may have the effect of limiting the "social outlook" of a child, it is doubtful whether society will permit him to remain excluded from its grasp for long; for wherever a man goes, Thoreau wrote in *Walden,* "men will pursue him with their dirty institutions, and, if they can, constrain him to belong to their desperate oddfellow society." If as a result of his private education the child will grow into a man who, contrary to Santayana's expectations, will like to go alone for a walk and stand alone in his opinion, his eccentricity will enrich his neighbors and advance the human endeavor toward freedom.

## B. COMPULSORY LISTENING

Capital Transit, a privately owned public utility corporation, operated the street railway and bus system in the District of Columbia, under a franchise from Congress. In 1948 the company experimented with a music program in a number of its vehicles; and a poll of passengers who heard these programs showed that 92 per cent favored their continuance; soon thereafter the company began to install radio reception equipment in its buses, streetcars, waiting rooms and other facilities. The programs consisted of 90 per cent music and 10 per cent announcements and commercial advertising. The Public Utilities Commission of the District of Columbia ordered an investigation and then concluded that the radio programs were "not inconsistent with public convenience, comfort, and safety"; that they tended "to improve the conditions under which the public ride."

In the *Pollak* case [12] it was contended on behalf of passengers that the order of the commission approving the radio programs violated liberties of the mind embraced in the guaranty of liberty by the First and Fourteenth Amendments; that forced listening in the buses and streetcars operated by a public utility corporation that enjoyed a legal monopoly violated the rights of riders under the First Amendment by forcing them to hear speech which they did not wish to hear, by making it difficult or impossible for them to read or to converse with others; that forced listening, supported by an order of a governmental agency, was an exercise of collective force at its most dangerous incidence—the mind; that the radio program was an unconstitutional "taking" of the property of objecting passengers, for it meant the "taking" of their attention and the free use of their time.

The United States court of appeals agreed with these arguments insofar as they affected "commercials" and "announcements," but did not decide whether broadcasts limited to music would infringe constitutional rights. "If Transit obliged its passengers to read what it liked or get off the car," said Judge Edgerton, "invasion of their freedom would be obvious." The court saw no difference between coerced reading and coerced listening.

The Supreme Court, however, held that the facts did not show a violation of a constitutional guaranty. The Court said there was no proof that the programs interfered substantially with the conversation of passengers or "with rights of communication constitutionally protected in public places." There was no proof that the programs were used "for objectionable propaganda"—the few announcements were not enough to sustain an objection.

In his opinion for the Court, Justice Burton contended that the Constitution does not guaranty to a passenger on a public vehicle a right of privacy equal that which he may enjoy in his own home. If the interests of "all concerned" are advanced by the radio programs, the objector must give way: "The liberty of each individual in a public vehicle or public place is subject to reasonable limitations in relation to the rights of others." The powers of the corporation and of the commission were not "arbitrarily and capriciously exercised." The Court thus sustained the right of a public utility commission to approve broadcasts of music, commercial advertising, and announcements in buses and streetcars.

Justice Black, concurring, made it clear that while he agreed that there was no violation of the Constitution in this case, it would be a violation of the First Amendment to broadcast news, public speeches, views, or propaganda of any kind.

Justice Douglas dissented. He argued that "the right to be let alone is indeed the beginning of all freedom." A person does not lose this right by leaving his home; he takes with him "immunities from controls bearing on privacy." What are some of these immunities?

He may not be compelled against his will to attend a religious service; he may not be forced to make an affirmation or observe a ritual that violates his scruples; he may not be made to accept one religious, political, or philosophical creed as against another. Freedom of religion and freedom of speech guaranteed by the First Amendment give more than the privilege to worship, to write, to speak as one chooses; they give freedom not to do nor to act as the government chooses.

Justice Douglas saw the case as one involving coercion to make people listen. People who ride on buses and streetcars are compelled to do so by their circumstances, and, of course, they may not complain of the noises normally made by fellow passengers. But here the right of privacy has been invaded beyond the normal risks of travel. Today the government may approve or authorize use of the radio in public vehicles for cultural ends, but tomorrow the radio may be used for political purposes. But in either case the right of privacy has been invaded; for "the music selected by one bureaucrat may be as offensive to some as it is soothing to others. The news commentator chosen to report on the events of the day may give overtones to the news that please the bureau head but which rile the streetcar captive audience." At home, the offending program may be turned off. "But the man on the streetcar has no choice but to sit and listen, or perhaps to sit and to try *not* to listen."

The government, said Douglas, should never be permitted to force people to listen to *any* radio program. The right of privacy, he said,

should include the right to pick and choose from competing entertainments, competing propaganda, competing political philosophies. If people are let alone in those choices, the right of privacy will pay dividends in character and integrity. The strength of our system is in the dignity, the resourcefulness, and the independence of our people. Our confidence is in their ability as individuals to make the wisest choice. That system cannot flourish if regimentation takes hold. The right of privacy . . . is a powerful deterrent to any one who would control men's minds.

It is noteworthy that Justice Frankfurter, saying that his feelings were "so strongly engaged as a victim of the practice in controversy," decided that it was better to take himself out of the case.

As important as speech is—and freedom of speech—silence, too, must be given a high place among the values in a people's culture and in a man's life. "Silence is original and self-evident like the other basic phenomena," Max Picard has said, "like love and loyalty and death and life itself. But it existed before all these and is in all of them. Silence is the firstborn of the basic phenomena. It envelops the other basic phenomena— love, loyalty, and death." [13] Language, he says, should have a double echo—from the silence whence it came and from the place of death. But today language is far from both these worlds of silence: "It springs from noise and vanishes in noise. Silence is today no longer an autonomous world of its own; it is simply the place into which noise has not yet penetrated." [14] And the world of noise today is based upon the world of radio, for

radio has occupied the whole space of silence. There is no silence any longer. Even when the radio is turned off the radio-noise still seems to go on inaudibly. . . . And the type of man formed by the constant influence of this noise is . . . formless, undecided, inwardly and externally, with no definite limits and standards. . . . It is as if men were afraid that silence might break out somewhere and destroy the noise of radio. . . . There is no more silence, only intervals between radio-noises.[15]

In an ideal world, I suppose, freedom of silence would be regarded as important as freedom of speech. But we are far removed from such a world. There is nothing in our Bill of Rights, or in the Universal Declaration of Human Rights, or in any constitution, that mentions any such freedom. This is a freedom that remains to be won, though it is perhaps too late to assert the freedom of silence in a world of radio-noises: Justice Douglas asks for too much too late.

But what Justice Black projects is perhaps to be expected, not freedom of silence, but freedom of thought—the freedom to think quietly one's own thoughts without being forced by an act of the government to be a member of a captive audience coerced to listen to radio programs of news reports, speeches, views, or propaganda of any kind.[16]

## ☆ 16 ☆

# The Right to Be Let Alone

"THE right to be let alone," Justice Douglas has said in the *Pollak* case, "is indeed the beginning of all freedom." If, he argued, "liberty" as used in the Fifth Amendment is to be a repository of freedom, it must include privacy as well as freedom from unlawful governmental action. This right to privacy, or the right to be let alone, can be traced back to an article by Louis D. Brandeis and Samuel D. Warren, published in 1890, that remains the classic statement on the subject.[1]

### A. THE FOUNDATION OF THE RIGHT OF PRIVACY

Why is it necessary to recognize the existence of the right to be let alone, the duty to protect a person's privacy? The answer provided by Brandeis and Warren deserves to be given *in extenso:*

The press is overstepping in every direction the obvious bounds of propriety and decency. Gossip is no longer the resource of the idle and of the vicious, but has become a trade, which is pursued with industry as well as effrontery. To satisfy a prurient taste the details of sexual relations are spread broadcast in the columns of the daily papers. To occupy the indolent, column upon column is filled with idle gossip, which can only be procured by intrusion upon the domestic circle. The intensity and complexity of life, attendant upon advancing civilization, have rendered necessary some retreat from the world, and man, under the refining influence of culture, has become more sensitive to publicity, so that solitude and privacy have become more essential to the individual; but modern enterprise and invention have, through invasion upon his privacy, subjected him to mental pain and distress, far greater than could be inflicted by mere bodily injury. Nor is the harm wrought by such invasions confined to the suffering of those who may be made the subjects of journalistic or other enterprise. In this, as in other branches of commerce, the supply creates the demand. Each crop of unseemly gossip, thus harvested, becomes the seed of more, and, in direct proportion to its circulation, results in a lowering of social standards and of morality. Even gossip apparently harmless, when widely and persistently circulated, is potent for evil. It both belittles and perverts. It belittles by inverting the relative importance of things, thus dwarfing the thoughts and aspirations of a people. When personal gossip attains the dignity of print, and crowds the space available for matters of real interest to the community, what wonder that the ignorant and thoughtless mistake its relative importance. Easy of comprehension, appealing to that weak side of human nature which is never wholly cast down by the misfortunes and frailties of our neighbors, no one can be surprised that it usurps the place of interest in brains capable of other things. Triviality destroys at once robustness of thought and delicacy of feeling. No enthusiasm can flourish under its blighting influence.

These words were written, it should be noted, before the invention of radio and television, before the days of the movie, Walter Winchell, wire tapping, brain-washing, and the nightmarish world projected by George Orwell's *Nineteen Eighty-Four*.

The right of privacy required no new legal principle, Brandeis and Warren contended, but only the application of an existing principle to a new state of facts: the right to life and property should encompass the "right to enjoy life," the right of a person to protect "his private life, which he has seen fit to keep private." The underlying principle is that of "an inviolate personality," which includes the right to the privacy of one's thoughts, emotions, and sensations, expressed in writing, conduct, conversation, attitudes, facial expressions, personal appearance, sayings, acts, and personal relations—the right to "the immunity of the person,—the right to one's personality."

Privacy should include, said Brandeis and Warren, the right of a person who has remained a private individual to prevent publication of his portrait, and discussion by the press of one's private affairs. This freedom from publicity—freedom from another person's asserted freedom of speech or press—is not to prevent injury to reputation, but injury to one's sensitivity, the unsettling of a person's "peace of mind." [2] A person should have the right not to have his life embittered by intrusion upon his private affairs, just as he has "the right not to be assaulted or beaten, the right not to be imprisoned, the right not to be maliciously prosecuted, the right not to be defamed."

There should, however, be limits on the right to be let alone, said Brandeis and Warren. Chiefly, there should be no prohibition upon publication of matter which is of public or general interest. The law should

protect those persons with whose affairs the community has no legitimate concern, from being dragged into an undesirable and undesired publicity and to protect all persons, whatsoever their position or station, from having matters which they may properly prefer to keep private, made public against their will. . . . The general object in view is to protect the privacy of private life, and to whatever degree and in whatever connection a man's life has ceased to be private, before the publication under consideration has been made, to that extent the protection is to be withdrawn. . . . Some things all men alike are entitled to keep from popular curiosity, whether in public life or not.

The right of privacy should obtain even if the statements are true and are made without malice; for privacy implies "the right not merely to prevent inaccurate portrayal of private life [or portrayal with sinister intent], but to prevent its being depicted at all."

This right of privacy, as formulated by Brandeis and Warren, it should be noted, does not on the surface involve any provision of the Bill of Rights, for the guaranties of the Bill of Rights are directed only against governmental action, while what these writers had in mind was a right of privacy asserted against the "idle or prurient curiosity" of private persons; but basically the

First Amendment is involved, because if a state recognizes the right of privacy, it thereby limits the freedom of speech and press of commentators, columnists, photographers, and others. Thus the right of privacy involves a clash between basic values: the right to be let alone and the right freely to speak and print the truth. In this clash, especially today when the media of communication have the power to crush a man's personality in an instant, the right of privacy should be afforded a pre-eminent position—the privacy of private life must be protected, preserved, and enhanced; for unless personality is held inviolate, the truth, as well as all other values, may crumble to nothingness. An individual's right to his individuality is the rock bottom of all ideals, values, rights, and freedoms. Neither the state nor society can claim any rights that deserve a position of priority over this right of privacy.

More recently William Faulkner has made a similar plea on behalf of privacy.[3] The American Dream, he said, had been "a sanctuary on earth for individual man," freedom for the individual from "the old-established closed-corporation hierarchies of arbitrary power" and from the "mass" into which these hierarchies had compressed the individual. Americans lived this Dream. It became a condition of life. "We did not live *in* the dream: we lived the Dream itself." But then we lost the dream. "It is gone now. We dozed, slept, and it abandoned us." As a symptom of what has happened, Faulkner relates that about ten years ago a friend of his who was a well-known writer told him that "a wealthy widely circulated weekly pictorial magazine" had offered the friend a good price to write an article about him—"not about my work or works, but about me as a private citizen, an individual." Faulkner said

No, and explained why: my belief that only a writer's works were in the public domain, to be discussed and investigated and written about. . . . But that, until the writer committed a crime or ran for public office, his private life was his own; and not only had he the right to defend his privacy, but the public had the duty to do so.

Eight years later he heard that the magazine had started work on the article, to be written by someone other than his friend.

He told the magazine and the writer that he strongly objected and asked them to stop. The article was published. Faulkner says that the "terrifying" thing is "not what the writer said, but that it was said," and that he, the victim, was completely helpless to prevent it. Nor did he have any remedy after the act, because we have no laws against bad taste. And even if he had a right to recover damages, "the matter would still have remained on the black side of the ledger since the publisher could charge the judgment and costs to operating loss and the increased sales from the publicity to capital investment. The point is," says Faulkner,

that in America today any organization or group, simply by functioning under a phrase like Freedom of the Press or National Security or League Against Subversion, can postulate to itself complete immunity to violate the individualness . . . of anyone who is not himself a member of some organization or group numerous enough or rich enough to frighten them off.

Americans, says Faulkner, seem bent on reducing individuals to an "identityless anonymous unprivacied mass," "destroying the last vestige of privacy without which man cannot be an individual."

The right of privacy, it has been said, is

the right of an individual to live a life of seclusion and anonymity, free from the prying curiosity which accompanies both fame and notoriety. It presupposes a desire to withdraw from the public gaze, to be free from the insatiable interest of the great mass of men in one who has risen above—or fallen below—the mean. It is a recognition of the dignity of solitude, of the majesty of man's free will and the power to mold his own destiny, of the sacred and inviolate nature of one's innermost self.[4]

Has the law come to recognize this right to be let alone, the right to the protection of the privacy of one's private life, as against the competing claims of freedom of speech and of the press? The right exists in three states by statute and in nineteen other states by judicial decision.[5] Several cases may here be cited as illustrations of factual situations that have come before the courts.

In one case, a woman who had been a prostitute had been tried for murder and had been acquitted. She abandoned her life of shame, married, and was living among friends who were ignorant of her past—she was a respectable woman in respectable society. Seven years after her trial for murder a movie was made based on her former life and using her maiden name —the movie had the lurid title *The Red Kimono*. She sued for damages, basing her action on the right of privacy. The California courts held that the incidents in the woman's past life, insofar as they were matters of public record, could be freely used; but she could recover for the use of her name in the advertisements and in the picture itself.[6]

In another case a man, employed as a chauffeur, was held up by a robber and shot. The incident seriously affected his nerves. A year and a half later the radio program "Calling All Cars" presented a dramatization of the holdup and shooting and used the victim's name. When he heard the program, he suffered mental anguish, which was aggravated by telephone calls from sympathetic friends. The court held that these facts were enough to show that the plaintiff's right to be let alone had been violated.[7]

Had the name of the plaintiff not been used in either of these cases, it is doubtful if the court would have allowed recovery. This was made clear in a case [8] in which it appeared that the plaintiff had been convicted of bank robbery in 1919. After serving nine years in prison, he was paroled and pardoned. In 1933 he was convicted of murder and sentenced to death. His sentence was commuted to life imprisonment. In 1940 he received a conditional release, and in 1945 a presidential pardon. Until 1940 his story was given much publicity; but following his release he obtained employment and lived an obscure life. In 1952 a commercial entertainment program, "The Big Story," telecast a fictionalized dramatization based on the plaintiff's conviction and pardon. The plaintiff's name was not used; but the name of the reporter of the Washington newspaper who led the campaign to save the plaintiff's life was used. The plaintiff claimed, however, that, although his true name was not used, the actor who portrayed him resembled him physically, and that the plaintiff's words and actions were reproduced visually and aurally, so that he and his friends and acquaintances clearly identified him. Five days before the program was televised he heard about it, and he called and wrote the National Broadcasting Company requesting them not to broadcast the program. The program was put on the air as scheduled.

The court held that these facts did not constitute an invasion of the right of privacy. "This court agrees," said Judge Keech,

that we are not so uncivilized that the law permits, in the name of public interest, the unlimited and unwarranted revival by publication of a rehabilitated wrongdoer's past mistakes in such a manner as to identify him in his private setting with the old crime and hold him up to public scorn. Persons formerly public, however, cannot be protected against disclosure and re-disclosure of known facts through the reading of old newspaper accounts and other publication, oral repetition of facts by those familiar with them, or reprinting of known facts of general interest, in a reasonable manner and for a legitimate purpose. . . . Though fairness and decency dictate that some boundary be fixed beyond which persons may not go in pointing the finger of shame at those who have erred and repented, reasonable freedom of speech and press must be accorded. . . . Public identification of the present person with past facts, however, would constitute a new disclosure and, if unwarranted, would infringe upon an existing privacy. Thus, it would appear that the protection which time may bring to a formerly public figure is not against repetition of the facts which are already public property, but against unreasonable public identification of him in his present setting with the earlier incident.

But the principle laid down by the court in this case, commendable as it is in approximating a balance between the right to be let alone and freedom of the press, is not universally recognized; for the courts have, in some cases, gone so far as to uphold the right of "public identification of the present person with past facts"—the "public identification of him in his present setting with the earlier incident." Thus the *New Yorker* was sustained in its asserted right to publish an article on the life of a person who had achieved fame as a child prodigy about twenty-five years before but had since lived the life of an obscure person. The "present person" was identified in the magazine article by name, and was identified in his present setting with the earlier incidents of his life. The article went beyond *The Red Kimono,* which used the plaintiff's maiden name; for it used the name by which the plaintiff was known as a child prodigy and as an inconspicuous clerk.[9]

The right of privacy, as broadly contemplated by Brandeis and Warren and for which William Faulkner has pleaded, has by no means been accepted by the courts. There is no tendency to recognize the distinction between "public" and "private" characters (e.g., the distinction drawn by Faulkner between politicians and criminals, on the one hand, whose characters have fallen into the public domain by their voluntary choice, and other persons, on the other hand). Any person can instantly become a public character, perhaps through the very individuality which he would eagerly keep from the public eye— the present obscurity of the former child prodigy was the very fact that made him a fit subject for public exposure! "There is no hiding place," as the Negro spiritual puts it. Nor is there protection for the privacy of the private life of a public character (nor was there in England for Princess Margaret when she was considering marriage to Captain Townsend). Nor will the law shield the right to be let alone of persons who themselves have not acted in any public drama—Faulkner gives as an example the parents of a man accused of the murder of his wife, or her parents, whom publicity might drive to suicide or sudden death.[10] Almost everything has become newsworthy; and the "candid camera" is everywhere.

The right of privacy, it has been well said,

is the protective bulwark built up against the threatened annihilation of man's personal life by unprecedented advances in communication. . . . It gives expression to an ideal which conceives of the individual as a unit not to be obliterated by society. Everyone has a right to live his own life in quiet and solitude. Modesty and reticence need not be sacrificed entirely to public clamor. No one owes an obligation to permit others to profit by his mistakes or his success. One's home is his castle, and one's private life is a precious possession which cannot be wrested from him.[11]

Although a limitation of freedom of speech and the press, the right of privacy should be universally recognized and given ample scope as a basic—perhaps as the most basic—human right. What Justice Brandeis wrote thirty-eight years after publication of his famous article is relevant not only to the right of privacy as guarantied by the Fourth Amendment against invasion by the Federal Government, but also, and no less, to the right of privacy against invasion by a private person: "The makers of our Constitution," said Brandeis,

undertook to secure conditions favorable to the pursuit of happiness. They recognized the significance of man's spiritual nature, of his feelings and of his intellect. They knew that only a part of the pain, pleasures and satisfactions of life are to be found in material things. They sought to protect Americans in their beliefs, their thoughts, their emotions and their sensations. They conferred, as against the Government, *the right to be let alone—the most comprehensive of rights and the right most valued by civilized men.*[12]

## B. LIBEL AND SLANDER

Related to the right of privacy is the right to the integrity of one's reputation, accomplished through the law of libel and slander. This law protects a person from injury which would follow from a lowering of his prestige in the community by oral or written communication (slander and libel, respectively), subjecting him to ridicule, hatred, or contempt, and thereby injuring him in his business, profession, or vocation. The injury is to the victim's property or material interests. Libel and slander differ from a violation of the right of privacy in that privacy protects a person in his spiritual interests—the publication of his private affairs hurts him in his estimation of himself, in his own feelings; while libel or slander hurts him in the estimation of his fellows, in his honor or reputation, in the feelings others have about him. A man's honor or reputation is a business or professional asset; a man's private life is a spiritual asset. The right of privacy should protect a person in his private life; the law of libel and slander protects him in his social life.

Generally, authorities have seen in the law of libel and slander

an effort to protect an interest of property or substance; but
Roscoe Pound is, I believe, right in considering this law as
the protection of an interest in personality—"the inviolability
of the spiritual person"—thus bringing close together the right
of privacy and protection against defamation of character. "On
the one hand," says Pound,

there is the claim of the individual to be secured in his dignity and
honor as part of his personality in a world in which one must live
in society among his fellow men. On the other hand there is the
claim to be secured in his reputation as a part of his substance, in
that in a world in which credit plays so large a part the confidence
and esteem of one's fellow men may be a valuable asset.[13]

In fact, Pound has shown, historically injury to personality came
to be recognized before injury to interests of substance; and
honor is perhaps a more ancient legal conception than is
property. For primitive law treated all injuries to personality as
injuries to honor; the "primitive tendency was to treat all
wrongs as injuries to personality, and all injuries to personality
as insult." The term *iniuria* originally meant "insult" and was
used in Roman law to designate all infringements of interests
of personality. Slowly jurists came to distinguish three different
types of *iniuria:*

Those of the first type were . . . injuries to the physical person.
Here, although the interest was originally regarded as one of honor,
the law soon came to see that in truth it was an interest in body and
life, in other words, an interest in the physical person. . . . Injuries
of a second type are called symbolic injuries, that is, injuries to the
honor or, as the Roman books said, to the dignity of the person.
Examples of symbolic injuries are insulting words addressed to the
person, insulting gestures, and the like. Here the injury is to the
feelings of the complainant and the interest is an interest in his
honor. . . . Injuries of the third type were . . . injuries to reputation, to credit, to social or business standing. Here there is injury
to an interest of substance.[14]

We will see a little later how injuries of the second type, the
so-called "symbolic injuries," became our constitutional doctrine of "fighting words." Here it needs to be pointed out that

the right of privacy, as projected by Brandeis, is based on the same principle as that which is basic to injuries of this type, that it is an application of an existing principle to a new state of facts. But here our main concern is with injuries of the third type—injuries to reputation.

Why does the law punish or permit recovery for injuries to reputation? Because, says Pound,

men will fight in defense of their honor no less than in defense of their physical persons. Hence, the most elementary of social interests, the interest in general security, demands that the one individual interest be secured no less than the other and for much the same reasons. The exaggerated importance of individual honor in primitive and in pioneer society illustrates this. In a condition of feeble law adequate securing of this interest . . . is quite impossible, and the insistence of the individual on protecting and vindicating it for himself becomes a serious menace to the peace and order of society.[15]

For this reason the law of libel and slander has struck deep roots in our legal order, and is not affected by the constitutional guaranty of freedom of speech and of the press. The rationale for the exclusion of libelous or slanderous words from constitutional protection has been expressed as follows by a unanimous Supreme Court:

There are certain well-defined and narrowly limited classes of speech, the prevention and punishment of which has never been thought to raise any Constitutional problem. These include the lewd and obscene, the profane, the libelous, and the insulting or "fighting" words—those which by their very utterance inflict injury or tend to incite an immediate breach of the peace . . . such utterances are no essential part of any exposition of ideas, and are of such slight social value as a step to truth that any benefit that may be derived from them is clearly outweighed by the social interest in order and morality. "Resort to epithets or personal abuse is not in any proper sense communication of information or opinion safeguarded by the Constitution, and its punishment as a criminal act would raise no question under that instrument."[16]

The injury resulting from the speech or publication of the types referred to by the Supreme Court may be tangible and immediate, while the public good effected by the words may be conjectural and remote.

Libel was a misdemeanor at common law, was a criminal offense in the American colonies, and is punished today as a crime in every American jurisdiction. A Star Chamber decision of 1605 stated the principle which has persisted to this day:

If it [the libel] be against a private man it deserves a severe punishment, for although the libel be made against one, yet it incites all those of the same family, kindred, or society to revenge, and so tends *per consequens* to quarrels and breaches of the peace.[17]

The purpose of the criminal libel statutes is not so much protection of a person's reputation as prevention of breaches of the peace and maintenance of public order. From this it follows that the truth by itself is not a sufficient defense to a prosecution; indeed, "the greater the truth, the greater the libel." With respect to this point, criminal libel and the right of privacy are in agreement. But in a criminal libel prosecution the truth *is* a defense *if* coupled with a showing that the publication was made with good motives and for justifiable ends. In the case of civil libel (a suit for damages), in some jurisdictions the truth is a complete defense; in other states the truth alone is not a defense unless the words were published with good motives and for justifiable ends.[18]

Statements which would normally be libelous or slanderous or an invasion of privacy may be, under certain circumstances, *privileged.*

Early in the history of Parliament some members of the House of Commons were prosecuted for statements that the Crown considered offensive. These prosecutions were a source of conflict between King and Parliament. Early in the seventeenth century James I and Parliament fought bitterly over this issue. In 1621 James wrote to the Speaker of the House of Commons, saying that word had come to him that the "fiery and popular spirits" of some members of Commons had led these members "to argue and debate publicly of the matters far above their reach and capacity, tending to our high dishonour and breach of prerogative royal." He then went on to warn that no one "shall presume henceforth to meddle with anything concerning our government or deep matters of state." He said that he knew very well how to punish "any man's misdemeanours in Parliament, as well during their sitting as after—which we mean not to spare hereafter upon any occasion of any man's insolent behaviour there." In response to this message from the King, the Commons adopted a protest, in which it was stated that Parliament enjoyed "liberties, franchises, privileges and jurisdictions" that are "the ancient and undoubted birthright and inheritance of the subjects of England"; that "the making and maintenance of laws, and redress of mischiefs and grievances, which daily happen within this realm, are proper subjects and matter of counsel and debate in Parliament," and that in the handling of these matters, "every member of the House hath and of right ought to have freedom of speech," and that every member has "freedom from all impeachment, imprisonment, and molestation (other than by the censure of the House itself) for or concerning any bill, speaking, reasoning, or declaring of any matter or matters touching the Parliament or Parliament business." [19] Conflict over this issue continued, until, finally, absolute freedom of speech and debate in Parliament was recognized by the Bill of Rights (1689), which stated "that the freedom of speech and debates or proceedings in Parliament ought not to be impeached or questioned in any court or place out of Parliament." [20]

With this history in mind, it is no surprise that in drafting the Articles of Confederation in 1777, Congress provided for absolute freedom of speech and debate in Congress,[21] and that Article I, Section 6 of the Constitution provides that "for any speech or debate" in Congress, members of Congress "shall not be questioned in any other place." The Supreme Court has given the widest reach to this *absolute privilege,* saying that a member of Congress cannot be brought before any court of justice for any statement he may make, "though to the last degree calumnious, or even if it brought personal suffering upon individuals." [22] The purpose of this absolute privilege is not the protection of members of Congress for their own benefit, "but to support the rights of the people, by enabling their representatives to execute the functions of their office without fear of prosecutions, civil or criminal." The privilege is not limited to words spoken in debate; it extends also to voting, to the making of a written report, "and every other act resulting from the nature and in the execution of the office," and extends to acts even when they violate the rules of the House of which the person is a member.[23] The Constitution thus permits "unlimited freedom" to members of Congress in speeches, debates, committee hearings, reports and other such activities; the courts will not entertain actions for defamation or for invasions of rights of privacy against members of Congress when there is available to them as a defense the plea of absolute privilege. "The claim of an unworthy purpose does not destroy the privilege. Legislators are immune from deterrents to the uninhibited discharge of their legislative purpose. . . . Self-discipline and the voters must be the ultimate reliance for discharging or correcting . . . abuses." [24]

Absolute privilege extends to members of state legislatures, and to proceedings in civil and military courts. Substantially the same protection is given to counsel, witnesses, and parties as to judges, for it is considered "sound policy to send such individuals [in legal proceedings] . . . to their tasks unhampered by any lurking fear that they may later be called to account for what they say." [25]

Suppose a newspaper reports what has been said by someone on an occasion when the speaker enjoyed absolute privilege? The newspaper has a *qualified privilege*. If the newspaper publishes a fair and true report of a judicial, legislative, or other public official proceedings, or of speeches, debates, or arguments made in the course of such proceedings, it is not liable, criminally or civilly, unless the person whose reputation has been defamed can prove malice in the publication of the report.[26]

The reason for the existence of this rule of qualified privilege with respect to the reporting of judicial proceedings has been stated by Justice Holmes. The privilege arises from the fact, he said, that it is desirable that the trial of causes should take place under the public eye, not because the controversies of one citizen with another are of public concern, but because it is of the highest moment that those who administer justice should always act under the sense of public responsibility, and that every citizen should be able to satisfy himself with his own eyes as to the mode in which a public duty is performed.[27]

The qualified privilege is thus an extension of the right to a public trial guarantied by the Sixth Amendment. Equally strong reasons obtain with respect to the reporting of legislative and other public proceedings in a democracy. "It seems to us impossible to doubt," Lord Chief Justice Cockburn has said,

that it is of paramount public and national importance that the proceedings of the houses of Parliament shall be communicated to the public, who have the deepest interest in knowing what passes within their walls, seeing that on what is there said and done the welfare of the community depends. Where would be our confidence in the government of the country or in the Legislature by which our laws are framed, and to whose charge the great interests of the country are committed, where would be our attachment to the constitution under which we live, if the proceedings of the great council of the realm were shrouded in secrecy and concealed from the knowledge of the nation? [28]

It apparently was argued in the case before Cockburn that while it may be in the public interest generally that legislative proceedings be made public, the line should be drawn where the character of individuals is brought into question. To this argument the Chief Justice replied that, first, it would be too difficult to scan debates to see if there is in them any defamatory matter; second, that there is perhaps no subject of deeper public interest than that of the conduct of public servants—there is no subject of legislative discussion "which more requires to be made known than an inquiry relating to it." But suppose the defamatory matter published relates to a private person; e.g., the newspapers report what a senator said at a committee hearing about a university professor? If the report published is a fair and true account of what was said, and is published without malice (that is, without an intent to injure the subject of the speech or remarks), then it should be considered privileged; for what private persons do is often of public concern; but even more (adapting the words of Justice Holmes quoted above), because it is of the highest moment that our legislators should always act under a sense of public responsibility, and that every citizen should be able to satisfy himself with his own eyes as to the mode in which a public duty is performed; for when a legislator exposes an individual, he at the same time exposes himself, to the same public gaze and scrutiny. "Were it left to me to decide whether we should have a government without newspapers," wrote Jefferson, "or newspapers without government, I should not hesitate a moment to prefer the latter." [29] This may or may not be a wise choice; but certainly it is true that a government of laws is not possible if the government by men is not exposed for public examination. If innocent men are in the process injured in their reputations, the fault is not with the newspaper that attempts to report news truly and fairly; the fault should be traced to its source, the legislator who acts without regard to truth or fairness. His statements are absolutely privileged; and as to him, "the voters must be the ultimate reliance for discharging or correcting . . . abuses" [30] of which he is guilty.

In addition to qualified privilege, newspapers have the right of *fair comment,* and may use this right as a defense to a charge of libelous defamation. Without the right of fair comment there would be no freedom of the press. This right is enjoyed by any individual; it is not restricted to newspapers; and is available whether the statement is oral or written. The defense of fair comment must possess the following elements: The comment must be founded on facts, or what to a reasonable man would be acceptable as facts; it must be fair; it must not be made out of malice, but must be the result of honest opinion; the comment must be upon a subject of public interest.[31] If the comment possesses these elements, it may be severe, caustic, bitter, and even intemperate, for the comment does not purport to report objective facts but to be a subjective reaction to facts. The comment must be on a matter of public interest; it may not invade the privacy of a person under the guise of a comment on public affairs. The subject of the comment may be candidates for public office, public officials, books, dramas, concerts, or any other public presentation.

In its origin, Charles Beard has said, freedom of the press had little or nothing to do with truth-telling; "most of the early newspapers were partisan sheets devoted to savage attacks on party opponents. If we are to take George Washington's own statement at face value, it was scurrilous abuse by the press which drove him into retirement at the end of his second term." [32]

It was Philip Freneau, the poet, and Benjamin Franklin Bache, Franklin's grandson, who were the chief offenders. When Washington complained to Jefferson, his Secretary of State, especially of the acts of Freneau (to whom Jefferson gave a job in his department), Jefferson wrote that he was not concerned with "the merits or demerits" of Freneau's newspaper. "No government," he went on, in his letter to Washington, "ought to be without censors." If the government is virtuous, "it need not fear the fair operation of attack and defence. Nature has given to man no other means of sifting out the truth either in religion, law or politics. I think it is as honorable to the government neither to know, nor notice, its sycophants or censors, as it would be undignified and criminal to pamper the former and persecute the latter." [33]

The time came when Jefferson himself was abused by the press—he was accused of theft, atheism, cowardice, immorality, and seduction. "Nothing can now be believed," he wrote, "which is seen in a newspaper." He said that he looked with commiseration upon his fellow citizens who, reading newspapers, "live and die in the belief, that they have known something of what has been passing in the world in their time." The man who never reads newspapers, he added, "is better informed than he who reads them." [34]

But Jefferson did not abandon his principled belief in a free press even when the press abandoned all principles of truth and fairness and attempted to victimize him. "I have lent myself willingly as the subject of a great experiment," he wrote, "which was to prove that an administration, conducting itself with integrity and common understanding, cannot be battered down, even by the falsehood of a licentious press." What was the experiment to the conduct of which he lent himself as the subject? It was, he said, "to demonstrate the falsehood of the pretext that freedom of the press is incompatible with orderly government." [35]

Freedom of the press is compatible with orderly government; more than that, it is essential to free government and to a society that values differences of points of view, intellectual and artistic ferment, originality, the cultivation of a critical faculty, and an open mind on the part of its citizens. Since the days of Washington and Jefferson the press has developed a sense of responsibility, in part due to the legal limits on freedom of expression which we have been discussing—e.g., the right of privacy. "Freedom of the press," wrote Charles Beard, "means the right to be just or unjust, partisan or non-partisan, true or false, in news column or editorial column." [36] This is not the case today. Freedom of the press does not mean freedom to commit libels, to invade the privacy of a private life, to comment unfairly or maliciously, to be unjust or false. It does not mean irresponsibility. The press "has lost the common and ancient human liberty to be deficient in its function or to offer half-truth for the whole." [37]

### C. GROUP LIBEL

As we have seen, the First Amendment offers no protection to a person when he makes libelous statements about another person. The libel may be the basis of a civil suit for damages or for a prosecution for criminal libel. In some states the truth is a defense in a criminal libel prosecution only if it can be shown that the statement was published with good motives and for justifiable ends.

Suppose, instead of a named individual, a group is libeled and no individual is identified in the statement by name? Can a member of the group recover damages for libel? The answer has been authoritatively stated as follows:

A libel directed at a group may form the foundation of an action by an individual if the group is small enough so that a person reading the article may readily identify the person as one of the group. The familiar illustration is that if one should say that the members of a City Council are all corrupt, any member of the Council could, even though not designated by name, sue the publication. However, if the group is so large that there is no likelihood that a reader would understand the article to refer to any particular member of the group, it is not libelous.[38]

Under this rule it has been held that a statement that "31,000 Workers' Alliance members and their officials divert their membership dues to further Communist agitation under direct orders from the Third International headquarters in Russia" could not serve as a basis for a suit for damages by the president of the named organization, for the group was too large.[39]

What of the group itself, as an entity—could it recover? The law found little difficulty in extending the law of libel to protect business corporations. Then the courts found that charitable organizations should also be protected, for they had the same interest in reputation as the business corporation. Then the right was extended to unincorporated trade unions. It has been urged that any organization should be allowed to recover if it depends upon good reputation for success in its field of endeavor.[40]

A moment's reflection will, however, disclose great difficulties with a principle so sweepingly inclusive. For under it the Democratic Party could sue and recover damages arising from the "twenty years of treason" libel.[41] It has been said that

libelous words become dangerous words for democracy when calculated to inflame public indignation against others by arousing community hatreds. Political vilification of individuals or groups of individuals can conceivably destroy the climate of tolerance so necessary for the survival of free expression and substitute an atmosphere of unreasoned passion. Totalitarian forces operating within European democracies found group libel a most effective method to attack mercilessly their enemies and incite antipathies between various classes of society. . . . Private groups could certainly be smeared out of existence if with impunity they could be mislabeled as "communist," "Fascist" or pink.[42]

Since the arguments on behalf of group libel laws tend to support criminal sanctions even more than civil suits for damages, we should consider the *Beauharnais* case [43] before weighing or answering these arguments.

The Illinois legislature in 1917, following some race riots, passed a law, sometimes spoken of as the "Anti-Hate Law," making it unlawful for anyone to make, publish or exhibit in any public place any publication or exhibition that "portrays depravity, criminality, unchastity, or lack of virtue of a class of citizens of any race, color, creed or religion," and exposes "the citizens of any race, color, creed or religion to contempt, derision, or obloquy or which is productive of breach of the peace or riots." The statute was not used until 1925, when it was applied to a movie. Then it was used in 1941 and 1942 against Jehovah's Witnesses. Then it was invoked for the fourth time against Joseph Beauharnais in 1950.

As president of the White Circle League, Beauharnais published and distributed on a Chicago street corner a leaflet which called on the mayor and council "to halt the further encroachment, harassment and invasion of white people, their property, neighbors and persons by the Negro," and it appealed for a million white persons to unite and to contribute to the White Circle League, and argued that "if persuasion and the need to prevent the white race from becoming mongrelized by the Negro will not unite us, then the aggression . . . rapes, robberies, knives, guns and marijuana of the Negro surely will." Beauharnais was convicted by the Illinois courts, and his conviction was sustained by a five-to-four decision of the Supreme Court.

In his opinion for the majority, Justice Frankfurter pointed out that the Illinois courts treated the statute as "a form of criminal libel law," which contemplated that the truth shall be a defense only if the statement was published with good motives and for justifiable ends, that they found the statement of a libelous character as a matter of law, and that they found the justification in punishing libels criminally in the tendency of the publication to cause a breach of the peace.

The state, said Justice Frankfurter, may constitutionally make it a criminal offense to publish libels directed at "designated collectivities"; for "if an utterance directed at an individual may be the object of criminal sanctions, we cannot deny to a State power to punish the same utterance directed at a defined group." Justice Frankfurter recalled that nine years before the statute was adopted the first Northern race riot occurred in Chicago, and that in 1951 there were race riots in Cicero, Illinois. In the face of these and similar facts, said Frankfurter,

we would deny experience to say that the Illinois legislature was without reason in seeking ways to curb false or malicious defamation of racial and religious groups, made in public places and by means calculated to have a powerful emotional impact on those to whom it was presented.

There may well be, said Frankfurter, sharp differences of opinion as to the wisdom of the means chosen by Illinois to meet the evil; but states have the right to deal with social evils on a trial-and-error basis. A person's opportunities may depend on the reputation of his racial or religious group no less than on his own merits; it follows that the courts are "precluded from saying that speech concededly punishable when immediately directed at individuals cannot be outlawed if directed at groups with whose position and esteem in society the affiliated individual may be inextricably involved."

But the Court, in approving as constitutional a group libel law that prohibits the defamation of a group identified by creed or race, expressly said that the opinion was not to be interpreted as approving also the prohibition of a libel of a political party.

Justice Frankfurter summarized the majority view by saying:

Libelous utterances, not being within the area of constitutionally protected speech, it is unnecessary . . . to consider the issues behind the phrase "clear and present danger." Certainly no one would contend that obscene speech, for example, may be punished only upon a showing of such circumstances. Libel, as we have seen, is in the same class.

In the dissenting opinions one finds the arguments against the constitutionality of group libel laws. Justice Black contended that the Illinois statute should have been tested against "the unequivocal First Amendment command that its defined freedoms shall not be abridged." The "peace and well-being" of a state, or the "rational basis" of a statute are not constitutional standards when a First Amendment freedom is curtailed. A state has no right to "experiment" in the area of the basic freedoms—an area constitutionally excluded from legislative concern or action. "My own belief is," said Black,

that no legislature is charged with the duty or vested with the power to decide what public issues Americans can discuss. In a free country that is the individual's choice, not the state's. State experimentation in curbing freedom of expression is startling and frightening doctrine. . . . I reject the holding that either state or nation can punish people for having their say in matters of public concern.

Justice Black thought that the majority were giving wider scope and more respectable status to libel laws than even the Court of Star Chamber had done; for now it has become dangerous to say something critical of racial or religious groups.

Mr. Justice Douglas, while concurring in the dissenting opinion of Justice Black, wrote his own opinion, in which he said that

Hitler and his Nazis showed how evil a conspiracy could be which was aimed at destroying a race by exposing it to contempt, derision, and obloquy. I would be willing to concede that such conduct directed at a race or group in this country could be made an indictable offense. For such a project would be more than the exercise of free speech. Like picketing, it would be free speech plus.

He conceded that even without the element of conspiracy, there might be times and occasions when the government might call a halt to inflammatory talk; but then "the peril of speech must be clear and present, leaving no room for argument, raising no doubts as to the necessity of curbing speech in order to prevent disaster." The right of free speech is an absolute right; it is not subject to regulation "within reasonable limits"; free speech and freedom of the press are "above and beyond the police power; they are not subject to regulation in the manner of factories, slums, apartment houses, production of oil, and the like."

One of the strongest arguments against the decision was put by Douglas as follows:

Today a white man stands convicted for protesting in unseemly language against our decisions invalidating restrictive covenants. Tomorrow a Negro will be hailed before a court for denouncing lynch law in heated terms. Farm laborers in the west who compete with field hands drifting up from Mexico; whites who feel the pressure of orientals; a minority which finds employment going to members of the dominant religious group—all of these are caught in the mesh of today's decision. . . . Intemperate speech is a distinctive characteristic of man. Hot heads blow off and release destructive energy in the process. . . . The Framers of the Constitution knew human nature as well as we do. They too had lived in dangerous days; they too knew the suffocating influence of orthodoxy and standardized thought. They weighed the compulsions for restrained speech and thought against the abuses of liberty. They chose liberty. That should be our choice today no matter how distasteful to us the pamphlet of Beauharnais may be.

The decision of the Court is limited to the proposition that a statute may put the libel of a religious or a racial group outside the protection of the First Amendment. It does not go beyond this to include the libel of any other group. But the decision goes quite far in excluding from constitutional protection speech that relates to subjects that have always been—shall we say?—in the public domain. Incitement to a race riot or a pogrom can certainly be punished; but when there is no immediate threat to life or limb or public order, there should be no assumption that the group libel does such grave injury to an important public interest that in the face of it the Constitution should be ignored.[44]

If group libel statutes are constitutional when limited to attacks on races or creeds, "why should we stop with quarrels among racial and religious groups?" Professor Zechariah Chafee, Jr., has asked. For, he points out,

the community is equally imperiled by class warfare, by strikes which cut off the necessities of life from great cities, by the miseries of sharecroppers. . . . Once you start group libel laws, every influential body of men will urge that it has an equal claim to be protected by such legislation. And the wider the protection, the narrower becomes the field for unimpeded discussion of public affairs.[45]

Secondly, asks Chafee,

what is truth in group libel? Any group can be defamed by dragging up obnoxious acts by some of its members. Suppose an attempt to stir up racial prejudice by a lurid but accurate description of actual crimes by thirty different Negroes. Every fact is true, but the imputation that all Negroes are responsible for these outrages is utterly false. Can the defendant maintain a plea of truth or not? [46]

Thirdly, there is a great risk in a prosecution for group libel, for if the defendant should be convicted, his supporters and sympathizers will consider and treat him as a martyr or hero, or if he is acquitted, he and his organization will be strengthened and emboldened. Fourthly, when a group libel law was enacted in New Jersey in 1939,[47] the statute was applied in one town to Jehovah's Witnesses for attacks on Catholics. "Whereas previously no Catholic issue has arisen in the community, now the town became divided into pro-Catholics and anti-Catholics just because of this law. In general, the more you bring group prejudices into the arena of legal controversy, the more you raise the issues you are trying to allay." [48] Fifthly, group libel laws are thought to be urgently needed precisely at times when such laws will prove useless; for then such laws will touch only the symptom and not the cause; because if there are antagonisms, "it is useless to stamp out the public expression" of them.[49] Not only is it useless, but it is even harmful to do so, for, as Justice Douglas has said, the release of destructive energy when hot heads blow off in intemperate speech is socially useful. It is better that social hatreds be expressed openly than through whispering or underground conspiracies. "The less one can say publicly, the more he will say in private. . . . The very suppression of publications and meetings is made a fresh cause for hatred. . . . Group vilification is superseded by group violence." [50]

Libels of individuals seldom involve social or political issues; but group libels, it has forcefully been pointed out, almost invariably relate to such issues.

The really dangerous disseminators of group hatred are those who use it to further social, economic, and political arguments. It is difficult to draw a line between pure abuse and honest though derogatory, malignant, and wrong-headed criticism. The subtler the propaganda, the more it represents rational argument, and consequently the more plausible and dangerous it is. . . . Much public criticism, moreover, is not susceptible of proof or disproof—it lies in the realm of opinion rather than fact. If men may advance derogatory opinions only at the risk of being hailed into court and forced to cite substantiating chapter and verse to the satisfaction of a jury, vigorous criticism might soon cease to be voiced.[51]

These arguments against the wisdom and constitutionality of group libel laws seem thoroughly convincing; and the fact is that legislative bodies, both before and after the Supreme Court's decision in the *Beauharnais* case, have been much more impressed with the arguments against such laws than those in their favor. Time and again Congress has refused to enact group libel laws.[52] Of the criminal group libel laws in eight states, three show no successful prosecutions, two are of such limited scope as to merit no consideration, one has not been used, and one has been declared unconstitutional for vagueness.[53] Only the Illinois act has won success, first as a weapon with which to harass Jehovah's Witnesses, and later in the *Beauharnais* case, in which the majority of the Court, had it won a following, would have undone the commendable, traditional position of the courts not to extend the law of libel.

# ☆ 17 ☆

# Fighting Words

ON A busy Saturday afternoon a Jehovah's Witness named Chaplinsky was distributing the literature of his sect on the street of a town in New Hampshire. Some townsmen complained to the city marshal that Chaplinsky was denouncing all religion as a "racket." The officer warned him that the crowd was getting restless. Then a disturbance occurred and the traffic officer at the busy intersection started with Chaplinsky for the police station, but Chaplinsky was not told that he was under arrest or that he would be arrested. In the meantime the city marshal, having been told that a riot was under way, hurried to the scene, and on his way, near the city hall, he met Chaplinsky and the traffic officer. The city marshal then repeated his warning to Chaplinsky. In reply, Chaplinsky, it was claimed, exclaimed: "You are a God damned racketeer, and a damned Fascist and the whole government of . . . [the town] are Fascists or agents of Fascists."

At this point Chaplinsky was arrested and charged with violation of a statute that provided that it shall be an offense to address to another person on a street or in a public place "any offensive, derisive or annoying word," or to call him by "any offensive or derisive name." Chaplinsky was convicted. On appeal, the United States Supreme Court, in an opinion by Justice Murphy, unanimously affirmed the conviction.[1] In his opinion Justice Murphy made the following statement, which we have previously quoted and which has been quoted in numerous subsequent opinions:

There are certain well-defined and narrowly limited classes of speech, the prevention and punishment of which have never been thought to raise any Constitutional problem. These include the lewd and obscene, the profane, the libelous, and the insulting or "fighting" words—those which by their very utterance inflict injury or tend to incite an immediate breach of the peace. It has been well observed that such utterances are no essential part of any exposition of ideas, and are of such slight social value as a step to truth that any benefit that may be derived from them is clearly outweighed by the social interest in order and morality.

Then Justice Murphy quoted from an earlier case to the effect that "epithets or personal abuse" is not communication of information or opinion protected by the First Amendment, and punishment for the use of such expressions involves no constitutional question.[2]

As construed by the state court, the offense under the New Hampshire statute was limited to words which, when addressed to a person of common intelligence, would likely cause him to fight. Some words, by common consent, said the state court, are " 'fighting words' when said without a disarming smile." There are such things as "disorderly words," which, when spoken face to face, are likely to cause a breach of the peace or which when spoken are themselves a breach of the peace.

The statute, as thus construed, said Justice Murphy, is constitutional; it punishes "verbal acts" or "the use in a public place of words likely to cause a breach of the peace." The words used by Chaplinsky clearly fell within the scope of the statute.

At the trial Chaplinsky offered to prove provocation and also the truth of his words, but his testimony was excluded. The Supreme Court held that the exclusion raised no constitutional issue.

Here, then, is another instance of speech that is beyond the range of the First Amendment, and where even the truth of the utterance will not give the speaker the constitutional freedom to speak.

"Speak ye every man the truth to his neighbor," said the prophet Zechariah. American law obviously does not choose to follow this precept, for telling the truth may land one in jail. "I wish," Jefferson wrote in a letter, "that not only no act but no thought of mine should be unknown." [3] This is a surprising statement from a man of affairs sixty-five years of age; for certainly many of Jefferson's thoughts when expressed in face-to-face encounters would have constituted fighting words; and Jefferson knew better than to act on his "wish."

It should be noted that fighting words are not the same as libelous or slanderous words. Language may be abusive and insulting and yet fall short of the tests that obtain in the law of defamation. Generally, the law will not allow recovery of damages in a suit based on the use of merely insulting language. [4] In an Ohio case, for example, it appeared that the parties had a dispute concerning the sale of a farm; when they met on a street, defendant began to abuse the plaintiff in the presence of other people, and in a loud and angry voice called her "a God damned son of a bitch," "a dirty crook," and other endearing terms. It was held that such epithets, not being slanderous per se, constituted no legal basis for recovery. [5] The decision is typical of the general rule: the law of libel and slander is for the protection of reputation, not peace of mind; if the words spoken are only insulting epithets, they constitute no tort. [6]

New Hampshire is not the only state that punishes fighting words as a criminal offense; and several of the statutes impose criminal punishment when the insult is to a member of the addressee's family or concerning his female relatives; or when the insulting language is used in the addressee's home or on his property; or when the insulting language is addressed to women or children in a public place (not on the theory, I suppose, that the women or children will fight, but that others standing by may respond violently to the fighting words); and some statutes have extended the coverage to include especially soldiers, members of the national guard, public speakers, prisoners, teachers, and female telephone operators; and the general rule is that provocation or the truth is no defense. [7]

It has been urged that the law recognizes insult or insulting language as a new tort. Liability, it has been argued,

should exist for either oral or written words. Insulting gestures may also be included. There need, of course, be no publication other than to the person about whom they were spoken. But they need not be uttered face-to-face; statements to third persons which are relayed to the plaintiff should be treated as tortious. . . . If the plaintiff started the verbal brawl, his act may be regarded as a provocation, and this is one occasion in which provocation should be treated as a complete defense. . . . Shall truth be a defense? It is so recognized in actions for defamation but not in actions for invasion of the right of privacy. This action [for insult] is somewhere in between the two, and the decision is a difficult one to reach.[8]

There is much to be said for this proposal for the recognition of freedom from insult which causes mental disturbance—insult to a person's sense of dignity. Once the right to privacy becomes firmly and widely recognized, many courts will extend the principles of that right to allow recovery for insult to a person's sense of dignity. One is reminded of Lincoln's remark that one should always tell the truth, but should not always be telling it.

# ☆ 18 ☆

# Obscene Literature

IN OUR quotation from the Supreme Court's opinion in the *Chaplinsky* case,[1] it will be recalled, Justice Murphy put "the lewd and obscene" in the class of speech the prevention and punishment of which has "never been thought to raise any Constitutional problem." In that passage Justice Murphy placed obscene, profane, and libelous language, together with fighting words, all in the same class—types of speech that are beyond the pale of the First Amendment. And in the *Beauharnais* case,[2] too, Justice Frankfurter put group libel on a par with obscenity as outside "the area of constitutionally protected speech." In each instance the reference to obscene language was an obiter dictum. Justice Frankfurter offered no explanation for assimilating obscenity to group libel, or vice versa; but Justice Murphy attempted a rationale in a paraphrase of some passages in *Free Speech in the United States* by Zechariah Chafee, Jr.

Professor Chafee, in discussing "the normal criminal law of words," distinguishes verbal crimes that are outside the protection of the Constitution from the expression of ideas that are constitutionally protected. Obscenity, notwithstanding the First Amendment, is a crime, and the "true explanation" for this, says Chafee in a significant passage—the one which Justice Murphy paraphrased in part and which he cited—is that

profanity and indecent talk and pictures, *which do not form an essential part of any exposition of ideas,* have a very slight social value as a step toward truth, which is clearly outweighed by the social interests in order, morality, the training of the young, and the peace of mind of those who hear and see. Words of this type offer little opportunity for the usual process of counter-argument. The harm is done as soon as they are communicated, or is liable to follow almost immediately in the form of retaliatory violence. *The only sound explanation of the punishment of obscenity and profanity is that the words are criminal, not because of the ideas they communicate, but like acts because of their immediate consequences to the five senses.* The man who swears in a street car is as much of a nuisance as the man who smokes there. Insults are punished like a threatening gesture, since they are liable to provoke a fight. *Adulterated candy is no more poisonous to children than some books.* Grossly unpatriotic language may be punished for the same reasons. The man who talks scurrilously about the flag commits a crime, not because the implications of his ideas tend to weaken the Federal Government, but because the effect resembles that of an injurious act such as trampling on the flag, which would be a public nuisance and a breach of the peace.[3]

On one side, Chafee would place "nasty talk or the sale of unsuitable books to the young," which are likely to cause *present injury,* and on the other side, words that express ideas, which may cause "bad future consequences." This does not mean, however, that any expression of an unpopular view may be punished because a listener or reader may lack self-control and cannot refrain from violence:

A man does not become a criminal because some one else assaults him, unless his own conduct is in itself illegal or may be reasonably considered a direct provocation to violence. Thus all these crimes of injurious words must be kept within very narrow limits if they are not to give excessive opportunities for outlawing heterodox ideas.[4]

Apparently Justices Murphy and Frankfurter had these distinctions in mind when they spoke of obscenity and libel in the same breath—that obscene words or pictures which, in their context, have the effect of *acts,* may be punished as criminal acts; but that when words form an essential part of an exposition of ideas, and are used to communicate ideas, and are not intended to have immediate consequences, then, without regard to whether the ideas communicated are conventional or unconventional, popular or unpopular, religious or antireligious, moral or immoral, the words are *speech* in the constitutional sense rather than *acts* in the criminal law sense.

No American critic was more distinguished than Edmund Wilson when in 1946 Doubleday published his second novel, *Memoirs of Hecate County*. The book was widely reviewed in literary journals. Some 70,000 copies were printed and sold.[5] The New York Society for the Suppression of Vice (now the New York Society for the Improvement of Morals) attacked the book as obscene, and Doubleday was charged with a criminal offense for publishing and selling the book. The trial before three judges in New York City resulted in a two-to-one vote for conviction. At the trial Lionel Trilling, a distinguished critic, testified on behalf of the defense. When the state's attorney on cross examination read to this witness two passages, written in the first person, which described sexual intercourse, Professor Trilling stated that there was a close relationship between these passages and the theme of the book. The conviction was upheld by the upper courts of New York.[6] The case went up to the United States Supreme Court, and for the first time in such a case the constitutional issue was squarely raised. The Court, by a four-to-four vote, affirmed the conviction;[7] and, as is the practice in such instances, no opinions were written. It is reasonable to infer that four members of the Supreme Court voted for reversal of the judgment of conviction on the ground that the publisher was constitutionally protected notwithstanding the passages in which sexual intercourse was treated candidly.[8] But equal weight, at least, is to be given to the fact that four Justices voted to sustain the conviction for obscenity, thus perpetuating the broad proposition that obscenity is beyond the pale of constitutional protection; and thus distinctions between obscene words that are *acts* (and punishable, like libelous or fighting words) and obscene words that are *speech* (and constitutionally protected as such) are not recognized in our law.

Only in two cases have courts held that the constitutional test applies to literature allegedly obscene. First is the case of

*Commonwealth v. Gordon,*[9] decided by Judge Curtis Bok in the Court of Quarter Sessions in Philadelphia in 1949.

In the case before Judge Bok booksellers were charged with violating the state law that prohibits the sale of "any obscene, lewd, lascivious, filthy, indecent or disgusting book, . . . or any written or printed matter of an indecent character." The books involved in the case were the *Studs Lonigan* trilogy and *A World I Never Made,* by James T. Farrell; *Sanctuary* and *The Wild Palms,* by William Faulkner; *God's Little Acre,* by Erskine Caldwell; *End as a Man,* by Calder Willingham; and *Never Love a Stranger,* by Harold Robbins. The books had been published by reputable publishers—Vanguard Press, Random House, and Alfred A. Knopf.

Judge Bok, after recognizing the fact that the Supreme Court has not applied constitutional principles to an obscenity statute, quoted the following oral statement by Justice Rutledge in the *Doubleday* case:

> Yes, you must first ascertain the substantive evil at which the statute is aimed, and then determine whether the publication of this book constitutes a clear and present danger.
>
> It is up to the state to demonstrate that there was a danger, and until they demonstrate that, plus the clarity and imminence of the danger, the constitutional prohibition would seem to apply.

This appeared to Judge Bok to be "much closer to a correct solution of obscenity cases than several general dicta by the Supreme Court to the effect that obscenity is indictable just because it is obscenity." Adapting the constitutional test to the statute and the books before him, Judge Bok held that only the commission of criminal behavior, or its imminence, resulting from the reading of a book can bring the book within the criminal statute. "The causal connection between the book and the criminal behavior," said Judge Bok, "must appear beyond a reasonable doubt." Since there was no such proof in the case, the defendants were acquitted.

Like Professor Chafee, Judge Bok distinguished allegedly obscene literature from obscenity that is not speech but an act. Obscene books of the latter type he refers to as books which use obscenity as "erotic allurements or as an excuse for selling the volumes," books that "have the effect of inciting to lewdness, or of inciting to any sexual crime," or that are "sexually impure and pornographic, i.e., 'dirt for dirt's sake.' " How does one decide that a book falls into one category or the other? According to Judge Bok, the constitutional test, as he has formulated it, will separate the permissible from the prohibited; in other words, a publication may be punished as obscene "only where there is a reasonable and demonstrable cause to believe that a crime or misdemeanor has been committed or is about to be committed as the perceptible result of the publication and distribution of the writing in question."

Although Judge Bok's decision was made in 1949, no other court has gone so far in an effort to afford constitutional protection to allegedly obscene literature, and it remains to be seen if the decision will exert an influence on the judiciary in the years to come. A committee of the House of Representatives, perhaps in an effort to dissuade courts from looking to the Bok opinion as a reputable precedent that deserves serious consideration, has attempted to cast a shadow of moral doubt upon the decision in the *Gordon* case by suggesting that Judge Bok or his family had financial interests in the publication of pocket books; [10] but a minority committee report said that this suggestion of personal pecuniary interest was "a gratuitous and unjust reflection upon the distinguished jurist." [11] This incident is mentioned to show that the issues are enmeshed with moral overtones, and that it is often difficult to disengage the cant and hypocrisy from the reasonable and sincere. Judge Bok deserves recognition for his rational analysis, bold conclusion, and for the courage to make a plea on behalf of literary freedom as falling within the guaranty of the First Amendement. The constitutional test will still condemn "dirt for dirt's sake," but it will give the American people the untrammeled freedom to publish, distribute, and buy books written by its leading literary critic, by Nobel Prize winners like Faulkner, Sinclair Lewis, Eugene O'Neill, and Ernest Hemingway, and by authors of the stature of Theodore Dreiser, James T. Farrell, E. E. Cummings, Lillian Smith, and John Steinbeck.[12]

The second case, while more restricted in its constitutional reach or claims, is even more important. This is *Butler v. Michigan*,[13] decided by the Supreme Court in 1957.

The case involved the sale, to a policeman in Detroit, of a copy of a Pocket Book edition of *The Devil Rides Outside*, by John H. Griffin. The vendor was convicted for violation of the Michigan statute that provided that any person who shall sell or distribute any book or other publication

containing obscene, immoral, lewd or lascivious language, or obscene, immoral, lewd or lascivious prints, pictures, figures or descriptions, tending to incite minors to violent or depraved or immoral acts, manifestly tending to the corruption of the morals of youth, . . . shall be guilty of a misdemeanor.

On appeal, the Supreme Court unanimously reversed the judgment of conviction.

In a brief opinion for the Court, Justice Frankfurter pointed out that the Michigan statute, as interpreted and applied in this case, prohibited the sale of a book to the *general public,* while the test of the offensive or criminal character of the book is its tendency to affect the morals of *youth.* The state thus, in order to shield the innocence of youth, made it impossible for grown men and women to read certain books. "Surely," said Justice Frankfurter, "this is to burn the house to roast the pig." Michigan, indeed, had a statute that made it a criminal offense to sell or give to a minor child any book containing obscene language or pictures "tending to the corruption of the morals of the youth"; but the state had not proceeded under this statute: here the sale of the book had been to an adult, in fact a police officer.

"We have before us," said Frankfurter,

legislation not reasonably restricted to the evil with which it is said to deal. The incidence of this enactment is to reduce the adult population of Michigan to reading only what is fit for children. It thereby arbitrarily curtails one of those liberties of the individual, now enshrined in the Due Process Clause of the Fourteenth Amendment, that history has attested as the indispensable conditions for the maintenance and progress of a free society.

In this decision, the Supreme Court for the first time extended constitutional protection to books alleged to be obscene; for now at least this liberty has been established—the liberty of a parent to read a book that may be unfit for his young son or daughter. The decision is a notable gain for literary freedom.

The modern law of obscene literature takes as its point of departure Lord Campbell's Act, adopted by Parliament in the middle of the nineteenth century. In urging the adoption of his bill, Lord Campbell said that "the measure was intended to apply exclusively to works written for the single purpose of corrupting the morals of youth, and of a nature calculated to shock the feelings of decency in any well regulated mind." [14] According to this statement the intent or purpose of a book was a paramount consideration: a book written "for the single purpose of corrupting the morals of youth"; and the subject to be tested by the book was not the moron or the nymph or satyr, but "any well regulated mind."

About ten years after the act was adopted it was applied in the leading case of *Queen v. Hicklin*, in which Lord Chief Justice Cockburn misinterpreted the intention of the statute as stated by its sponsor.[15] The test for obscenity, said Cockburn, was "whether the tendency of the matter charged as obscenity is to deprave and corrupt those whose minds are open to such immoral influences, and into whose hands a publication of this sort may fall." According to this statement of the law, the purpose or intent of the author is irrelevant; and the book need not be tested upon "any well regulated mind," but is to be tested upon a mind that is "open to such immoral influences."

This law of obscene libel, as formulated by Cockburn, still obtains in England; but judicial and literary voices have been raised in protest. The *Times Literary Supplement* (London) has raised the question whether, if prosecution for obscenity is to take place, it is possible to draw a line which would leave on the side of decency literature that extends from the Book of Genesis to Aldous Huxley's *Point Counter Point*, and would exclude matter the tendency of which is "to deprave and corrupt those whose minds are open to such immoral influences." For, said the *Times* writer,

a weak stomach is not necessarily proof of strong principles, and there is something more than ordinarily anomalous about a law which can pounce upon a work of the imagination, aspiring, perhaps, to the high estate of a Rabelais, Shakespeare or Swift, while it passes unheeded the highly coloured versions of reality which are inflicted upon the Sunday reading public. Some years ago, it was suggested in *The Times* that, although the adult reader ought to be able to protect himself against suggestions of depravity, children, under a fixed age limit, should be denied access in bookshops and libraries to literature coming within the Cockburn definition. Even at that, they would find a wide range of literary misbehaviour still open to them, for murder, robbery, hatred and treason have never been considered corrupting in modern times. If our countrymen go to the dogs through reading books, they go to the dogs, apparently, in one particular alone.[16]

In an English case that attracted much notice in 1954, Justice Stable, while giving the appearance of using the Cockburn test, in fact undermined it. The case in the Central Criminal Court (Old Bailey) involved the charge of obscene libel for publication of *The Philanderer*, a novel by the American writer Stanley Kauffmann and published by the reputable firm Secker and Warburg. The theme of the book, Justice Stable told the jury of nine men and three women,

is the story of a rather attractive young man who is absolutely obsessed with his desire for women [hence the title of the book]. It is not presented as an admirable thing, or a thing to be copied. It is not presented as a thing that brought him happiness or any sort of permanent satisfaction. Throughout the book you hear the note of impending disaster. He is like the drunkard who cannot keep away from drink, although he knows where it will land him in the end. So far as his amatory adventures are concerned, the book does deal, with candour or if you prefer it crudity, with the realities of human love and human intercourse. There is no getting away from that, and the Crown say: "Well, that is sheer filth."

Members of the jury, is it? Is the act of sexual passion sheer filth? It may be an error of taste to write about it. . . . But is it sheer filth?

There is a difference, said Justice Stable, between filth, or pornography, and literature. Books that fall in the former classification, against which the obscene libel law is directed, "have got no message; they have got no inspiration; they have got no thought. They have got nothing. They are just filth, and, of course, that ought to be stamped out." But if an author has "an honest purpose and an honest thread of thought," and does not merely try to camouflage the crudity so as to fool the authorities, then his book is not an obscene libel.

Justice Stable charged the jury in the words of Cockburn but added:

The charge is not that the tendency of the book is either to shock or to disgust. That is not a criminal offence. The charge is that the tendency of the book is to corrupt and deprave. Then you say: "Well, corrupt or deprave whom?" To which the answer is: Those whose minds are open to such immoral influences and into whose hands a publication of this sort may fall.

But a book may fall into the hands of a "decently brought up young female aged fourteen"; or it may fall into the hands of a child in the nursery. This is not relevant, said Justice Stable, for it is not a question of books putting ideas into young people's heads. "Really, members of the jury, is it books that put ideas into young heads, or is it Nature? . . . Are we going to say in England that our contemporary literature is to be measured by what is suitable for the fourteen-year-old schoolgirl to read?" The judge pointed out that there are two extreme schools of thought. There are those who consider "that sex is sin; that the whole thing is dirty; that it was a mistake from beginning to end (and if it was, members of the jury, it was the great creator of life who made the mistake, and not you or I), and the less that is said about this wholly distasteful topic the better; let it be covered up and let us pretend it does not exist." Then there are the nudists. Somewhere between these two extremes "the average, decent, well-meaning man or woman takes his or her stand." Here Justice Stable clearly implied that while the bars are not completely down, it was not to be assumed in 1954 (as distinguished from 1868) that the English law is to reflect the attitude to sex that one may find in some of the teachings of the mediaeval Church. He himself, said Justice Stable, did not believe that we could get away from sex. "It is not our fault," he said, "that but for the love of men and women and the act of sex, the human race would have ceased to exist thousands of years ago." And, he added, if the time should ever come when sex will cease to be a great motive force in human life, then the human race will cease to exist.

One more important point was made by Justice Stable: he stressed his belief that novels are not to be belittled. In the first place, they are a source of much information concerning the lives of people in past centuries; and they are valuable as such sources because they attempt to portray the thought and behavior of real people. Secondly, for the contemporary world, novels afford us insights into how people in other countries live and think. And is this not important if we are concerned with the question in which direction humanity is moving "and in what column we propose to march"? If the Englishman wants to understand how life is lived in the United States, and he lacks the opportunity to go there to observe for himself, why should he not have the freedom to read the novels written by American authors who attempt to depict the lives of people as they live in New York, and to portray their speech, and turns of phrase, and their attitudes? If the facts are not palatable, should we close our eyes to them for that reason? [17] (The same argument could be used in favor of contemporary novels written about one's own countrymen—e.g., Erskine Caldwell's *Tobacco Road* and John Steinbeck's *The Grapes of Wrath*.)

The jury in the case of *Regina v. Warburg* returned a verdict of "Not guilty." A leading British periodical probably spoke for most persons who have given thought to the matter when it said editorially: "Mr. Justice Stable earned the gratitude of all of us in his summing-up . . . when he pointed out that public taste must not be held at the level of the adolescent—or, he might have added, the fetichist and senile pervert." [18] The editorial made the following important points: (1) It is wrong to lump as obscene libels the peddling of dirty books and the publication, by "a world famous firm of publishers, of unimpeachable good name," of a book that "had been seriously reviewed by distinguished reviewers in reputable journals and had established itself in the circulating libraries without previous complaint." (2) "No strict definition of obscenity can stand logical scrutiny. . . . There are no absolute canons in this field. . . . Each generation sets its own standards of taste. . . . Events, which one generation will blush to hear, make normal Sunday reading to the next." (3) When a jury is assisted by an able judge, and their standard is not "the dangers to the abnormal and the unstable," and the appeal is to their common sense, freed from the absurdities of judicial prejudice, they are better equipped than any other authority "to judge what is permissible at any given moment." (4) A line must be drawn somewhere. It should be drawn between "that which is produced merely to stimulate sexual interest and that which has a broader, artistic purpose. It is a question of 'intent'." (5) Much trouble would be avoided if the prosecuting authorities would use better judgment and a sense of discrimination, for often the chief absurdity is in the decision to prosecute.

Much of the difficulty with the law is the result of the dictum of Cockburn in the *Hicklin* case that "intention" is not an essential ingredient of the crime. Why, it has been cogently asked, if intention is a necessary ingredient of the crime of sedition, should it not be in the case of obscenity? If intention were made an essential ingredient of the offense, then obscenity could be defined as the crime of publishing matter "for the sole purpose of gain by exciting sexual passions, and thus corrupting public morals." Much would still remain dependent on "the good sense of judges and juries." [19]

To a considerable degree the opinions of Justice Stable, Judge Bok, and Justice Frankfurter owe their insights and appeal to opinions of Judges Woolsey, Learned Hand, and Augustus N. Hand, which we should consider briefly.

The Cockburn test was taken over by Massachusetts courts, which in 1909 banned Elinor Glyn's *Three Weeks* [20] and in 1930 Dreiser's *An American Tragedy*.[21] In the latter year the New York courts banned Arthur Schnitzler's *Reigen* (or *Hands Around*); [22] but on the whole the courts of this state were less

severe than those of Massachusetts.[23] In the federal courts two
acts of Congress were relevant: an act regulating imports,[24]
and an act concerning nonmailable matter.[25] The latter act,
passed in 1873, in response to the campaign in its favor by
Anthony Comstock,[26] indiscriminately lumps "obscene" books
with "filthy" pictures, contraceptive instruments and drugs, and
advertisements by abortionists; and the term "indecent" is defined by the statute to include "matter of a character tending to
incite arson, murder, or assassinations"; the former act prohibits
the importation of "obscene" books, as well as books that advocate treason or insurrection, "obscene or immoral" pictures,
figures, or instruments, contraceptives, lottery tickets—however,
the Secretary of the Treasury may, in his discretion, admit "the
so-called classics or books of recognized and established literary
or scientific merit," but he has the further discretion to allow
the entry of such books only when they are imported for non-
commercial purposes. A more indecent statutory hodgepodge
can scarcely be imagined. The federal courts relied on the
Cockburn test as well as on these sweeping statutes.

A voice of protest was, however, heard in a case decided in
1913,[27] in which Judge Learned Hand said that the Cockburn
test did not seem to answer the understanding and morality of a
later day, and he questioned the wisdom of mutilating truth
and beauty in the interest of those most likely to pervert them
to base uses, and of reducing the treatment of sex to the
standard of a child's library. We should not, he said, forbid all
"which might corrupt the most corruptible," and accept for our
own limitation that which may perhaps be necessary to the
weakest members of society. "To put thought in leash to the
average conscience of the time," said Judge Hand, "is perhaps
tolerable, but to fetter it by the necessities of the lowest and
least capable seems a fatal policy."

Then, twenty years later, came the opinions of Judge Woolsey
and Judge Augustus N. Hand in the case involving the importation of *Ulysses* by James Joyce.[28] Judge Woolsey held that the
book, in spite of its "unusual frankness," was not pornographic.
Although the book contains many words "usually considered
dirty," it could not be considered, said Judge Woolsey, "dirt

for dirt's sake." Joyce, "a real artist," sought to draw "a true picture of the lower middle class in a European city"—"ought it to be impossible for the American public legally to see that picture?" The test is the effect of the book "on a person with average sex instincts. . . . It is only with the normal person that the law is concerned." He held that the book may be admitted.

In affirming the decision, Judge Augustus N. Hand said that the proper test is the book's "dominant effect." In applying this test,

relevancy of the objectionable parts to the theme, the established reputation of the work in the estimation of approved critics, if the book is modern, and the verdict of the past, if it is ancient, are persuasive pieces of evidence. . . . We think that *Ulysses* is a book of originality and sincerity of treatment and that it has not the effect of promoting lust.

Despite these commendable decisions, the Cockburn test still persists. Just as Justice Stable could assert the Cockburn test and yet escape from it, so courts have avoided asserting it and yet have applied it. Through such judicial legerdemain the Supreme Judicial Court of Massachusetts banned Lillian Smith's *Strange Fruit* in 1945 and Erskine Caldwell's *God's Little Acre* in 1950;[29] federal courts have banned Henry Miller's *Tropic of Cancer* and *Tropic of Capricorn;*[30] and, as we have seen, the New York courts have banned Edmund Wilson's *Memoirs of Hecate County,* and the United States Supreme Court has, by an evenly divided vote, affirmed the ban on this book.

Eventually, one may hope, the Supreme Court will put literary works squarely and fully under the protection of the First Amendment. It will be impressed with the contention that there is little or no information supporting the belief in a causal relationship between reading a book "that suggests or incites sexual thoughts and the conduct of the reader";[31] that a line should be drawn between dirt-for-dirt's sake, or "under-the-counter" pornography, and literary works like Edmund Wilson's novel.[32] The views of Justice Stable, of Judges Learned Hand, Augustus N. Hand, and Bok, and of Justice Frankfurter offer sufficient elements for the construction of a constitutional doctrine that will protect "this vast and significant area of human thought and conduct." [33] The Supreme Court may fail, as others have failed, to agree on a definition of "obscenity" that will work successfully in all situations to separate literature from pornography, but it can help clear the air by manifesting an attitude which will show an awareness of the truth of the statements we have quoted from some of the cases—like those, e.g., concerned with *Ulysses* and *The Philanderer,*—and an awareness "that stamping on a fire often spreads the sparks, that many past suppressions are now considered ridiculous, that the communication of ideas is just as important in this field as in any other, and that healthy human minds have a strong natural resistance to emotional poisons." [34]

A number of times in our discussion we have pointed to the difficulty, if not impossibility, of defining "obscenity." This is an important constitutional point that requires special consideration.

The first essential of due process, the Supreme Court has said, is that a statute which forbids or requires the doing of an act must not be written in terms "so vague that men of common intelligence must necessarily guess at its meaning and differ as to its application." [35] If people want to be law-abiding, a statute must be sufficiently definite in its terms to serve as "adequate guidance" to them.[36] The standard of certainty in statutes punishing for offenses is that

The crime "must be defined with appropriate definiteness." . . . There must be ascertainable standards of guilt. Men of common intelligence cannot be required to guess at the meaning of the enactment. The vagueness may be from uncertainty in regard to . . . the applicable tests to ascertain guilt.[37]

In *Winters v. New York,*[38] from which the above passage was quoted, the Supreme Court considered a statute of the State of New York which, as interpreted by the highest state court, prohibited, as "indecent or obscene" publications, collections of criminal deeds of bloodshed or lust "so massed as to become vehicles for inciting violent and depraved crimes against the person." The Supreme Court held that the statute was "too uncertain and indefinite" to be constitutional. At the same time, however, the opinion by Justice Reed spoke of a "permissible uncertainty in statutes caused by describing crimes by words well understood through long use in the criminal law—obscene, lewd, lascivious, filthy, indecent or disgusting." He made it clear that had the New York statute been construed as limiting punishment to "the indecent and obscene, as formerly understood," it would not have been constitutionally condemned for want of definiteness.

Justice Frankfurter wrote a dissenting opinion, in which he contended that a majority of the Court had confused "want of certainty as to the outcome of different prosecutions for similar conduct, with want of definiteness in what the law prohibits. But diversity in result for similar conduct in different trials under the same statute is an unavoidable feature of criminal justice."

Four years later there came before the Supreme Court the *Miracle* case,[39] which will be discussed in our next section; it is relevant here only for the concurring opinion of Justice Frankfurter, in which he held—for himself and Justices Jackson and Burton—that the New York statute that made it unlawful to exhibit a motion picture film without a license, and that provided that a license was not to be issued if the film or a part thereof was "sacrilegious," was unconstitutional for indefiniteness. He pointed out that not one case, barring the instant case before the Court, had been found which considered the meaning of the term "sacrilegious" in any context; and the meaning given to it by the New York Court of Appeals left the term "unconstitutionally vague."

The reasoning of Justices Reed and Frankfurter in the *Winters* case and of the latter in the *Miracle* case does not serve as a basis for the conclusion that the term "obscenity" is unconstitutionally vague or indefinite. The term has been used too long and too often in statutes and judicial opinions to be exposed to this line of attack. All that can be said is "that no legal definition of obscenity is very satisfactory," and that "no attempt to frame a definition which will work in all situations is likely to succeed." [40] But the same thing could be said of "negligence," or "restraint of trade." [41] The law is full of words that are scarcely "as hard as cannon-balls," to use an Emersonian expression. What is reasonable to expect is not a decision that statutes punishing for "obscenity" are unconstitutional because of vagueness, but a decision that such statutes are to be interpreted and applied by courts so that their prohibitions will not nullify the freedoms guaranteed by the First Amendment. The decision of the Supreme Court and the opinion of Justice Frankfurter in *Butler v. Michigan* in 1957 went a considerable distance toward satisfying this expectation.

# ☆ 19 ☆

# Previous Restraint

HISTORICALLY, censorship meant the official *licensing* of books, plays or news *before* publication, or their suppression *before* publication. The author or publisher was required to submit the manuscript to a censor—a licensing official—and his approval had to be procured or the publication would be a criminal offense.

### A. CENSORSHIP OF PUBLICATIONS

Soon after the introduction of printing in England in 1476, the government began to assert a power to suppress or censor publications that officials found offensive for one cause or another. In 1529 Henry VIII made up the first list of prohibited books, and in the following year he established the first licensing system under secular authority. This first licensing system, based on the royal prerogative, extended only to books "concerning holy scripture." Ecclesiastics were the licensers. Licensing as a way of controlling authors and publishers continued, in one way or another, to 1695, a period of 165 years.[1] It was against licensing as a form of previous restraint on publication that John Milton wrote his classic *Areopagitica*.[2]

In colonial America efforts were made to transplant the system of licensing. In 1662 the General Court of Massachusetts ordered that nothing shall be printed without the previous license of two named censors.[3] It was not until 1723 that licensing received a deathblow in Massachusetts,[4] a generation later than in the mother country. The situation in Virginia may be judged from the following statement of Governor William Berkeley: "I thank God we have no free schools nor printing; and I hope we shall not have these hundred years. . . . God keep us from both." [5]

Except for the "Minnesota gag law," which the Supreme Court invalidated in 1931,[6] there have been no attempted previous restraints on publishing since the end of the colonial period; however, there have been numerous, though largely unsuccessful, attempts to control, through licensing devices, the distribution or sale of publications.

In 1925 the Minnesota legislature adopted an act for the abatement, as a public nuisance, of any "malicious, scandalous and defamatory" newspaper or other periodical. Publishers of such a newspaper or periodical were to be enjoined in an action brought by the county attorney or the attorney general, or, upon their failure, by any citizen of the county. The court was empowered to issue a permanent injunction to abate the "nuisance." After the injunction was issued, publication in violation of its terms was to constitute contempt, and the disobedience was to be punished by fine or imprisonment. An anti-Semitic scandal sheet published articles charging the chief of police with gross neglect of duty, connivance with gangsters, and participation in graft. Some of the articles implicated the county attorney and other officials. The former proceeded under the statute against the publisher, and a permanent injunction was issued against him. The United States Supreme Court reversed the judgment.

Chief Justice Hughes in his opinion for the Court pointed out that the object of the statute was not punishment but suppression of the offending periodical; more than this, the statute put the publisher under an effective censorship, for once an injunction is issued, resumption of publication of what the court might consider scandalous or defamatory was punishable as a contempt. "This is of the essence of censorship." There may be *subsequent* punishment, by criminal or civil action, of one who commits a libel, but there may be no *previous* restraint upon publication, such as Minnesota attempted. The only exceptions to the prohibition upon previous restraint, said the Court, may be such as a war may make necessary—the government may prevent the publication, e.g., of the sailing dates of transports, or the number and location of troops; but the exceptions, said the Court, only serve to place in a strong light the general conception of freedom of the press, which means principally, though not exclusively, *immunity from previous restraints or censorship.*

It was insisted by the state that the statute was designed to prevent the circulation of scandal which tended to disturb the public peace, to provoke assaults and the commission of crime. Charges of reprehensible conduct unquestionably create a public scandal, said the Court, "but the theory of the constitutional guaranty is that even a more serious public evil would be caused by authority to prevent publication." The Court declared the act unconstitutional.

The case settled the proposition that if a publisher, before he may resume publication of his periodical, is required by law to satisfy a public official that in the future he will behave decently, he is subject to previous restraint or censorship, and the law that so restricts him is unconstitutional.

## B. CENSORSHIP OF DISTRIBUTION

About a century and a half passed from the founding of the Nation to the appearance of the first instance of an attempt at a previous restraint of *publication,* and this effort, as we have just seen, failed. But only seven years after the decision in *Near v. Minnesota* the Supreme Court was called upon to consider a series of cases in which attempts had been made by state or municipal governments to impose some form of previous restraint on the public *distribution or sale* of publications. The pattern for the Court's decisions had, however, been set by the opinion of Chief Justice Hughes in the "Minnesota gag law" case.

The first case to reach the Court was *Lovell v. Griffin,* in which it appeared that the city of Griffin, Georgia, had adopted an ordinance which prohibited the free distribution or sale of circulars or other literature without prior written permission from the city manager; distribution or sale without a permit was declared a "nuisance," which the police authorities were required to "abate." [7] Alma Lovell, regarding herself as sent "by Jehovah to do His work," set out to distribute tracts concerning the gospel of the "Kingdom of Jehovah" without having applied for a permit. The Supreme Court, again in an opinion by Chief Justice Hughes, unanimously held the ordinance unconstitutional. The Court pointed out that the "broad sweep" of the ordinance reached all types of publications; nor was there any limitation as to time or place, or as to "ways which might be regarded as inconsistent with the maintenance of public order, or as involving disorderly conduct, the molestation of the inhabitants, or the misuse or littering of the streets." The ordinance was declared "invalid on its face." Its character was such as to strike "at the very foundations of the freedom of the press by subjecting it to license and censorship." Freedom from previous restraint upon publication does not exhaust the guaranty of freedom of the press, said Chief Justice Hughes, but the prevention of such restraint was a leading purpose in the adoption of the First Amendment. "Legislation of the type of the ordinance in question would restore the system of license and censorship in its baldest form." Liberty of the press, said the Court, is not limited to newspapers and periodicals. It embraces pamphlets and leaflets, in fact "every sort of publication which affords a vehicle of information and opinion." It embraces distribution or circulation no less than publication.

This very significant decision and opinion by no means put an end to the attempts by municipalities to censor the distribution of literature on the streets. In 1939 the Court had to consider an ordinance of the town of Irvington, New Jersey, that prohibited distribution of circulars from house to house without first having received a license from the chief of police. The applicant had to furnish information about himself and the project for which he was canvassing, he had to be fingerprinted and photographed; and the license was to be refused if the officer was not satisfied that the applicant was of good character or that his project was not free from fraud.

The Supreme Court declared the ordinance unconstitutional, saying,

It bans unlicensed communication of any views or the advocacy of any cause from door to door, and permits canvassing only subject to the power of a police officer to determine, as a censor, what literature may be distributed from house to house and who may distribute it. . . . In the end, his liberty to communicate with the residents of the town at their homes depends upon the exercise of the officer's discretion. . . . To require a censorship through license which makes impossible the free and unhampered distribution of pamphlets strikes at the very heart of the constitutional guarantees.[8]

The law may not vest in any official the discretionary power to say that "some ideas may, while others may not, be carried to the homes of citizens; some persons may, while others may not, disseminate information from house to house." The law may punish frauds and trespasses after they are committed, but it may not seek to prevent them by a censorship or licensing requirement. So, too, the law may fix reasonable hours when canvassing may be done, and may otherwise regulate the use of streets and the conduct of persons using streets—e.g.,

a group of distributors could not insist upon a constitutional right to form a cordon across the street and to allow no pedestrian to pass who did not accept a tendered leaflet; nor does the guarantee of freedom of speech or of the press deprive a municipality of power to enact regulations against throwing literature broadcast in the streets;

but if the ordinance goes beyond reasonable regulation and becomes in fact a law subjecting distribution of pamphlets to license or censorship, then—whatever the motive of the authorities—it is an abridgment of freedom of the press and is unconstitutional.

### C. CENSORSHIP OF SPEECH

As we have seen, there may be no previous restraint or licensing or censorship of publications or of distribution of printed matter. Does the same constitutional prohibition apply to speech in public places? In recent years the Supreme Court has had to consider this question.

In 1951 the Court had before it the *Kunz* case, in which a Baptist minister had been convicted in New York City for holding a religious meeting at Columbus Circle without a permit, contrary to the provisions of an ordinance.[9] Carl Kunz in 1946 applied for and received a permit, which was good for only one year. Before the end of the year, however, his permit was revoked after a hearing by the police commissioner on evidence that he had denounced and ridiculed other religious beliefs. In 1947 and again in 1948 he applied for permits, but his applications were disapproved; then he spoke without a permit in September 1948, and was arrested and convicted. His conviction was reversed by the United States Supreme Court.

In his opinion for the Court, Chief Justice Vinson stated that while Kunz had been convicted for speaking without a permit in 1948, he had been denied a permit on the ground that in 1946 his permit had been revoked "for good reasons." But the ordinance was silent as to the reasons for which a permit may be denied. The interpretation of the ordinance in 1948 by the police commissioner allowed him, an administrative official, "to exercise discretion in denying subsequent permit applications on the basis of his interpretation, at that time, of what is deemed to be conduct condemned by the ordinance." Thus construed and administered, the ordinance gave the police commissioner "discretionary power to control in advance the right of citizens to speak on religious matters on the streets of New York." As such, the ordinance was held to be "clearly invalid as a prior restraint on the exercise of First Amendment rights." The public authorities may regulate streets and parks, said the Court, but they may not institute a licensing system which vests in an administrative official discretion to grant or withhold a permit "upon broad criteria unrelated to proper regulation of public places." In this case it was apparent that the police commissioner had denied the permit because he had focused his attention on the contents of the speeches or sermons that Kunz was likely to deliver, and not on police considerations relating to the prevention of "serious interference with normal usage of streets and parks." Prior restraints on the right of free speech in public parks or streets are unconstitutional. (The Court made it clear that it was concerned only with the question of *suppression* of speech; the propriety of punitive measures for a speech *after* it has been delivered was not before the Court.)

Justice Jackson alone dissented and wrote a strong opinion. He pointed out that New York City made no attempt to limit the freedom of Kunz to make speeches on private property; nor would Kunz have had any difficulty with the authorities with respect to sermons or speeches on public property had he confined himself to preaching his own religion or "making any temperate criticism or refutation of other religions." But Kunz did not do this. At his meetings he denounced the Pope as "the anti-Christ," and Jews as "Christ-killers." Kunz said that all the Jews should have been burned in incinerators as "garbage that didn't believe in Christ," and "It's a shame they all weren't." These and similar utterances "stirred strife and threatened violence." Language such as this in street meetings, said Justice Jackson, is not immune from *prior* municipal control.

There is "a world of difference," said Jackson, between Kunz saying these things in his own pulpit or hall and his saying them on the street, for, he said,

the street preacher takes advantage of people's presence on the streets to impose his message upon what, in a sense, is a captive audience. A meeting on private property is made up of an audience that has volunteered to listen. The question, therefore, is not whether New York could, if it tried, silence Kunz, but whether it must place its streets at his service to hurl insults at the passerby.

The city may, said Jackson, *prevent* or punish insulting or "fighting" words or utterances which "tend to incite an immediate breach of the peace." The words used by Kunz against Catholics and Jews "are always, and in every context, insults which do not spring from reason and can be answered by none. Their historical associations with violence are well understood, both by those who hurl and those who are struck by these missiles." To use such words on a New York street, said Jackson, was like shouting fire in a theatre and causing a panic.

At the hearing to revoke Kunz's permit, eighteen complainants appeared, and Kunz stated that he intended to go on saying what he always said and admitted that, unless a police officer was present at his meetings, he had trouble. The city has a right to prevent fighting or riots; it may, therefore, said Justice Jackson, *prevent* or punish speech which creates a clear and present danger of a fight or a riot. If, however, the speech is "temperate and reasoned," a hostile reception of it would not end the protection afforded to it by the Constitution; the constitutional protection could not be defeated, said Jackson, by persons who would break up meetings that they do not relish. But where the speech is temperate and reasoned, a crowd that should be tolerant might be prejudiced, angry, and malicious, and the situation may threaten to get out of hand. In such an emergency, said Jackson,

I think the police may require the speaker, even if within his rights, to yield his right temporarily to the greater interest of peace. Of course, the threat must be judged in good faith to be real, immediate and serious. But silencing a speaker by authorities as a measure of mob control, is like dynamiting a house to stop the spread of conflagration. It may be justified by the overwhelming community interest that flames not be fed as compared with the little interest to be served by continuing to feed them. . . . It is well to be vigilant to protect the right of Kunz to speak, but is he to be sole judge as to how far he will carry verbal attacks in the public streets? Is official action the only source of interference with religious freedom? Does the Jew, for example, have the benefit of these freedoms when, lawfully going about, he and his children are pointed out as "Christ-killers" to gatherings on public property by a religious sectarian sponsored by a police bodyguard? . . . Is the Court, when declaring Kunz has the *right* he asserts, serving the great end for which the First Amendment stands? . . . Of course, as to the press, there are the best of reasons against any licensing or prior restraint. Decisions . . . hold any licensing or prior restraint of the press unconstitutional, and I heartily agree. . . . Publishing . . . reaches only those who choose to read, and, in that way, is analogous

to a meeting held in a hall where those who come do so by choice.
Written words are less apt to incite or provoke to mass action than
spoken words, speech being the primitive and direct communication
with the emotions.

Justice Jackson, it seems, went in his criticism far beyond the
reach of the Court's decision. In the first place, the Court did
not hold that Kunz has the constitutional *right* to use fighting
words in a speech on a public street; it only held that the city
could not, by *prior restraint,* through the refusal to give him a
permit, *prevent* him from making his speech. This does not
mean that Kunz has the constitutional right to make a speech
which incites to disturbance or riot; for if he should make such
a speech, he might be punished for his act. Because an act may
not be prevented does not mean that it may not subsequently
be punished.

Because there is *more* reason for the constitutional ban on
prior restraints of publications than for the constitutional ban
on prior restraints of speech, it does not follow that there is *no*
reason for the latter. Justice Jackson conceded that there may
be no prior restraint on a speech to be delivered on private
property. The difference seems to be that the speaker on the
street or in the park has a captive audience—people cannot
help but hear the speaker's invective and insults. But this is
rarely the case; normally one does not hear what the soapbox
orator says unless one chooses to listen by joining his audience,
and then one is a voluntary rather than a captive auditor.
Furthermore, as we know from the *Terminiello* case,[10] speaking
in a private hall—when the speaker is a rabble-rouser, full of racial or religious prejudice and hatred—is no guaranty against a
public disturbance or a riot. Nor is it a relevant fact that
eighteen persons appeared as complainants at the hearing which
the police commissioner gave Kunz; one may be sure that in
the 1930's Mayor Frank Hague could have gotten out more than
eighteen complainants against Norman Thomas or C.I.O. or-
ganizers speaking in private halls, let alone on the public streets,
of Jersey City. The freedom to speak is not dependent on a
public opinion poll or on the outcome of a popularity contest.

If a speaker knowingly incites a riot, he may be *punished* for his act, whether his speech was delivered under the stars or in a rented auditorium. But if freedom of speech is constitutionally guarantied, it ought not to be in any way conditioned by the necessity to get a permit from public officials who may demand satisfactory proof that the speaker will not offend, insult, arouse, disgust, or shock anyone.

The purpose of the constitutional guaranty is, said Justice Jackson, "to foster peaceful interchange of all manner of thoughts, information and ideas. Its policy is rooted in faith in the force of reason." But the "force of reason" has many ways in which to express itself. One could hardly say that Martin Luther always spoke in the soft tones and mild language of Jeremy Taylor or Richard Hooker. Were the speeches of Amos or Jeremiah, of Jesus or Paul, always free of epithets or personal abuse? One might suppose that the priests, publicans and tax-gatherers would have been happier if the prophets had not been free to speak or preach without a permit from city hall. "We should weigh the value of insulting speech," said Jackson, "against its potentiality for harm." The potentiality for harm in the use of *this* rule or doctrine is immeasurable; there is in it no less danger than there is in a licensing law.

The outdoor meeting, it has been noted, is especially well adapted to the promotion of unpopular causes by persons who lack the financial resources to rent a hall or buy time on the radio.[11] In this connection it may be argued that it is clearly in the public interest that unpopular causes be kept above ground by affording them freedom of speech and outdoor assembly without prior restraint; any other rule is likely to drive them underground, beyond public knowledge and criticism. It should also be noted that in recent years the outdoor meeting has gained respectability by the institution of the "whistle-stop" technique in national political campaigns, first by President Truman, and later by Adlai Stevenson and President Eisenhower. A permit system today that would go beyond the barest necessities of traffic regulation of the streets and parks would be likely to conflict with powerful as well as with weak causes.

At the same time that the Supreme Court decided the *Kunz*

case, it also decided the *Niemotko* case.[12] At the invitation of the Jehovah's Witnesses of Havre de Grace, Maryland, two persons undertook to deliver Bible talks in the city's public park. There was no city ordinance requiring a permit, but it had become the custom to obtain a permit from the park commissioner for meetings or celebrations in the park. Jehovah's Witnesses applied for a permit to use the park on certain consecutive Sundays; the park commissioner denied the application. In compliance with custom, an appeal was taken to the mayor and city council; after a hearing, the application was again denied. Niemotko then proceeded to hold a meeting in the park without a permit. As soon as the meeting opened, he was arrested. On the next Sunday the other speaker was arrested in the park before he began his lecture. They were tried for disorderly conduct under a state statute and convicted. The Supreme Court unanimously reversed the convictions.

In his opinion for the Court, Chief Justice Vinson pointed out that there was no evidence of disorder, or threats of violence or riot; there was no breach of the public peace. There was no licensing requirement in accordance with an ordinance or statute that provides "narrowly drawn, reasonable and definite standards" that officials must follow in passing on an application for a permit. All that appeared here was a custom or practice, with the public officials enjoying a limitless discretion. There was here no evidence that could serve as a valid basis for the refusal of a permit, in view of the fact that the city allowed other religious groups to use the park. The conclusion is "inescapable," said the Court, "that the use of the park was denied because of the City Council's dislike for or disagreement with the Witnesses or their views." Such treatment of Jehovah's Witnesses, the Court held, was a denial of equal protection of the laws in the exercise of freedom of speech and religion protected by the First and Fourteenth Amendments.

In 1953, the Supreme Court decided another case that involved similar discrimination against Jehovah's Witnesses by the public officials of Pawtucket, Rhode Island.[13] Jehovah's Witnesses conducted a religious meeting in a city park. Of the four hundred persons who attended, one hundred and fifty were members of the sect. The meeting was addressed by Fowler, a visiting member of the sect, over two loud speakers. It was a quiet, orderly meeting. Fowler spoke for only a few minutes when he was arrested and charged with violating an ordinance which provided that no person shall address any political or religious meeting in any public park. He was convicted. The Supreme Court unanimously reversed the conviction.

In his opinion for the Court, Justice Douglas pointed out that the ordinance had been construed by the city officials as not prohibiting church services in the park; and church services normally. include prayer, singing, and preaching. Public officials may not classify the speaking by the minister of one denomination as "preaching" or a "sermon" and that of a minister of another denomination as an "address," and to regulate the latter while allowing the former. To permit such discrimination would be to prefer one religion over another. Sermons are as much a part of religious services as are prayers, and no public authority may undertake to "approve, disapprove, classify, regulate, or in any manner control sermons delivered at religious meetings."

These cases settle the proposition that no licensing ordinance or law may, under guise of regulating public places in the interests of public welfare and order, vest discretion in any official to permit or to prohibit a public lecture, sermon, or speech. There may be no previous restraint on speech.

## D. CENSORSHIP OF MOTION PICTURES

Edison in 1889 invented the kinetoscope, which led to the modern motion picture. By 1913 the motion picture screen had won popularity, and in the next five years the foundations of the motion picture industry were established. At the end of World War I, when the movies began to exploit the new post-war morals and manners, and some pictures dared to defy the old-fashioned canons of decency and morality, a demand for restrictive legislation got underway.

The evils of the movies were compared with the evils of the saloon, and the opposition to deviant moral behavior was organized and eager for another victory [upon the heels of their success in putting the prohibition amendment into the Constitution]. Religious, civic, and women's groups swelled the wave of protest, and the demand for the reform of the movies became a national movement. . . . Religious leaders of all denominations raised their voices against the evils of the contemporary movie. . . . The movies were under fire from all sides.[14]

As today, movie advertising often was more sensational than were the movies themselves, and scandals involving Hollywood stars aggravated the situation. The result was "wholesale condemnation of Hollywood and the motion picture industry by all kinds of public bodies." [15] The industry successfully fought against federal legislation, but on the state and municipal level the reform pressures succeeded. Chicago in 1907 was the first city, and Pennsylvania in 1911 was the first state, to adopt restrictive legislation. The Pennsylvania act, which became the pattern for other states, created a state board of censors, composed of two men and one woman, appointed by the governor; no film could be exhibited in the state unless it had been first submitted to and approved by the censors; and all advertising matter was subject to the same requirements of submission and approval. Ohio and Kansas adopted similar laws in 1913.

The constitutionality of these censorship laws was challenged in a case that came before the Supreme Court in 1915.[16] The Court upheld these laws and said that the exhibition of moving pictures was "a business pure and simple, originated and conducted for profit," and that movies were not to be regarded as part of the press of the country or as organs of public opinion.

The decision of the Court was not universally approved. The movie industry sponsored an amendment to the Constitution providing for freedom of the screen, but this undertaking made no progress.[17] Professor Chafee attacked the decision of the Court, saying: "All the objections to a press censorship apply as well to film censorship, especially in an age when more persons probably go to the movies than read books. Are not grown men and women to be trusted to tell bad from good when it is in plain sight?" [18] Chafee pointed out that although movie censorship existed in only six states,[19] the action of censors in any one of them could affect the exhibition of the film in all other states; and that censorship by local policemen was even worse, because they were much more susceptible to local pressures. He referred to censors as "big and little despots," and said that the wonder was "that we get some of the magnificent films we do." [20] He pointed out that in two states prolabor newsreels were banned; that in one state a senator's speech opposing enlargement of the Supreme Court had been cut from the *March of Time* until popular outcry had forced a reversal; that one state objected to showing girls smoking, that another state would not approve a kiss beyond a fixed duration ("no kiss over five feet long"); that one state permitted a scene showing a woman killing a man, but would not allow a scene showing a man killing a woman. The time had come, said Chafee, for the Court to recognize the fact that motion pictures are important to the thought of the nation. Freedom of speech, he said,

covers much more than political ideas. It embraces all discussion which enriches human life and helps it to be more wisely led. . . . Motion pictures have already taken their place beside the novel and the stage drama as one of the great arts. . . . Therefore, if we are to have unhampered criticism of life from motion pictures, the state censorship should be completely abolished.[21]

In 1952 the Supreme Court responded to these and similar criticisms and decided that it would no longer adhere to its 1915 decision. In the *Miracle* case the Court held that the basic constitutional principles of freedom of speech and the press applied to motion pictures.[22]

*The Miracle* had been banned by the New York state censors on the ground that it was "sacrilegious." The statute under which the censors acted provided that they shall not approve a film that is "obscene, indecent, immoral, inhuman, sacrilegious, or is of such a character that its exhibition would tend to corrupt morals or incite to crime." The Supreme Court held that the banning of a film on the basis of a censor's conclusion that it is "sacrilegious" is a violation of the First and Fourteenth Amendments. The term "sacrilegious" was not defined by the statute, nor was it limited narrowly by the New York courts; thus, the censor was "set adrift," said the Supreme Court, "upon a boundless sea amid a myriad of conflicting currents of religious views, with no charts but those provided by the most vocal and powerful orthodoxies."

Justice Clark's opinion for the Court, however, left the door open for a testing of the constitutionality of movie censorship on grounds other than those involved in the *Miracle* case. Opportunities for such tests came soon. The Ohio censors prohibited showing of a picture entitled *M* "on account of being harmful," and New York refused to license *La Ronde* on the ground that it was "immoral" and that it "would tend to corrupt morals." In a per curiam opinion, and in reliance on its decision in the *Miracle* case, the Supreme Court in 1954 set aside the bans on these films.[23] And in 1955, again without an opinion, the Supreme Court set aside the ban on *The Moon Is Blue*, that had been imposed by the Kansas censors on the grounds that the film was "obscene, indecent, and immoral and such as to tend to debase or corrupt public morals." [24]

In none of these cases did the Court hold, in broad terms, that movie censorship is as unconstitutional as is press censorship. The Court has held in these cases that censorship or previous restraint of a movie on the ground that it is "sacrilegious," or "harmful," or "immoral," or "obscene," when these terms are not carefully defined by statute or narrowly limited by state court interpertation, is unconstitutional. Yet it can hardly be doubted that the constitutional base of movie censorship has been badly shaken, if not removed altogether. The basic principles of freedom of speech and the press now protect movies, and freedom of expression through this medium and the absence of previous restraint must be the rule, and for a state or a municipality to justify making an exception to the rule is now extremely difficult. Movies are, of course, and ought to be, subject to the ordinary processes of the criminal law after they have been exhibited, just as books and newspapers are after publication, and our previous discussion of obscenity laws is relevant at this point.

### E. CENSORSHIP OF NEWS—PREVIOUS RESTRAINT ON SOURCES OF INFORMATION

As we have seen, in *Near v. Minnesota* Chief Justice Hughes, in holding the "Minnesota gag law" unconstitutional as a previous restraint on newspapers, said that such restraint may be justified under exceptional circumstances; and as an instance of such circumstances he cited prohibition of the publication of the sailing dates of transports, or the number and location of troops.[25] Unfortunately, government censorship extends far beyond the obvious instances cited by Chief Justice Hughes; such terms as "top secret," "secret," "confidential," and "restricted" have become familiar to the public, and it is common knowledge that these terms are not limited to security data but take in many nonmilitary subjects which government officials wish to keep from public knowledge. No reasonable person can question the need of laws against espionage,[26] or of other carefully considered wartime and security measures.[27] But, as an authoritative study points out, "wartime repressive measures are like dead hands that do not relax their grasp upon the republic after the occasion which has created them has passed"; for wartime repressive measures have been carried over into peacetime (or the twilight zone of cold war) "for the sake of stifling political, economic, and social reform." [28] It is no longer shocking to learn that there is source censorship which keeps information not only from the public, but which keeps information from other government officials or from another branch of the government —thus, Executive departments may keep information from Congress or its committees, the Department of Justice may keep information from the federal courts, and a government agency may keep information from its employees even when it acts to dismiss them on the basis of the information in its files.

Some of these matters will be gone into later, and the entire subject of "the people's right to know" is much too complex to be considered fully here; but we shall attempt a brief statement of the problem.[29]

That suppression of news at the source has become a grave problem can scarcely be doubted. Congressman John E. Moss, chairman of a House subcommittee investigating Government information practices, asserted at the end of 1955 that there was "a clear need" for legislation to break down official barriers on news. The free flow of information to the people and to Congress is, he said, a matter of "the utmost significance under our form of government," yet much information is being withheld by many barriers to "the free circulation of facts, opinions and ideas." [30] Testifying before this committee, James S. Pope, executive editor of the *Louisville Courier-Journal,* said that the public's right to freedom of information had been "invaded and flouted" by Government agencies. "There is," he said, "a state of mind of arrogance and contempt for the public on the part of some officials of the Government. The fact that we have to fight for freedom of information is a disgrace." James Reston, Washington correspondent of the *New York Times,* spoke of the Government's "growing tendency to manage the news." He condemned efforts of the Bureau of the Budget to conceal facts concerning purely domestic matters.[31]

In connection with observance of National Newspapers Week in October 1955, a significant statement was made by J. R. Wiggins, executive editor of the *Washington Post and Times Herald,* and chairman of the freedom of information committee of the American Society of Newspaper Editors.[32] In this statement Mr. Wiggins emphasized the intimate relation that exists between the right of citizens to know and their right to govern themselves, for political acts are the result of information; therefore,

the acts and judgments of those who are fully informed are their own acts. The acts and judgments of those who are only partly informed are, in reality, the acts and judgments of those who partly inform them. . . . People who have the power to make decisions [the electorate and Congress] must be given information that will enable them to make the right political decisions. This information must be in the hands of the whole people; not just available to a select few or to a privileged elite whose word must be blindly accepted.

As instances of "how fear of external danger is expanding the area of secrecy," Mr. Wiggins cited, among other events, the following:

1. In June 1955 Defense Department officials said that newspaper editors on their own should withhold publication of information that is not secret at all but which, in their judg-

ment, might prove helpful to an enemy. "If editors took this request seriously," commented Mr. Wiggins,

their readers would be deprived of a great deal of routine information which citizens need to have to conduct their business, pursue their normal lives, and discharge their public duties. All information about the life of a country is of some possible use to an enemy; it is of overwhelming use to the citizens themselves and the minor risk of informing an enemy must be taken, if life is to go on in a reasonably normal way.

2. In September 1955 the Government recommended rules to be observed by private firms having defense contracts. These firms (like the newspaper editors) were urged to withhold many unclassified facts, so that "publication of that segment of information of possible value to a potential enemy can be prevented."

3. The Commerce Department set up an Office of Strategic Information, which has made an effort to keep publishers from disclosing technical information which might be useful to an enemy even though not secret enough to be classified.

4. In June 1955 General Matthew B. Ridgway wrote a letter to the Secretary of Defense in which he expressed grave doubts concerning our national military policy. The Defense Department classified the document "confidential," and the contents became public when the document was published in violation of the restriction. The letter, said Mr. Wiggins, was "indispensable to Americans really trying to understand current military issues."

These and other events illustrate, said Mr. Wiggins, "the development of a climate of secrecy." They followed from the fears of conscientious and responsible public officials; however, "one man's fears are not the proper measure of another man's rights."

In November 1955 the American Civil Liberties Union made public a report by Allen Raymond on secrecy in government.[33] Mr. Raymond pointed out that since 1949 newspaper editors have been actively promoting "freedom of information"; but "the tide still runs against the editors. Censorship increases."

Three inquiries by committees of Congress have failed to produce notable improvements; on the contrary, the situation has
become aggravated. The examples cited by Mr. Raymond were
not confined

to areas of secrecy in which the military security of the nation as
against some foreign foe would be a consideration in the formulation of Executive policy. They extend through regions of silence
in which the security of the citizen as against official corruption,
or against danger to life, liberty and property in communities and
homes through[out] the United States is an issue at stake. It is in
these domestic regions as well as in foreign affairs that the Federal
government's secrecy is seen by the newsmen as a menace to everyone.

As an instance of information withheld from the public, well
outside the kind of circumstances that Chief Justice Hughes had
in mind when he spoke of the Government keeping secret the
sailing dates of transports or the number and location of troops,
Mr. Raymond cited the following incident. In 1951 reporters
discovered that investigators for the Bureau of Internal Revenue
had found that liquor was being adulterated in 368 saloons in
the Albany, New York, area, and that the Bureau had levied
fines totalling $37,465.33 upon the offending saloon keepers,
without bringing them into court, by a process known as "confidential compromise." The editor of an Albany newspaper tried
to learn from the Federal Government the names of the guilty
saloon keepers and the details of the fines, but he had no success. Then James S. Pope, in his capacity as chairman of the
freedom of information committee of the American Society of
Newspaper Editors, attempted to get information from the
Government, but without success. Mr. Raymond, commenting
on this incident, asked:

In such an atmosphere of secrecy do all the so-called settlements
find their way into the U.S. Treasury? Or are agents of the Alcohol
Tax Unit of the Internal Revenue Bureau periodically shaking
down saloon keepers all over the United States . . . and permitting
these tavern keepers to go on robbing the public as long as they
settle for a few dollars occasionally [in the Albany incident the

settlement came to an average of $100 per saloon keeper, hardly more than a token penalty for adulterating liquor, which means cheating customers and defrauding the Government of taxes] after some star chamber trial from which the public is barred? As long as trials are in secret, is there any guarantee that revenue agent and saloon keeper are not whacking up the small sum of shakedowns, as petty graft to protect illicit enterprise?

Summarizing the facts as he found them, Mr. Raymond in part said:

It is a fair consensus among Washington correspondents that abuses of the power in Federal agencies to suppress information of value and interest to the nation were never so rampant as now; . . . [that] this widespread abuse of Executive power is exercised in the great majority of instances by many agencies on matters having nothing whatever to do with national security; . . . that these abuses have already curtailed the power of the press and of Congress itself to be of service to the people by finding out what goes on in government; that they have been accompanied by an arrogation of powers within the Executive of doubtful constitutionality, so far inadequately challenged; that they have advanced to the point where the civil liberties of the people themselves are threatened; and that some prudent remedial action by Congress is necessary.

The press in the United States is unlicensed. To this extent it is free from previous restraint and conforms to the ideal projected by John Milton in his *Areopagitica*. But, as we have seen, other forms of previous restraint have been devised to keep secret facts which ought to be publicly known. The efforts of the American Society of Newspaper Editors, the American Newspaper Publishers' Association, and the American Civil Liberties Union to establish firmly, in law and in public devotion, the people's right to know, or freedom of information, will eventually bear fruit.

In his study of the legal aspects of this subject, prepared for the American Society of Newspaper Editors, Harold L. Cross rightly states that the language of the First Amendment is broad enough to embrace the right of access to information of government action, "without which the freedom to print could be fettered into futility." The First Amendment provides for freedom to acquire the news as well as to publish and to distribute the news. "The public business," says Mr. Cross,

is the public's business. The people have the right to know. Freedom of information about public records and proceedings is their just heritage. Citizens must have the legal right to investigate and examine the conduct of their affairs. They must have a simple, speedy means of enforcement. These rights must be raised to the highest sanction. The time is ripe. The First Amendment points the way. The function of the press is to carry the torch.[34]

And the function of the people, one might well add, is to support the press in its claims of freedom of information, for in this matter the press can act only on behalf of its constituents —the citizens, numbering more than 54,000,000, who buy a newspaper every day.[35] For James Madison was largely right when he argued that freedom of access to information, and its publication, "is the only effectual guardian of every other right."[36]

# Picketing in Labor Disputes

IN THE opening address at the celebration of the two-hundredth anniversary of the birth of Chief Justice Marshall, Justice Frankfurter remarked that in a study of the "evolution of social policy by way of judicial application of Delphic provisions of the Constitution, recession of judicial doctrine is as pertinent as its expansion." As an illustration of a movement of recession of judicial doctrine, Justice Frankfurter called attention to the fact that while in 1940 the Supreme Court looked upon picketing as an aspect of the constitutionally protected freedom of discussion, in 1949 the Court "retreated from this position and recognized that picketing, as the weapon of strikes, is not merely a means of communication." [1] The story of this recession of judicial doctrine with respect to picketing can be told briefly.

For our purposes we might well begin our discussion with Justice Brandeis' opinion in *Senn v. Tile Layers Protective Union*, decided in 1937.[2] Senn conducted, from his home, a small tile laying business. He employed one or two tile layers and one or two helpers, and he himself often worked as a tile layer or helper. Neither Senn nor any of his employees belonged to the union. He competed for contracts with unionized contractors, who paid higher wages than Senn. Because the industry consisted of employers with small numbers of employees, the union agreement provided that the employer will not himself work as a tile layer or as a helper. The union tried to induce Senn to become a union contractor. He indicated a willingness provided there would be no prohibition upon himself as a worker; but the union said that this was impossible, since all other employers had accepted the restriction. The union then picketed his shop, declaring on the placards that Senn was "unfair" to the union and appealing to the public to "let the Union tiler layer install your tile work." Senn sought an injunction against the picketing, but the Wisconsin state courts denied him this relief on the ground that the state statue prohibited issuance of an injunction against peaceful picketing.

Senn appealed to the Supreme Court, contending that the Fourteenth Amendment guaranteed him a right to work with his own hands; that the union sought to destroy this right; that the state could not allow picketing which sought to coerce him to refrain from exercising his constitutional right. The union's defense was that since Senn's exercise of the right to work was harmful to the interests of union members, the union had the right to seek to induce him, by legal means, to unionize his shop and to agree not to exercise the right to work with his own hands.

The state court had found that the end sought by the union was legal and that the means used to achieve this end were also legal. The Supreme Court agreed.

The end sought by the union, said Justice Brandeis, is not forbidden by the Constitution; for there was no evidence that the prohibition upon self-employment was arbitrary or capricious, or malicious, or that the union sought to impose it out of a desire to injure Senn. The end sought was not illegal: "There was no effort to induce Senn to do an unlawful thing." The means used also were lawful: "There was no violence, no force was applied, no molestation or interference, no coercion. There was only the persuasion incident to publicity."

As to the end sought by the union, said Justice Brandeis, the laws of the state permit unions to seek to induce employers to give up their right to self-employment. "Whether it was wise for the State to permit the unions to do so is a question of its public policy—not our concern. The Fourteenth Amendment does not prohibit it." As to the means used, Justice Brandeis said: "Exercising its police power, Wisconsin has declared that in a labor dispute peaceful picketing and truthful publicity are means legal for unions." The use of these means may have annoyed, or even injured, Senn; but such annoyance or hurt is not an invasion of a constitutional right.

Now, thus far the reasoning of Justice Brandeis has made the following contributions, which, as we shall see, appear to be of permanent relevance for the legal analysis of picketing cases: (1) The Court analyzed the facts and issues from the standpoint of means and ends. The end sought to be achieved by the picketing was legal under the laws of Wisconsin. The picketing (the means used) was conducted in a lawful manner, without force or violence.[3] (2) It was up to the state, through its legislature or courts, to declare whether or not the end sought by the union was to be considered lawful or unlawful. This was a question of wisdom or policy, a question for the state and not for the Supreme Court as long as the Fourteenth Amendment "does not prohibit it."

What of the free speech aspect of picketing? There is nothing in the Constitution, said Brandeis, "which forbids unions from competing with nonunion concerns for customers by means of picketing." Wisconsin, he pointed out, "has declared that in a labor dispute peaceful picketing and truthful publicity are means legal for unions." These statements mean that since the Constitution *does not prohibit* a union from seeking the end sought by the tile layers union, Wisconsin did not violate the Constitution when it declared that a union may use peaceful (and truthful) picketing to achieve this end. But does the Constitution *guaranty* picketing by a labor union as an exercise of free speech? Suppose the Wisconsin legislature or courts had said that, although the end sought by the tile layers union was not unlawful, the union could not engage in peaceful and truthful picketing to achieve this end, though it could employ other means of publicity (such as handbills, newspaper advertising, appeals on the radio)? Would Justice Brandeis have held that *prohibition* of picketing under those circumstances would have been a denial of a constitutional liberty? "Members of a union

might," said Justice Brandeis, "without special authorization by
a State, make known the facts of a labor dispute, for freedom
of speech is guaranteed by the Federal Constitution." This proposition does not *necessarily* imply a constitutional status for
picketing, for the facts of a labor dispute may be made known
in other ways.

Three years later, in *Thornhill v. Alabama,* the Supreme
Court explored this question and placed picketing under the
protection of the Constitution.[4] Together with the *Senn* case,
*Thornhill* is basic to an understanding of the problem of picketing.

An Alabama statute had the significant title: "Loitering or
picketing forbidden." The words of the statute as interpreted
by the courts of Alabama gave literal meaning to the title—
picketing in any form and under all circumstances was prohibited. Even if a single individual had walked slowly and peace-
fully on the sidewalk in front of the employer's place of
business, carrying a sign which truthfully stated the fact that
the employer did not engage union men affiliated with the
American Federation of Labor, he would have violated the law
and have been guilty of a misdemeanor. This sweeping, comprehensive prohibition upon picketing, said Justice Murphy for the
Supreme Court, violated the constitutional guaranty of freedom
of speech and the press. Workers, he said, have the right "effectively to inform the public of the facts of a labor dispute." A
state may not impair "the effective exercise of the right to discuss freely industrial relations which are matters of public concern." "In the circumstances of our times," said Justice Murphy,
"the dissemination of information concerning the facts of a labor
dispute must be regarded as within that area of free discussion
that is guaranteed by the Constitution." The opinion, however,
left the door open for a statute narrowly drawn to prohibit or
punish picketing that is a breach of the peace, or a "serious invasion of rights of property or privacy at the scene of a labor
dispute."

As Justice Frankfurter has said, the opinion in the *Thornhill*
case assimilated picketing to speech that is constitutionally protected. But it was not long before the Court departed from this

position and went back to the Brandeis means-ends approach.

In *Ritter's Cafe* case it appeared that the owner of the cafe, in Houston, Texas, had made an agreement with a building contractor under which the latter was to construct a building for Ritter a mile and a half away from the cafe.[5] The new building, as far as the record showed, was wholly unconnected with the cafe business. The building contractor was free to make his own arrangements regarding the employment of labor in the construction of the building. He employed nonunion carpenters and painters. All of Ritter's employees in the cafe belonged to the union of hotel and restaurant workers. Members of the carpenters' and painters' unions picketed—not the construction site—but the cafe; one picket from each union walked back and forth carrying placards which read, "The Owner of This Cafe Has Awarded a Contract to Erect a Building to W. A. Plaster Who Is Unfair to the Carpenters Union 213 and Painters Union 130, Affiliated with the American Federation of Labor" (the picketing was peaceful and truthful). On the day picketing began the cafe workers quit, and union drivers refused to deliver supplies, and the cafe business slumped 60 per cent. The Texas court issued an injunction prohibiting the picketing as a restriction on "the free pursuit" of business contrary to the state antitrust laws. The injunction did not forbid picketing the construction site but only the cafe.

The Supreme Court upheld the injunction. In his opinion for the Court, Justice Frankfurter rejected the claim that there is "a constitutional command that peaceful picketing must be wholly immune from regulation" by the state and that the state is powerless "to confine the use of this industrial weapon within reasonable bounds." Texas had the right to draw a line to confine the area of industrial warfare; it had the right "to localize" the conflict by prohibiting picketing of the cafe business, which was "wholly outside the economic context of the real dispute." The "real adversary" of the picketing unions was the building contractor; Texas could reasonably "insulate" from the dispute the cafe which had "no connection with the dispute." In brief, a state may confine picketing to "the sphere . . . directly related to the dispute." A state is not compelled by the Constitution to allow a union "to conscript neutrals having no relation to either the dispute or the industry in which it arose. . . . To hold otherwise would be to transmute vital constitutional liberties into doctrinaire dogma." In other words, the end sought to be achieved by the picketing was the "conscription" of Ritter, who was a "neutral" in the dispute between the building contractor and the picketing unions, and picketing for this end could be declared by a state to be illegal without violating any constitutional guaranty.

In another case that was decided on the same day, Justice Douglas, in a concurring opinion, while arguing strongly for the *Thornhill* doctrine, formulated briefly a position which has in fact guided the Court in picketing cases since 1942.[6] Picketing by a union, said Justice Douglas,

is more than free speech, since it involves patrol of a particular locality and since the very presence of a picket line may induce action of one kind or another, quite irrespective of the nature of the ideas which are being disseminated. Hence those aspects of picketing make it the subject of restrictive regulation.

Thus, picketing, in the words of Justice Frankfurter, "is not merely a means of communication";[7] and insofar as it is something else, it is not protected by the First Amendment. The Brandeis approach in the *Senn* case has displaced the Murphy approach in the *Thornhill* case: picketing the end of which is to compel violation of a state's antitrust act may be enjoined;[8] picketing the end of which is to frustrate a state's policy to help self-employer businessmen remain in business may be enjoined;[9] picketing the end of which is to compel an employer to coerce his employees to join a union contrary to their wishes may be enjoined;[10] picketing the end of which is to compel an employer to violate a state statute which outlaws the union shop may be enjoined;[11] picketing the end of which is to compel an employer to hire Negro clerks in proportion to the number of his Negro customers, contrary to a state's public policy, may be enjoined.[12]

The proposition formulated by Justice Douglas and the methodological contribution made by Justice Brandeis have both been clearly adopted and expressed by Justice Frankfurter for the Court in *Hughes v. Superior Court:* [13]

But while picketing is a mode of communication[,] it is inseparably something more and different. . . . It has been amply recognized that picketing, not being the equivalent of speech as a matter of fact, is not its inevitable legal equivalent. Picketing is not beyond the control of a State if the manner in which picketing is conducted or the purpose which it seeks to effectuate gives ground for its disallowance.

Why is picketing different from other media of communication? Justice Frankfurter has supplied the answer:

Publication in a newspaper, or by distribution of circulars, may convey the same information or make the same charge as do those patrolling a picket line. But the very purpose of a picket line is to exert influences, and it produces consequences, different from other modes of communication. The loyalties and responses evoked and enacted by picket lines are unlike those flowing from appeals by printed word.[14]

It follows from this view of the nature and effects of picketing that states have considerable discretion to limit picketing, even when it is peaceful and truthful, to the achievement of purposes which the state considers lawful.

Yet the *Thornhill* doctrine remains: a state may not ban picketing altogether; "because of its element of communication," picketing under some circumstances will find sanction in the Constitution.[15] The specific situation will control the decision. The constitutional boundary line between picketing as "communication" and picketing as "something more and different" cannot be established by general phrases.[16] But the opinions of the Court make it clear that while a state may prohibit picketing when its end is the achievement of an unlawful purpose, other means of communication must remain open to the labor organization to make known its side of the dispute—other means of communication from which are absent "the compulsive features inherent in picketing." [17]

At one time it was possible for a federal court to say: "There is and can be no such thing as peaceful picketing, any more than there can be chaste vulgarity, or peaceful mobbing, or lawful lynching." [18] The courts then saw only "the compulsive features inherent in picketing." Then for some years it looked as if peaceful picketing not only was possible but was constitutionally protected as "the working man's means of communication." Now peaceful picketing is in a twilight zone: there is and there is not such a thing as peaceful picketing; it is and it is not a means of communication; it is and it is not constitutionally protected. It is likely to remain in this situation of constitutional uncertainty for a long time.

# Taxes on Knowledge

IN 1955 the British press observed the centenary of the disappearance from the statute books of the British stamp tax on publications—a "tax on knowledge" which was imposed from 1712 to 1855. Its end marked a milestone in the history of freedom of the press.

Following the end of previous restraints on publication, with the expiration of the Regulation of Printing Act in 1694,[1] new methods of controlling publications were sought. A special effort was made to reduce the circulation of newspapers by forcing them to increase the sales price. The press was accused by Queen Anne and her ministers of being "licentious, schismatical, and scandalous." In 1712 Parliament enacted the first in a series of notorious stamp acts. "It is obvious that the bill was designed to check the publication of those newspapers and pamphlets which depended for their sale on their cheapness and sensationalism."[2] The act imposed a tax on newspapers and pamphlets, on advertisements, and on paper. In the first year after its enactment, approximately half of the newspapers were forced out of existence.[3] Loopholes were, however, soon discovered in the act, with the result that the tax fell more heavily on printers who supported the government and felt themselves compelled not to evade payment of the tax. A census of the political affiliations of London newspapers conducted for the government in 1723 disclosed that 34 were favorable to King George and 34 were opposed to the existing administration. Walpole felt that the situation was intolerable, and so in 1724 another stamp act was passed. While the first act was aimed primarily at pamphlets and secondarily at newspapers, the second act reversed the emphasis. Again there were evasions and stampless publications appeared. In 1757 another stamp act was passed with increased taxes on newspapers and advertisements. In 1765 Parliament established a stamp tax on American newspapers and pamphlets; but the violent opposition by the American colonists forced a repeal of the American stamp tax in 1766.[4] Parliament kept on enacting a whole procession of stamp acts,[5] until it abolished the tax on advertisements in 1853 and the tax on newspapers in 1855.[6]

These taxes, it has been said, operated as an effective control over the periodical press. "By making it difficult to operate newspapers at a profit, the government forced the publishers to accept subsidies and political bribes." [7] The exorbitant prices led to the practice of renting out newspapers to readers for a limited period of time. A single copy would be hired out to twenty or thirty readers in London, and would then be sent into the country at a reduced price—a practice which the stamp act of 1789 attempted to stop.[8] The stamp tax prohibited the existence of the cheap newspaper and prevented the general spread of knowledge.[9] When one considers the fact that these taxes were in existence for nearly one hundred and fifty years it becomes apparent that it would be impossible to measure the detrimental effect that they had on the political, social, intellectual, and spiritual development of the English people.[10]

Before the adoption of the Constitution, Massachusetts in 1785 and 1786 ventured to impose taxes on newspapers, magazines, and advertisements; but the opposition was so violent that the tax on newspapers and magazines had to be repealed in 1786 and on advertisements two years later.[11]

Nothing more was heard of these odious taxes on knowledge until Louisiana, under the control of Huey Long, enacted a law which imposed a tax of 2 per cent on the gross receipts derived from advertisements in Louisiana newspapers having a circulation of over 20,000 copies per week. This figure had been chosen to hit the newspapers opposed to Long and exempt the small papers, which supported him.[12] The thirteen newspapers that were affected by the law sought an injunction to restrain its enforcement. The Supreme Court unanimously sustained a permanent injunction.[13]

The Court held that the Louisiana tax was an abridgment of freedom of the press. Significantly, the Court spoke of "the natural right of the members of an organized society, united for their common good, to impart and acquire information about their common interests." The tax law operated, the Court said, as a double restraint: (1) it curtailed the amount of income realized from advertising, and (2) it restricted circulation. In his opinion for the Court, Justice Sutherland reviewed the English experience with taxes on knowledge and said that it was the intention of the First Amendment to outlaw such taxes as well as previous censorship; for "the restricted rules of the English law in respect of freedom of the press in force [in England] when the Constitution was adopted were never accepted by the American colonists."

Owners of newspapers are not immune from the ordinary forms of taxation, but the tax here involved was bad not because it took money from the publishers' pockets, but because it was "a deliberate and calculated device in the guise of a tax to limit the circulation of information to which the public is entitled in virtue of the constitutional guaranties." To allow the press to become fettered "is to fetter ourselves."

A few years later the Court was called upon to apply these principles to ordinances which imposed taxes on the right of Jehovah's Witnesses to sell their pamphlets and books. The city of Opelika, Alabama, required book agents or peddlers to procure a license for an annual fee of $10, and the fee for transient book peddlers was $5; the license fee in Casa Grande, Arizona, was $25 per quarter; that in Fort Smith, Arkansas, ranged from $2.50 per day to $25 per month. In each of these cities Jehovah's Witnesses were arrested and convicted for selling pamphlets or books without a license. The Supreme Court in 1942 sustained the convictions,[14] with Chief Justice Stone and Justices Black, Douglas, and Murphy dissenting.

In the majority opinion, written by Justice Reed, the position was taken that what was involved here was "a suitably calculated occupational license" or the payment of "reasonable fees for the privilege of canvassing." The Constitution interdicts "prohibition and unjustifiable abridgement [of religion, speech, or press], not taxation." Perhaps municipalities should permit "the poor and weak to draw support from the petty sales of religious books without contributing anything for the privilege of using the streets," but this was a question of wisdom and not of constitutional law.

Chief Justice Stone, dissenting, contended that Jehovah's Witnesses spread their religious doctrines in conformity to the teachings of St. Matthew by going from town to town, from house to house, to proclaim them. Funds collected were used for the support of their religious movement and no one personally derived a profit from the publication and distribution of the literature. The only activities involved in these cases were "the dissemination of ideas, educational and religious, and the collection of funds for the propagation of those ideas," which are subject to constitutional protection. In significant passages Chief Justice Stone said:

The First Amendment is not confined to safeguarding freedom of speech and freedom of religion against discriminatory attempts to wipe them out. On the contrary, the Constitution, by virtue of the First and Fourteenth Amendments, has put those freedoms in a preferred position. Their commands are not restricted to cases where the protected privilege is sought out for attack. They extend at least to every form of taxation which, because it is a condition of the exercise of the privilege, is capable of being used to control or suppress it. . . . The taxes are insupportable either as a tax on the dissemination of ideas or as a tax on the collection of funds for religious purposes. . . . It seems fairly obvious that if the present taxes, laid in small communities upon peripatetic religious propagandists, are to be sustained, a way has been found for the effective suppression of speech and press and religion despite constitutional guaranties. The very taxes now before us are better adapted to that end than were the stamp taxes which so successfully curtailed the dissemination of ideas . . . and which were a moving cause of the American Revolution. . . . In its potency as a prior restraint on publication the flat license tax falls short only of outright censorship or suppression. The more humble and needy the cause, the more effective is the suppression.

Justice Murphy, in his dissenting opinion, emphasized that newspaper space and radio time are expensive; therefore, the pamphlet has become the convenient vehicle of persons with limited resources; but such persons must depend on contributions for their literature; solicitation of contributions should not weaken the constitutional guaranties, for the freedom guarantied by the Constitution "cannot and must not mean freedom only for those who can distribute their broadsides without charge." Furthermore, the taxes were a burden on the right of Jehovah's Witnesses to worship God in their own fashion and to spread their gospel—not by preaching from a pulpit, but by distribution of religious literature. He noted an "arresting parallel" between the troubles of Jehovah's Witnesses and the struggle of various dissenting groups in colonial times. If "the accepted" clergymen of a town may stand in their pulpits and preach without let or hindrance, then the "heavy burden" imposed upon this "new set of itinerant zealots, the Witnesses," should not be allowed to stand. Rather than err in evaluating the First Amendment rights in such a way that they may be invaded, it is far better that we "err in being overprotective of these precious rights."

Soon after *Jones v. Opelika* was decided, Justice Byrnes resigned and was succeeded by Justice Rutledge. The Court ordered the case re-argued and then vacated its earlier judgment, again by a five-to-four vote, with, this time, Justices Reed, Roberts, Jackson, and Frankfurter the dissenters.[15] It is of interest to note that the American Newspaper Publishers Association filed a brief as *amicus curiae* on behalf of Jehovah's Witnesses. The reasons for the Supreme Court's dramatic reversal of position are set forth in the opinion for the majority by

Justice Douglas in *Murdock v. Jeannette*,[16] which we shall consider briefly.

The city of Jeannette, Pennsylvania, required a canvasser or solicitor to procure a license for which he was to pay $1.50 for one day, $7 for one week, $12 for two weeks, or $20 for three weeks. The Court set aside the convictions of Jehovah's Witnesses for violation of the ordinance. The judgment in *Jones v. Opelika,* said Justice Douglas for the Court, "has this day been vacated. Freed from that controlling precedent, we can restore to their high, constitutional position the liberties of itinerant evangelists who disseminate their religious beliefs and the tenets of their faith through distribution of literature." The mere fact that these "itinerant preachers" "sold" rather than "donated" their tracts or books, said the Court, did not "transform evangelism into a commercial enterprise"; for, if it did, "then the passing of the collection plate in church would make the church service a commercial project." It should be remembered, said the Court, that Tom Paine's pamphlets were not distributed free of charge. An itinerant evangelist does not become a mere book agent by selling his religious tracts to help defray expenses. "Freedom of speech, freedom of the press, freedom of religion are available to all, not merely to those who can pay their own way." The hand distribution or sale of religious tracts enjoys "the same claim to protection as the more orthodox and conventional exercises of religion."

The decision, it was made clear by Justice Douglas, was not intended to throw doubt upon the constitutionality of taxes on the income or property of clergymen. Such taxes are quite different from a tax on the privilege of delivering a sermon or distributing a religious publication; for there may be no tax "on the exercise of a privilege granted by the Bill of Rights."

In dissenting from the decision, Justice Reed argued that the rites which are protected by the First Amendment "are in essence spiritual—prayer, mass, sermons, sacrament—not sales of religious goods." Fortunately, the Court rejected this effort to "freeze" religion into a fixed definition; for what is spiritual or godly to one sect or person may be secular or satanic to another.

The case settled the proposition that the First Amendment prohibits taxes on knowledge that are an invasion of freedom of religion or of speech and press. This does not mean that religion or that persons engaged in the book or newspaper business must be subsidized by exemption from burdens to which all other citizens are subject.[17] What it means is that no license or privilege taxes may be imposed as a condition for the exercise of First Amendment freedoms.[18]

# ☆ 22 ☆

# Limited Abridgments of Speech and Press

IN RECENT years the Supreme Court seems to have evolved the principle that if the government seeks to meet an evil, and it attempts to meet that evil in a way which only indirectly, marginally, or "not unduly" abridges the First Amendment freedoms, or if the abridgment "touches only a relative handful of persons" and leaves the rest "completely free from restraint," then the action of the government will be considered constitutional.

The clearest instance of this approach is the case of *American Communications Association v. Douds,*[1] which deserves careful consideration.

The Labor Management Relations Act of 1947 (Taft-Hartley)[2] provides in section 9(h)[3] that a union shall not enjoy the privileges afforded by the act unless each officer file an affidavit with the National Labor Relations Board that he is not a member of or affiliated with the Communist Party. This is commonly known as the non-Communist affidavit provision. The Supreme Court in the *Douds* case upheld the constitutionality of this provision.[4]

In the important opinion for the Court by Chief Justice Vinson, it was contended that the constitutional justification for the Labor Management Relations Act was the power of Congress to protect interstate commerce by removing obstructions to the free flow of commerce caused by strikes and other forms of industrial unrest. The policy of the act is to strengthen unions and to encourage collective bargaining, as factors that will contribute to the achievement of industrial peace. In line with these basic policies, Congress sought to remove the likelihood of political strikes. Congress had found that Communist officers of unions subordinated legitimate union objectives to strikes ordered by party leaders in support of policies of the U.S.S.R.; thus, Congress had facts that showed that before the Nazis attacked the U.S.S.R. and before the United States declared war, Communist leaders of unions called strikes in American defense plants, and that this was done solely in response to party orders. In brief, Communist leaders of unions were not interested to achieve the objectives of the Labor Management Relations Act; their concern was to make unions a device by which commerce would be disrupted and the policy of Congress would be frustrated "when the dictates of [Communist or Russian] political policy required such action."

Against the action of Congress, the unions contended that the non-Communist affidavit requirement violated fundamental rights guarantied by the First Amendment: the right of union officers to associate with whatever political groups they will, and the right of union members to choose their officers without government interference.

Facing these contentions of the unions directly, Chief Justice Vinson said that it cannot be denied that the practical effect of the act on noncomplying unions was not restricted to a withholding of statutory benefits from them, for a failure to enjoy the statutory benefits might make it difficult for the unions to remain effective organizations. As a consequence, the question before the Court was "whether, consistently with the First Amendment, Congress, by statute, may exert these pressures upon labor unions to deny positions of leadership to certain persons" who are members of or affiliated with the Communist Party.

Congress certainly has the right to seek to prevent political strikes; the non-Communist affidavit provision bears "reasonable relation" to the apprehended evil. But by enacting this provision Congress "has undeniably discouraged the lawful exercise of political freedoms as well [as lessened the threat to interstate commerce]." The "grave and difficult problem" was whether Congress could seek to control interstate commerce in such a way that its action would have the "necessary effect of discouraging the exercise of political rights protected by the First Amendment."

This, then, admittedly presented a free speech issue. In such an instance, the unions contended, it is up to the Government to prove that joining the Communist Party or that political strikes constituted a clear and present danger. Not at all, said Chief Justice Vinson. The clear and present danger test would apply if Congress had undertaken to prevent the dissemination of Communist doctrine because it feared that unlawful action would follow if free speech were practiced. But this is not what happened here. In this instance the interest of Congress is to protect the free flow of commerce "from what Congress considers to be substantial evils of conduct that are not the products of speech at all." The non-Communist affidavit provision is not a congressional attempt to curtail speech out of a fear of what would follow if free speech were practiced; the provision "regulates harmful conduct" which is carried on by Communists. The theory of the act of Congress is not that political strikes follow from the advocacy of Communist *doctrine;* such strikes are the products of the *actions* of persons who have the will and power to achieve such strikes *"without* advocacy or persuasion that seeks acceptance in the competition of the market." [5] Said Chief Justice Vinson:

Speech may be fought with speech. Falsehoods and fallacies must be exposed, not suppressed, unless there is not sufficient time to avert the evil consequences of noxious doctrine by argument and education. That is the command of the First Amendment. But force may and must be met with force. Section 9(h) is designed to protect the public not against what Communists . . . advocate or believe, but against what Congress concluded they have done and are likely to do again.

Congress here directed its efforts against *conduct* by Communists—the calling of political strikes by Communist officers of labor unions. The First Amendment would have no bearing at all on this congressional action if this action did not, incidentally, discourage "the lawful exercise of political freedoms." Here is the critical point at which constitutional doctrine must be applied—the point at which the constitutional power of Congress "to protect interstate commerce by removing obstructions to the free flow of commerce" is crossed by the limits on Congress found in the First Amendment. The Court resolved the crisis by holding that when "the effect of a statute or ordinance upon the exercise of First Amendment freedoms is relatively small and the public interest is substantial," the clear and present danger test has no relevance, and the statute is constitutional. Congress here did not attempt to circumvent the First Amendment by cloaking censorship of ideas as a regulation of conduct; Congress did not attempt to protect the public from "the remote possible effects of noxious ideologies"; Congress, on the contrary, sought to protect the public from "present excesses of direct, active conduct." The action of Congress "results [only] in an indirect, conditional, partial abridgment of speech." Weighing "the probable effects of the statute upon the free exercise of the right of speech and assembly against the congressional determination that political strikes are evils of conduct which cause substantial harm to interstate commerce and that Communists . . . pose continuing threats to that public interest when in positions of union leadership," the non-Communist affidavit provision is constitutional. This is the resolution achieved because

we have here no statute which is either frankly aimed at the suppression of dangerous ideas nor one which, although ostensibly aimed at the regulation of conduct, may actually "be made the instrument of arbitrary suppression of free expression of views. . . ." In this legislation, Congress did not restrain the activities of the Communist Party as a political organization; nor did it attempt to stifle beliefs. . . . Section 9(h) touches only a relative handful of persons [members of the Communist Party who are officers of unions]. . . . And it leaves those few who are affected free to maintain their affiliations and beliefs subject only to possible loss of positions [in unions] which Congress has concluded are being abused to the injury of the public by members of . . . [the Communist Party].

We would summarize the views of Chief Justice Vinson as follows: Congress constitutionally may remove obstructions to the free flow of commerce. Industrial peace contributes to the free flow of commerce. Politically inspired strikes disrupt commerce. Congress has found that Communist officers of unions will involve their unions in strikes when such strikes will serve the interests of the U.S.S.R. Congress may attempt to prevent such strikes by requiring the non-Communist affidavit from officers of unions as a condition prior to affording unions the facilities of the National Labor Relations Board and other rights under the Labor Management Relations Act. The non-Communist affidavit requirement will have the effect of discouraging the exercise of political freedoms, but this was not what Congress intended to accomplish; this is a side effect—the intent of the legislation was the prevention of political strikes and not the discouragement of the exercise of freedoms guaranteed by the First Amendment. Finally, the discouragement in the exercise of fundamental freedoms will be felt by only few persons.

Justice Black alone dissented.[6] The Commerce Clause, he said, cannot restrict the freedoms guaranteed by the First Amendment. "On the contrary," he said, "the First Amendment was added after adoption of the Constitution for the express purpose of barring Congress from using previously granted powers to abridge belief or its expression." The Court has allowed compromise in a field "where the First Amendment forbids compromise." Justice Black attacked vigorously the application of the *de minimis* doctrine to the Bill of Rights. "The Court assures us," he said,

that today's encroachment on liberty is just a small one, that this particular statutory provision "touches only a relative handful of persons, leaving the great majority of persons of the identified affiliations and beliefs completely free from restraint." But not the least of the virtues of the First Amendment is its protection of each member of the smallest and most unorthodox minority.

Furthermore, said Justice Black, laws aimed at one minority generate hatreds which rapidly get out of control. Then, too, the reasoning of the Court that upholds the bar on Communists as union officers would apply just as forcibly to laws barring them from election to public offices, from mere membership in unions, "and in fact from getting or holding any jobs whereby they could earn a living." Justice Black also attacked the opinion of the majority for suggesting that Congress could single out Communists for special treatment because of the evidence that as a group they act in obedience to the commands of a foreign power. This, he said,

was the precise reason given in Sixteenth-Century England for attainting all Catholics unless they subscribed to test oaths wholly incompatible with their religion. Yet in the hour of crisis, an overwhelming majority of the English Catholics thus persecuted rallied loyally to defend their homeland against Spain and its Catholic troops. And in our own country Jefferson and his followers were earnestly accused of subversive allegiance to France. . . . Penalties should be imposed only for a person's own conduct, not for his beliefs or for the conduct of others with whom he may associate. Guilt should not be imputed solely from association or affiliation with political parties or any other organization, however much we abhor the ideas which they advocate. . . . Like anyone else, individual Communists who commit overt acts in violation of valid laws can and should be punished. But the postulate of the First Amendment is that our free institutions can be maintained without proscribing or penalizing political belief, speech, press, assembly, or party affiliation.

The differences between the views of the majority and of Justice Black are fundamental and complex. At the center of the debate between them, it seems to me, is the following difference in their views: Chief Justice Vinson saw Congress directing its efforts at *conduct*—at the prevention of political strikes— and not at Communists. In order to prevent such strikes, Congress enacted legislation which is directed at Communist officers of unions—to encourage unions to remove them from office, and to discourage unions from electing them to office. Justice

Black saw Congress enacting legislation "coercing union members not to elect any Communist as an officer" because of the "testimony of an ex-Communist that some Communist officers had called 'political strikes.'" This legislation, he held, is ostensibly aimed at the prevention of such strikes, but is really directed at certain persons because of their political beliefs or affiliation. It is not enough that *some* Communists in official positions in unions would use their power to foster industrial strife; a Communist, like any other person, is to be judged only on the basis of *his own conduct,* and not for the conduct of others: "like anyone else, individual Communists who commit overt acts in violation of valid laws can and should be punished." Until he violates a valid law, the individual Communist, according to Justice Black, should be let alone.

This constitutional debate is of crucial importance in our day. We shall need to come back to it later. In the context of the *Douds* case, however, it seems that the debate would have been avoided if Congress had merely outlawed political strikes. If fomenting such a strike had been declared an unfair labor practice, or even a crime, then the union or officers responsible for the strike could be punished or restrained. Admittedly, the definition of "political strikes" would offer great difficulties to the legislative draftsmen; but our labor legislation has in it many terms that are difficult to define with precision, with the result that many of them are the subject of frequent litigation.[7]

This argument was advanced before the Court— "that a statute aimed at political strikes should make the calling of such strikes unlawful but should not attempt to bring about the removal of union officers, with its attendant effect upon First Amendment rights." Chief Justice Vinson met this point by contending that

the legislative judgment that interstate commerce must be protected from a continuing threat of such strikes is a permissible one in this case. The fact that the injury to interstate commerce would be an accomplished fact before any sanctions could be applied, the possibility that a large number of such strikes might be called at a time of external or internal crisis, and the practical difficulties which would be encountered in detecting illegal activities of this kind are factors which are persuasive that Congress should not be powerless to remove the threat, not limited to punishing the act.

But one may question how really "persuasive" are these factors. When Congress was concerned with strikes that may "imperil the national health or safety"—national emergency disputes—it made provision regarding them in the same act which requires the non-Communist affidavits; [8] and in the *Steel Seizure* case,[9] decided in 1952, the Court held that, even in case of a national emergency, the President has no constitutional power to seize private property; and Congress has conducted many committee hearings to consider proposals for the handling of national emergency labor disputes within the framework of the Constitution. The entire record with respect to this matter shows a commendable sensitivity on the part of Congress and the Court to preserve constitutional guaranties. And yet, when it came to political strikes, even those that may fall far short of creating national emergencies, the Court was persuaded that Congress could enact *preventive* legislation, despite candid recognition of the fact that this legislation would impair First Amendment freedoms. In spirit, if not in form, the non-Communist affidavit requirement is censorship or previous restraint on the exercise of such freedoms.[10]

# ☆ 23 ☆

# Test Oaths and the Freedom
# to Think and Believe

AS WE have seen, in *American Communications Association
v. Douds*,[1] the Supreme Court, by a five-to-one vote, upheld
the constitutionality of the requirement of the Labor Management Relations Act that a union shall not enjoy the privileges
afforded by the act unless each officer file an affidavit that he is
not a member of or affiliated with the Communist Party. But
there was much more to the non-Communist affidavit requirement, and also to the *Douds* case. In addition to the membership
and affiliation provision, the act required that the affidavit state
that the union officer "does not believe in, and is not a member
of or supports any organization that believes in or teaches, the
overthrow of the United States Government by force or by
any illegal or unconstitutional methods." This provision goes
much further than the membership requirement, for membership is an objective, tangible, overt act. It does not even relate
to his speech, or to a book or handbill he may have written.
The provision delves into the person's *beliefs*, which are in his
mind or heart. The six members of the Court who decided the
case had much more difficulty with this part of the affidavit requirement; and its constitutionality was sustained only by a
three-to-three vote.[2]

In his opinion sustaining the constitutionality of the belief provision, Chief Justice Vinson said that Congress had evidence supporting the view that "some union leaders who hold to a belief in violent overthrow of the Government for reasons other than loyalty to the Communist Party" regard strikes as means toward ultimate revolutionary goals.[3] Congress, he said, "could rationally find" that such persons are "likely to resort to such tactics when, as officers, they formulate union policy." Under some circumstances, he said, beliefs may justify inferences when the inferences are drawn by Congress on the basis of its investigations.

"Beliefs are inviolate," said Chief Justice Vinson. But Congress has not taken action against beliefs; the statute only "regulates harmful conduct [political strikes] which Congress has determined is carried on by persons who may be identified by their political affiliations and beliefs." The statute is not designed to protect the public against the beliefs of certain persons, "but against what Congress has concluded they have done and are likely to do again." Congress is intent on regulating *conduct* and not on penalizing or suppressing *beliefs;* and conduct which affects interstate commerce may constitutionally be regulated by Congress; and Congress, not the Court, has the final judgment as to the need or desirability to regulate any particular form of conduct which affects interstate commerce. Admittedly, the statute has discouraging effects upon the exercise of First Amendment freedoms; but the "discouragements" proceed not against persons or beliefs, but only against the "combination" of the beliefs "with occupancy of a position of great power over the economy of the country." Congress did not set out to "stifle beliefs." The affidavit requirement "touches only a relative handful of persons"; and even these few persons are left free to maintain their beliefs, "subject only to possible loss of positions [as officers of unions]."

Chief Justice Vinson interpreted the belief provision as applying to persons "who believe in violent overthrow of the Government as it presently exists under the Constitution as an objective, not merely a prophecy." Congress "might well find" that persons with this objective "would carry that objective into their conduct of union affairs by calling political strikes designed to weaken and divide the American people, whether they consider actual overthrow of the Government to be near or distant."

"Of course we agree," said Vinson, "that one may not be imprisoned or executed because he holds particular beliefs." But there is no need to suggest that "thought control" is involved here, for the sole effect of the statute upon one who believes in the overthrow of the Government "is that he may be forced to relinquish his position as a union leader." The "loss of a particular position is not the loss of life or liberty." It is inaccurate to speak of the oath requirement "as 'punishing' or 'forbidding' the holding of beliefs, any more than it punishes or forbids membership in the Communist party."

There are circumstances under which the public has a right to ascertain a certain person's beliefs, for "beliefs are springs to action." Thus, a statute might provide that no person may become a member of the Secret Service force assigned to protect the President unless he swears that he does not believe in assassination of the President.

But where, then, will the line be drawn? Is the power of government over beliefs as unlimited as its power over conduct, and is the door wide open now to force disclosure of beliefs respecting economic, moral, and political issues? This, said Vinson, does not follow "while this Court sits." [4]

The First Amendment, said Vinson, "requires that one be permitted to advocate what he will unless there is a clear and present danger that a substantial evil will result therefrom. It does not require that he be permitted to be the keeper of the arsenal."

Justices Frankfurter and Jackson, while willing to uphold the constitutionality of the membership requirement, dissented from the decision respecting the belief requirement; Justice Black dissented from the decision respecting the entire affidavit provision. We have already discussed the opinion of Justice Black; now we turn to the important dissenting opinions of the other two members of the Court.

In the provision relating to beliefs, said Justice Frankfurter, Congress "has cast its net too indiscriminately." The provision asks "assurances from me regarding matters that open the door too wide to mere speculation or uncertainty." It would be one thing if the statute required an oath disavowing "active belief, as a matter of present policy, in the overthrow of the Government of the United States by force"; this might be constitutional; but the statute goes beyond this, it asks for a disavowal of belief in the overthrow of the Government "by force *or by any* illegal or unconstitutional methods." Who can with certainty say that a method is "illegal" or "unconstitutional"? Such questions are "frequently determined by this Court by the chance of a single vote." A person is constitutionally protected "to the largest possible extent in his thoughts and in his beliefs as the citadel of his person." Government may enter that citadel, "if at all," only if the entry "is strictly confined so that the belief that a man is asked to reveal is so defined as to leave no fair room for doubt that he is not asked to disclose what he has a right to withhold."

But what has a man a right to withhold? In his dissenting opinion, Justice Jackson answered this question in terms as sweeping as those used by Justice Black. "I think we must let his mind alone," said Jackson.

Congress, he said, has no power to proscribe *any opinion or belief* which has not manifested itself in an overt act. Membership in or affiliation with the Communist Party is an overt act. But the belief requirement asks for revelation and denial of "mere beliefs or opinions, even though they may never have matured into any act whatever or even been given utterance."

If one is accused of perjury by falsely swearing that he was not a member of the Communist Party, then the Government would need to prove "visible and knowable overt acts or courses of conduct" sufficient to establish his membership. But if one is accused of perjury by falsely swearing as to his beliefs, then the trial would need to concern itself with his mental states for the purpose of establishing, not some overt act, like membership, but a mental state—his beliefs. "Attempts of the courts to fathom modern political meditations of an accused would be as futile and mischievous as the efforts in the famous heresy trials of old to fathom religious beliefs." Even when it comes to treason, the Constitution provides that no person shall be convicted "unless on the testimony of two witnesses *to the same overt act.*" [5] Said Justice Jackson:

Only in the darkest periods of human history has any Western government concerned itself with mere belief, however eccentric or mischievous, when it has not matured into overt action; and if that practice survives anywhere, it is in the Communist countries whose philosophies we loathe. . . . Efforts to weed erroneous beliefs from the minds of men have always been supported by the argument which the Court invokes today, that beliefs are springs to action, that evil thoughts tend to become forbidden deeds. Probably so. But if power to forbid acts includes power to forbid contemplating them, then the power of government over beliefs is as unlimited as its power over conduct and the way is open to force disclosure of attitudes on all manner of social, economic, moral and political issues.

These suggestions may be discounted as fanciful and farfetched. But we must not forget that in our country are evangelists and zealots of many different political, economic and religious persuasions whose fanatical conviction is that all thought is divinely classified into two kinds—that which is their own and that which is false and dangerous. Communists are not the only faction which would put us all in mental strait jackets. Indeed all ideological struggles, religious or political, are primarily battles for dominance over the minds of people. It is not to be supposed that the age-old readiness to try to convert minds by pressure or suppression, instead of reason and persuasion, is extinct. Our protection against all kinds of fanatics and extremists, none of whom can be trusted with unlimited power over others, lies not in their forbearance, but in the limitations of our Constitution.

Is there a right to think revolutionary thoughts? Of course there is, said Jackson; for "we cannot ignore the fact that our own Government originated in revolution and is legitimate only if overthrow by force may sometimes be justified. That circumstances sometimes justify it is not Communist doctrine but an old American belief." As evidence of this "old American belief" Jackson quoted from the Declaration of Independence, the Pennsylvania Declaration of Rights, the diary of John Adams, the correspondence of Thomas Jefferson, speeches by

Henry Clay and Abraham Lincoln, the Maryland Declaration of Rights, and the writings of Thoreau and of President Grant. Although personally convinced that revolution does not serve the cause of liberty as well as does nonviolence, Jackson pointed out that revolutionary sentiments have a "strong appeal to the impetuous and are deeply imbedded in American tradition," and have been expressed by Americans of undoubted patriotism. Congress may, of course, make it a crime to take one overt step to use or to incite violence against the Government, yet, said Jackson,

I do not see how in the light of our history a mere belief that one has a natural right under some circumstances to do so can subject an American citizen to prejudice any more than possession of any other erroneous belief. . . . I think neither [state nor Federal Government] has any power, on any pretext, directly or indirectly to attempt foreclosure of any line of thought. Our forefathers found the evils of free thinking more to be endured than the evils of inquest or suppression. . . . This is not only because individual thinking presents no danger to society, but because thoughtful, bold and independent minds are essential to wise and considered self-government. . . . A free man must be a reasoning man, and he must dare to doubt what a legislative or electoral majority may most passionately assert. . . . Our Constitution relies on our electorate's complete ideological freedom to nourish independent and responsible intelligence and preserve our democracy from that submissiveness, timidity, and herd-mindedness of the masses which would foster a tyranny of mediocrity. The priceless heritage of our society is the unrestricted constitutional right of each member to think as he will. Thought control is a copyright of totalitarianism, and we have no claim to it. It is not the function of our Government to keep the citizen from falling into error; it is the function of the citizen to keep the Government from falling into error.

In a Communist state, said Justice Jackson, the government exacts a profession of belief or nonbelief; individuals are permitted to have only the ideas that the ruling group approves. But our Constitution protects individual nonconformity, and excludes government from "the realm of opinions and ideas, beliefs and doubts, heresy and orthodoxy, political, religious or scientific." Under our system, said Justice Jackson, "it is time enough for the law to lay hold of the citizen when he acts illegally, or in some rare circumstances when his thoughts are given illegal utterance. I think we must let his mind alone."

This dissenting opinion by Justice Jackson is especially forceful because it was written by a member of the Court who did not generally identify himself with the civil liberties absolutists —Justices Murphy, Rutledge, Black, and Douglas.[6] Here he spoke as an absolutist: the Government has no power, "on any pretext, directly or indirectly," to ask a person to disclose what is in his mind; as to thoughts and beliefs, the Government has no power of inquest or of suppression.

The opinion of Chief Justice Vinson does not meet the powerful argument of this dissenting opinion. "Beliefs are inviolate," said Vinson; yet his opinion attempted to justify an oath requirement in which a person was asked to disavow certain beliefs. The decision of the Court stands for the proposition that Congress *may* probe a man's mind to discover his thoughts and beliefs. True, Vinson tried hard to hedge the decision. Lines will be drawn; the door may be opened to force disclosure of what is in a person's mind, but the door will not be altogether removed— "while this Court sits." But this means that a citizen's protection against governmental efforts at thought control is to be found in the Court rather than where it was put originally—in the Constitution. Justice Douglas has stressed that the First Amendment provides that "Congress *shall make no law* . . . abridging the freedom of *speech*." "The Constitution," he has said, "provides no exception." [7] Justice Jackson would not say this, but he did say in the *Douds* case that the First Amendment provides that Congress *shall make no law* abridging the freedom of *thought or belief,* and that the Constitution provides *no exception* to this prohibition. With respect to the inviolability of what is within a man's mind or heart, Justice Jackson was an absolutist. He here reaffirmed his position in the *Barnette* flag salute case.

In his opinion in the *Douds* case Chief Justice Vinson relied, to some degree or at least argumentatively, on two cases, only one of which, however, involved a test oath; namely, *Re Sum-*

*mers,* decided in 1945.[8] This case ought to be examined briefly.

Clyde Summers had complied with all prerequisites for admission to the bar of Illinois except that he had been denied a certificate of the committee on character and fitness. Summers was described by a member of the Court as follows:

He is honest, moral and intelligent, has had a college and a law school education. He has been a law professor and fully measures up to the high standards of legal knowledge Illinois has set as a prerequisite to admission to practice law in that State. He has never been convicted for, or charged with, a violation of law. That he would serve his clients faithfully and efficiently if admitted to practice is not denied.[9]

Yet Summers was denied admission to the Illinois bar because he was a conscientious objector to war and the use of force. Because of this belief, the committee on character and fitness held that Summers could not swear in good faith to support the Illinois constitution, and therefore could not be admitted to the bar. Illinois had a constitutional provision that required service in the state militia in time of war, and Summers was unwilling to say that he would serve in the militia. But Illinois had not drafted men into the militia since 1864; and the state constitution prohibited the draft of conscientious objectors except in time of war, and also excepted from militia duty persons who were exempted by federal law ( and federal law permitted conscientious objectors to substitute for active military service nonwar work of national importance). Notwithstanding these facts, the state maintained that Summers, though he was willing to take an oath to support the state constitution, ought not to be permitted to take the oath because his beliefs would make it impossible for him to observe that oath.

The Supreme Court upheld the state, saying merely that Illinois had the right to interpret in its own way the oath to support the state constitution, and that this interpretation did not violate the First Amendment.

Four Justices dissented—Black, Douglas, Murphy, and Rutledge. In his opinion, Justice Black rightly observed that "the probability that Illinois would ever require the petitioner to serve in a war has little more reality than an imaginary quantity in mathematics." The exclusion of Summers from the practice of law in Illinois was based, then, solely on his *thoughts or religious beliefs* as to resort to war or force. Illinois in fact insisted on Summers taking an oath, not respecting what he would *do*—for he was willing to swear or affirm that he would support the state constitution—but respecting what he *thought or believed*. A state, said Justice Black, cannot penalize Summers' belief

through the circuitous method of prescribing an oath, and then barring . . . [him] on the ground that his present belief might later prompt him to do or refrain from doing something that might violate that oath. Test oaths, designed to impose civil disabilities upon men for their beliefs rather than for unlawful conduct, were an abomination to the founders of this nation. . . . Under our Constitution men are punished for what they do or fail to do and not for what they think and believe.

The majority opinion, by Justice Reed, relied on the *Schwimmer* and *Macintosh* cases,[10] which deserve consideration in connection with the test oath, at least for their notable dissenting opinions—which eventually became the majority view.

Rosika Schwimmer, when she was fifty years of age, appeared before a federal district court to obtain her naturalization papers. The oath of allegiance, which an act of Congress required her to take, affirmed that the person will "bear true faith and allegiance to the Constitution." She was willing to take this oath without reservations. But she was not permitted to do so because she was a pacifist. In answer to a question, she said that she would not be willing to take up arms in defense of this country. She was denied naturalization, and the Supreme Court sustained the decision against her. Justices Holmes, Brandeis, and Sanford dissented. It was in his dissenting opinion in this case that Holmes wrote the following words which have been frequently quoted:

If there is any principle of the Constitution that more imperatively calls for attachment than any other it is the principle of free thought—not free thought for those who agree with us but freedom for the thought that we hate. I think that we should adhere to that principle with regard to admission into, as well as to life within this country.

In the *Macintosh* case, a Canadian, who was a Baptist minister and a professor of divinity at Yale, applied for naturalization. He was willing to take the oath of allegiance. When asked, however, "If necessary, are you willing to take up arms in defense of this country?" he answered, "Yes; but I should want to be free to judge of the necessity." He explained that he was willing to give this country all the allegiance he ever could give to any country, but he could not put allegiance to the government of any country before allegiance to the will of God. This position, he said, was the only one he could take consistently with his moral and Christian principles. The Supreme Court upheld the denial of naturalization to him.

This time Chief Justice Hughes and Justices Holmes, Brandeis, and Stone dissented. In his dissenting opinion Hughes contended that the statutory oath of allegiance, which Macintosh was willing to take, simply promised that the person taking it was willing to support and defend the Constitution and the laws of the United States against all enemies, foreign and domestic, and to bear true faith and allegiance to the United States. The oath did not imply a promise to bear arms notwithstanding religious beliefs, nor a promise to put allegiance to temporal power above obedience to God. The oath—like other oaths prescribed by acts of Congress—was not intended to impose any religious test. "I think," said Hughes, "that the requirement of the oath of office [which the Constitution requires of members of Congress, members of state legislatures, and all executive and judicial officers of the United States and of the states] should be read in the light of our regard from the beginning for freedom of conscience." This, he said, is equally true of the form of oath, including the naturalization oath, prescribed by Congress. While government may enforce laws regardless of scruples or beliefs, in the forum of the conscience duty to a moral power that is higher than the state remains. The attempt to exact oaths or to subject persons to tests that are contrary to their conscience "has been the cause of many deplorable conflicts"; and it is not to be assumed that it was the intention of Congress to disregard these conflicts when it prescribed the naturalization oath. And the requirement of "attachment to the principles of the Constitution" should be construed as in accord with, rather than in opposition to, "the theory and practice of our government in relation to freedom of conscience."

These cases were decided in 1929 and 1930, respectively. In 1946, the year following the decision in the *Summers* case, the Supreme Court[11] overruled the *Schwimmer* and *Macintosh* decisions. James Louis Girouard, a Canadian, filed his petition for naturalization. He was willing to take the oath of allegiance; but in answer to the question if he was willing, when necessary, to take up arms in defense of this country, he explained that he was a Seventh Day Adventist and would not take up arms, but would be willing to serve in the army and render noncombatant military duty. This time the Court held that the applicant should be naturalized. Justice Douglas, in his opinion for the Court, said that the dissenting opinions of Holmes and Hughes had demonstrated the fallacies in the earlier cases. The naturalization oath, said Douglas, is in essentials not different from the oath of office required of public officials: "It is hard to believe that one need forsake his religious scruples to become a citizen but not to sit in the high councils of state." Expressly reversing previous decisions, Justice Douglas said:

The struggle for religious liberty has through the centuries been an effort to accommodate the demands of the State to the conscience of the individual. The victory for freedom of thought recorded in our Bill of Rights recognizes that in the domain of conscience there is a moral power higher than the State. . . . The test oath is abhorrent to our tradition. Over the years Congress has meticulously respected that tradition.[12]

Despite the decision in the *Girouard* case, the Court in the *Douds* case relied on the decision in the *Summers* case. This fact adds force to our thought that the decision in the *Douds* case, at least with respect to the belief requirement of the non-

Communist affidavit provision, rests on very weak constitutional ground—and on the vote of only three Justices of the Supreme Court.[13]

Except for the test oath relating to beliefs, in the Labor Management Relations Act of 1947, it seems to be the fact that Congress over the years has respected the tradition which has made such test oaths abhorrent. The opinion may be ventured that the dissenting opinions in the *Douds* case give considerable strength to that tradition.[14]

# ☆ 24 ☆

# Loyalty Oaths and Guilt by Association

AS WE have seen in our discussion of the *Douds* case, the Labor Management Relations Act provided in effect that a union officer who was a member of the Communist Party could not make the affidavit needed as a condition precedent to the union enjoying the opportunities offered to unions complying with the non-Communist affidavit requirement.[1] Mere membership of the officer in the Communist Party disqualified the union. This is an instance of a loyalty oath that is widely used today, especially by states with respect to teachers and other public employees. It is not, technically, a test oath, for it does not inquire into thoughts or beliefs; it is an inquiry into objective facts, overt acts—membership in the Communist Party or in some other subversive organization. The loyalty oath of this type involves the problem of guilt by association—guilt by mere membership. This problem has many facets—questions that involve the First Amendment freedoms of assembly and of political activity, and procedural questions that involve other guaranties of the Constitution. The problems are many and complex. We shall limit our discussion to the most significant problems touching this subject, and only insofar as they revolve around the First Amendment.

American experience with loyalty oaths goes back to the days of the Revolution.² In Pennsylvania a loyalty oath law was enacted, which affected Quakers in particular, since they refused to take the oath. Some Quakers continued to teach without taking the oath, and were, as a consequence, thrown into jail. Massachusetts, on the other hand, exempted Quakers from the oath and even from the duty to affirm that they would "defend" the state. During the Civil War, and in the years immediately following, a number of states enacted laws requiring a loyalty oath from all public employees, including teachers; and the Federal Government ³ required members of Congress to swear before admission that they had never borne arms against the United States, given aid, countenance or counsel to the enemy, or yielded a voluntary support to any government—the oath was directed against only overt acts.

Nevada seems to be the first state after the Civil War to have adopted a loyalty oath for teachers. In 1866, two years after Nevada was admitted to the Union, it enacted a law which required teachers to swear that they will support, protect, and defend the constitutions and governments of the United States and of the state, and that they will bear true faith, allegiance, and loyalty to the same; and further, that they will "well and faithfully perform all the duties of teacher." ⁴ New York in 1921 adopted laws (the Lusk Laws) directed at teachers—they must be "loyal and obedient" and they "shall be removed . . . for the utterance of any treasonable or seditious word"—but they were so notoriously offensive that two years later the legislature, prodded by Governor Alfred E. Smith, repealed them. Rhode Island adopted a loyalty oath law for teachers in 1917, Ohio in 1919, and seven other states adopted similar laws in the 1920's. By 1940 twenty-one states had such laws. Substantially these laws (except for the Lusk Laws of the State of New York) followed the pattern of the Nevada statute.

In a study of these loyalty oath laws, the American Civil Liberties Union pointed out that no court test of these laws could be made, for lawyers felt that the Supreme Court would uphold the states in requiring an oath of loyalty by any class of citizens, and teachers would be regarded as reasonably subject to such an oath. The study reported that "numerous dismissals, refusals of promotion and transfers" followed from application of the laws.[5] At the time this study was made (1940), the demand for conformity by teachers made it hazardous in most communities for teachers to discuss in the classroom, and often outside, subjects that were the chief topics of conversation: "Communism, Soviet Russia, Socialism, pacifism, trade unions, public ownership of industry, free trade, government regulation of industry, dishonest banking, civil liberties for radicals, racial equality, birth control, and sex hygiene." [6]

Teachers and professors strongly objected to these laws, Why? The reasons were effectively formulated in the statement on teachers' oath laws prepared for the American Association of University Professors in 1936 by a committee comprising A. J. Carlson, Arthur O. Lovejoy, and Zechariah Chafee, Jr.[7] The principal objects of these laws, the statement pointed out, are three:

1. *"Supporting the Constitution."* To single out teachers for an oath to support the Constitution was "an offensive aspersion upon their citizenship." Such oaths were not demanded of clergymen, journalists, or members of other professions. Are teachers peculiarly prone to violate the law? The false assumption that teachers are prone to violate the Constitution and the laws makes teachers regard the oath laws as offensive. Unless or until the oath requirement is made general, teachers will continue to object to laws that make teaching into a suspect profession.

Furthermore, proponents of teachers' oath laws favored such laws because they construed an oath to "support" the Constitution as a pledge to refrain from advocating changes in the Constitution or the laws generally. They wanted to prevent "subversion," and by this they meant a proposal to make any change to which the oath law sponsors were strongly opposed.

While the oath laws probably created no actionable offense once the oath was taken, their legal futility did not render them harmless, for they gave to school and university authorities a quasi-legal basis for the dismissal of a teacher whose political views or activities they regarded as inconsistent with "support" of the Constitution. The fate of teachers thus was placed in the hands of legally irresponsible persons who had the means to compel teachers to surrender fundamental freedoms.

2. *"Propaganda."* While political proselytizing has no place in the school, the oath laws had the effect of narrowing the subject matter of study and devitalizing the work of teachers of government and other social sciences. Pupils in high schools should become acquainted with facts concerning important contemporary issues and controversies, and should be encouraged to think about such matters; and teachers should have opportunities to demonstrate by example the scientific mind in the analysis of problems, the principle of the open mind where evidence is lacking or debatable, and the principle of the tolerant mind where opinions differ. But the oath laws discouraged even the mere exposition of any opinions, or movements, or governmental or economic systems of which some citizens disapproved.

3. *"Teaching American principles."* Supporters of the oath laws often contended that propaganda in favor of certain American traditions and institutions should be made compulsory. While it is desirable to pass on from generation to generation certain common loyalties and traditions, this principle was subject to abuse when rival groups claimed to have a monopoly of "American" traditions and principles and desired to win control of the schools as instruments of their own faction. They were not interested in inculcating respect for the fundamental freedoms of speech and press, equality in rights before the law, the exclusion of religious beliefs and practices from the province of government, equality of opportunity, and tolerance as a quality of spirit and temper. On the contrary, persons who sponsored teachers' oath laws had no conspicuous respect for civil liberties, they were not tolerant of dissent, they showed no confidence in the value of free discussion. The movement for such laws was, in the main,

a manifestation of an essentially un-American temper on the part of a fraction of our citizenship. It is a phase of a tendency which, in some other countries, has finally resulted in an abandonment of the democratic method, the establishment of governments based upon terrorism, and the general suppression of freedom of inquiry, of speech, of the press, and of the suffrage. And it is above all for this reason that American teachers are opposed to such laws.[8]

The period that generated the teachers' loyalty oaths expressed a "cult of loyalty" which found expression in "hollow rituals of affirmation," in patriotic societies that were "censors of other people's public virtue."

The country was not content to look for the overt forms of disloyalty in treasonable conduct; it sought subtler traces in ideas and ideologies. This was a dangerous course, rendered more so by our disparate traditions. What creed could define Americanism? What social or political stance was manifestly loyal or disloyal? The tendency was for loyalty to become that belief which the inquirer took for granted, disloyalty that belief which raised doubts in some beholder.[9]

As we have seen, by the end of 1940 there were twenty-one states that had teachers' loyalty oath laws. In the next decade, six additional states passed such laws.[10] By 1953 the total number of states with laws requiring special teachers' loyalty oaths was thirty-two.[11] And now something relatively new appeared in such laws: some states specifically forbade membership by teachers in subversive organizations. In a few cases the Communist Party was specified by name; e.g., the Georgia law enacted in 1949 required an oath stating "that I am not a member of the Communist Party and that I have no sympathy for the doctrines of Communism and will not lend my aid, my support, my advice, my counsel nor my influence to the Communist Party or to the teachings of Communism." The words "Communist" or "Communist Party" also appeared in the Arkansas, Maryland, Oklahoma, and Texas statutes.

A brief summary of developments in the State of New York will be instructive, especially in view of the fact that this state's teachers' loyalty oath has been passed upon by the United States Supreme Court.[12]

In 1934, eleven years after the repeal of the Lusk Laws, the New York legislature adopted a law that required teachers in all public schools and in tax-exempt private schools to take the following oath: "I do solemnly swear (or affirm) that I will support the Constitution of the United States and the Constitution of the State of New York, and that I will faithfully discharge, to the best of my ability, the duties of the position to which I am now assigned." This statute is still in force. In 1939 the legislature adopted the Devaney Law, which barred from public employment and from teaching in tax-supported educational institutions any person who advocated, advised, or taught the doctrine that government should be overthrown by force or any unlawful means.

At the same time there were exaggerated charges of "immoral," "ungodly," and "un-American" activities in the public schools and the municipal colleges of New York City. In 1940 the New York State Senate adopted a resolution protesting the appointment of Bertrand Russell to teach mathematics and philosophy at the College of the City of New York. The appointment was voided by Judge McGeehan of the New York Supreme Court, in an opinion which spoke of the "norms and criteria" which are "the laws of Nature and of Nature's God," and of the appointment of Bertrand Russell as the establishment of a "chair of indecency" at the college. He spoke of "the filth" contained in Russell's books; he said that Russell was not a person of "good moral character," that the appointment was "an insult" to the people of the city; the fact that Russell was an "extraordinary" person made him, said the judge, "the more dangerous." [13]

The New York legislature, responding to the wild claims and exaggerated charges made by some of its members and by others, authorized a committee of investigation that became known as the Rapp-Coudert committee, which functioned in 1940 and 1941. The committee concentrated on the Teachers Union, sought to get the union to disclose its membership lists, and conducted public and private hearings in its investigation of subversive activities in the New York City public schools. Since the membership list, which the courts compelled the union to disclose to the committee, did not show who was and who was not a Communist, the committee's efforts to obtain the list led to the suspicion that the committee was antiunion. The committee set the pattern for congressional committees by engaging a research staff that got together a good deal of documentary and other materials relating to the operations of the Communist Party. The committee compiled a list of teachers and other school employees who were allegedly Communists. Many of these persons were subpoenaed to testify at executive and public hearings. Witnesses who testified at the public hearings named over fifty college associates as Communists, each of whom appeared before the committee and was given only a few minutes to meet the charges. There is strong support for the view that the committee members

were not looking upon these hearings as sources of further information. Quite apparently they had already made up their minds concerning the guilt of those appearing before them. Additional support of this view was supplied by the almost invariable failure of the committee to cross-examine the responding witnesses as they presented their evidence. . . . It seems highly likely that along with a number of persons correctly identified as Communists were a number of others who should never have been named. The committee did not exercise sufficient care before accepting an unsupported opinion in view of the seriousness of the accusation and the possibility that it might do irrevocable harm to an innocent person.[14]

The committee defended its procedures by saying that it was not a judicial tribunal trying people on criminal charges but a legislative committee seeking information.

On narrowly technical grounds this was correct. When viewed realistically this was not the case. In the first place, the committee was not limiting itself to eliciting information. It was at the very least attempting in effect to pin indictments upon particular individuals. Moreover, the committee had already gone on record publicly and especially in its communications to the school authorities to the effect that no Communist should be permitted to retain his job. . . . The committee had already so definitely made up its mind that *all persons publicly named* were guilty as charged that it in effect prevented them from proving their innocence during the public hearings.[15]

In 1941 the Board of Higher Education of the City of New York adopted the following resolution: "Resolved that it is the purpose of the Board of Higher Education not to retain as members of the collegiate staffs members of any Communist, Fascist or Nazi group or society, or to retain any individual who, or members of any group which, advocates, advises, teaches or practises subversive doctrines or activities." A month later, responding to sharp criticism of the resolution, the board added a proviso "that it is the intention of the Board to adhere to its established policy not to discharge any member of its staffs (1) merely because of membership in a political organization unaccompanied by any of the activities or elements referred to in the resolution above or (2) merely because of any differences of opinion on political, economic or social matters."

Every person who was named a Communist and who appeared before the legislative committee denied the charge under oath. The Board of Higher Education then suspended the person. If he had no tenure, he was dismissed or not re-employed. If he had tenure, he was tried before a committee of the board. Every person tried in 1941 or 1942 was dismissed. No case reached the courts.[16]

Despite these results, the Rapp-Coudert committee charged that the school authorities showed a lack of wholehearted support of the committee's objectives and threatened to ask the legislature to take strong measures. In 1949 the threat was carried out by the enactment of the Feinberg Law.[17] This statute provides that the Board of Regents shall make up a list of "organizations which it finds to be subversive" in that they teach or advocate that government shall be overthrown by force or violence or any unlawful means. This list may be amended from time to time. In making up the list, the board may utilize any list prepared by any agency of the Federal Government. Membership in any organization on the list "shall constitute prime facie evidence of disqualification" for appointment to or retention in any position in the public schools or the state-supported colleges.[18] The board adopted rules and regulations under the terms of the act, which provide that each year officials of school districts must report to the board that each teacher has not violated the law; and school authorities must make annual reports to the state commissioner of education. Following promulgation of the rules, the commissioner of education issued a memorandum implementing the rules, in which he stated:

The writing of articles, the distribution of pamphlets, the endorsement of speeches made or articles written or acts performed by others, all may constitute subversive activity.

Nor need such activity be confined to the classroom. Treasonable or subversive acts or statements outside the school are as much a basis for dismissal as are similar activities in school or in the presence of school children.

The events we have related show a line of development that may be briefly summarized as follows: (1) Teachers were required to take an oath that they will support the Constitution and that they will faithfully perform their duties. (2) The oath was changed to include a statement that the teacher did not belong to any organization that teaches or advocates overthrow of the government by force or violence or any unlawful means. (3) The oath was changed to include a denial of membership in the Communist Party. (4) In addition to the oath law, the legislature enacted laws—implemented by administrative rules and regulations—prohibiting employment of teachers who belong to the Communist Party or other subversive organizations the names of which are on a list prepared by a designated official or agency. (5) There was reliance on legislative investigating committees to discover and disclose the names of persons who were charged by witnesses with membership in the Communist Party. (6) There was use of the legislative hearings as pressure on the legislature and educational authorities to adopt more stringent measures against persons alleged to have violated the oath or loyalty laws. (7) Reporting procedures were adopted that require frequent or constant review of teachers' conduct in and outside the school, including their membership in organizations, their writings and speeches, their affiliations, and the views of others which they allegedly endorse.

There are procedural aspects of the topic that involve the Fifth Amendment privilege against self-incrimination and other procedural guaranties which fall outside the scope of our discussion. Limiting ourselves to First Amendment freedoms, we propose to discuss the impact of the teachers' oath and loyalty laws on these freedoms. The problem has been concretized in the phrase "guilt by association," which, unfortunately, has emotional overtones.

Now let us face up to the constitutional issue directly, within the limits of the decisions and opinions of the Supreme Court: May a teacher be removed from his position merely on the basis of proof that he is a member of the Communist Party or of any other organization proscribed as subversive by some agency acting under legislative authority?

The first Supreme Court case in which there was a discussion of some aspects of this question was the *Schneiderman* case, decided in 1943.[19] William Schneiderman came to the United States when he was three years of age. At the age of sixteen he joined the Young Workers League, a Communist group, and three years later, in 1924, he joined the Workers Party of America,[20] which was another name for the Communist Party. In 1927 he became a citizen of the United States. Twelve years later, in 1939, the Government brought proceedings to denaturalize Schneiderman. The complaint charged that Schneiderman, at the time of his naturalization, and during the statutory period of five years preceding that event, was not a person attached to the principles of the Constitution and well disposed to the good order and happiness of the United States. When Schneiderman was naturalized the law prohibited the naturalization of members of organizations that taught disbelief in organized government.

The Government did not show that Schneiderman had ever written or spoken to advocate overthrow of the Government; only his membership in the Communist organizations was shown. At the trial he did testify, however, that he subscribed to the principles of those organizations.

The Supreme Court held that Schneiderman could not be denaturalized.[21] Limiting ourselves to the question of guilt by association, we note that Justice Murphy, in his opinion for the Court, said: "Under our traditions beliefs are personal and not a matter of mere association, and . . . men in adhering to a political party or other organization notoriously do not subscribe unqualifiedly to all of its platforms or asserted principles."

The Government contended that the party literature showed advocacy of and belief in the overthrow of the Government by force and violence. Reliance on some pasages in party literature was held by the Court insufficient insofar as the method involved indiscriminate imputation of party dogmas to a member. Said Justice Murphy:

The difficulties of this method of proof are here increased by the fact that there is, unfortunately, no absolutely accurate test of what a political party's principles are. Political writings are often over exaggerated polemics bearing the imprint of the period and the place in which written. . . . Every utterance of party leaders is not taken as party gospel. And we would deny our experience as men if we did not recognize that official party programs are unfortunately often opportunistic devices as much honored in the breach as in the observance.

Since the party's program was subject to two interpretations, the Court held that it would not be justified in canceling the certificate of citizenship by imputing to a member a reprehensible interpretation "in the absence of overt acts indicating that such was his interpretation." The fact that the party exercised strict discipline over its members and that Schneiderman was not a mere "rank and file or accidental member" but "an intelligent and educated individual" who filled the role of a party leader, said the Court, was not enough proof to meet the test of "clear, unequivocal, and convincing evidence" necessary for setting aside a naturalization decree.

In brief, Justice Murphy's opinion for the Court discredited the guilt by association theory on which the suit was based. The Government had not satisfied the Court that the Communist Party stood unequivocally for certain proscribed doctrines, that Schneiderman was aware of the proscribed character of the tenets of the organization, and that he had adopted them as his own: "Beliefs are personal and not a matter of mere association."

In his dissenting opinion, Chief Justice Stone said that the record showed that Schneiderman's devotion to the party was not transitory but consistent with his genuine and settled convictions, and that his desire was to advance the party's principles. It was preposterous, he said, to maintain that vigorous aid given by Schneiderman in disseminating party teachings was compatible with attachment to the principles of the Constitution. Schneiderman's pledge of adherence to the party's principles and tactics, and his membership in Communist organizations, "were neither passive nor indolent." The facts in the case precluded the possibility that he did not know the character of the party's teachings and that he did not aid in their advocacy. Said Chief Justice Stone:

It might as well be said that it is impossible to infer that a man is attached to the principles of a religious movement from the fact that he conducts its prayer meetings, or, to take a more sinister example, that it could not be inferred that a man is a Nazi and consequently not attached to constitutional principles who, for more than five years, had diligently circulated the doctrines of *Mein Kampf.*

In neither case of course is the inference inevitable. It is possible, though not probable or normal, for one to be attached to principles diametrically opposed to those, to the dissemination of which he has given his life's best effort. But it is a normal and sensible inference which the trier of fact is free to make that his attachment is to those principles rather than to constitutional principles with which they are at war. *A man can be known by the ideas he spreads as well as by the company he keeps.*[22]

It should be noted that naturalization and denaturalization are statutory matters, and that the statute that controlled the *Schneiderman* case did not provide that membership in the Communist Party, standing alone, shall be sufficient to disqualify an alien from naturalization; [23] and that while Chief Justice Stone said that a man can be known by the company he keeps, he did not rely on this proposition alone for his belief that the trial court had sufficient ground to conclude that Schneiderman was not attached to the principles of the Constitution at the time of, and for five years prior to, his naturalization—he relied on the trial record which showed many Communist activities by Schneiderman.

In a subsequent case,[24] involving an attempt to denaturalize a Nazi, Justice Douglas in his opinion for the Court said that the trial court had "properly ruled that membership in the Bund was not in itself sufficient to prove fraud which would warrant revocation of a decree of naturalization. Otherwise, guilt would rest on implication, contrary to the rule of the *Schneiderman* [case]." Here, said the Court, "we have much more than that. We have a clear course of conduct, of which membership in the Bund was a manifestation, designed to promote the Nazi cause in this country."

In the *Douds* case, however, as we have seen, the Court held that Congress could disqualify unions from the opportunities offered by the Labor Management Relations Act of 1947 if their officers refused or failed to sign affidavits that they were not members of the Communist Party.[25] Congress intended that membership in the Communist Party, *standing alone,* shall disqualify the union; and the Court upheld the congressional act. Affiliation of this kind, said Chief Justice Vinson, provides "rational ground for the legislative judgment" that Communist Party members would be subject to " 'tempting opportunities' to commit acts deemed harmful to the national economy." In this respect the affidavit requirement "is not unlike a host of other statutes which prohibit specified groups of persons from holding positions of power and public interest because, in the legislative judgment, they threaten to abuse the trust that is a necessary concomitant of the power of office." Congress could find that Communists, "unlike members of other political parties, . . . represent a continuing danger of disruptive political strikes when they hold positions of union leadership." Joining the Communist Party is an overt act.

Justice Jackson, concurring in only that aspect of the Court's opinion that sustained the membership part of the affidavit, made some remarks regarding guilt by association that are important:

There has recently entered the dialectic of politics a cliché used to condemn application of the conspiracy principle to Communists. "Guilt by association" is an epithet frequently used and little explained, except that it is generally accompanied by another slogan, "guilt is personal." Of course it is; but personal guilt may be incurred by joining a conspiracy. That act of association makes one responsible for the acts of others committed in pursuance of the association. It is wholly a question of the sufficiency of evidence of association to imply conspiracy. *There is certainly sufficient evidence that all members owe allegiance to every detail of the Communist Party program and have assumed a duty actively to help execute it, so that Congress could, on familiar conspiracy principles, charge each member with responsibility for the goals and means of the Party.*[26]

In his dissenting opinion, Justice Black rejected the concept that a person can constitutionally be in any way penalized for political association or affiliation. Penalties, he said, may be imposed "only for a person's own conduct," not "for the conduct of others with whom he may associate."

Guilt should not be imputed solely from association or affiliation with political parties or any other organization, however much we abhor the ideas which they advocate. *Schneiderman v. United States.* Like anyone else, individual Communists who commit overt acts in violation of valid laws can and should be punished. But the postulate of the First Amendment is that our free institutions can be maintained without proscribing or penalizing political belief, speech, press, assembly, or party affiliation. This is a far bolder philosophy than despotic rulers can afford to follow. It is the heart of the system on which our freedom depends.

Of the six members of the Court who participated in the *Douds* case, only Justice Black dissented from the Court's decision on the ground that the membership provision in the affidavit requirement violated a prohibition on guilt by association implied in the First Amendment. Even if it were admitted that the Communist Party advocated violent overthrow of the Government, it could not be punished for advocating peaceful changes, or for doing other things which it has a right to do; so, too, argued Justice Black, a member of the party may be punished for a criminal offense committed by him, but not for any act that is not criminal, nor for any act done by others. This was in 1950.

Two years later all nine members of the Court considered the Feinberg Law of the State of New York. In *Adler v. Board of Education* [27] the Court upheld the law as constitutional, with only Justices Black and Douglas dissenting on the merits. We turn to a consideration of this case.

In his opinion for the Court, Justice Minton referred to the preamble of the Feinberg Law, which makes elaborate findings that members of the Communist Party and its affiliated organizations have been infiltrating into the public schools, notwithstanding the existence of statutes designed to prevent the employment in public office of members of organizations that teach or advocate that government shall be overthrown by force or violence or other unlawful means; as a result, propaganda can be disseminated among school children. The legislature also found that members of such organizations use their positions to advocate and teach subversive doctrines, and that they are bound to follow and teach a prescribed party line without regard to truth. This propaganda, the legislature declared, is sufficiently subtle to escape detection in the classroom, and so it is difficult to measure the menace of infiltration into the classroom. The legislature declared that the prohibition upon teachers who are members of the party or affiliated organizations must be rigorously enforced. To carry out this policy and these purposes, the legislature enacted the Feinberg Law, which provides that the Board of Regents shall, after notice and hearing, make a list of organizations which advocate that government should be overthrown by force or violence or other unlawful means. The board is authorized to provide that membership in any listed organization "shall constitute prima facie evidence for disqualification" for employment in the school system.

Justice Minton found that on the freedom of speech and assembly question the case was similar to the *Douds* case. A person has no constitutional right to be a school teacher, any more than to be an officer of a union that enjoys the opportunities afforded by an act of Congress. A union may enjoy the statutory opportunities on the terms fixed by law, and a person may work for a public agency on the terms fixed by law. If the members of a union do not choose to take advantage of the statutory facilities on the terms fixed by Congress, they may still elect Communists to union offices and thus enjoy freedom to assemble, speak, think, and believe as they will; if persons do not choose to work for the state on the terms fixed by the Feinberg Law and cognate legislation, "they are at liberty to retain their beliefs and associations and go elsewhere."

It was not disputed at the trial that persons who advocate overthrow of government by force or violence may be disqualified from teaching in the public schools. The conflict was over the membership provision. The Court held that the membership provision did not deprive teachers of the right of free speech and assembly—they may be barred "by unexplained membership in an organization found by the school authorities, after notice and hearing, to teach and advocate the overthrow of the government by force or violence, and known by such persons to have such purpose." For a teacher, said Justice Minton,

works in a sensitive area in a school-room. There he shapes the attitude of young minds towards the society in which they live. In this, the state has a vital concern. . . . *One's associates, past and present, as well as one's conduct, may properly be considered in determining fitness and loyalty. From time immemorial, one's reputation has been determined in part by the company he keeps. In the employment of officials and teachers of the school system, the state may very properly inquire into the company they keep, and we know of no rule, constitutional or otherwise, that prevents the state, when determining the fitness and loyalty of such persons, from considering the organizations and persons with whom they associate. . . .*

If under the procedure set up in the New York law, a person is found to be unfit and is disqualified from employment in the public school system because of membership in a listed organization, he is not thereby denied the right of free speech and assembly. His freedom of choice between membership in the organization and employment in the school system might be limited, but not his freedom of speech or assembly, except in the remote sense that limitation is inherent in every choice.[28]

Under the terms of the statute, it will be noted, the question is not whether *in fact* the teacher has exploited his position to insinuate the party line into his teaching, or that he has attempted to influence his pupils outside of class in party activities; and with regard to a person who seeks employment in the school system, such questions cannot even arise. On the contrary, the legislature, as we have seen, found that Communist propaganda is sufficiently subtle to escape detection in the classroom. If the organization is on the list prepared by the Board of Regents, and membership with knowledge of the organization's purpose is established, then prima facie disqualification has been shown. The teacher or applicant is still entitled to a hearing, but what he can expect from it except a decision barring him from employment is difficult to see. Superficially it looks as if the statute provides due process, but actually the procedures can have only one end in view; namely, the establishment of the fact of membership in a proscribed organization with knowledge of its purpose; and once this fact is proved, then "disqualification" follows—not presumptively, but conclusively. Whether one agrees or disagrees with the Court's decision, it seems to me that one ought to see here a case of guilt by association, *in the literal sense;* and Justice Minton's opinion, in the passage we have quoted in italics, admits as much and attempts to justify the conclusion.

Three members of the Court—Justices Black, Douglas, and Frankfurter—disagreed with the majority.

To Justice Douglas, the decision placed public employees in a category "of second class citizens by denying them freedom of thought and expression." Everyone has these freedoms, and no one needs them more than does the teacher. The Feinberg Law "proceeds on a principle repugnant to our society—guilt by association."

Once membership in a proscribed organization is shown, said Justice Douglas, the only question that can be raised is whether the teacher knew the purpose of the organization. Innocence, then, will depend on ignorance or knowledge; but "when the witch hunt is on, one who must rely on ignorance leans on a feeble reed."

Furthermore, and even more important, the law will restrict the intellectual freedom of the teacher in several ways: (1) The existence of the law is bound to limit academic freedom, for teachers will fear that an organization, howsoever innocent it may appear to them, may in time become suspect to others, for Communists may infiltrate into it, and the organization may be put on the list, and teachers who were members may find themselves automatically condemned. In the light of so grave a danger, it is better not to join an organization. "In that manner freedom of expression will be stifled." (2) The law makes a teacher's opinions and thoughts crucially important for the maintenance of his employment; for, once membership is shown, his views become relevant to the question of knowledge or ignorance. (3) To effectuate the law, periodical reports on the teachers will need to be made out. The school principals will need to become detectives, and the students will become informers. As a consequence, the law

inevitably turns the school system into a spying project. . . . Ears are cocked for tell-tale signs of disloyalty. The prejudices of the community come into play in searching out the disloyal. This is not the usual type of supervision which checks a teacher's competency; it is a system which searches for hidden meanings in a teacher's utterances.

A teacher's past will be "combed for signs of disloyalty"; his utterances will be watched

for clues to dangerous thoughts. A pall is cast over the classrooms. There can be no real academic freedom in that environment; . . . there can be no exercise of the free intellect. . . . A deadening dogma takes the place of free inquiry; . . . discussion often leaves off where it should begin. . . . This system of spying and surveillance with its accompanying reports and trials cannot go hand in hand with academic freedom. It produces standardized thought, not the pursuit of truth. Yet it was the pursuit of truth which the First Amendment was designed to protect. . . . The Framers knew the danger of dogmatism; they also knew the strength that comes when the mind is free, when ideas may be pursued wherever they lead.

The test should be "overt acts," said Justice Douglas; but this phrase does not encompass membership in an organization—an exercise of the right of free association is no more an "overt act" than is an exercise of the right of free speech or press. Said Justice Douglas:

> Of course the school systems of the country need not become cells for Communist activities; and the classrooms need not become forums for propagandizing the Marxist creed. *But the guilt of the teacher should turn on overt acts.* So long as she is a law abiding citizen, so long as her performance within the public school system meets professional standards, her private life, her political philosophy, her social creed should not be the cause of reprisals against her.[29]

Justice Black's dissent also was based squarely on the guaranties of the First Amendment. The Feinberg Law, he said, was

another of those rapidly multiplying legislative enactments which make it dangerous—this time for school teachers—to think or say anything except what a transient majority happen to approve at the moment. Basically these laws rest on the belief that government should supervise and limit the flow of ideas into the minds of men. The tendency of such governmental policy is to mould people into a common intellectual pattern. Quite a different governmental policy rests on the belief that government should leave the mind and spirit of man absolutely free. Such a governmental policy encourages varied intellectual outlooks in the belief that the best views will prevail. This policy of freedom is in my judgment embodied in the First Amendment and made applicable to the states by the Fourteenth. Because of this policy public officials cannot be constitutionally vested with powers to select the ideas people can think about, censor the public views they can express, *or choose the persons or groups people can associate with.* Public officials with such powers are not public servants; they are public masters.[30]

The New York law, sustained by the Court, effectively penalized school teachers, said Justice Black, "for their thoughts and *their associates*." [31]

Justice Frankfurter's dissenting opinion was devoted almost entirely to the proposition that the suit was wanting in the necessary basis for review by the Court; but in passing he remarked that

it may well be of constitutional significance whether the reporting system contemplates merely the notation as to each teacher that no evidence of disqualification has turned up, if such be the case, or whether it demands systematic and continuous surveillance and investigation of evidence. The difference cannot be meaningless, it may even be decisive, if our function is to balance the restrictions on freedom of utterance and of association against the evil to be suppressed.

Since the laws and regulations require annual reports on each teacher with a view to discovering evidence of violations, and annual reports to the legislature on measures taken for their enforcement, it is difficult to see how it is possible to avoid "systematic and continuous surveillance and investigation of evidence." Indeed, the reports submitted by the authorities in 1955 showed that in the municipal colleges of the City of New York twenty-four members of the faculties, and in the public schools seventy-nine persons, had been under investigation.[32] The laws and regulations, taken together, it would seem, cannot but weaken the morale of teachers and professors; for many of them must feel themselves to be under constant observation, and accountable to superiors from day to day, and must feel the necessity to avoid saying or doing anything that may tend to arouse the suspicions or curiosity of an investigator, an informer, or an overzealous administrator who must look out for his own position or future. As John Lord O'Brian has said: "No one familiar with the administration of a government department . . . can doubt that the mere existence of any law or order authorizing secret investigations will encourage suspicion, distrust, gossip, malevolent tale-bearing, character assassination and a general undermining of morale."[33]

The Court's failure to declare the Feinberg Law and the regulations adopted under it unconstitutional on their face[34] is difficult to understand and even more difficult to justify.

Shortly after the decision in the *Adler* case, Justice Frankfurter took advantage of an opportunity to make some very notable observations concerning the nature of academic freedom in a case in which the Court unanimously agreed that guilt by association must be somewhat circumscribed. That was done in the case of *Wieman v. Updegraff.*[35]

Oklahoma, by statute enacted in 1951, required its twenty thousand state employees to subscribe to a loyalty oath which included, *inter alia,* a statement (a) that the employee is not "affiliated directly or indirectly with the Communist Party," or with any group determined by the Attorney General of the United States to be a Communist front or a subversive organization; (b) that he has not been a member of such party or listed group at any time within the five years preceding the taking of the oath; and (c) that as long as his public employment will continue, he will not join any organization that advocates overthrow of the Government of the United States or the state by force or violence or other unlawful means. Some members of the faculty and staff of a state college refused to take the oath and challenged the constitutionality of the act.

The Court held that the act could not be upheld as it was interpreted by the state courts, which held that the law excluded persons from public employment solely on the basis of organizational membership, regardless of their knowledge or ignorance of the character of the organizations to which they had belonged. Membership alone, said Justice Clark for the Court, cannot constitutionally be made a disqualification. For, he said, "membership may be innocent." A person may join an organization unaware of its purposes and activities. Persons have been known to sever their membership after learning of the character of an organization. Also, at the time of joining, the organization may have been innocent, and may later have been captured for subversive ends; and an organization may have been subversive and may later have freed itself of its guilty elements. For all these reasons it is a denial of constitutional right to make mere membership, as distinguished from *knowing membership*, a disqualification from public employment. To fail to distinguish between innocent and knowing membership, said the Court, "is to stifle the flow of democratic expression and controversy at one of its chief sources."

Justice Black, concurring, would have gone further. "Test oaths," he said, "are notorious tools of tyranny. When used to shackle the mind they are, or at least should be, unspeakably odious to a free people." Test oaths are especially dangerous, he said, when they act retroactively to "impose pains and penalties for past lawful associations and utterances."

In a notable concurring opinion, Justice Frankfurter pointed out that a right of association is peculiarly characteristic of the American people. Joining an organization "is an exercise of the rights of free speech and free inquiry," which all Americans have but which teachers especially need to have. An unwarranted inhibition "upon the free spirit of teachers" affects not only those directly involved in litigation over legislation, but it also has "an unmistakable tendency to chill that free play of the spirit which all teachers ought especially to cultivate and practice; it makes for caution and timidity in their associations by potential teachers."

Democracy rests upon public opinion; but public opinion can be relied on only if it is disciplined and responsible; and public opinion can be disciplined and responsible "only if habits of open-mindedness and of critical inquiry are acquired in the formative years of our citizens"; and it is the special task of teachers and professors "to foster those habits of open-mindedness and critical inquiry which alone make for responsible citizens, who, in turn, make possible an enlightened and effective public opinion." How can teachers accomplish this task? Teachers, said Justice Frankfurter,

must fulfill their function by precept and practice, by the very atmosphere which they generate; they must be exemplars of open-mindedness and free inquiry. They cannot carry out their noble task if the conditions for the practice of a responsible and critical mind are denied to them. They must have the freedom of responsible inquiry, by thought and action, into the meaning of social and economic ideas, into the checkered history of social and economic dogma. They must be free to sift evanescent doctrine, qualified by time and circumstance, from that restless, enduring process of extending the bounds of understanding and wisdom, to assure which the freedom of thought, of speech, of inquiry, of worship are guaranteed by the Constitution.

To function properly, a university must be a center of independent thought; it must attract men of the greatest capacity, and encourage them to exercise their independent judgment, and afford them the freedom to think and to express themselves.

The spirit of Justice Frankfurter's concurring opinion would seem logically to put him on the side of Justices Black and Douglas; but, as we have seen in the *Adler* case, he was not willing to go so far as to declare the Feinberg Law and the regulations adopted to implement its provisions unconstitutional on their face.

Nor should the Court's insistence on scienter—that is, that membership in an organization named by the Attorney General as in some sense subversive must be with knowledge, at the time of membership, of the purpose and nature of the organization— be sufficient to validate the test oath under the broad principle of academic freedom as expounded by Justice Frankfurter; for the element of scienter involves a probing into the mind of the teacher as to what he knew, how much he knew, whom he knew, what he read, what periodicals he subscribed to or purchased, and possibly even an invasion into the privacy of his relations with his wife and other members of his family and their associations with persons suspected of having subversive opinions. As I see it, the element of scienter, present in the *Adler* case, should not have saved the statutory scheme constructed by New York State authorities. The majority in that case held, it will be recalled, that "one's associates, past and present," "may properly be considered in determining fitness and loyalty"; that there may be guilt by association, for "from time immemorial, one's reputation has been determined in part by the company he keeps"; that in passing on the fitness and loyalty of teachers, officials may consider "the organizations and persons with whom they [the teachers] associate."

I do not see how it is possible to achieve both ends simultaneously: preserve the teacher's freedom of association as an integral part of his right—and duty—of free inquiry, and yet make his position as a teacher dependent upon his ability to prove that his membership in an organization proscribed by the Attorney General was acquired and maintained with innocence of mind. Academic freedom—as broadly envisioned by Justices Frankfurter, Black, and Douglas—and guilt by association cannot both be maintained at the same time. One or the other must give way.

It should not be assumed, however, that, because the Supreme Court has found that guilt by association may constitutionally be used as a test of a teacher's fitness or loyalty, academic freedom has come to an end in the United States. The situation is much more complex than one would think from a mere analysis of legal concepts. While in recent years there have been many instances of successful and unsuccessful attempts to restrict academic freedom, never before have professors and teachers been as keenly aware of the meaning of academic freedom and of its important social role, and never before have they so valiantly and militantly stood up in its defense.[36] In their struggle they have found more solace and strength in the dissenting and concurring opinions of Justices Frankfurter, Black, and Douglas than in the decisions of the Court.

The loyalty oath, implemented by the device of finding guilt by association, has affected teachers and professors more than members of other callings—first, because they have frequently and invidiously been singled out for subjection to the oath by legislation aimed at them, and second, because, as Justice Frankfurter has explained, the nature of their vocation, if it is to serve the needs of a democratic society, calls for the largest measure of intellectual freedom. But others, too, have felt the impact of the legislative demand for anti-Communist oaths and affidavits.[37] We shall consider this subject briefly.

Except for the Oklahoma oath, which did not require scienter, the Supreme Court has upheld as constitutional every act requiring an anti-Communist oath or affidavit that has been challenged before that tribunal.

In 1951 the Court had before it a Maryland statute, interpreted as requiring that every candidate for public office, as a prerequisite to having his name appear on the ballot, file an affidavit that he is not knowingly a member of an organization engaged in an attempt, in one way or another, to overthrow government by force or violence. In a per curiam opinion the Court unanimously upheld the act as constitutional.[38]

A more difficult question came before the Court in the *Garner* case.[39] An ordinance of the City of Los Angeles required all city employees to swear that, within five years prior to the effective date of the law, they had not advocated or taught the overthrow of the government by force or violence or any other unlawful means, that they had not been members of or affiliated with any organization which advocated or taught the overthrow of government, and that they would not, while in the public service, advocate or teach the overthrow of government or join an organization that has this purpose. In addition, each employee was required to file an affidavit stating whether he is a member of the Communist Party, or if he was a member in the past, stating the years when he was a member. Some employees took the oath but refused to make the affidavit, and some refused to do either.

*As to the affidavit requirement,* seven members of the Court held this section of the ordinance valid on the ground that the city was not constitutionally forbidden to require its employees to disclose their past or present membership in the Communist Party. Whether the city might discharge an employee whose affidavit admitted past or present membership was not decided; but the Court probably would have sustained also the right of the city to discharge an employee for past or present membership.

"Past conduct," said Justice Clark for the Court, "may well relate to present fitness; past loyalty may have a reasonable relationship to present and future trust. Both are commonly inquired into in determining fitness for both high and low positions in private industry and are not less relevant in public employment."

*As to the oath requirement,* five members of the Court sustained this section of the ordinance against the objection that it was a bill of attainder, an ex post facto law, and that it deprived persons of freedom of speech and assembly and of the right to petition for redress of grievances. The essential points in Justice Clark's opinion which attempted to dispose of these objections were the following:

1. What was involved here was a law which set up standards of qualification and eligibility for public employment. No one who fails to meet the legal standards is "penalized," in any constitutional sense; he merely does not get or continue in a government job. Since bills of attainder and ex post facto laws are legislative enactments that impose "punishment," the ordinance does not fall into either of these categories.[40] A law may prescribe reasonable qualifications for a vocational pursuit, private or public in character, even though it may have the necessary effect of disqualifying some persons presently engaged in it.

2. As to the First Amendment guaranties, Justice Clark said that a government may seek to protect the integrity and competence of the public service, and to achieve this end it may regulate the political activities of its employees. Here the Court relied on its decision in the important *Mitchell* case,[41] which we shall consider at a later point in our discussion.

With respect to the decision regarding the affidavit requirement, only Justices Black and Douglas dissented; and as to the oath requirement decision, these two members of the Court, and Justices Frankfurter and Burton as well, dissented.

Justice Frankfurter dissented on the ground that the lack of scienter provisions in the oath rendered it a violation of due process, and that there was nothing in the record to warrant the Court's assumption that scienter would be a required element in the administration of the ordinance. Not only does the oath make an irrational demand, he said, but

it is bound to operate as a real deterrent to people contemplating even innocent associations. How can anyone be sure that an organization with which he affiliates will not at some time in the future be found by a State or National official to advocate overthrow of government by "unlawful means"? All but the hardiest may well hesitate to join organizations if they know that by such a proscrip-

tion they will be permanently disqualified from public employment. These are considerations that cut deep into the traditions
of our people. Gregariousness and friendliness are among the most
characteristic of American attitudes. Throughout our history they
have been manifested in "joining." . . .

The needs of security do not require such curbs on what may
well be innocuous feelings and associations. Such curbs are indeed
self-defeating. They are not merely unjustifiable restraints on individuals. They are not merely productive of an atmosphere of
repression uncongenial to the spiritual vitality of a democratic
society. The inhibitions which they engender are hostile to the best
conditions for securing a high-minded and high-spirited public
service.

All this is true, but the argument, as we have shown, can be
pushed one step further; for if scienter is required, so that only
guilty knowledge of the proscribed character of an organization
will disqualify a person from public employment, a person who
joins today an organization which, three years later, may be declared subversive, must begin to build up a record which will
later manifest his innocence; and instead of being an inactive
but sympathetic member, since he is merely a "joiner," he is
compelled to become an active member, so that he may possibly
recognize the first signs of subversion as they may manifest themselves in the organization. These are burdens which the average
mortal, preoccupied with the everyday demands of life, will find
it impossible to undertake or sustain. The effect in many instances must be to discourage free association, which the Constitution guaranties, and to produce "an atmosphere of repression uncongenial to the spiritual vitality of a democratic society."

It may be different when the ban is limited to the Communist
Party, at least for the reason that the employee knows the name
and the reputation of the organization that is proscribed, and
the prohibition does not run over to repress the exercise of his
constitutional freedom of association with regard to all other
groups.

The dissenting opinion of Justice Douglas relied heavily on

two cases that involved test oaths that were resorted to in the days of the Civil War. His views should be considered for the light they throw upon our contemporary situation.

In 1862 and 1865 Congress adopted legislation that provided that every person elected or appointed to any federal office, except the President, and that every lawyer who wished to practice in any federal court, shall take an oath that he never voluntarily bore arms against the United States, that he never gave counsel, aid, or encouragement to persons engaged in armed hostility against the United States, and that he never sought or held office or supported any authority or government in hostility to the United States.[42] The constitutionality of this legislation was attacked by Augustus Hill Garland, who sought the right to practice law in the federal courts although he could not take the legislative oath, for he had been a member of the Confederate House of Representatives and of the Confederate Senate.[43] The Supreme Court, in a notable opinion by Justice Field, declared the legislation unconstitutional.[44] Exclusion "from any of the professions or any of the ordinary avocations of life for past conduct," said Justice Field, "can be regarded in no other light than as punishment for such conduct." Enactments of this kind, said the Court, partake of the nature of bills of attainder or ex post facto legislation, for they either impose punishment for acts which were not punishable at the time they were committed, or they add a new punishment to the one previously prescribed. While a legislature may prescribe qualifications for the pursuit of any of the ordinary avocations of life, it may not, however, exercise this power as a means for the infliction of punishment.

In the other case to come before the Supreme Court involving test oaths, it appeared that the new Missouri Constitution of 1865 provided that every state or municipal official, attorney, and clergyman shall take an oath that he had always been loyal "on the side of the United States against all enemies thereof, foreign and domestic," and that he will always protect and defend "the Union of the United States" and will not allow its government to be destroyed or overthrown.[45] Taking office or performing official or professional functions without having taken the oath was declared a criminal offense. A priest of the Roman Catholic Church refused to take the oath and was convicted after he preached and taught in his church.

The Supreme Court held the test oath unconstitutional. Disqualification from office or from the pursuit of a lawful profession or vocation is, the Court held, a punishment; and the Missouri law imposed a punishment for an act which was not punishable under Missouri law at the time it was committed, or at least imposed an additional punishment to what had previously been prescribed; the test oath law was, therefore, an ex post facto law; it was also a bill of attainder. Justice Field, in his opinion for the Court, made the following notable statement:

The theory upon which our political institutions rest is, that all men have certain inalienable rights—that among these are life, liberty and the pursuit of happiness; and that in the pursuit of happiness all avocations, all honors, all positions, are alike open to everyone, and that in the protection of these rights all are equal before the law. Any deprivation or suspension of any of these rights for past conduct is punishment, and can be in no otherwise defined.

Counsel for the state contended that "punishment" is a term restricted to the deprivation of life, liberty, or property. This contention was expressly denied by the Court: it embraces also deprivation or suspension of political or civil rights.

Furthermore, said Justice Field, the state laws in question

subvert the presumptions of innocence, and alter the rules of evidence, which heretofore, under the universally recognized principles of the common law, have been supposed to be fundamental and unchangeable. They assume that the parties are guilty; they call upon the parties to establish their innocence; and they declare that such innocence can be shown only in one way—by an inquisition, in the form of an expurgatory oath, in the consciences of the parties.

Punishment can follow only conviction in a court of law; it cannot follow, said the Court, a mere refusal to take an oath. Otherwise, said the Court, quoting Alexander Hamilton, it would mean to invert the order of things; and, instead of obliging the State to prove the guilt [in a court], in order to inflict the penalty, it was to oblige the citizen to establish his own innocence to avoid the penalty. It was to excite scruples in the honest and conscientious, and to hold out a bribe to perjury. . . . It substitutes for the established and legal mode of investigating crimes and inflicting forfeitures, one that is unknown to the Constitution, and repugnant to the genius of our law.

In the *Garner* case, said Justice Douglas, we find, too, that "the presumption of guilt can only be removed by the expurgatory oath." There was no essential difference between the Los Angeles law and the laws that came before the Court in the years immediately after the Civil War. Yet in 1951 the Court was able to say: "We are unable to conclude that punishment is imposed by a general regulation which merely provides standards of qualification and eligibility for employment." Did the post–Civil War laws do anything other than "merely" provide "standards of qualification and eligibility for employment"? While the Court in the *Garner* case did not expressly overrule the *Garland* and *Cummings* decisions, the effect is the same, and this effect is, I believe, indeed unfortunate.

If the *Garner* case may be spoken of as a whirlwind, we may say that the wind was sown by Justice Holmes in an opinion he wrote in 1892, when he was a member of the Supreme Judicial Court of Massachusetts. The mayor of New Bedford had removed a policeman for violating a police regulation that prohibited members of the police force from soliciting funds for political purposes and from serving on political committees. The policeman contended that the regulation violated his right to express his political opinions. In upholding the mayor, Justice Holmes wrote for the court: "The petitioner may have a constitutional right to talk politics, but he has no constitutional right to be a policeman. There are few employments for hire in which the servant does not agree.to suspend his constitutional right of free speech, as well as of idleness. . . . The servant cannot complain, as he takes the employment on the terms which are offered him." [46]

This reasoning provided at least a part of the rationale of the decision in the *Douds* case: A union may have a constitutional right to choose Communists as its officers, but it does not have a constitutional right to enjoy the privileges offered to unions by an act of Congress; the union accepts the privileges on the terms which are offered it by Congress.

Does this mean that government may offer rights and privileges on any conditions, no matter how offensive they may be? The Court has said that it would not go so far, but it has failed to draw a definite line beyond which Congress or the agencies of government may not go.

The Hatch Political Activities Act makes it unlawful for employees in the executive branch of the Federal Government to take any active part in political management or in political campaigns, out of, as well as in, working hours,[47] and a regulation of the Civil Service Commission makes such conduct ground for removal of civil service employees. In the leading case involving the constitutionality of this act, the *Mitchell* case, it appeared that George P. Poole was a roller in the Mint—an industrial worker who in his job was remote from contact with the public or from policy making; but off hours he was a ward executive committeeman of a political party, and on election day was active as a worker at the polls.[48] Could Poole be disciplined for these violations of the Hatch Act? The Court held that Poole's activities subjected him to disciplinary sanctions.

In his opinion for the Court, Justice Reed said that, under the Bill of Rights, Poole had the right, as a citizen, to act as a party official or worker to further his own political views; but Congress had the right to prohibit such activities by government employees during their working hours or during their free time; and the Court will not review the judgment of Congress that such a prohibition was necessary. "Of course," said Justice Reed, "it is accepted constitutional doctrine that these fundamental human rights are not absolutes. . . . Again this Court must balance the extent of the guarantees of freedom against a congressional enactment to protect a democratic society against the supposed evil of political partisanship by classified employees of government." Apart from the exercise of political privileges such as the ballot, Congress may require political neutrality for classified public servants in the interests of efficiency.

Poole argued that, since he was protected by the Bill of Rights, Congress may not provide that no Republican, Jew, or Negro shall be appointed to federal office, or that no federal employee shall attend Mass, or that he may not take an active part in missionary work. "None," commented Justice Reed,

would deny such limitations on congressional power but, because there are some limitations, it does not follow that a prohibition against acting as ward leader or worker at the polls is invalid. . . . For regulation of employees it is not necessary that the act regulated be anything more than an act reasonably deemed by Congress to interfere with the efficiency of the public service. . . . Congress may regulate the political conduct of Government employees "within reasonable limits," even though the regulation trenches to some extent upon unfettered political action.

Courts will interfere only when the regulation passes "beyond the general existing conception of governmental power." Where does this "conception of governmental power" come from? It develops, said Justice Reed, from "practice, history, and changing educational, social and economic conditions."

Dissenting, Justice Black pointed out that millions of persons [49] were prohibited by law from taking part in campaigns "that may bring about changes in their lives, their fortunes, and their happiness." All they could do legally was vote in silence, "carefully and quietly express a political opinion at their peril," and be silent spectators at campaign gatherings; but democratic government must contemplate, permit, and encourage "much wider political activity by all the people." Laws which limit the First Amendment freedoms, he said,

should be narrowly drawn to meet the evil aimed at and to affect only the minimum number of people imperatively necessary to prevent a grave and imminent danger to the public. . . . Legislation which muzzles several million citizens threatens popular government, not only because it injures the individuals muzzled, but also because of its harmful effect on the body politic in depriving it of the political participation and interest of such a large segment of our citizens. . . .

There is nothing about federal and state employees as a class which justifies depriving them or society of the benefits of their participation in public affairs. . . . I think the Constitution guarantees to them the same right that other groups of good citizens have to engage in activities which decide who their elected representatives shall be. . . .

It is argued that it is in the interest of clean politics to suppress political activities of federal and state employees. It would hardly seem to be imperative to muzzle millions of citizens because some of them, if left their constitutional freedoms, might corrupt the political process.

If, said Justice Black, facts would show that some persons in high government positions might coerce their subordinates along political lines, then laws can be drawn to punish coercion, or to prohibit political activities by officials in positions of power over subordinates, but the Hatch Act is not so limited— it punishes millions of employees and deprives the nation of their contribution to public affairs.

Justice Douglas said that constitutionally Congress might prohibit political activities by administrative employees— those "who have access to the files, who meet the public, who arrange appointments, who prepare the basic data on which policy decisions are made." But there is no reason for putting industrial workers under the ban.[50] Political rights are too basic and fundamental in our society to be sacrificed or qualified "for anything short of a clear and present danger to the civil service system." In the absence of a clear and present danger, their "political sterilization" and their relegation to second-class citizenship is a violation of the First Amendment freedoms.

The net result of the cases involving restrictions on the exercise of basic freedoms by public employees is that the Government and the states may go as far as they like in imposing such restrictions, in conditioning employment upon the surrender of basic freedoms, as long as the restrictions do not impress the Court as being "patently arbitrary or discriminatory." This is how the principle was stated for the Court by Justice Clark: "We need not pause to consider whether an abstract right of public employment exists. It is sufficient to say that constitutional protection does extend to the public servant whose exclusion pursuant to a statute is patently arbitrary or discriminatory." [51]

The harmful degrees to which this principle has been carried by the courts may be illustrated by the case of *Bailey v. Richardson*,[52] which involved the procedures of loyalty review boards under the federal security program, and the impact of these procedures on fundamental constitutional freedoms.

Congress in 1939 provided that it shall be unlawful for any person employed by the Federal Government to have membership in any political group which advocates the overthrow of our constitutional form of government in the United States; and if already employed, such person was to be immediately removed from his position.[53] Starting with 1941, every appropriation act has carried the provision that no part of any appropriation is to be used to pay the salary or wages of any person who advocates, or is a member of any organization that advocates, the overthrow of the Government of the United States by force or violence. Also in 1941 the Civil Service Commission issued a regulation which provided that a person may be disqualified for appointment or for examination if there exists a reasonable doubt as to his loyalty.[54]

The next important development came in 1947 with the issuance of Executive Order 9835 by President Truman, which provided for formal loyalty procedures and for the dismissal of an employee from the service of the Federal Government if "on all the evidence, reasonable grounds exist for the belief that the person involved is disloyal to the Government of the United States." [55] In 1951 this order was amended by President Truman to require dismissal if on the whole record there was "a reasonable doubt as to the loyalty of the person involved to the Government of the United States." [56] Under this amendment it was thought that dismissal would be more easily effected.

In 1953 President Eisenhower issued an executive order which did away with "loyalty" as a test and substituted in its place "security." [57] This order provided that an employee was to be dismissed if his employment "may not be clearly consistent with the interest of the national security." The order was to cover all "security risks" for whatever ground—any "criminal,

infamous, dishonest, immoral, or notoriously disgraceful conduct, habitual use of intoxicants to excess, drug addiction, or
sexual perversion," as well as commission of "any act of sabotage, espionage, treason, or sedition," or membership in "or
affiliation or sympathetic association with" any group or combination of persons "which is totalitarian, Fascist, Communist,
or subversive." This order was soon amended to provide an
additional "security risk"; namely, "refusal by the individual,
upon the ground of constitutional privilege against self-incrimination, to testify before a congressional committee regarding charges of his alleged disloyalty or other misconduct." [58]

The *Bailey* case came up under President Truman's executive
order of 1947, but in all its essential aspects the case would
have been the same had it come up under any of the executive
orders subsequently made. In 1949 Dorothy Bailey was dismissed from a nonsensitive position as a loyalty risk after a
hearing before the Loyalty Review Board at which no one
testified against her and at which no affidavits against her were
presented for the record. Miss Bailey testified in her own
behalf and presented some seventy supporting affidavits. She
was not given the names of those who had informed against
her.

In sustaining the Government's refusal to reinstate her, the
United States court of appeals held that, except insofar as
legislation may impose limitations, government employees
"hold office at the pleasure of the appointing authority." An
applicant for appointment to government service "has no constitutional right to a hearing or a specification of the reasons
why he is not appointed." Nor is "mere dismissal" from government service "punishment" in a constitutional sense; nor is
"dismissal for suspicion of disloyalty" an exception entitling
the person to confrontation of witnesses or other rights.

The dismissal did not, said the court, impinge on the employee's First Amendment freedoms, for

the plain hard fact is that so far as the Constitution is concerned
there is no prohibition against the dismissal of Government employees because of their political beliefs, activities or affiliations. . . .
The situation of the Government employee is not different in this

respect from that of private employees. A newspaper editor has a constitutional right to speak and write as he pleases. But the Constitution does not guarantee him a place in the columns of a publisher with whose political views he does not agree. . . .

The clear and present danger rule does not help us in this matter, because Government employ[ment] . . . is not a right. . . . No one denies Miss Bailey the right to any political activity or affiliation she may choose. What is denied her is Government employ-[ment].

It was contended for Miss Bailey that without a judicial hearing, the Government had no right to label her a loyalty risk, and thus seriously impair her chances of finding lucrative employment. The court answered this charge by saying that "it has long been established that if the Government, in the exercise of a governmental power, injures an individual, that individual has no redress." Since she has no constitutional right to her job, and the executive officers had power to dismiss her, the fact that she was injured gave her no right to redress. "It is our clear opinion," said the court, "that the President, absent congressional restriction, may remove from Government service any person of whose loyalty he is not completely convinced. He may do so without assigning any reason and without giving the employee any explanatory notice."

Dissenting, Judge Edgerton contended that "dismissal for disloyalty is punishment and requires all the safeguards of a judicial trial." [59] Dismissal for incompetence or for some other reason—such as to make room for members of the party that was successful in the election—or for no reason at all, is not punishment; but dismissal for wrong conduct or for wrong views is punishment; for a "person dismissed as disloyal can obtain no normal employment, public or private." Miss Bailey was, therefore, entitled to all the safeguards of a judicial trial, including trial by jury, clear information of the charges against her, and confrontation of accusing witnesses.

Miss Bailey's dismissal, said Judge Edgerton, abridged her freedom of speech and assembly. He said that Justice Holmes's famous statement that "the petitioner may have a constitutional right to talk politics, but he has no constitutional right to be a policeman," was a great oversimplification. In the granting of a privilege, the Government may not impose conditions which require the surrender of constitutional freedoms; e.g., Congress may not condition the grant of a second-class mailing privilege on the requirement that certain economic or political ideas shall not be disseminated. "Similarly, the premise that government employment is a privilege does not support the conclusion that it may be granted on condition that certain economic or political ideas not be entertained."

Judge Edgerton pointed out that in loyalty hearings employees have been asked questions such as the following:

Do you read a good many books?
What books do you read?
What magazines do you read?
What newspapers do you buy or subscribe to?
Do you think that Russian Communism is likely to succeed?
How do you explain the fact that you have an album of Paul Robeson records in your home?
Do you ever entertain Negroes in your home?
Did you ever write a letter to the Red Cross about the segregation of the blood?

Government employees, he said, have been put "under economic and social pressure to protect their jobs and reputations by expressing in words and conduct only the most orthodox opinions on political, economic and social questions." The loss of employment, reputation, and earning power involves a very substantial restriction on the free exercise of fundamental freedoms. Here, Miss Bailey's freedom of thought as well as freedom of speech had been invaded—she was dismissed, said Judge Edgerton, "for thinking prohibited thoughts." Furthermore, her dismissal attributed to her guilt by association, and thus she was denied the freedom of assembly guaranteed by the First Amendment. She was believed to be a member or an associate of the Communist Party. "Undoubtedly many such persons are disloyal in every sense to the government of the United States." But "beliefs are personal and not a matter of mere association." To interdict all members of a "named political party" is an abridgment of free speech, press, and assembly. Judge Edgerton concluded his opinion with these words:

Even if her services were on the whole undesirable, to oust her as disloyal on rumor and without trial is to pay too much for protection against such harm as she could do in such a job. The cost is too great in morale and efficiency of government workers, in appeal of government employment to independent and inquiring minds, and in public confidence in democracy. But even if such dismissals strengthened the government instead of weakening it, they would still cost too much in constitutional rights. We cannot preserve our liberties by sacrificing them.

By an equally divided vote the Supreme Court affirmed the decision of the court of appeals. The judgment of the latter court, which substantially narrows the constitutional freedoms of a government worker—freedoms which other citizens may enjoy—remains the law of the land.

That nongovernment workers have a larger measure of constitutional freedom than have government workers has been made clear by the decision of United States court of appeals in *Parker v. Lester*,[60] which the Government decided not to appeal.

During the Korean war, and acting under authority of an act of Congress and an executive order,[61] the Coast Guard adopted regulations that seamen should not be employed on American merchant vessels unless they had validated documents which the Commandant of the Coast Guard was not to issue "unless the Commandant is satisfied that the character and habits of life of such person are such as to authorize the belief that the presence of the individual on board would not be inimical to the security of the United States." The Coast Guard was not required to disclose the sources of information, nor to disclose its data with such specificity that the identity of informers could be inferred. In brief, the procedures of the Coast Guard to screen persons who sought private employment on merchant vessels was substantially the same as that described in the *Bailey* case as applicable to government employees. But the court in the *Parker* case decided that the security procedures for the screening of private employees fell short of constitutional standards. The court distinguished private from public employment:

The liberty to follow their chosen employment is no doubt a right more clearly entitled to constitutional protection than the right of a government employee to obtain or retain his job. It has been suggested that the latter is not entitled to protection of the due process clause. *Bailey v. Richardson.* . . . Even the alien lawfully residing in the United States is entitled to this protection. . . . The plaintiffs here are citizens of the United States and the rights and liberties which they assert relate not to any public employment present or prospective, but to their right to pursue their chosen vocations as merchant seamen.

The court relied heavily on the decision of the Supreme Court in *Truax v. Raich,* in which it was held that a state may not deny to aliens (a fortiori to citizens) the ordinary means of earning a livelihood.[62] "It requires no argument to show," said the Court, "that the right to work for a living in the common occupations of the community is of the very essence of the personal freedom and opportunity that it was the purpose of the [Fourteenth] Amendment to secure."

Certainly, said the court in the *Parker* case, the Government has the right to provide for the screening of persons who are security risks on merchant vessels; but the question is: "Is this system of secret informers, whisperers and tale-bearers of such vital importance to the public welfare that it must be preserved at the cost of denying to the citizen even a modicum of the protection traditionally associated with due process?" The court answered this question with an emphatic "No." A process directed to the prevention of future misconduct rather than the punishment of crimes already committed must include the right to know a charge, to be confronted with the accusers, to cross-examine informers, and to produce evidence in one's behalf; otherwise our system will be no different from the Nazi and Communist systems of "protective custody." Just as officials are not helpless to go out and procure proofs for criminal prosecutions, so, too, officials are not prevented from procuring proofs when screening security risks. The burden on officials may be greater if they will need to respect the constitutional rights of citizens, but "surely it is better that these agencies suffer some handicap than that the citizens of a freedom loving country shall be denied that which has always been considered their birthright."

The court pointed out that if the procedures respecting merchant seamen are constitutional, then the same procedures could be applied to millions of other workers—e.g., the enginemen and trainmen hauling the cargo to the docks, railroad track and bridge inspectors, switchmen and dispatchers, workers in shipping rooms of factories, all workers on transportation facilities and on docks.

The impact of the security procedures on First Amendment freedoms was considered by the court:

Furthermore, in considering the public interest in the preservation of a system under which unidentified informers are encouraged to make unchallengeable statements about their neighbors, it is not amiss to bear in mind whether or not we must look forward to a day when substantially every one will have to contemplate the possibility that his neighbors are being encouraged to make reports to the FBI about what he says, what he reads and what meetings he attends. . . . But the time has not come when we have to abandon a system of liberty for one modeled on that of the Communists. Such a system was not that ordained by the framers of our Constitution. It is the latter we are sworn to uphold.

It should be clear from this statement, as well as from Judge Edgerton's dissenting opinion in the *Bailey* case,[63] that there is an intimate relation between procedural due process and the First Amendment freedoms. A whittling down of due process can easily undermine the constitutional freedoms of speech, press, and assembly. If persons in private employment are entitled to these freedoms, it is hard to see why government workers are expected to forfeit them.

Furthermore, if "the right to work for a living in the common occupations of the community" is constitutionally protected, why should government employment be viewed differently? In 1956 there were about 56,000,000 people engaged in nonagricultural civilian employment; of this number, 2,350,000 were civilian employees of the Federal Government, and about another 5,000,000 persons worked for state and local governments. This means that about 13 per cent of our nonagricultural civilian labor force were in public jobs.[64] The federal establishment includes over sixty great and varied enterprises; its work force possesses fifteen thousand different basic skills; and nearly one-third of all federal employees are industrial type, blue-collar, hourly-pay employees.[65] In the light of these facts, can public employment rationally be excluded from "the common occupations of the community"? Hundreds of thousands of our young men and women attend our colleges and universities to prepare themselves for a career in the public service. Why should we assume that by choosing the public service they intend to give up freedoms which, in American theory, are thought to be "unalienable"?

In 1956, twelve states and thirty-two cities had fair employment laws barring discrimination in employment; [66] and since 1935 we have had federal laws that substantially limit the power of employers to impose on their workers terms and conditions of employment on a take-it-or-leave-it basis. A person may not have a constitutional right to a particular job or in a particular shop, but many laws nonetheless give him an opportunity to be considered fairly when a job is available, and give him an opportunity to have a voice in establishing the conditions under which he will be employed. In American theory, private property and private enterprise are not derivative from government; on the contrary, government has been instituted to protect property and business; yet we have imposed sharp restrictions on the businessman in order to give more rights to his workers. On the other hand, in American theory government is derivative from the will of the people and has only delegated powers, as an agent or servant of the people; it is the recipient, rather than the source, of rights and powers; yet we hesitate to say that there are restrictions on the powers of government in its capacity as an employer, as if it were the master and not the servant of the people—with the paradoxical result of decisions as in the *Bailey* case, which was decided against the government employee, and the *Parker* case, which was decided in favor of the private employee.

The Bill of Rights marks off an area into which government may not enter. This should mean that the Government, when it exercises a power delegated to it by the Constitution, has no right to set up "privileges" and condition their enjoyment on relinquishment by the citizen of freedoms preserved for him by the Bill of Rights. The Government ought not to have the right to say: "All freedoms abandon, ye who enter here!"

The position taken by the Supreme Court in the *Douds* case that, "when the effect of a statute or ordinance upon the exercise of First Amendment freedoms is relatively small and the public interest to be protected is substantial, it is obvious that a rigid test requiring a showing of imminent danger to the security of the nation is an absurdity," if taken seriously and if made into a rule of conduct for the governing of men by the various branches and agencies of government, would reduce the First Amendment to almost a nullity. Our constitutional guide must be the conviction that ways can be found to protect the public interest without invading the fundamental freedoms of Americans, whether the invasion be large or small, whether the number of Americans affected by the invasion be large or small. It is not enough for Congress to show that "reasonable grounds" exist for enactment of a law that will affect First Amendment freedoms; it ought to be compelled to show that there is no other way to protect the public interest, and that the specific public interest is more important than the sacrifice of the freedom in question. If this means giving the Bill of Rights a "preferred" position in the Constitution, then so be it. Any other position given the Bill of Rights exposes it to gradual reduction to a mere rule of reason, which would hardly be more than a plea to Congress and the other instruments of government to practice moderation, not to hurt too many people, not to make big invasions into basic freedoms. But here one recalls Maeterlinck's observation:

Let us not say to ourselves that the best truth always lies in moderation, in the decent average. . . . The average, the decent moderation of today, will be the least human of things tomorrow. At the time of the Spanish Inquisition, the opinion of good sense and of the good medium was certainly that people ought not to burn too large a number of heretics; extreme and unreasonable opinion obviously demanded that they should burn none at all.

If the *Douds* decision points toward "decent moderation," the test of "not too much," [67] it is the expression, I would say, of a disposition toward lukewarmness in an area where we should find "roses and raptures" rather than "lillies and languors." It may be that Emerson was right when he said that "most of the great results of history are brought about by discreditable means," [68] though I doubt it; but certainly the meaning of the Bill of Rights is that government in the United States may not use "discreditable means" to achieve commendable results, and that invasions of basic freedoms are "discreditable means" and are always instances of excess and never of moderation.

PART III

# Freedom of Speech, Press, and Assembly: The Clear and Present Danger Doctrine

# The Original Meaning
# of the Doctrine

IN PRECEDING pages we discussed conflicts between, on the one hand, speech, press, and assembly, and, on the other hand, competing interests protected by the state, such as the interest in privacy, reputation, public peace, and order. We also discussed the constitutional prohibition upon previous restraint or censorship, and upon "taxes on knowledge." With respect to these and the other matters we have considered, the scope of the protection of speech, press, and assembly offered by the Constitution was not ordinarily tested by the clear and present danger standard—libel and slander, group libel, privacy, obscenity, fighting words, picketing, and other situations we have considered are settled by doctrines or reasons more or less peculiar to such situations, to which the clear and present danger doctrine has no relevance.[1] We shall now consider the conception of freedom of speech, press, and assembly as understood in the light of this doctrine. This will involve us in an area in which freedom of speech, press, and assembly is asserted for the unmolested dissemination of unpopular economic, political, and social views, where the conflict often is between freedom and national security.

The wide scope of our discussion of free speech and press up to this point discloses how little has been left for disposition by the clear and present danger doctrine. Most problems in this area are settled without reference to this doctrine. And the meaning and importance of the clear and present danger doctrine have been whittled down substantially even in the instances where it concededly has relevance.

In the light of the types of cases with regard to which the doctrine is irrelevant, and in the light of the fact that in the situations in which the doctrine is relevant it is not very significant, the doctrine has lost most of its "punch." It no longer occupies the center of interest in an analysis of the constitutional law regarding the First Amendment freedoms. The exceptions to the rule are today more important than the rule itself. If what is excluded from the clear and present danger doctrine is the tail, and the doctrine is the dog, then the tail wags the dog; but the doctrine is not even the dog. Today no doctrine can be said to be the dog. In this area, the Supreme Court is literally not doctrinaire; it decides issues as they arise, often by divided vote, and often without resort to broad doctrines. Justices Black and Douglas stand in awe of the Bill of Rights; the other members of the Court tend to create the impression that they are too sophisticated and worldly-wise to stand in awe of anything—to stand in awe of anything, that is, but the tremendous power of the other branches of the Government. The rule for themselves is self-denial of power. But they hesitate to impose the same rule on the legislative and executive branches, fearing, I suppose, that holding the others to the rule of self-denial of power would involve the assertion of power by the Court; and the Court is afraid of asserting power, knowing that it could be checked, or that its prestige could be lessened by malicious attacks, and that in either case the Rule of Law would be weakened.

Of course the Supreme Court could be checked, but not easily. The Court-packing adventure of Franklin D. Roosevelt demonstrated to him and to the country that while the power to check the Court theoretically exists, the countervailing forces are great, and are perhaps insurmountable. The most serious challenge to the power of the Court has come from the Southern

States and not from Congress or the President; but these states challenge the power of the Federal Government and not only of the Court; they stand in the way of enactment of civil rights laws no less than of the enforcement of a court decree.

A hundred years ago, John Stuart Mill wrote with wonderful perspicacity, in his essay *On Liberty,* that the disposition of mankind is "to impose their own opinions and inclinations as a rule of conduct on others," and that this disposition is "hardly ever kept under restraint by anything but want of power"; and since "the power is not declining, but growing, unless a strong barrier of moral conviction can be raised against the mischief, we must expect, in the present circumstances of the world, to see it increase." In our system of government, the Bill of Rights can be that "strong barrier of moral conviction." If it is not that, it is nothing. But if it is that, then it marks off an area where government may not trespass; and when it does trespass, a self-denial of power by the Court means a validation of power in the trespasser; and then our system of checks and balances works in only one way—the Court is checked, but the other branches of the Government, while they may check and balance one another, and may threaten to check the Court, themselves remain unchecked by the Court—unchecked by the Bill of Rights, unchecked by the "strong barrier of moral conviction" the Bill of Rights should be.

These considerations should be helpful as we turn to a consideration of the clear and present danger doctrine.

In an important opinion in *Whitney v. California,*[2] written with the concurrence of Justice Holmes, Justice Brandeis formulated the clear and present danger doctrine in the following terms: The "fundamental rights"—such as "the right of free speech, the right to teach, and the right of assembly" —he said,

may not be denied or abridged. But, although the rights of free speech and assembly [which were involved in the case before the Court] are fundamental, they are not in their nature absolute. Their exercise is subject to their restriction, if the particular restriction proposed is required in order to protect the state from destruction or from serious injury, political, economic or moral. . . . The necessity which is essential to a valid restriction does not exist unless speech would produce, or is intended to produce, a clear and imminent danger of some substantive evil which the state constitutionally may seek to prevent.

Where the restriction upon speech or assembly follows from a statute, adopted by the legislature because of its conviction that the exercise of the right to speech or assembly creates a clear and present danger of substantive evil, the Court is not bound by the legislative findings—"the enactment of the statute," said Justice Brandeis, "cannot alone establish the facts which are essential to its validity." The Court must determine for itself whether the prohibitory legislation was in fact necessary; and it is not bound or controlled by the fact that a vast majority of a state's citizens believe that the dissemination of certain doctrines is "fraught with evil consequences." It is not enough to sustain a restriction on free speech to show that a majority of the citizens, acting through their representatives, feared serious injury unless the restriction were imposed; for at one time "man feared witches and burned women. It is the function of speech to free men from the bondage of irrational fears."

To justify, constitutionally, suppression of free speech, said Brandeis, there must be "reasonable ground to fear that serious evil will result if free speech is practiced; reasonable ground to believe that the danger apprehended is imminent; reasonable ground to believe that the evil to be prevented is a serious one."

Suppose the statute is directed toward the suppression or punishment of speech that has as its purpose propagation of the idea that certain laws should be violated, that certain criminal acts should be accomplished? With respect to this problem, Brandeis distinguished advocacy from incitement, and said that

even advocacy of violation, however reprehensible morally, is not a justification for denying free speech where the advocacy falls short of incitement and there is nothing to indicate that the advocacy would be immediately acted on. The wide difference between advocacy and incitement, between preparation and attempt, between assembling and conspiracy, must be borne in mind.

Moreover, even if it is shown that the speech has created an imminent or immediate danger, that alone is not sufficient to sustain the restriction or punishment; for it must also be shown that the feared evil is "relatively serious";—society may not limit free speech merely to avert "a relatively trivial harm to society."

In a word, only an emergency can justify a limitation on the right of speech and press. Said Justice Brandeis:

Those who won our independence by revolution were not cowards. They did not fear political change. They did not exalt order at the cost of liberty. To courageous, self-reliant men, with confidence in the power of free and fearless reasoning applied through the processes of popular government, no danger flowing from speech can be deemed clear and present, unless the incidence of the evil apprehended is so imminent that it may befall before there is opportunity for full discussion. If there be time to expose through discussion the falsehood and fallacies, to avert the evil by the processes of education, the remedy to be applied is more speech, not enforced silence. Only an emergency can justify repression. Such must be the rule if authority is to be reconciled with freedom. Such, in my opinion, is the command of the Constitution. It is, therefore, always open to Americans to challenge a law abridging free speech and assembly by showing that there was no emergency justifying it.

This may be taken to be a statement of the doctrine in its "classic" form, as expressed by Justices Holmes and Brandeis. In practice it meant that a defendant had the right to challenge a statute as an unconstitutional abridgment of his freedom of speech, press, or assembly, and to ask the court or jury to decide "whether there actually did exist at the time a clear danger; whether the danger, if any, was imminent; and whether the evil apprehended was one so substantial as to justify the stringent restriction imposed by the legislature."

# ☆ 26 ☆

# History of the Doctrine

ACCORDING to Justice Rutledge,[1] the first official declaration of the clear and present danger doctrine may have been Jefferson's statement in the Virginia Statute for Establishing Religious Freedom (1786), "that it is time enough for the rightful purposes of civil government, for its officers to interfere when principles break out into overt acts against peace and good order."[2] Clearly related to this statement is the passage in *Notes on Virginia* (1801) in which Jefferson says that government has authority only over such "natural rights as we have submitted to them"; and

the rights of conscience we never submitted, we could not submit. We are answerable for them to our God. The legitimate powers of government extend to such acts only as are injurious to others. But it does me no injury for my neighbor to say there are twenty Gods or no God. It neither picks my pocket nor breaks my leg.[3]

Similarly relevant is Jefferson's statement in his famous "wall of separation between Church and State" letter (1802), "that the legislative powers of the Government reach actions only, and not opinions."[4]

As a lawyer, Jefferson would have had to admit that, while it may not injure me if my neighbor says there are twenty gods, he does, in a sense, pick my pocket if he calls me a thief, and he does in a sense, break my leg if he calls me a moral pervert.

Here words, opinions, or principles have become overt acts, actions, which the law may reach. But apart from instances of libel and slander and fighting words, and similar cases that we have already considered, in which words themselves are actionable because the law assimilates them to actions, Jefferson envisaged a broad area in which government would have no power to concern itself with a person's words or opinions; however, he made no effort to treat this problem systematically and in such a way that the courts could make effective use of constitutional principles that would clearly mark off words from acts. Intent primarily to achieve freedom of religion, Jefferson took a stand in favor of freedom of speech, press, assembly, and religion and argued that "reason and free inquiry are the only effectual agents against error." Reason and free inquiry are "the natural enemies of error, and of error only. . . . It is error alone which needs the support of government. Truth can stand by itself." [5]

Holmes's belief in "free trade in ideas" was explicitly avowed by Jefferson; and before Jefferson, by John Milton; but the clear and present danger doctrine was only vaguely foreshadowed by Jefferson. It was Justice Holmes who first formulated the doctrine as a principle of constitutional law.

It was not until 1919, in *Schenck v. United States,* that Holmes first formulated the doctrine; [6] but the basis for it was prepared in his mind some forty years before, in his lectures at the Lowell Institute in Boston, that were published in 1881 as *The Common Law.* [7]

In his second lecture, in which he was concerned with uncovering the roots of the criminal law, he came to grips with the concept "intent." To prove murder, says Holmes, it is enough to show knowledge that the act will probably cause death; intent in such a case is foresight of the consequences of the act; foresight, however, is not what this very criminal foresaw, but what a man of reasonable prudence would have foreseen. A man is chargeable with the reasonable inferences, whether he draws them or not; e.g., if a workman on a housetop in midday knows that the space below is a city street, and if he throws down a heavy beam, and a death is caused, he is guilty

of murder, for a person of ordinary prudence would have foreseen the consequence of the act, and so the workman must be
dealt with "as if he foresaw it, whether he does so in fact or
not." But the law may go further.

If certain acts are regarded as peculiarly dangerous under certain
circumstances [e.g., abduction of a girl under sixteen], a legislator
may make them punishable if done under these circumstances, although the danger was not generally known. The law often takes
this step. . . . It sometimes goes even further, and requires a man
to find out facts, as well as to foresee future harm, at his peril,
although they are not such as would necessarily be inferred from
the facts known.

A man may have every right to make a fire if one takes into
account only the immediate consequences of his act; but the
act becomes arson "by reason of more remote consequences
which were manifestly likely to follow, whether they were
actually intended or not."

*Intent,* actual or imputed, however, is not itself criminal.
"The law deals only with conduct." An *attempt,* however, is
conduct, is "an overt act." Therefore, if an act is done, "of
which the natural and probable effect under the circumstances
is the accomplishment of a substantive crime, the criminal law
. . . can hardly abstain altogether from punishing it, on any
theory. . . . Acts should be judged by their tendency under the
known circumstances, not by the actual intent which accompanies them."

At this point Holmes makes observations in a very significant
passage, which I feel compelled to quote in full:

Some acts may be attempts or misdemeanors which could not
have effected the crime unless followed by other acts on the part of
the wrong-doer. For instance, lighting a match with intent to set
fire to a haystack has been held to amount to a criminal attempt
to burn it, although the defendant blew out the match on seeing
that he was watched. So the purchase of dies for making counterfeit coin is a misdemeanor, although of course the coin would not
be counterfeited unless the dies were used.

In such cases the law goes on a new principle, different from that
governing most substantive crimes. The reason for punishing any

act must generally be to prevent some harm which is foreseen as likely to follow that act under the circumstances in which it is done. In most substantive crimes the ground on which that likelihood stands is the common working of natural causes as shown by experience. But when an act is punished the natural effect of which is not harmful under the circumstances, that ground alone will not suffice. The probability does not exist unless there are grounds for expecting that the act done will be followed by other acts in connection with which its effect will be harmful, although not so otherwise. But as in fact no such acts have followed, it cannot, in general, be assumed, from the mere doing of what has been done, that they would have followed if the actor had not been interrupted. They would not have followed it unless the actor had chosen, and the only way generally available to show that he would have chosen to do them is by showing that he intended to do them when he did what he did. The accompanying intent in that case renders the otherwise innocent act harmful, because it raises a probability that it will be followed by such other acts and events as will all together result in harm. The importance of the intent is not to show that the act was wicked, but to show that it was likely to be followed by hurtful consequences.

It will be readily seen that there are limits to this kind of liability. The law does not punish every act which is done with the intent to bring about a crime. If a man starts from Boston to Cambridge for the purpose of committing a murder when he gets there, but is stopped by the draw and goes home, he is no more punishable than if he had sat in his chair and resolved to shoot somebody, but on second thoughts had given up the notion. On the other hand, a slave who ran after a white woman, but desisted before he caught her, has been convicted of an attempt to commit rape. We have seen what amounts to an attempt to burn a haystack; but it was said in the same case, that, if the defendant had gone no further than to buy a box of matches for the purpose, he would not have been liable.

Eminent judges have been puzzled where to draw the line, or even to state the principle on which it would be drawn, between the two sets of cases. But the principle is believed to be similar to that on which all other lines are drawn by the law. Public policy, that is to say, legislative considerations, are at the bottom of the matter; the considerations being, in this case, *the nearness of the danger, the greatness of the harm, and the degree of apprehension felt.* When a man buys matches to fire a haystack, or starts on a journey meaning to murder at the end of it, there is still a considerable chance that he will change his mind before he comes to the point. But when he has struck the match, or cocked and aimed the pistol, there is very little chance that he will not persist to the end, and the danger becomes so great that the law steps in. With an object which could not be used innocently, the point of intervention might be put further back, as in the case of the purchase of a die for coining.

*The degree of apprehension may affect the decision, as well as the degree of probability that the crime will be accomplished.* No doubt the fears peculiar to a slave-owning community had their share in the conviction which has just been mentioned.

In this discussion in *The Common Law* Holmes prepared the ground for his clear and present danger doctrine, and even, as we shall see, for its revision by later Justices of the Supreme Court. All the key terms and conceptions are here: intent; foreseeable consequences of an act; a person acting at his peril; the natural and probable effects of an act; acts to be judged by their tendency under the circumstances without regard to the actual intent; the difference between preparation and attempt; probability of consequences; public policy or legislative considerations; the nearness of the danger, the greatness of the harm, and the degree of apprehension felt; an object which could not be used innocently; degree of probability; fears peculiar to a community. The only important element not considered was the First Amendment.

In the *Schenck* case Justice Holmes had an opportunity to bring to a focus the analysis he had previously made of the elements of a criminal act, and to see how the elements combine when the First Amendment is thrown into the mixture.

Charles Schenck and Elizabeth Baer, general secretary and member of the executive board, respectively, of the Socialist Party, were convicted under the Espionage Act of 1917.[8] They were found guilty of three charges: (1) conspiracy by causing and attempting to cause insubordination in the armed forces, and to obstruct the recruiting and enlistment service when the

United States was at war with Germany, by printing and distributing a circular to men called and accepted for military service; (2) conspiracy to use the mails for distribution of the circular; (3) unlawful use of the mails in distribution of the circular.

On one side of the circular—of which the defendants printed around fifteen thousand copies—there were statements that conscription was a violation of the Thirteenth Amendment, and that a conscript was little better than a convict. It said: "Do not submit to intimidation." It asked for repeal of the military service act of 1917. In impassioned words it suggested that conscription was in the interest of Wall Street. On the other side of the circular it was argued that opposition to the draft was a constitutional right and duty, which only politicians and a mercenary capitalist press denied, and it denied the power of Congress to send Americans to fight on foreign land.

Justice Holmes wrote the opinion for a unanimous Court that affirmed the judgments of conviction. His opinion, though very brief, is one of the most important in constitutional law.

First, the question of intent. "Of course," said Holmes, "the document would not have been sent unless it had been intended to have some effect, and we do not see what effect it could be expected to have upon persons subject to the draft except to influence them to obstruct the carrying of it out."

Assuming that this was "the tendency" of the circular, was it not protected by the First Amendment? "We admit," said Holmes, that

in many places and in ordinary times the defendants, in saying all that was said in the circular, would have been within their constitutional rights. But the character of every act depends upon the circumstances in which it is done. . . . The most stringent protection of free speech would not protect a man in falsely shouting fire in a theater, and causing a panic. . . . The question in every case is whether the words used are of such a nature as to create a clear and present danger that they will bring about the substantive evils that Congress has a right to prevent. It is a question of proximity and degree. When a nation is at war many things that might be said in time of peace are such a hindrance to its effort that their utterance will not be endured so long as men fight, and that no court could regard them as protected by any constitutional right. It seems to be admitted that if an actual obstruction of the recruiting service were proved, liability for words that produced that effect might be enforced. The Statute of 1917, in section 4, punishes conspiracies to obstruct as well as actual obstruction. If the act (speaking, or circulating a paper), its tendency and the intent with which it is done, are the same, we perceive no ground for saying that success alone warrants making the act a crime.

What Holmes said here in effect was this: Congress may enact a law under the terms of which a speech or a publication may constitute a criminal offense even in the absence of proof that it in fact brought about a substantive evil. The words themselves may constitute a substantive evil. But whether or not they do will depend on the surrounding circumstances. The words will be punishable if they are uttered or published under such circumstances that they create a clear and present danger that they will cause the evil that Congress has a right to prevent. In other words, a speech may by itself be a crime just as an attempt may by itself be a crime. It makes a difference whether a speech is made in a time of excitement and stress, or whether it is made when people are composed and relaxed; for "the degree of apprehension felt" is important. When slavery was in existence, as Holmes pointed out, a slave who ran after a white woman, though he desisted before he caught her, was convicted of an attempt to commit rape; so, too, in a time of war, the degree of apprehension of danger is greater than in a time of peace, and, therefore, words may be more greatly feared—they come close to the line where the Court may say that they constitute a clear and present danger; for, "when a nation is at war many things that might be said in time of peace are such a hindrance to its effort that their utterance will not be endured so long as men fight, and that no court could regard them as protected by any constitutional right."

It must be noted that the defendants in the *Schenck* case were convicted, and that the Supreme Court unanimously affirmed the judgments: the clear and present danger doctrine was used to support a *denial* of free speech. With rare exception, this is the way the doctrine has been used by the Court. No federal statute has ever been invalidated by the doctrine.

A week after the decision in the *Schenck* case came the Court's decision in the *Frohwerk* case, in which again the judgment of conviction was affirmed by a unanimous Court, with Justice Holmes writing the opinion.[9] Frohwerk was indicted for conspiracy with another person in the preparation and circulation of twelve articles in a German-language newspaper in Missouri, by which he attempted to cause disloyalty, mutiny, and refusal of duty in the armed forces. Examining the articles, Justice Holmes found them similar to those in the *Schenck* case: that it was a mistake to send our troops to France, that we were in the war to help Wall Street, that Germany was unconquerable, and that we were led and ruled by England.

Again, Justice Holmes pointed out that the First Amendment could not have been "intended to give immunity for every possible use of language." This time, in place of shouting fire in a theatre, he gave as an example of a limit on free speech "the counseling of a murder."

Turning to the articles by the defendant, Holmes said: "It may be that all this [that Frohwerk wrote] might be said or written even in time of war in circumstances that would not make it a crime. We do not lose our right to condemn either measures or men because the country is at war." Nor did it appear that the defendant had made "any special effort to reach men who were subject to the draft." Then why did Holmes approve affirmance of the judgment of conviction? Because, he said, on the record it was "impossible to say that it might not have been found that the circulation of the paper was in quarters where a little breath would be enough to kindle a flame, and that the fact was known and relied upon by those who sent the paper out."

It is interesting to note that here Holmes does not speak of the shouting of fire in a theatre and causing a panic, but of a *little breath* that is enough to kindle a flame. He did not attempt to show how the facts in the case met the test of a clear and present danger; he merely referred several times to the *Schenck* case.

And on the same day this decision was made, the Court unanimously affirmed the conviction of Eugene V. Debs, and again the opinion was by Justice Holmes.[10]

Debs, a Socialist and pacifist, made a speech, the main theme of which was the growth of Socialism and a prophecy of its ultimate success. "With that," said Holmes, "we have nothing to do." But there were passages in his speech, Holmes concluded, that sustained the conviction for obstructing and attempting to obstruct the recruiting and enlistment service of the United States, in violation of the Espionage Act of 1917. The "immunity of the general theme" does not protect a speech if one purpose of the speech, "whether incidental or not does not matter," was to oppose "not only war in general, but this war," and if the opposition to "this war" was so expressed "that its natural and intended effect would be to obstruct recruiting." If obstruction of recruiting was intended, "and if, in all the circumstances, that would be its probable effect," the speech would not be—and was not—protected. Holmes approved the trial judge's charge to the jury that Debs could not be found guilty for advocacy of his opinions "unless the words used had as their natural tendency and reasonably probable effect to obstruct the recruiting service, etc., and unless the defendant had the specific intent to do so in his mind."

Holmes did not use the clear and present danger formula, but instead, as we have seen, spoke of the "probable effect" of the speech, and of the "natural tendency and reasonably probable effect" of utterances.

It should be apparent by now that the opinions of Holmes in the three cases, in which convictions for violations of the Espionage Act of 1917 were unanimously sustained, could hardly be said to lay down clear principles that are easy of application in speech or press cases. Nor could it be said that his opinions in these cases went far to protect free utterance; for neither Debs nor Schenck nor Frohwerk could be said to have shouted fire. Nor could it be said that in these cases Holmes considered his words in the *Schenck* opinion about a clear and present danger as the expression of a constitutional test or as the formulation of a doctrine; for in the *Frohwerk* and *Debs* opinions there was no mention at all of a clear and present danger test.

It was not long before Holmes (and Brandeis, too) felt compelled to move away from the other members of the Court, to give greater protection to speech and press than he and the Court had given in the three cases we have discussed, and to raise his language in the *Schenck* opinion about a clear and present danger to the dignity of a constitutional principle.

The first occasion to accomplish this was in the *Abrams* case,[11] decided eight months after the decision in the *Debs* case.

Jacob Abrams and four other persons were convicted of conspiring to violate the Espionage Act of 1917. The defendants had printed five thousand copies of two circulars, which they distributed in New York City by throwing some of them from a window and the rest "secretly." One circular had the caption: "The Hypocrisy of the United States and Her Allies." It attacked the sending of American troops into Russia and "the hypocrisy of the Plutocratic gang in Washington and vicinity." The circular concluded with the following phrases:

The Russian Revolution cries: "Workers of the World! Awake! Rise! Put down your enemy and mine!"

Yes friends, there is only one enemy of the workers of the world and that is Capitalism.

It is a crime, that workers of America, workers of Germany, workers of Japan, etc., to fight the Workers' Republic of Russia.

Awake! Awake, You
Workers of the World!

Revolutionists

P.S. It is absurd to call us pro-German. We hate and despise German militarism more than do your hypocritical tyrants. We have more reasons for denouncing German militarism than has the coward of the White House.[12]

The second leaflet, in Yiddish, attacked the United States, and the Allies generally, for sending troops into Russia. It said that the American workers' money was going to pay for bullets that would be used not only against the Germans, but also against "the Workers Soviet of Russia," and that the workers in ammunition factories were producing bullets "to murder not only the Germans, but also your dearest, best, who are in Russia and are fighting for freedom." The circular expressly appealed to the immigrants from Russia not to help in "the destruction of the Russian Revolution," and it called for a general strike, so that the United States Government may know "that not only the Russian Worker fights for freedom, but [that] also here in America lives the spirit of revolution." The circular ended with these words:

> Three hundred years had the Romanoff dynasty taught us how to fight. Let all rulers remember this, from the smallest to the biggest despot, that the hand of the revolution will not shiver in a fight.
> Woe unto those who will be in the way of progress. Let solidarity live!
>
> The Rebels

The Supreme Court, with Holmes and Brandeis dissenting, affirmed the convictions.

The defendants argued that their intent was only to aid the cause of the Russian Revolution, but the Court said that even if this were true, "the plan of action which they adopted necessarily involved, before it could be realized, defeat of the war program of the United States, for the obvious effect of this appeal, if it should become effective, as they hoped it might, would be to persuade persons of character such as those whom they regarded themselves as addressing, not to aid government loans and not to work in ammunition factories." The Court said that "the manifest purpose" of the second circular "was to create an attempt to defeat the war plans of the United States by bringing upon the country the paralysis of a general strike." Although there was no proof that any person was influenced by the circulars, or even that they reached any munitions worker, the Court stressed the fact that they had been distributed in New York City, from the port of which many soldiers were taking ship, and where war supplies were being manufactured. The Court referred to other writings found on the person of one of the defendants and in their meeting place to spell out the intent of the defendants to cause a revolution at home, so that troops might not be sent to quell the revolution in Russia.

No mention was made by the Court of the clear and present danger doctrine; and the contention that the circulars were protected by the First Amendment was quickly disposed of by mere reference to the *Schenck* and *Frohwerk* decisions. Ironically, the opinions in these decisions were by the member of the Court who now found it necessary to write a dissenting opinion that was destined to become one of the most celebrated dissenting opinions in the history of the Court.

The opinion of Holmes lays stress on two key concepts: intent, and clear and present danger.

As to intent: Ordinarily, a person may be punished if at the time of his act he knew facts from which common experience showed that certain consequences would follow, even if individually he could not actually foresee the consequences. This is the general rule with respect to both criminal and civil liability. But it is not the rule when the statute, such as the Espionage Act of 1917, requires a specific intent. In such a case it is necessary to show that the deed was done *with the aim* to produce the consequence: "he does not do the act with intent to produce it unless the aim to produce it is the proximate motive of the specific act, although there may be some deeper motive behind."

Holmes illustrated his point by the following example: A citizen whose patriotism is beyond question may think that we are wasting money on airplanes or by making more cannon of a certain kind than we need (or, in terms of our own day, more H-bombs than are needed), and may advocate curtailment, and his advocacy may even be successful. Suppose other people think that the curtailment is likely to hinder the country in prosecution of the war, and suppose, even more, that events prove that the curtailment in fact produced tragic consequences; yet would any one hold that the advocacy of curtailment was a crime?

Well, now, Abrams and his codefendants, said Holmes, had the specific intent to prevent interference with the revolution in Russia, but this "might have been satisfied without any hindrance to carrying on the war in which we were engaged." Their only object was to help Russia and stop American intervention there, but not to impede the United States in the war that it was carrying on. Specific intent cannot be proved by selecting from the leaflets several phrases that, when taken literally, "might import a suggestion of conduct that would have interference with the war as an indirect and probably undesired effect."

Turning to the import of the First Amendment, Holmes said that just as the Government may constitutionally punish persuasion to murder, so, too, it may constitutionally punish "speech that produces or is intended to produce a clear and imminent danger that it will bring about forthwith certain substantive evils that the United States constitutionally may seek to prevent."

We should make note of the fact that Holmes said here that the constitutional protection of speech stops when speech *produces* a clear and present danger, or when speech *is intended to produce* a clear and present danger. The question to Holmes (and Brandeis) [13] was whether the leaflets in fact *produced* a clear and present danger, or whether the leaflets were *intended* to produce a clear and present danger.

One can see here clearly how Holmes kept alive in his mind his discussion of intent in the second Lowell Institute lecture. When words *fall short of actually creating* a clear and present danger, the *specific intent* with which they were uttered is a question of paramount importance; and even when the words *actually do* create a clear and present danger, the *specific intent* of the speaker may still be of fundamental importance, as in the case of a national figure who may advocate curtailment of certain types of arms, or a change in military policy or tactics, and the advocacy may be successful—and detrimental to the war effort; yet the advocacy could not be said to have been criminal.

What of speech in time of war? The power to punish speech, said Holmes, undoubtedly is greater in time of war than in time of peace because war opens dangers that do not exist at other times.

But, as against dangers peculiar to war, as against others, the principle of the right to free speech is always the same. It is only the present danger of immediate evil or an intent to bring it about that warrants Congress in setting a limit to the expression of opinion. . . . Congress certainly cannot forbid all effort to change the mind of the country. Now nobody can suppose that the surreptitious publishing of a silly leaflet by an unknown man, without more, would present any immediate danger that its opinions would hinder the success of the government arms or have any appreciable tendency to do so.

However, added Holmes, if the opinions in the leaflets were published "for the very purpose" of obstructing the war effort, then the leaflets "might indicate a greater danger, and at any rate would have the quality of an attempt"; but then an "actual intent" would need to be established.

In this case, said Holmes,

sentences of twenty years' imprisonment have been imposed [14] for the publishing of two leaflets that I believe the defendants had as much right to publish as the government has to publish the Constitution of the United States, now vainly invoked by them. Even if I am technically wrong, and enough can be squeezed from these poor and puny anonymities to turn the color of legal litmus paper,— I will add, even if what I think the necessary intent were shown,— the most nominal punishment seems to me all that possibly could be inflicted, unless the defendants are to be made to suffer not for what the indictment alleges, but for the creed that they avow,—a creed that I believe to be the creed of ignorance and immaturity when honestly held, . . . but which, although made the subject of examination at the trial, no one has a right even to consider in dealing with the charges before the court.

Justice Holmes concluded his opinion with words that have been quoted times without number—words as wise as they are eloquent:

Persecution for the expression of opinions seems to me perfectly logical. If you have no doubt of your premises or your power and want a certain result with all your heart you naturally express your wishes in law and sweep away all opposition. To allow opposition by speech seems to indicate that you think the speech impotent. . . . But when men have realized that time has upset many fighting faiths, they have come to believe . . . that the ultimate good desired is better reached by free trade in ideas,—that the best test of truth is the power of the thought to get itself accepted in the competition of the market; and that truth is the only ground upon which their wishes safely can be carried out. That, at any rate, is the theory of our Constitution. It is an experiment, as all life is an experiment. Every year, if not every day, we have to wager our salvation upon some prophecy based upon imperfect knowledge. While that experiment is part of our system I think that we should be eternally vigilant against attempts to check the expression of opinions that we loathe and believe to be fraught with death, unless they so imminently threaten immediate interference with the lawful and pressing purposes of the law that an immediate check is required to save the country. . . . Only the emergency that makes it immediately dangerous to leave the correction of evil counsels to time warrants making any exception to the sweeping command, "Congress shall make no law abridging the freedom of speech." Of course I am speaking only of expressions of opinion and exhortations, which were all that were uttered here; but I regret that I cannot put into more impressive words my belief that in their conviction upon this indictment the defendants were deprived of their rights under the Constitution of the United States.

Despite their author's misgiving, these words, while not impressive enough to persuade seven of his colleagues in the *Abrams* case, in the long run came to be looked upon as indeed quite impressive.

Can one say that in the *Abrams* case the majority of the Court had abandoned the clear and present danger doctrine? It would not, I think, be correct to say this, for it could hardly be proved that the Court in the *Schenck* case had adopted the doctrine. In the first three cases involving the Espionage Act of 1917 there was no conflict over the decision to uphold the convictions. "The considerations that move a judge to yield concurrence in an opinion reaching an approved result through uncongenial doctrine are," Justice Frankfurter has said, "among the most teasing mysteries." [15] It is even hazardous to say that in these cases Holmes himself had been committed to the doctrine. The spirit of Holmes's opinions in the cases in which the convictions were upheld can scarcely be said to be that of a staunch defender of civil liberties.[16] Frohwerk, and Debs, it may be noted, had each been sentenced to ten years' imprisonment. That these were harsh sentences is borne out by the fact that President Wilson commuted the former's sentence to one year, and that Debs, after he had served two years in prison, was released by President Harding. Perhaps it was not until the *Abrams* case that Holmes—and Brandeis, too—felt himself challenged; and from this time on he used the clear and present danger test as a constitutional doctrine. But he had no opportunity to resort to the doctrine in an opinion for the Court.

It was not until 1937, in *Herndon v. Lowry,* that the Court used the language of the clear and present danger doctrine; [17] and even so, only obliquely. This was eighteen years after the *Schenck* case, and two years after the death of Holmes.[18]

And it was not until 1927, in *Fiske v. Kansas,* that the Court for the first time ruled in favor of a defendant in a free speech case; [19] after that, ten years passed before a defendant was again successful.[20]

In these cases it was state legislation that the Court invalidated.[21] As to federal legislation affecting First Amendment freedoms, the evidence supports the judgment of Commager:

It is safe to say . . . that the judicial record in the important . . . field of personal liberties is practically barren. . . . This is the record. . . . It discloses not a single case, in a century and a half, where the Supreme Court has protected freedom of speech, press, assembly, or petition against congressional attack.[22]

This was written in 1943, and the judgment has remained valid.

Following the *Abrams* case there came before the Court in the next year three more cases.[23] In the *Schaefer* and *Pierce* cases the Court sustained convictions under the Espionage Act of 1917, with Holmes and Brandeis dissenting.[24] In the third of these cases, the *Gilbert* case, the Court upheld a conviction under a statute of Minnesota which made it unlawful to advocate or teach that men should not enlist in the armed forces

or aid the Government in carrying on the war. Gilbert's purpose in a speech he delivered, said the Court, was "the discouragement" of aid or assistance of the Government in prosecution of the war. While the Court cited the *Schenck, Frohwerk,*
and *Debs* cases, it also cited cases in which Holmes had dissented—*Abrams* and *Schaefer;* and yet Holmes concurred in
the result in the *Gilbert* case, and Brandeis alone dissented.
Brandeis contended that the state statute was even more offensive to the Constitution than was the Espionage Act of 1917,
for the former applied to utterances made in time of war or
in time of peace, while the act of Congress was only a war
measure. The state statute, said Brandeis,

abridges freedom of speech and of the press, not in a particular
emergency, in order to avert a clear and present danger, but under
all circumstances. The restriction imposed relates to the teaching
of the doctrine of pacifism, and the legislature in effect proscribes
it for all time. . . . The prohibition is made to apply, whatever
the motive, the intention, or the purpose of him who teaches. It
applies alike to the preacher in the pulpit, the professor at the
university, the speaker at a political meeting, the lecturer at a
society or club gathering. Whatever the nature of the meeting, and
whether it be public or private, the prohibition is absolute. . . .
The reason given by the speaker for advising against enlistment is
immaterial.[25]

What went on in the mind of Holmes as he and Brandeis
parted company here, we cannot tell. But it is odd, indeed,
to see Brandeis arguing on the basis of a doctrine which he had
learned from Holmes, with his teacher in the opposing camp.
"No matter how rapidly we utter the phrase 'clear and present
danger,' or how closely we hyphenate the words, they are not a
substitute for the weighing of values," Professor Paul A.
Freund has said. "They tend to convey a delusion of certitude
when what is most certain is the complexity of the strands in the
web of freedoms which the judge must disentangle." [26] Freund
has suggested that in this instance Holmes chose to set a higher
value on freedom of experimentation by the state, while Brandeis set a higher value on experimentation in ideas.[27] But it is

hard to discover what "experiment" Holmes could possibly have seen in the Minnesota statute.

There would be little gained toward an understanding of the history of the clear and present danger doctrine from a detailed examination of the three other cases [28] involving the Espionage Act of 1917 that were decided before *Gitlow v. New York*.[29] The *Gitlow* case, however, is important enough to call for special consideration.

Following the assassination of President McKinley, the New York legislature enacted a statute against the teaching or advocacy of anarchy, which it defined as "the doctrine that organized government should be overthrown by force or violence" or by assassination "or by any unlawful means." The statute, it should be noted, was not directed at acts of violence, but only at the advocacy of a doctrine. Benjamin Gitlow was convicted under this statute. In 1919 the Socialist Party split into two sections, the moderates and the radicals. Gitlow, a leader of the latter, or Left-Wing section, as it was called, prepared a thirty-four page "Manifesto," which was published in the *Revolutionary Age,* the official organ of the Left-Wing section.

The "Manifesto" was a typical statement of Communist doctrines and program: that the class struggle is essential for the proletariat conquest of power; that revolutionary Socialism must destroy the parliamentary, bourgeois state and replace it with a dictatorship of the proletariat; that World War I has strengthened American capitalism, so that "this is not the moment of revolution, but it is the moment of revolutionary struggle. . . . The mass struggle of the proletariat is coming into being." It called for the organization of the unorganized workers.

The revolution starts with strikes of protest, developing into mass political strikes and then into revolutionary mass action for the conquest of the power of the state. . . . It is not a problem of immediate revolution. It is a problem of the immediate revolutionary struggle. The revolutionary epoch of the final struggle against Capitalism may last for years and tens of years; but the Communist

International offers a policy and program immediate and ultimate in scope. . . .

There was no evidence that the publication had any effect on anyone anywhere. It was the kind of Communist publication that could perhaps be found in many libraries; it was hardly comparable in appeal or influence to the *Communist Manifesto* of Marx and Engels, the publication of which the State of New York did not prohibit.

The Supreme Court, in 1925, upheld the conviction of Gitlow. In his opinion for the Court, Justice Sanford argued that the New York statute, as applied to Gitlow, did not penalize the publication of abstract doctrine or academic discussion. What the statute prohibits, he said, is "language advocating, advising, or teaching the overthrow of organized government by unlawful means. These words imply urging to action." The "Manifesto," he said, was not "mere prediction" that industrial disturbances and revolutionary mass strikes will inevitably occur; it "advocates and urges in fervent language mass action which shall progressively foment industrial disturbances" that will destroy parliamentary government.

Freedom of speech, said the Court, does not protect utterances "which tend to subvert or imperil the government, or to impede or hinder it in the performance of its governmental duties." A state may penalize "utterances which openly advocate the overthrow" of government by unlawful means. This is merely the state's right of "self-preservation." In the exercise of its police power, said the Court, the State of New York, through its legislature, has determined that utterances advocating overthrow of government "are so inimical to the general welfare, and involve such danger of substantive evil," that they must be penalized. This legislative determination "must be given great weight." There must be every presumption in favor of the act.

Utterances "inciting" overthrow of government "by their very nature" involve danger to the state.

They threaten breaches of the peace and ultimate revolution. And the immediate danger is none the less real and substantial because the effect of a given utterance cannot be accurately foreseen. The state cannot reasonably be required to measure the danger from every such utterance in the nice balance of a jeweler's scale. A single revolutionary spark may kindle a fire that, smoldering for a time, may burst into a sweeping and destructive conflagration. . . . [A state may, therefore, seek] to extinguish the spark without waiting until it has enkindled the flame or blazed into the conflagration. It cannot reasonably be required to defer . . . measures . . . until the revolutionary utterances lead to . . . imminent and immediate danger of its destruction; but it may . . . suppress the threatened danger in its incipiency.

In other words, said the Court, the legislature may decide that utterances of a certain kind are dangerous and are to be punished. Once the legislature has acted, the courts do not need to consider whether specific words used are likely to bring about the substantive evil (destruction of the government); it is enough if the utterance falls within the language prohibited by the statute.

The Court at this point distinguished two kinds of legislation. There is (1) a statute that punishes certain acts; e.g., attempts to destroy the government. It says nothing about utterances. If the state were to prosecute a person under such a statute, and if the prosecution were based on utterances, then it would be a question for the courts whether the defendant's utterances "involved such likelihood of bringing about the substantive evil as to deprive it of the constitutional protection." The utterances could be punished under the statute if their "natural tendency and probable effect were to bring about the substantive evil which the legislative body might prevent." And there is (2) a statute, like the one before the Court in the *Gitlow* case, that punishes certain kinds of utterances; e.g., utterances that teach or advocate the necessity or propriety of overthrowing government by force or violence. In a prosecution under such a statute, the only question is whether the utterances teach or advocate the prohibited doctrine. The courts need not consider "the tendency and probable effect" of the defendant's utterances. As we shall have occasion to see later when we consider the *Dennis* case,[30] these distinctions made by the Court in 1925 are still influential in the thought of some Justices of the Court.[31]

Justice Holmes, in a dissenting opinion in which Justice Brandeis joined, said that the Court's decision contradicted the test accepted by a unanimous Court in the *Schenck* case. If the correct test were applied, he said, then

it is manifest that there was no present danger of an attempt to overthrow the government. . . . It is said that this Manifesto was more than a theory, that it was an incitement. Every idea is an incitement. It offers itself for belief, and, if believed, it is acted on unless some other belief outweighs it, or some failure of energy stifles the movement at its birth. The only difference between the expression of an opinion and an incitement in the narrower sense is the speaker's enthusiasm for the result. Eloquence may set fire to reason. But whatever may be thought of the redundant discourse before us, it had no chance of starting a present conflagration. If, in the long run, the beliefs expressed in proletarian dictatorship are destined to be accepted by the dominant forces of the community, the only meaning of free speech is that they should be given their chance and have their way.

If the publication of this document had been laid as an attempt to induce an uprising against government at once, and not at some indefinite time in the future, it would have presented a different question. The object would have been one with which the law might deal, subject to the doubt whether there was any danger that the publication could produce any result; or, in other words, whether it was not futile and too remote from possible consequences. But the indictment alleged the publication and nothing more.

It is obvious that Holmes did not accept the majority's distinction between two kinds of statutes, one that punished acts and one that punished utterances. His refusal to accept the distinction is especially significant since it was Holmes, rather than his colleagues of the majority, who was a proponent of the view that courts must presume the reasonableness and the constitutionality of legislative acts.[32] Holmes would not declare the New York statute unconstitutional, but he would subject a prosecution under the act to the clear and present danger test, and he refused to conclude that the statute made this constitutional test redundant. We shall have more to say about this in our discussion of the *Dennis* case.

In the decade (1925–1935) immediately following the *Gitlow* decision, the clear and present danger doctrine was mentioned only twice—by Justice Brandeis in his concurring opinion in *Whitney v. California* (1927),[33] which we have already considered, and by Justice Cardozo in his dissenting opinion in *Herndon v. Georgia* in 1935.[34] Although First Amendment cases [35] were before the Court, the doctrine was not mentioned in any majority opinion, as we have said, until *Herndon v. Lowry* [36] in 1937—a case that deserves some consideration.

Angelo Herndon, a Negro Communist Party organizer in the South, was convicted for attempting to incite insurrection and was sentenced by Georgia courts to imprisonment for not less than eighteen years. The attempt to incite insurrection was made, according to the state's evidence, by calling and attending public meetings and by making speeches for the purpose of organizing the Communist Party of Atlanta, and with this intent, by circulating pamphlets and other publications. The statute, under which Herndon was convicted, broadly provided that "any attempt, by persuasion or otherwise, to induce others to join in any combined resistance to the lawful authority of the State shall constitute an attempt to incite insurrection." The statutory penalty was death, unless the jury recommended mercy.

When arrested, Herndon had with him Communist Party receipts and membership books, copies of the *Daily Worker,* and some party pamphlets and magazines. Some party literature was also found in his room. But there was no proof that he had distributed any of the literature except two circulars that the state supreme court characterized as "more or less harmless." The membership forms spoke of "the proletarian struggle" and of "the revolutionary theory of Marxism." They called for "equal rights for Negroes and self-determination for the Black Belt." The prosecution made a great deal of the party's call for Negro self-determination. They introduced into evidence pamphlets that were in Herndon's possession that called for the establishment of a Negro belt across some Southern states, to be accomplished by confiscation of the lands of white capitalists, and by the Negro majority wielding power over the white minority. Toward achieving these ends, there should be demonstrations, strikes, and tax boycotts; and Negro self-determination was to be viewed as only a step toward the ultimate end of a "National Rebellion." There was no evidence that Herndon distributed this literature or that he advocated any doctrine implying such violent subversion of law and order.

The state supreme court, upholding the conviction, said that to establish guilt the state need not prove that a defendant intended that an insurrection should follow instantly, "but it would be sufficient that he intended it to happen at any time, as a result of his influence, by those whom he sought to incite."

The United States Supreme Court, by a bare majority, reversed the conviction. In his opinion for the Court, Justice Roberts quoted the clear and present danger language from the *Schenck* opinion; but, he noted, the Georgia statute was quite different from the Espionage Act of 1917, and it was also quite different from the New York statute before the Court in the *Gitlow* case. In the instant case the statute was neither specific nor limited in its terms and application, and the facts proved against Herndon did not establish his guilty intent as judged by a standard of guilt clearly defined by a statute.

Some of the tenets of the party were lawful and others, it may be assumed, were unlawful; but there was no proof that Herndon brought the unlawful aims to the attention of persons whom he sought to induce to join the party, or that he approved the unlawful aims, "or that the fantastic program they envisaged was conceived of by anyone as more than an ultimate ideal."

As construed by the state courts, the statute under which Herndon was convicted did not furnish "a sufficiently ascertainable standard of guilt." The judge and jury, trying a person under the statute as construed by the state courts, "cannot appraise the circumstances and character of the defendant's utterances or activities as begetting a clear and present danger of forcible obstruction of a particular state function."

Does this passage import an approval of an application of the clear and present danger doctrine to the facts before the Court in the *Herndon* case? It is hard to say, especially in view of the fact that earlier in his opinion Justice Roberts differentiated sharply the Espionage Act cases from the instant case. It is easier to say what the Court did not approve. It did not approve of a conviction for utterances made with an intent that an insurrection should happen "at any time" as a result of the "influence" of the words upon those whom the speaker sought to influence, or for utterances made with an intent that an insurrection should happen "at any time" within which the speaker "might reasonably expect" his "influence" to be felt by those whom he sought to induce. For under this test of danger "at any time," said Justice Roberts, it would be sufficient for conviction if the jury thought that the defendant

reasonably might foretell that those he persuaded to join the party might, at some time in the indefinite future, resort to forcible resistance of government. The question thus proposed to a jury involves pure speculation as to future trends of thought and action. Within what time might one reasonably expect that an attempted organization of the Communist Party in the United States would result in violent action by that party? If a jury returned a special verdict saying twenty years or even fifty years the verdict could not be shown to be wrong. The law, as thus construed, licenses the jury to create its own standard in each case. . . . The statute, as construed and applied, amounts merely to a dragnet which may enmesh anyone who agitates for a change of government if a jury can be persuaded that he ought to have foreseen his words would have some effect in the future conduct of others. . . . So vague and indeterminate are the boundaries thus set to the freedom of speech and assembly that the law necessarily violates the guaranties of liberty embodied in the Fourteenth Amendment.

Taking Justice Roberts' opinion as a whole, it is hard to escape the feeling that Justice Roberts found himself in the middle between two poles. On the one hand there was the proposition that speech should be protected unless and until it could be shown that it created, or was intended to create, a clear and present danger. On the other hand there was the "bad tendency" test, under which speech would be protected unless and until it could be shown that it reasonably could be expected to cause somebody someday in the indefinite future to resort to the force and violence that the speaker thought he foresaw. While Justice Roberts was ready to reject the latter test, he was not willing to commit himself unambiguously to the former. As we shall see, it is doubtful if the conflict has thus far been resolved; the tension between the two poles remains.[37]

Starting with *Thornhill v. Alabama* in 1940,[38] the Court mentioned or relied on the clear and present danger doctrine with considerable regularity. In the *Thornhill* case, speaking for all members of the Court except Justice McReynolds, Justice Murphy said that discussion of matters of public interest may be abridged "only where the clear danger of substantive evils arises under circumstances affording no opportunity to test the merits of ideas by competition for acceptance in the market of public opinion"; and for this proposition he cited the opinions of Holmes in the *Schenck* and *Abrams* cases. And in *Cantwell v. Connecticut,* decided later in the same year, Justice Roberts said for a unanimous Court that although the contents of the phonograph record played by a Jehovah's Witness on a public street naturally aroused animosity,

we think that, in the absence of a statute narrowly drawn to define and punish specific conduct as constituting a clear and present danger to a substantial interest of the State, the petitioner's communication, considered in the light of the constitutional guaranties, raised no such clear and present menace to public peace and order as to render him liable to conviction.[39]

Roberts cited as authorities for this conclusion the *Schenck* case, *Herndon v. Lowry,* and the *Thornhill* case. Thus twenty-one years passed between the first acceptance, if one may call it that, of the doctrine by a unanimous Court and its renewed acceptance by a unanimous Court—a very uneven career, to say the least, for a constitutional doctrine—and in both *Thornhill* and *Cantwell,* unlike *Schenck,* the decision was for the defendants.

Between the *Cantwell* and the *Dennis* cases the doctrine wove itself into and out of majority and dissenting opinions. Only the specialist can have the patience to follow the path of the doctrine in detail in the intermediate cases.[40]

But we must take note that during these years the doctrine was subjected to serious question by Justice Frankfurter. Starting with his dissenting opinion in *Bridges v. California* in 1941,[41] Justice Frankfurter attacked what he thought was a doctrinaire use of the clear and present danger phrase. In the *Bridges* dissent he argued that the phrase was intended by Holmes and Brandeis as only a "rule of reason," the application of which still required "the exercise of good judgment." It was only a "short-hand" phrase, the recitation of which solved no problem; and the "literary difference" between it and "reasonable tendency" was "not of constitutional dimension."

While other members of the Court, as we have seen, had previously by-passed the doctrine, no one until this time had ventured to reduce it to a mere phrase.

In his dissenting opinion in the *Barnette* case in 1943 Justice Frankfurter spoke of clear and present danger as "a felicitous phrase" that must be considered only within the context in which Justice Holmes used it and only in relation to the situation for which Holmes adapted it.[42] Holmes was not, in the *Schenck* case, "enunciating a formal rule that there can be no restriction upon speech and, still less, no compulsion where conscience balks, unless imminent danger would thereby be wrought 'to our institutions or our government.'" And in 1946, in his concurring opinion in *Pennekamp v. Florida,* Frankfurter again said that clear and present danger "was never used by Mr. Justice Holmes to express a technical legal doctrine or to convey a formula for adjudicating cases. It was a literary phrase not to be distorted by being taken from its context." [43]

In 1951, in the *Dennis* case, Frankfurter's view became the view expressed for the Court by Chief Justice Vinson.[44] Using Frankfurter's words but not within quotation marks, Vinson said:

neither Justice Holmes nor Justice Brandeis ever envisioned that a shorthand phrase should be crystallized into a rigid rule to be applied inflexibly without regard to the circumstances of each case. . . . Nothing is more certain in modern society than the principle that there are no absolutes, that a name, a phrase, a standard has meaning only when associated with the considerations which gave birth to the nomenclature.

Then, having reduced clear and present danger from a doctrine to a phrase, the Court proceeded to decide what the phrase meant within the circumstances presented by the case of *Dennis v. United States.*

To a consideration of this landmark case we now turn.

# The Doctrine Reduced to a Phrase: Dennis v. United States

IN 1940 Congress enacted the Smith Act.[1] Sections 2 and 3 of the act, which alone are relevant here, provided as follows:

Sec. 2.

(a) It shall be unlawful for any person—

(1) to knowingly or wilfully advocate, abet, advise, or teach the duty, necessity, desirability, or propriety of overthrowing or destroying any government in the United States by force or violence, or by the assassination of any officer of such government;

(2) with the intent to cause the overthrow or destruction of any government in the United States, to print, publish, edit, issue, circulate, sell, distribute, or publicly display any written or printed matter advocating, advising, or teaching the duty, necessity, desirability, or propriety of overthrowing or destroying any government in the United States by force or violence;

(3) to organize or help to organize any society, group, or assembly of persons who teach, advocate, or encourage the overthrow or destruction of any government in the United States by force or violence; or to be or become a member of, or affiliate with, any such society, group, or assembly of persons, knowing the purposes thereof.

(b) For the purposes of this section, the term "government in the United States" means the Government of the United States, the government of any State, Territory, or possession of the United

States, the government of the District of Columbia, or the government of any political subdivision of any of them.

Sec. 3. It shall be unlawful for any person to attempt to commit, or to conspire to commit, any of the acts prohibited by the provisions of . . . this title.

Note should be taken of the fact that these sections do not punish *overthrow* of the government, or *attempts to overthrow* the government; they punish the knowing or wilful *advocacy or teaching* of the duty, necessity, desirability or propriety of overthrowing government; or the *publication* of matter that teaches or advocates the duty, necessity, desirability or propriety of overthrowing government, with the intent to cause the overthrow of government by such publication; or the *organizing* of a group to teach or advocate the overthrow of government, or to join such a group with knowledge of its purpose. A person could commit any of these criminal offenses by acting alone or by conspiring with others to commit them.

In 1948 the twelve top leaders of the Communist Party of the United States were indicted under the conspiracy provision of the act. Eleven of them were tried and convicted, and the judgments of conviction were upheld by the Supreme Court.[2] They were convicted for wilfully and knowingly conspiring (1) to organize the Communist Party as a group that would teach and advocate overthrow of the Government of the United States by force and violence, and (2) knowingly and wilfully to advocate and teach the duty and necessity of overthrowing and destroying the Government of the United States by force and violence.

The Communist Party was first organized in the United States in 1919.[3] On June 22, 1941, Nazi Germany attacked the U.S.S.R.; on December 11 of the same year Germany and the United States declared war on each other; so that then the United States and the U.S.S.R. were war allies. These events placed the party in the unusual position of being a supporter of a capitalist government. As the 1944 national election approached, the Communists decided that the word "Party" should be eliminated from the name of the Communist organization, so that Communists may vote for, and work for the re-election of, President Roosevelt, and thus endorse and support his war policies. At a national convention held in May 1944 the Communist Party became the Communist Political Association. On May 7, 1945, Germany surrendered. A few weeks later, on May 24, 1945, the *Daily Worker* reprinted an article by the French Communist, Jacques Duclos, "On the Dissolution of the Communist Party of the United States," in which the writer said: "It is clear that American Communists were right in supporting the candidacy of President Roosevelt in the last election but it was not at all necessary for this to dissolve the Communist Party." [4] This was interpreted by American Communists as a warning that Stalin was calling a halt to Russian collaboration with the United States; accordingly, at a convention of the Communist Political Association in July 1945 the organization again became the Communist Party of the United States.

On July 20, 1948, a federal grand jury indicted the persons elected by the 1945 party convention to constitute the party secretariat, several members of the party's national board, and several who were on the national committee. They were charged with conspiracy to organize the party in 1945, and with conspiracy, from that time until the date of the indictment, to teach and advocate the duty and necessity to overthrow the Government. The trial of the case before Judge Harold R. Medina in the federal district court in New York lasted nine months, six of which were given over to the taking of testimony. The trial record came to 16,000 pages. The defendants were found guilty by a jury, and the judgments were affirmed by the court of appeals.[5]

The opinion for the court of appeals was by Judge Learned Hand, one of the most respected and distinguished jurists of our time—a man of profound culture and scholarship, with wide interests and humane instincts. As we shall see, when the *Dennis* case came before the Supreme Court, Judge Hand's opinion was studied with care and was given much weight.

The first and most important issue, said Judge Hand, was whether the evidence was sufficient to support the jury's verdict that the defendants were guilty of the crime charged in the indictment. The defendants were engaged in a concerted effort to teach the doctrines of Marxism-Leninism. What are these doctrines? According to the prosecution, these doctrines, as summarized by Judge Hand, are

> that capitalism inescapably rests upon, and must perpetuate, the oppression of those who do not own the means of production: that to it in time there will succeed a classless society, which will make the paraphernalia of government unnecessary; but that there must be an intermediate and transitional period of "dictatorship of the proletariat," which can be established only by the violent overthrow of the existing government, if that be capitalistic. No entrenched bourgeoisie, having everything to lose and nothing to gain by the abolition of capitalism, . . . will ever permit itself to be superseded by . . . the ballot. . . . Therefore, the transition period involves the use of "force and violence," temporary it is true, but inescapable; and although it is impossible to predict when a propitious occasion will arise, one certainly will arise; . . . when the time comes the proletariat will find it necessary to establish its "dicatorship" by violence.

Opposed to this interpretation of Marxism-Leninism was the contention of the defendants that they had sought to achieve change only through constitutional means, that force and violence were no part of their program except that the proletariat would need to resort to such means in order to resist the efforts of the bourgeoisie to oust them from power won by constitutional actions; in other words, Communists will not resort to force to achieve power, but will meet force with force after they will have won power.

On this issue of fact, the court of appeals held that the Government had clearly established its case by the testimony of its witnesses and by the Communist publications that it had submitted to the jury. This meant that the defendants had made concerted efforts to teach and advocate the overthrow and destruction of the Government by force and violence as a means toward the establishment of Communism in the United States, and that they had formed the Communist Party to teach and advocate the principles of Marxism-Leninism.

The next question considered by Judge Hand was whether

these activities could be punished without abridging the First Amendment. After reviewing cases from *Schenck* through *Douds*, Judge Hand said that "the phrase, 'clear and present danger,' is not a slogan or a shibboleth to be applied as though it carried its own meaning; but that it involves in every case a comparison between interests which are to be appraised qualitatively." In each case courts, said Judge Hand,

must ask whether the gravity of the "evil," discounted by its improbability, justifies such invasion of free speech as is necessary to avoid the danger. We have purposely substituted "improbability" for "remoteness," because that must be the right interpretation. Given the same probability, it would be wholly irrational to condone future evils which we should prevent if they were immediate; that could be reconciled only by an indifference to those who come after us. It is only because a substantial intervening period between the utterance and its realization may check its effect and change its importance, that its immediacy is important. . . . We can never forecast with certainty; all prophecy is a guess, but the reliability of a guess decreases with the length of the future which it seeks to penetrate.

As Judge Hand developed this line of argument, it became clear that by a "present danger" he meant a "probable danger," and that the probability of a danger is established by the character of the actors and by the circumstances within which they act.

As to the actors, Judge Hand spoke of the defendants as the controlling spirits of a rigidly organized and ruthlessly disciplined group of persons who demand inflexible doctrinal orthodoxy; and one doctrine of their faith is the violent capture of all existing governments and the denial of the possibility of success by lawful means.

As to the circumstances within which the defendants acted at the time of the indictments (1948), Judge Hand said that our Government had been singled out by the Communist powers as the chief enemy of their faith, and that a single incident might have led to war. "We do not understand how one could ask for a more probable danger. . . . Such a conspiracy [by the defendants] creates a danger of the utmost gravity and of enough probability to justify its suppression. We hold," concluded Judge Hand, "that it is a danger 'clear and present.' "

Who decides whether the alleged acts of defendants constitute "a danger 'clear and present' "? Judge Medina ruled that this was a question for him, as trial judge, to decide. He instructed the jury:

I find as matter of law that there is sufficient danger of a substantive evil that the Congress has a right to prevent to justify the application of the statute under the First Amendment of the Constitution.

This is matter of law about which you have no concern. It is a finding on a matter of law which I deem essential to support my ruling that the case should be submitted to you to pass upon the guilt or innocence of the defendants.

This instruction to the jury was approved by Judge Hand. The question, he said, gets down to a choice between competing interests: "whether the gravity of the 'evil,' discounted by its improbability, justifies such invasion of free speech as is necessary to avoid the danger." Ordinarily a choice between competing interests (as was involved, e.g., in the *Douds* case) is for the legislature; but when it is impracticable to make the choice in general propositions, it may be left to administrative tribunals or to the courts. The choice may be left to juries when the competing interests concern only individuals involved in a private action, as, e.g., in a suit based on negligence; but it would be improper to put the question to a jury when the conflict is over "momentous public interests." [6]

Judge Hand's opinion was an attempt at finding a middle-of-the-road solution between two extreme positions which may be described as follows:

1. The position of the prosecution [7] was that the Supreme Court in the *Gitlow* case had decided that utterances advocating the violent overthrow of government may by legislation be punished as crimes. Advocacy and teaching of the overthrow of government are not part of the public opinion in a democracy; they are not to be tolerated in the market place of ideas; they are on a par with obscene and fraudulent utterances, which may be punished without the need to "wait and see" until they have created a clear and present danger. Such utterances do not

call for "freedom for the thought we hate." Just as Congress may punish an attempt to overthrow government, so, too, it may punish recruitment of volunteers for this attempt—it may strike at an attempt and also at the activities that are preparatory for the attempt. Whatever intellectual content there may be in utterances that teach overthrow of government, "such utterances"—as Justice Murphy said of "the lewd and obscene, the profane, the libelous, and the insulting or 'fighting' words" —"are no essential part of any exposition of ideas, and are of such slight social value as a step to truth that any benefit that may be derived from them is clearly outweighed by the social interest in order and morality."

2. The position of the defense [8] was that, assuming for the sake of argument that the defendants advocated and taught the overthrow of government, the First Amendment does not outlaw such utterances unless the facts and circumstances show that the utterances were part of an actual attempt to overthrow government. The First Amendment freedoms stand in a "preferred position"; therefore, no mere weighing of interests, no mere rule of reason or of reasonableness can condemn utterances as criminal as long as they are mere utterances and do not add up to an attempt, or part of an attempt, to overthrow government; it is only when utterances create an imminent danger of overthrow of government that they can be assimilated to an attempt to overthrow government. When the date of the revolution is far in the future, the revolutionary utterances are constitutionally protected.

Neither of these positions was accepted by Judge Hand. He did not put revolutionary utterances beyond the fence of the First Amendment, as if they were no better than lewd or obscene expressions; nor did he think that they are constitutionally protected unless they are part of an attempt to overthrow government or unless they create an imminent danger of such overthrow. If a concerted undertaking to teach and advocate overthrow of government creates a probability of danger, it may be punished as a criminal conspiracy. If the danger is improbable, the utterance is protected or privileged, and the organization of those who would advocate or teach the overthrow of government is not then a criminal conspiracy. Under the facts as produced at the trial, Judge Hand concluded that in the summer of 1948, when the indictments were found, there was probable danger from the actions of the defendant leaders of the Communist Party: they constituted a conspiracy that created "a danger of the utmost gravity and of enough probability to justify its suppression." The conspiracy was "a danger 'clear and present.' "

All of the essential points made by Judge Hand were accepted by Chief Justice Vinson in his opinion in which Justices Reed, Burton, and Minton joined.[9] The important points made by Chief Justice Vinson may be summarized as follows:

1. The Smith Act must be construed as requiring proof of intent to overthrow government by force and violence. Those who are charged with its violation must be shown to have this intent; and "certainly those who recruit [adherents or members] and combine for the purpose of advocating overthrow intend to bring about that overthrow." They may advocate *now* with the intent to overthrow "as speedily as circumstances permit."

2. There is no right to rebel against the Government of the United States, for the Government is not dictatorial but provides for orderly and peaceful changes.

3. Since there is no right of revolution, there is no right to prepare for a revolution. Acts that are intended to overthrow the Government by force and violence may be punished.

4. The Smith Act is directed at advocacy, not teaching in the sense of discussion. It does not, as interpreted by Judge Medina, stifle ideas or prohibit academic discussion of Marxism-Leninism. The free discussion of political theories, the "traditional rights of Americans to discuss and evaluate ideas" are left intact and constitutionally protected. Free discourse remains: speech can rebut speech, propaganda can answer propaganda.

5. But not all speech is constitutionally protected. There are other values, to which the value of speech must at times give way.

6. It must be remembered that in the *Schenck* case, in which

Holmes first used the clear and present danger phrase, there was no proof that there was a threat to the safety of the United States. The evidence showed only an "insubstantial gesture" toward attempting to cause insubordination in the armed forces and to obstruct recruiting. The prosecution was based only on the publication and circulation of a document. Yet the Court unanimously upheld the conviction. So, too, in subsequent decisions in which convictions were sustained: in *Debs* there was only one speech; in *Frohwerk* there were only twelve newspaper articles; in *Abrams* copies of only two socialist circulars had been distributed; in *Schaefer* there was the publication of a German-language newspaper with allegedly false articles that were critical of World War I and of capitalism; in *Pierce* there was distribution of a four-page pamphlet by a clergyman. In *Debs* and *Frohwerk* the decisions were unanimous; in the other cases Holmes and Brandeis dissented because they doubted the "probable effectiveness of the puny efforts toward subversion."

In all these cases the defendants were tried under statutes in which the offenses were specified in nonspeech or nonpress terms, but the prosecution relied on speeches or publications to prove the offenses. When Holmes and Brandeis dissented, it was only because they felt that the evidence was insufficient to establish the crime of interference with enlistment or some other such crime.

In the *Gitlow* case the situation was different, for there the New York statute was directed at speech: it made it a crime to advocate the necessity or propriety to overthrow government by force. The defendant had published a manifesto attacking the Government and capitalism. In sustaining the conviction, the Court held that the clear and present danger test did not apply because the legislature had found that a certain kind of speech was itself harmful and lawful. Since it was reasonable for a state to protect itself against revolution, it was also reasonable to protect itself against advocacy of revolution.

In dissenting in the *Gitlow* case Justices Holmes and Brandeis refused to make a distinction between (a) a statute which made certain acts unlawful—e.g., interference with military recruitment—and where the prosecution relied on utterances to prove the statutory offense, and (b) a statute which made utterance itself the crime. In either case, they contended, the clear and present danger test applies.

The Smith Act makes utterance itself criminal. Shall the Court follow the majority views of the Court in the *Gitlow* case or the views of Holmes and Brandeis? Chief Justice Vinson said that while *Gitlow* had not been expressly overruled, subsequent judicial opinion inclined toward the Holmes-Brandeis position. Clear and present danger is the test if a restriction on speech is involved.

7. But clear and present danger is not a rigid rule. "To those who would paralyze our Government in the face of impending threat by encasing it in a semantic straitjacket we must reply that all concepts are relative." What, then, does the "phrase" impart?

The Government may limit speech to protect itself against overthrow by force and violence. But at what point may it limit speech? "If Government is aware that a group aiming at its overthrow is attempting to indoctrinate its members and to commit them to a course whereby they will strike when the leaders feel the circumstances permit, action by the Government is required." Even though the attempt to overthrow may be doomed from the outset because of inadequate numbers or power of the revolutionists, and even if the Government is strong enough to crush a rebellion, the Government does not need to wait. Success or probability of success is not the test. Government may prevent the attempt, if there is a group ready to make the attempt "as speedily as circumstances would permit," by punishing the members of the group; for the existence of the group is itself the danger or the evil: "it is the existence of the conspiracy which creates the danger."

The clear and present danger means what Judge Hand said it means: "In each case [courts] must ask whether the gravity of the 'evil,' discounted by its improbability, justifies such invasion of free speech as is necessary to avoid the danger."

Here was a highly organized conspiracy, with members rigidly disciplined and subject to call when the defendants would feel that the time had come for action. These facts were "coupled with the inflammable nature of world conditions, similar uprisings in other countries, and the touch-and-go nature of our relations with countries with whom . . . [defendants] were in the very least ideologically attuned." The "ingredients of the reaction" were present; "we cannot bind the Government to wait until the catalyst is added." There was a clear and present danger of a substantive evil.

8. The Smith Act can constitutionally apply only if and when a clear and present danger exists. Whether or not such a danger exists is a question of law for the trial judge and not for the jury. If the judge rules that the act applies because of the existence of a clear and present danger, then the case can go to the jury on the question of fact, i.e., whether the evidence established beyond a reasonable doubt that the defendants violated the act.

Affirming the judgments of conviction, Chief Justice Vinson concluded that the defendants

intended to overthrow the Government of the United States as speedily as the circumstances would permit. Their conspiracy to organize the Communist Party and to teach and advocate the overthrow of the Government of the United States by force and violence created a "clear and present danger" of an attempt to overthrow the Government by force and violence. They were properly and constitutionally convicted for violation of the Smith Act.

It is difficult to simplify the foregoing line of reasoning; still, one must make the effort in the interest of worthwhile discussion. Reduced to elementary terms, Chief Justice Vinson's opinion, I think, stands for the following propositions:

When men actually stage a revolution—e.g., they take ammunition into the White House and the Capitol and start shooting—of course they may be punished. When their actions fall short of revolutionary deeds but add up to an attempt—e.g., they are armed and are in a cavalcade of automobiles on the way to Government buildings, with intent to commit assassinations and other acts of force and violence—of course they may be punished for the attempt. If they organize themselves for the purpose of teaching and advocating the necessity and desirability of overthrowing the Government, and they organize an association or party that will have as its purpose such advocacy and teaching, they constitute a conspiracy, which, though it falls short of being an attempt, may constitute a clear and present danger of an attempt to overthrow the Government.

An attempt is only one step removed from the substantive deed that persons may intend. Utterances, or the formation of an organization that would produce utterances, may be two steps removed from the ultimate deed (an actual use of force and violence with the intent to overthrow the Government). Persons caught at the point that is two steps removed may be punished as coconspirators if they created a clear and present danger of getting to the point that is only one step removed from the ultimate event. And "clear and present danger" means "clear and probable danger." Even though we may be certain that if the conspirators ever reached the point that is only one step removed from the ultimate event, their attempt would be a quick and decisive failure; since they could be punished for trying, they may also be punished for preparing to try, even though the preparation consists only in using speech and in organizing an association only for the use of speech.

In a concurring opinion, Justice Frankfurter protested against efforts to make an absolute of the First Amendment or of the clear and present danger rule. "It were far better," he said,

that the phrase [clear and present danger] be abandoned than that it be sounded once more to hide from the believers in an absolute right of free speech the plain fact that the interest in speech, profoundly important as it is, is no more conclusive in judicial review than other attributes of democracy or than a determination of the people's representatives that a measure is necessary to assure the safety of government itself.

There is no escape from the onerous task to weigh conflicting interests. The Government has the duty to preserve itself and the Nation; the Government has the duty to respect freedom of speech. These interests may, as in the instant case, conflict. Must free speech be preferred to preservation of the Government and the Nation? Yes, some authorities say, unless the speech creates a clear and present danger to the preservation of the Government or the Nation. But what does "clear and present danger" mean? Does it mean anything more than the demand to weigh, within the confines of the judicial process, the competing interests in free speech and in national security? In weighing these interests the courts must consider many complex factors, including "the relative seriousness of the danger in comparison with the value of the occasion for speech or political activity; the availability of more moderate controls than those which the state has imposed; and perhaps the specific intent with which the speech or activity is launched." [10] There is no escape, said Frankfurter, from the need to weigh one interest against another, and to do so in the light of many, varied, and complex factors: the clear and present danger is not to be used as an inflexible dogma for the solution of non-Euclidean problems. It is doubtful if the substitution of "probability" for "clear" and "present," by itself, helps the thought process.

Furthermore, the legislative judgment must be respected. To this extent the *Gitlow* opinion was correct. But respect for the legislative judgment was carried too far in that case, for the publication of the Left-Wing Manifesto in the circumstances could hardly have justified serious concern. In other words, Frankfurter believed that the New York statute that was before the Court in the *Gitlow* case—"nearly identical to the Smith Act"—was constitutional, but should not have been applied to the acts of the defendant. "In contrast," however, "there is ample justification for a legislative judgment that the conspiracy now before us [in the *Dennis* case] is a substantial threat to national order and security."

This line of thought involves the question where in the scale of values should be placed utterances that advocate overthrow of government; for the Smith Act is directed against such utterances. How much respect should be accorded the judgment of Congress expressed in the Smith Act? "On any scale of values which we have hitherto recognized," said Frankfurter, "speech of this sort ranks low."

Together with this judgment is the fact that the defendants, as found by the jury, formed the Communist Party, which at the time of the indictment was "of significant size [it had some 60,000 members], well-organized, well-disciplined, conditioned to embark on unlawful activity when given the command." The Court, said Frankfurter, could also take judicial notice that Communist doctrines were in the ascendency in powerful nations that were unfriendly to the United States. Membership in the party "was organized in small units, linked by an intricate chain of command, and protected by elaborate precautions designed to prevent disclosure of individual identity." Members of the party occupied positions of importance in political and labor organizations.

Despite these facts, if the question how to adjust the clash of interests were one for the Court to answer, it may well be that we, said Frankfurter, might choose to act differently; but the policy question was one for Congress and not for the Court, and Congress, acting in the light of many facts available to it, has exercised its judgment in the light of its responsibility. The Court ought not to translate "undesirable" into "unconstitutional." Especially is this so when the democratic process remains unimpaired even if the Smith Act remain on the statute book, and so Congress is free to repeal or change the law.

Justice Frankfurter made it clear that he doubted the wisdom of the Smith Act. Even when speech advocates overthrow of government, there may still be a public interest in leaving it free; for such advocacy, as in the case of Communist propaganda, is coupled with criticism of social defects; and without free criticism there may be no reform; and without reform a society may find it impossible to conserve its health. Furthermore, said Justice Frankfurter,

suppressing advocates of overthrow inevitably will also silence critics who do not advocate overthrow but fear that their criticism may be so construed. No matter how clear we may be that the defendants now before us are preparing to overthrow our Government at the propitious moment, it is self-delusion to think that we can punish them for their advocacy without adding to the risks run by loyal citizens who honestly believe in some of the reforms these defendants advance. It is a sobering fact that in sustaining the conviction before us we can hardly escape restriction on the interchange of ideas. . . . Liberty of thought soon shrivels without freedom of expression. Nor can truth be pursued in an atmosphere hostile to the endeavor or under dangers which are hazarded only by heroes.

Society, then, was paying a heavy price for the enforcement of the Smith Act; and Frankfurter doubted if the circumstances wisely called for the purchase at such a price. Was it true that national security was being purchased by imprisonment of the defendants? Frankfurter quoted with approval from a statement by George F. Kennan to the effect that Communism was an external, but not an internal, danger. The party, said Kennan, "represents a tiny minority in our country; it has no real contact with the feelings of the mass of our people; and its position as the agency of a hostile foreign power is clearly recognized by the overwhelming mass of our citizens." We create, said Kennan, an internal danger by the way we react to American Communists: we become "intolerant, secretive, suspicious, cruel, and terrified of internal dissension because we have lost our own belief in ourselves and in the power of our ideals." In combating Communists, we become like them; and this is our real internal danger. And Frankfurter quoted with approval a statement by Sir William Haley that suppression will never win a debate, and that if "the enemies of liberty are met with a denial of liberty, many men of goodwill will come to suspect that there is something in the proscribed doctrine after all. Erroneous doctrines thrive on being expunged. They die if exposed."

The Smith Act, as applied in the *Dennis* case, was, in the view of Justice Frankfurter, thoroughly unwise, but yet it was constitutional. "Much," he said, "that should be rejected as illiberal, because repressive and envenoming, may well be not unconstitutional." The concluding sentences of his opinion are: "Without open minds there can be no open society. And if society be not open the spirit of man is mutilated and becomes enslaved."

It is difficult to restate Justice Frankfurter's position, but as I read his opinion it comes to this:

1. When legislation is before the Court, and the question is

its constitutionality, the Court must try to see the need for the statute as Congress saw it. Although the Smith Act was adopted in 1940, the Court's judgment of the act must be made in the light of the facts available in 1948, when the defendants were indicted; for the question was not the constitutionality of the act on its face, but of the act as applied to the defendants in the light of the proofs and in the light of facts of which the trial court could take judicial notice. *All these facts were to be seen with the eyes of Congress.* As thus seen, it would appear that it may have been reasonable *for Congress* to conclude that the security of the United States was endangered by the existence of the Communist conspiracy in the United States.

2. For someone outside Congress—e.g., a British observer, or Mr. Kennan, or Felix Frankfurter as a private citizen—the action of Congress, as seen through the prosecution, may be unreasonable, or even dangerous nonsense. What such persons see—no matter how wise and well-informed they may be—has no bearing, however, on the constitutional issue.

3. But in enacting the Smith Act and in applying its terms to the defendants, Congress restricted free speech. Here again one must try to see the situation *as Congress saw it.* What Congress saw was speech that advocated overthrow of the Government, with intent that the speech be acted upon as speedily as circumstances would permit. *Congress reasonably could rank such speech low in the order of values.*

4. To a private citizen—e.g., Felix Frankfurter without his judicial robe—even such speech ought to be tolerated; for coupled with it is criticism of social and economic evils. Furthermore, if advocacy of overthrow is punished, persons who do not believe in overthrow of government will inevitably be silenced for fear that criticism will be confused with advocacy of overthrow. In other words, suppression of revolutionary speech will also suppress the speech of reformers. While the act and the prosecution are directed against the Communist conspiracy, nonetheless the interchange of ideas among non-Communist citizens will be restricted. But these considerations do not spell the unconstitutionality of the Smith Act as applied to the defendants.

The *constitutionality* is determined by the combination of the propositions in paragraphs (1) and (3) above; while the question of *wisdom* is determined by the combination of the propositions in paragraphs (2) and (4) above.

This line of reasoning involves assumptions, which Justice Frankfurter has made:

5. Congress has the duty to preserve the Nation and the Government and to choose the means which seem reasonable —seem reasonable to Congress—to achieve this end.

6. Congress must respect free speech and the other freedoms guarantied by the First Amendment. But these freedoms are not absolutes.

7. The guaranties of the First Amendment have no preferred constitutional position.

8. There is one extremely significant value that must be kept in mind; viz., the democratic processes must not be impaired or restricted: citizens must be free to choose their legislative representatives; so that if, in resolving a conflict between the constitutional value of national security and the constitutional value of free speech, Congress should err in judgment—though acting constitutionally—the people would find it possible to correct the error by enacting new legislation.

This line of reasoning, though admittedly impressive, is not invulnerable. Let us point to a number of difficulties.

Justice Frankfurter said that it is important constitutionally that the democratic processes be kept unimpaired and unrestricted. But he believed that the Smith Act, as applied in the *Dennis* case, had a silencing, repressive effect, for reformers will not speak for fear of being mistaken for revolutionaries. It may follow, then, that to speak for the amendment or repeal of the Smith Act might become dangerous after the convictions of the defendants. "But it is relevant to remind that in sustaining the power of Congress in a case like this nothing irrevocable is done," Justice Frankfurter said. But is this true? By his own testimony: "in sustaining the conviction before us we can hardly escape restriction on the interchange of ideas." Is not a restriction on the interchange of ideas detrimental to the democratic process that involves free citizens going freely to the polls to vote for candidates for Congress after free and open debates have informed the citizens on the issues and on the candidates' platforms? Again let us quote Frankfurter: "No matter how clear we may be that the defendants now before us are preparing to overthrow our Government at the propitious moment, it is self-delusion to think that we can punish them for their advocacy without adding to the risks run by loyal citizens who honestly believe in some of the reforms these defendants advance." Truth, said Frankfurter, cannot "be pursued in an atmosphere hostile to the endeavor or under dangers which are hazarded only by heroes." Was it not precisely to avoid the creation of such hazards and of such a hostile atmosphere that the First Amendment was adopted? "Without open minds there can be no open society," Frankfurter said. But if an act of Congress contributes to a closing of minds, and thus to a closed society, is it not interfering with the "democratic process," without which there can be no "open society"? Without an atmosphere conducive to open minds— not only for "heroes" but for the ordinary citizens—there can be no "democratic process," and no "open society." The last sentence of his opinion, as we have seen, states that "if society be not open the spirit of man is mutilated and becomes enslaved." Is not this truth basic to an understanding of the rationale of the First Amendment? And does it not follow that if an act of Congress affects the open spirit of man (who is not a hero), so that it becomes mutilated and may become enslaved, it is in conflict with the First Amendment?

What we have here is the following situation:

(a) Congress thought that the Communist conspiracy was a serious menace, a substantial threat to national security. (b) Frankfurter thought that Communism, while an external threat, was not in fact a domestic danger.

(c) Congress thought that utterances that advocate overthrow of the Government are not worthy of constitutional protection. (d) Frankfurter thought that such utterances also entail criticism of existing evils and cannot, out of hand, be placed outside the pale of the First Amendment.

(e) Congress thought that punishment of the defendants

will not restrict free speech. (f) Frankfurter thought that the judgments of conviction will restrict interchange of ideas.

Here is direct opposition on and contradiction of every significant proposition; yet Justice Frankfurter, in order to avoid the charge of lack of "judicial self-restraint," and in order not to lay the Court open to the charge of acting as a "super-legislature," concluded that the convictions did not violate the First Amendment.

Does this mean complete abdication of the power to hold acts of Congress unconstitutional as in conflict with the First Amendment? Not at all; for Frankfurter said that if an attempt were made to apply the Smith Act to facts like those in the *Gitlow* case, he might come to a different conclusion. Judicial self-restraint stops short of judicial abdication. "It requires excessive tolerance of the legislative judgment," he said, "to suppose that the Gitlow publication in the circumstances could justify serious concern."

What we are left with is a balancing of interests or values, which is by and large a legislative function or obligation; and the door of judicial review is left open, but only very slightly. Congress may be wrong in all its essential judgments with respect to a matter like the Communist Party of the United States, and in its legislative enactment may do more harm than good, and may even seriously restrict First Amendment freedoms, without contributing to national security (which was not seriously endangered anyway!)—yet the legislation, from Justice Frankfurter's standpoint, would be constitutional.

In the *Dennis* case Frankfurter was following the line he took in the majority opinion in the *Gobitis* case [11] and in the minority opinion in the *Barnette* case.[12] While in those cases he might have argued with some reason that the democratic process remained unimpaired by a law that compelled pupils that were Jehovah's Witnesses to salute the flag in school exercises, he could not sustain this position in the *Dennis* case without denying the facts of life as he knew them.

Justice Frankfurter, as we have seen, makes a distinction between wisdom and constitutionality—an act of Congress may be unwise and yet constitutional. I feel sure that no matter how many times Frankfurter may repeat this proposition, American citizens will tend to think that what is constitutional is wise and that what is wise is constitutional. And this feeling cannot and ought not to be brushed aside as one based on ignorance or foolishness; for a constitution ought to be an expression of the wisest political thought of the people—it ought to be framed so as to maximize legislative and judicial wisdom and to minimize idiocy. Was it not for this purpose that the Constitution was ordained and established for the United States? Children in the public schools and high school are taught, in the words of the Preamble to the Constitution, that the Constitution was adopted "in order to form a more perfect union, establish justice, insure domestic tranquility, provide for the common defence, promote the general welfare, and secure the blessings of liberty to ourselves and our posterity. . . ." The normal assumption made by the average citizen is that a law that does not promote the general welfare or that does not secure the blessings of liberty to ourselves and our posterity is in conflict with the Constitution; and since the law was made by the legislature, it will need to be unmade by the Court. From this point of view it is, of course, the duty of the Court to decide whether or not the act of the legislature conforms with the purposes of the Constitution; and while the Court should respect the judgment of Congress, it is the Court's judgment that the country must respect.

Students of Supreme Court opinions may know, with Justice Frankfurter, that this is folklore but not good constitutional law. Citizens who are strongly opposed to a decision of the Court may agree that there may be a wide and deep gulf separating wisdom and constitutionality—this is how white people in the South have reacted to the decisions of the Court that have declared state segregation laws unconstitutional. But the American consensus is different; it affirms the identity of the Constitution with wisdom—and sometimes even with the laws of God. When this identity breaks down, as happened in the case of the Eighteenth (Prohibition) Amendment, the Constitution will be changed, and so the Twenty-First Amendment repealed the Eighteenth; but the common assumption is that such an operation is seldom necessary—witness the fact that the Constitution has only twenty-two amendments, of which the first ten were adopted almost simultaneously with the original Constitution; thus only twelve times has the Constitution been amended in a period of over one hundred and fifty years. The conventional explanation of this extraordinary phenomenon is that the Constitution is the embodiment of wisdom, and that the Supreme Court on the whole has been its effective guardian. "The American Constitution," said Gladstone, "is the most wonderful work ever struck off at a given time by the brain and purpose of man"—and the American people agree with this judgment. How, then—the common man wants to know—is it possible that what is constitutional, according to the Supreme Court, shall nonetheless be foolish and even be a *denial* of the blessings of liberty and a *harm* to the general welfare? Subtle thoughts, finespun arguments in long judicial concurring opinions do not touch the mind of the common man for whom the Constitution was framed. The common man, if he knew what was involved, probably would say to Justice Frankfurter: "If, Sir, you agree with Mr. Kennan that Communism is not an internal but only an external threat to our national security, and if you think that the Smith Act convictions will restrict free speech, then your official duty is clear: declare the act, as applied in this case, unconstitutional, and no nonsense!— begging your pardon, Sir."

Much of the trouble flows from the fact that Justice Frankfurter's mind in such cases works along legislative rather than judicial lines. He takes his stand against thinking within a system of concepts, rules, principles, presuppositions, and seeks to think within the framework of problems—not the problems that one finds in the marketplace of ideas, but the problems one finds where the fight is thickest and rough. Considering the elements of such problems, his mind looks for a solution, but not for a permanent answer. His attitude is experimental; he is willing to test an hypothesis. If it works, all right; if not, he will try something else. He thus places himself in the shoes of a legislator. He looks for practical solutions to practical (and not merely theoretical) problems; and often the problems involve conflicts of interests—boards of education against parents of pupils,[13] national security against freedom of speech, crime detection against rights of privacy,[14] the needs of fair judicial administration against freedom of the press.[15] He would leave the practical solution of the practical problems of life to the officials who are assumed to be practical men. If the citizens find that their officials are not practical enough, they will replace them with others. In their experimentation legislators are bound to adopt laws that will affect adversely freedom of thought and speech and that will "offend a free-spirited society." But these· experiments—e.g., the Smith Act—will yet be constitutional. "Reliance for the most precious interests of civilization [like the freedoms of the First Amendment], therefore, must be found outside of their vindication in courts of law." [16]

This attitude probably comes from Justice Frankfurter's depreciation of moral and other absolutes. With William James, he would cry out: "Damn the absolute!" Absolutes, he believes, imprison or paralyze the mind. The mind needs to be free to move, by trial and error, from one hypothesis to another, from one experiment to another. But an absolute puts a high wall around thoughts or actions; it says, "Thus far and no further!" The demands of life are for tough-minded relativities, not soft-minded absolutes. Those who fear life cling to the securities of absolutes; those who are courageous go in search of solutions which they know to be only temporary, tentative, partial. The absolutist will pontificate, mistaking the word for the deed; while the relativist will experiment and do the world's hard and dirty work.

This attack on absolutes is largely justified, but Justice Frankfurter carries it too far, to the point where he would have nothing to do with them. Thus he starts out by denying that the First Amendment guaranties free speech as an absolute. Is the clear and present danger doctrine an absolute? No, not any more than is the First Amendment. Are matters improved by substituting "probable" for "present"? Hardly, for one absolute is no better than another—all are equally dangerous delusions. The result is that he dispenses with both doctrines—clear and present, and clear and probable. Neither plays any role in his *Dennis* opinion.

Three things need to be pointed out here:

1. As in his opinions in the flag salute cases, so, too, in the *Dennis* case, Justice Frankfurter clings to a proposition which he fails to recognize as an absolute; namely, the democratic process—by which he means, broadly, keeping the way open for the election of new legislators who may change the law—e.g., do away with the Smith Act, or repeal laws which permit boards of education to require the flag salute.

2. He does not sufficiently see that for the effective and intelligent operation of the democratic process the First Amendment freedoms are indispensable. If the end is the democratic process, then the means are these freedoms; and there are no other means; means and end are here inextricably, organically connected.

3. Absolutes can be valuable tools of thought if used pragmatically. They can be used to imprison thought, true enough; but they can also be used to liberate thought. An absolute can be a thought arrested at an arbitrary point. In that case it is an enemy of the intelligence. But an absolute can also be a living, throbbing thought, in which the process of the intelligence continues to function as the thought, in all its sensitivity, reaches out to touch and to react to facts, truths, problems. It may start out as an hypothesis, but it ends—if ever it ends— as James would say, as an ultimate, but as an ultimate that generates other truths, and which itself changes, becomes enriched in meaning, in its never-ending process of becoming. It is only in this way that we can live under a Constitution, because it is a living Constitution under which we live. Belief in absolutes in this pragmatic sense is perhaps not essential in the legislative process, but it is indispensable, I think, in the judicial process, especially when the judicial process involves constitutional interpretation. If we had parliamentary supremacy, we could dispense with this method of thought; but our system is founded on a belief in *constitutional* supremacy, and this must mean that there are limits on legislative experimentation—espe-

cially, as Justice Frankfurter would admit, when the experiment adversely affects the democratic process by creating fears when the need is for courage, by creating insecurity when the need is for confidence, by restricting deliberation and communication when the need is for freedom of thought and exchange of ideas. Perhaps something can be said for an experiment on behalf of national security if it succeeds in its purpose even though in the process First Amendment freedoms are to a degree sacrificed. But what can possibly be said for such an experiment when one believes, as Justice Frankfurter apparently does, that it is a misconceived remedy for a nonexistent ailment? [17]

A further blow to the clear and present—or probable—danger doctrine was given by Justice Jackson in his concurring opinion. He contended that the clear and present danger test was "an innovation" of Justice Holmes for cases brought under statutes that were designed to punish anarchists and that were misapplied to socialists, pacifists, and Left-wing adherents. Since the charges brought under these antianarchy statutes often rested on "far-fetched inferences which, if true, would establish only technical or trivial violations," Holmes proposed clear and present danger "as a test for the sufficiency of evidence in particular cases." The test is good enough for the kind of case for which it was devised. It should not be applied in a case based on speech that directly or explicitly advocates a crime. Where the speech does not directly or explicitly advocate a crime, and the issue is a

hot-headed speech on a street corner, or circulation of a few incendiary pamphlets, or parading by some zealots behind a red flag, or refusal of a handful of school children to salute our flag, it is not beyond the capacity of the judicial process to gather, comprehend, and weigh the necessary materials for decision whether it is a clear and present danger of substantive evil or a harmless letting off of steam.

To try to apply the test to Communists, however, is to make the Government captive in a "judge-made verbal trap." In previous cases in which the clear and present danger test was used the courts faced "trivialities" that were being prosecuted and which could be checked by this "rule of reason."

But the *Dennis* case, said Jackson, involves facts and issues that are quite different. Holmes and Brandeis never had a case like this before them.

The Constitution does not protect the right of an individual to advocate or teach the overthrow of government. Such speech is not constitutionally protected, and the clear and present danger test has no application to such speech. The facts in the *Dennis* case, said Jackson, go even beyond this proposition, for what the case really involves

is a conviction for conspiracy, after a trial for conspiracy, on an indictment charging conspiracy, brought under a statute outlawing conspiracy. . . . The Constitution does not make conspiracy a civil right. . . . The basic rationale of the law of conspiracy is that a conspiracy may be an evil in itself, independently of any other evil it seeks to accomplish. . . . Congress may make it a crime to conspire with others to do what an individual may lawfully do on his own. . . . Although one may raise the prices of his products, and many, acting without concert, may do so, the moment they conspire to that end they are punishable. The same principle is applied to organized labor. Any workman may quit his work for any reason, but concerted actions to the same end are in some circumstances forbidden.

To make out the crime of conspiracy no overt act need be proved; the act of conspiring may itself be the crime. This is not to say, Justice Jackson stated, that Congress could punish conspiracy to advocate something the doing of which it could not punish. But since Congress could punish the teaching or advocacy of overthrow of government, it has the power to punish a conspiracy for the purpose of so teaching or advocating.

While Jackson thought that the conspiracy weapon as against Communists was "an awkward and inept remedy," he could see no constitutional ground for depriving the Government of this weapon. "There is no constitutional right to 'gang up' on the Government." Jackson concluded by saying that he had little faith in the long-range effectiveness of the convictions to stop the rise of Communism. "Communism will not go to jail with these Communists."

The opinion by Justice Jackson has a flavor of hardheaded realism, for it points up the conspiratorial aspect of the Communist Party; but when examined closely, the opinion offers very little constructive thought.

As to the clear and present danger test, Jackson was factually mistaken in claiming that its origin was in cases which had nothing to do with conspiracies. In the *Schenck* case, in which the doctrine was first stated by Holmes, two of the three charges were based on conspiracy; and in *Frohwerk* the conviction was for conspiracy; so, too, in *Abrams*—and in this case the dissenting opinion of Holmes used the clear and present danger test. Jackson's effort to differentiate, on historical grounds, free speech cases that involved solitary individuals, in which the clear and present danger test may be applied, and free speech cases that involved a charge of conspiracy, in which the test may not be applied, is without support in the decisions.

Jackson trivialized the test by limiting it to cases in which the issue is "criminality of a hot-headed speech on a street corner, or circulation of a few incendiary pamphlets, or parading by some zealots behind a red flag, or refusal of a handful of school children to salute our flag."

Furthermore, he exaggerated the legal significance of conspiracy in free speech cases, thereby endangering the First Amendment freedoms. For suppose that instead of an individual, acting on his own initiative, making a hotheaded speech on a street corner, two persons agree that each will make a hotheaded speech on separate street corners, or on the same street corner on different days. The agreement could spell out a criminal conspiracy. While in the case of the solitary individual the clear and present danger test would apply, according to Jackson, in the conspiracy case it would not apply, and the defendants could be punished as coconspirators even if no act followed their agreement to make the speeches. Although Justice Jackson recognized the fact that criminal conspiracy could become "a dragnet device capable of perversion into an instrument of injustice," he left the doctrine of criminal conspiracy unprotected by the guaranties of the First Amendment. On the contrary, the main weight of his opinion seems to be on the proposition that conspiracy may be punished without regard to the First Amendment.

The only exception to this principle that Jackson recognized was that a legislature could not punish a "conspiracy to advocate something, the doing of which it may not punish." Since, e.g., an individual has the right to advocate the doctrine of communal property ownership not to be achieved by force, advocacy of this doctrine could not be punished through a conspiracy prosecution. This exception relates to the content of a speech, and is an important exception to the conspiracy doctrine as broadly conceived by Jackson, but it does not, I think, go far enough to remove the danger inherent in the doctrine when applied to concerted exercises of free speech, press, and assembly. The way the criminal conspiracy doctrine was used in the preceding century against efforts of organized labor should serve as a warning that the doctrine lends itself to abuse and can easily become an instrument of oppression against unpopular groups.[18] This is not said to throw a shadow on its justifiable use in restraint of trade cases, or in ordinary criminal situations (e.g., conspiracy to kidnap, or to murder); I mean only to question the propriety of extending widely the conspiracy doctrine to situations marked off as sanctuaries by the First Amendment.

Justice Jackson was wrong, too, in urging that Congress could make it a crime for an *individual* to teach or advocate overthrow of government, without regard to the clear and present danger test.[19] This was the holding of the Court in the *Gitlow* case; but in the *Dennis* case only Justice Jackson in the Supreme Court and Judge Chase in the court of appeals accepted the *Gitlow* decision as a binding precedent; [20] the others adopted, rather, the Holmes-Brandeis dissents, and affirmed, however interpreted, the clear and present danger test. Justice Jackson was wrong for the same reason that the majority in the *Gitlow* case were wrong: Gitlow's "Manifesto," as Holmes said, was a "redundant discourse"; it had no chance of starting anything, let alone a revolution.

# ☆ 28 ☆

# The Loss of a

# Constitutional Jewel?

THE prosecution of the Communist Party leaders was based on the charge that they had *conspired* to teach and advocate overthrow of the Government and that they had organized the party for the purpose of teaching and advocating this revolutionary doctrine. Professor Sidney Hook has made the very telling criticism that Congress, the prosecution, and the Supreme Court had misconceived the danger of the Communist conspiracy. The point is important enough to call for careful consideration.

Communism is an international movement, says Professor Hook,[1] with headquarters in Moscow. The Communist Party of the United States is an integral part of this movement. When viewed as an organization in isolation from the U.S.S.R., the party "would have only nuisance value, its members would be ineffectual, candidates for the political psychopathic ward." The party, when viewed, however, as part of the international movement, constituted "a clear and present threat" to national security; for it recruited members for espionage work and other unlawful activities. "Of course, considered in isolation, the Communist Party [of the United States] has not the slightest chance of succeeding in its aims"; but as part of the international movement, its recruits would commit acts of sabotage and espionage upon orders from Moscow, and it would not be up to the American Communists to decide whether the acts they are called upon to perform would be likely to succeed. "An unsuccessful attempt can be productive of great mischief. One plant needlessly struck, one atomic installation sabotaged, some key state secrets betrayed, in conjunction with the general strategy of the Soviet assault, may have effects out of all proportion to their apparent proximate causes." Members of the party thus "are literally the fifth column of the Red Army." They are "a para-military fifth column of a powerful state, ready to strike whenever their foreign masters give the word."

It is these facts which make the party a clear and present danger to national security. *"It is not the speech of members of the Communist Party which makes them dangerous but their organizational ties [to Moscow]."*

From this point of view it follows—Professor Hook draws this inference—that legislation was needed to destroy the Soviet fifth column in the United States. But then the "proscription should have been placed, not on *speech* to achieve revolutionary overthrow, but on *organization* to achieve it [i.e., revolutionary overthrow], and not merely any organization but *an organization set up and controlled by a foreign power.*"

While the Smith Act, then, had the right purpose—destruction of the Communist fifth column—it was misdirected at speech. The provisions and wisdom of the act, says Professor Hook, are of doubtful character. The party and its members could have been proceeded against as agents of a foreign power.[2]

This analysis of the nature of the Communist danger, it seems to me, is supported by the facts. If one accepts Professor Hook's line of reasoning, as I think one should, it would follow that the application of the Smith Act to the Communist leaders unduly strained the act and the First Amendment, and has gotten constitutional theory and doctrine into a predicament that could and should have been avoided. The act should never have been adopted. Having been adopted, it should not have been resorted to as a basis for prosecution of the Communist leaders.[3] To have convicted them for *teaching*—whatever the proscribed doctrines of their teaching may be—was to pay them an undeserved compliment, and to resort to a subterfuge in an instance where everything could and should have been crystal clear.

In the *Dennis* case there were only eleven defendants. The logic of the convictions was such, however, that the Government could not stop with this case. It had to proceed against other Communists. In the eight years following July 1948, when the *Dennis* indictments were procured, 131 Communists have been indicted for conspiracy; and of this number, 98 have been convicted.[4] How long can this keep up? If the party is a clear and present (or probable) danger, can the Nation afford to allow so much time to pass until all Communist Party members have been punished?[5] And after party members have served their prison terms, are they to be allowed to resume their party work where they left off?[6] It seems that the logic of prosecutions under the Smith Act can have as their end harassment of party leaders and members, rather than effective ruin of the party. This is perhaps what the Justices of the Court had in mind when they said that they doubted the wisdom of the act and the prosecutions.

It is "the existence of the conspiracy which creates the danger," said Chief Justice Vinson. Yet years after this was written the conspiracy continues to exist. One cannot help but ask: does the danger continue to exist? Prosecutions and convictions of Communist Party leaders, functionaries, hacks, lackeys, and drudges continue to be ground out, and Congressional committee reports on the nature and danger of the Communist conspiracy continue to be published—yet the party, though "outlawed" by a solemn act of Congress,[7] continues to exist, and the F.B.I. purports to know exactly how many members the party has,[8] and the party continues to publish newspapers and to make noises that one associates with life—or at least with existence. This existence of the party must occupy the attention of a great number of government employees and officials and must cost the American taxpayer a handsome penny. Can it be that the party harasses the Government even as the Government harasses the party, and that an equilibrium of reciprocal vexation has been established between them? To many observers, one suspects, the scene, at first a sea of troubles, has become just a bother and a bore. It was certainly important to awaken the American people to the nature and danger of the Communist Party, and at one time it looked as if actions initiated by all branches of the Government had succeeded in doing this; but now the dragged-out fight, with apparently no possibility of any knockout or end, has become a silly side show that attracts no interest and brings no honor or dignity to the Government or the Nation.

In 1950 Congress adopted the Internal Security Act,[9] and in Section 2 of this act Congress declared that Communists "in effect repudiate their allegiance to the United States and in effect transfer their allegiance to the foreign country in which is vested the direction and control of the world Communist movement," and that the party is a "clear and present danger to the security of the United States and to the existence of free American institutions." The Communist Control Act,[10] adopted four years later, declared the party a "clear, present and continuing danger to the security of the United States"; therefore, Congress concluded, "the Communist Party should be outlawed." Despite the grave, and even somber, tone of Congress, serious doubts may be expressed as to the effectiveness and wisdom of its enactments in combating Communism. Much of it is like catching rain in a sieve.

While the clear and present danger may continue, it is doubtful if much has been left of the clear and present danger doctrine as Holmes and Brandeis understood it in their opinions in the *Abrams, Gitlow,* and *Whitney* cases. The Cheshire cat has disappeared, only its grin remains.

This is the main point made by Justices Black and Douglas in their dissenting opinions in the *Dennis* case.

The Court, said Justice Black, has repudiated, directly or indirectly, the clear and present danger doctrine. The First Amendment, he said, is "the keystone of our Government," and the clear and present danger rule does no more " 'than recognize a minimum compulsion of the Bill of Rights.' "

So long as this Court exercises the power of judicial review of legislation, I cannot agree that the First Amendment permits us to sustain laws suppressing freedom of speech and press on the basis of Congress' or our own notions of mere "reasonableness." Such a doctrine waters down the First Amendment to little more than an admonition to Congress. The Amendment as so construed is not likely to protect any but those "safe" or orthodox views which rarely need its protection.

With respect to the clear and present danger issue Justice Douglas made the following points:

1. The issue, it will be recalled, was kept from the jury by Judge Medina. The trial judge ruled that there was a clear and present danger. Justice Douglas (with Justice Black agreeing with him on this point) said that this should be a question of fact for the jury.

I think that the dissenters were right in this matter. I agree with the statement of the American Civil Liberties Union that "both common sense and legal tradition dictate that a conclusion about the general state of the social order should be a conclusion as to fact, and should be made by the representatives of society who sit upon a jury." [11]

Judge Medina—and Chief Justice Vinson, agreeing with him —made the question, as to whether there was a clear and present danger of a substantive evil that Congress had a right to prevent, one for the judges; it was not to go to the jury. Now, as we have seen, Congress has twice declared, in 1950 and 1954, that *it* found that the Communist Party was a "clear and present danger" or a "clear, present and continuing danger." Thus Congress is attempting to take the question away from both the jury and the judges. If Congress should succeed in this attempt, it is difficult to see how it will be possible to raise the constitutional issue of free speech in cases brought under acts of Congress affecting Communist activities, especially under the Internal Security Act of 1950 and the Communist Control Act of 1954. This might make Congress the final tribunal on constitutional issues. We must strongly hope that deference to legislation and that judicial self-restraint will not be allowed to reach this extreme point.

2. Assuming, said Justice Douglas, that the question whether there was a clear and present danger was one for the trial judge, he could have decided this issue in the affirmative (a) on the basis of facts produced at the trial or (b) on the basis of facts of which he could take judicial notice. As to clause (a), Douglas said that the record was bare of facts showing the positions of Communists in industry and government, and the extent to which they have infiltrated the police, the armed services, transportation, stevedoring, power plants, munitions works, and other critical places. As to clause (b), Douglas said that he could not conclude that the efforts of Congressional committees, the Attorney General, state legislatures, loyalty boards, and labor unions were "so futile as to leave the country on the edge of peril." Furthermore, he believed that Communists were known to the F.B.I.; that in case of war with the U.S.S.R., they would be picked up overnight; and that "the invisible army" of Communists was "the best known, the most beset, and the least thriving of any fifth column in history." But, said Douglas, action on such an issue should not be based on judicial notice; there should have been "plain and objective proof of danger that the evil advocated is imminent."

Justice Douglas touches here on a vulnerable aspect of the theory of the *Dennis* case; that is, the charge that the defendants advocated and taught overthrow of government, and that they organized the Communist Party for such teaching and advocacy. As we have said, it was not this teaching and advocacy by the defendants or the party that made the conspiracy a clear and present danger. The Communist leaders were a danger because they stood ready to carry out orders from Moscow to commit acts of sabotage, espionage, or other criminal activities. Without regard to whether these acts would prove successful or abortive, they might still have caused havoc or serious damage. But the wording of the Smith Act is not such as to have centered the *Dennis* case on this point and its "plain and objective proof" beyond any reasonable doubt. The conspiracy that was a real danger was not the conspiracy to speak—to teach or advocate— but to attempt seditious acts when the signal would be given by the U.S.S.R. The peril was not *from* speech, yet, ironically, the Court's decision, while not meeting the real peril, has itself created a peril *to* speech. Congress and the courts have thus, tragically, twisted a rope of sand and have made a mockery of an awesome constitutional doctrine. For the clear and present danger doctrine, despite its difficulties and limitations, was a constitutional jewel [12]—and now it is almost lost in a sea of obfuscating words.

It is possible to say, when one has studied and brooded on the *Dennis* case, that the defendants were punished because it was inferred from the nature of their doctrines and from the conduct of Lenin and Stalin, who held the same doctrines, that they would, if they had an opportunity, commit a crime. According to Macaulay,[13] though the inference may be right, such punishment is persecution. This was the judgment, too, of Justices Black and Douglas. If driven to take a final position, I would agree; but I would add that the prosecution was a beast that could neither bear nor throw off its load, and that now we are in the same predicament with respect to the conviction: we can neither bear nor throw off its load. This is another instance of the justness of Thoreau's bitter observation: "Things are in the saddle and ride mankind." For, after all is said and done, I believe that wisdom supports the judgment of Chief Justice Hughes, expressed in a case unanimously supporting the right of the Communist Party to conduct an open meeting in Portland, Oregon:

The greater the importance of safeguarding the community from incitements to the overthrow of our institutions by force and violence, the more imperative is the need to preserve inviolate the constitutional rights of free speech, free press, and free assembly in order to maintain the opportunity for free political discussion, to the end that government may be responsive to the will of the people and that changes, if desired, may be obtained by peaceful means. Therein lies the security of the Republic, the very foundation of constitutional government.[14]

This, in effect, rightly gives to the First Amendment freedoms a preferred position, as constituting "the very foundation" of our Government. In these freedoms "lies the security of our

Republic." This, in effect, means, too, that when legislation restricts these freedoms, the Court must at times consider the question of the wisdom of the statute. If national unity can be attained without compelling little children to salute the flag in violation of their religious scruples, then the Court must say to the legislature—and this it did in the *Barnette* case—that it must think and work a bit harder and come up with other means to achieve a legitimate end. I do not see that the situation is different when Congress attempts to regulate interstate commerce or to strengthen the security of the Nation.

# Appendix, Notes,
# Table of Cases, Index

# Appendix:
# Adoption of the Bill of Rights

WRITING from Paris on December 20, 1787, Thomas Jefferson told James Madison that there were many things about the proposed Constitution that pleased him; some of the proposals even "captivated" him. Then he added: "I will now tell you what I do not like." First among the things he did not like, he said, was

the omission of a bill of rights, providing clearly, and without the aid of sophism, for freedom of religion, freedom of the press, protection against standing armies, restriction of monopolies, the eternal and unremitting force of the habeas corpus laws, and trials by jury in all matters of fact triable by the laws of the land. . . .[1]

He knew, Jefferson continued, that James Wilson thought that a bill of rights was not necessary because the new government was to have only the powers delegated to it, and the powers not delegated were to be understood as having been reserved by the states to themselves. But, argued Jefferson, it was dangerous to take this position, for there was nothing to prevent anyone from saying just the reverse; namely, that the states had only delegated powers, while the National Government had both delegated and reserved powers. Without a bill of rights it might be argued that the National Government will have the power to take away the right to trial by jury, or any of the other basic rights; and "I have a right to nothing, which another has a right to take away. . . . Let me add that a bill of rights is what the people are entitled to against every government on earth, . . . and what no just government should refuse," nor should its existence be permitted to "rest on inference."

Jefferson was not alone in thinking that the Constitution without a bill of rights would be gravely defective. Just a month before he wrote to Madison, he had received a letter from John Adams asking: "What think you of a Declaration of Rights? Should not such a thing have preceded the model?" [2] George Mason thought the absence of a bill of rights a fatal objection to the Constitution.[3]

Madison, however, was not convinced of the necessity of a bill of rights. "Is a bill of rights a security for religion?" he asked in 1788 in the Virginia convention. If all the people belonged to one sect, he said, "a bill of rights would be a poor protection for liberty." If the states enjoy freedom of religion, this is due to the "multiplicity of sects . . . which is the best and only security for religious liberty in any society." [4] In a letter to Jefferson written several months later, Madison said that although he had always favored a bill of rights, he did not consider it important, for the following reasons: (1) federal powers are delegated, while the subject-matter of a bill of rights is reserved or withheld from the grant of federal powers; (2) there was reason to fear that "a positive declaration of some of the most essential rights" could not then be obtained in the desired breadth; (3) security is found in the limited powers of the Federal Government and in the jealousy of the state governments, which will keep the Federal Government from asserting powers not granted by the Constitution; and (4) bills of rights are only "parchment barriers" against the will of "overbearing majorities"; they are ineffective on the occasions when their influence is most needed; for the real power in a community is in the majority, and a government will invade private rights when its acts are supported by the people; there is no effective appeal to a bill of rights from "the tyrannical will of the Sovereign" people. Notwithstanding these objections, Madison added, a bill of rights may be useful in the following ways:

1. The political truths declared in that solemn manner acquire by degrees the character of fundamental maxims of free Government, and as they become incorporated with the national sentiment, counteract the impulses of interest and passion.

2. Although it be generally true . . . that the danger of oppression lies in the interested majorities of the people rather than in usurped acts of the Government, yet there may be occasions on which the evil may spring from the latter source; and on such, a bill of rights will be a good ground for an appeal to the sense of the community.

Madison concluded his letter with a word of caution: he doubted the wisdom of *"absolute* restrictions in cases that are doubtful, or where emergencies may overrule them." The reason for this caveat was to him plain:

The restrictions however strongly marked on paper will never be regarded when opposed to the decided sense of the public, and after repeated violations in extraordinary cases they will lose even their ordinary efficacy. Should a Rebellion or insurrection alarm the people as well as the Government, and a suspension of the Hab. Corp. [habeas corpus] be dictated by the alarm, no written prohibition on earth would prevent the measure. . . . The best security ag[ain]st these evils is to remove the pretext for them.[5]

A year later found Madison, as a member of the House of Representatives of the first Congress of the United States, leading the movement for the incorporation of a bill of rights into the Constitution. On March 4, 1789, the Senate and the House of Representatives went into session for the first time. On May 4 Madison "gave notice," the official report states, "that he intended to bring on the subject of amendments to the Constitution."[6] On June 8 he made a motion that the House of Representatives resolve itself into a "committee of the whole on the state of the union" to consider his amendments. He said that a consideration of amendments to the Constitution should have been the first order of business; "it would have stifled the voice of complaint, and made friends of many who doubted the merits of the Constitution." For the fact was that some states had demanded important amendments, and a number of state conventions had ratified the Constitution only after they had been assured that amendments would be adopted as soon as the new government would be organized.[7]

The Constitution, as ratified, contained some important provisions that could easily be placed in a bill of rights, such as a prohibition against suspension of the privilege of the writ of habeas corpus, against ex post facto laws, and against the enactment of bills of attainder. There was a guaranty of trial by jury for criminal offenses. There was a prohibition against a religious test as a qualification for public office. But these provisions were generally considered insufficient; for there was no guaranty of freedom of religion, or of the press, or of speech, or of assembly, or of the right of petition, and there were no safeguards for due process in the administration of justice.

Over a hundred amendments had been suggested by state conventions.[8] Madison, however, proposed eight resolutions, only five of which are relevant here. Those resolutions offered by Madison that were concerned with fundamental freedoms read, in his own language and style, and according to his own numbering, as follows:

1. That all power is originally vested in, and consequently derived from, the people.

That government is instituted and ought to be exercised for the benefit of the people; which consists in the enjoyment of life and liberty, with the right of acquiring and using property, and generally of pursuing and obtaining happiness and safety.

That the people have an indubitable, unalienable, and indefeasible right to reform or change their government, whenever it be found adverse or inadequate to the purposes of its institution.

4. The civil rights of none shall be abridged on account of religious belief or worship, nor shall any national religion be established, nor shall the full and equal rights of conscience be in any manner, or on any pretext, infringed.

The people shall not be deprived or abridged of their right to speak, to write, or to publish their sentiments; and the freedom of the press, as one of the great bulwarks of liberty, shall be inviolable.

The people shall not be restrained from peaceably assembling and consulting for their common good; nor from applying to the Legislature by petitions, or remonstrances, for redress of their grievances.

The right of the people to keep and bear arms shall not be infringed; a well armed and well regulated militia being the best security of a free country: but no person religiously scrupulous of bearing arms shall be compelled to render military service in person.

No soldier shall in time of peace be quartered in any house without the consent of the owner; nor at any time, but in a manner warranted by law.

No person shall be subject, except in cases of impeachment, to more than one punishment or one trial for the same offence; nor shall be compelled to be a witness against himself; nor be deprived of life, liberty, or property, without due process of law; nor be obliged to relinquish his property, where it may be necessary for public use, without a just compensation.

Excessive bail shall not be required, nor excessive fines imposed, nor cruel and unusual punishments inflicted.

The rights of the people to be secured in their persons; their houses, their papers, and their other property, from all unreasonable searches and seizures, shall not be violated by warrants issued without probable cause, supported by oath or affirmation, or not particularly describing the places to be searched, or the persons or things to be seized.

In all criminal prosecutions, the accused shall enjoy the right to a speedy and public trial, to be informed of the cause and nature of the accusation, to be confronted with his accusers, and the witnesses against him; to have a compulsory process for obtaining witnesses in his favor; and to have the assistance of counsel for his defence.

The exceptions here or elsewhere in the constitution, made in favor of particular rights, shall not be so construed as to diminish the just importance of other rights retained by the people, or as to enlarge the powers delegated by the constitution; but either as actual limitations of such powers, or as inserted merely for greater caution.

5. No state shall violate the equal rights of conscience, or the freedom of the press, or the trial by jury in criminal cases.

7. The trial of all crimes (except in cases of impeachments, and cases arising in the land or naval forces, or the militia when on actual service, in time of war or public danger) shall be by an impartial jury of freeholders of the vicinage, with the requisite of unanimity for conviction, of the right of challenge, and other accustomed requisites; and all crimes punishable with loss of life or member, presentment or indictment by a grand jury shall be an essential preliminary, provided that in cases of crimes committed within any county which may be in possession of an enemy, or in which a general insurrection may prevail, the trial may by law be authorized in some other county of the same State, as near as may be to the seat of the offence. . . .

In suits at common law, between man and man, the trial by jury, as one of the best securities to the rights of the people, ought to remain inviolate.

8. The powers delegated by this constitution are appropriated to the departments to which they are respectively distributed: so that the legislative department shall never exercise the powers vested in the executive or judicial nor the executive exercise the powers vested in the legislative or judicial, nor the judicial exercise the powers vested in the legislative or executive departments.

The powers not delegated by this constitution, nor prohibited by it to the States, are reserved to the States respectively.[9]

In offering these amendments to the Constitution, Madison called attention to the fact that the Constitution of Great Britain went no further than to raise a barrier against encroachment by the Crown, while the power of Parliament was left "altogether indefinite." True, whenever a great right—like trial by jury or freedom of the press—was questioned in Parliament, able advocates defended these rights; "yet their Magna Charta does not contain any one provision for the security of those rights, respecting which the people of America are most alarmed." Whatever may be the situation in the mother country, in the United States the people want a barrier against their own legislatures, "against power in all forms and departments of Government." The amendments reserve out of the grant of power "those cases in which the Government ought not to act, or to act only in a particular mode." They are intended as restraints against some branch of the Government, or "against the community itself," that is, "against the majority [and] in favor of the minority."

In the United States it is, perhaps, less necessary to guard against abuse of power by the executive because it is "not the stronger branch of the system, but the weaker." Safeguards must be leveled against the legislative branch, "for it is the most powerful, and most likely to be abused." Yet, having said this, Madison went on: In our system of government, "the great danger lies rather . . . in the body of the people, operating by the majority against the minority." Admittedly, "paper barriers" are weak against the majority, yet they may have value for their tendency to impress some degree of respect for the rights they seek to protect, to establish public opinion in their favor, and to rouse the attention of the whole community. In this way a bill of rights may be a means to restrict the majority.

It was contended by some, said Madison, that a bill of rights has been found ineffectual in the constitutions of some of the states. Madison admitted that only in a few states have the most important guaranties not been violated at some time or other; but it did not follow from these abuses that a bill of rights does not have, "to a certain degree," a salutary effect. If the amendments should be adopted, independent judges

will consider themselves in a peculiar manner the guardians of those rights; they will be an impenetrable bulwark against every assumption of power in the legislative or executive; they will be naturally led to resist every encroachment upon rights expressly stipulated for in the constitution by the declaration of rights.

There is, said Madison, an additional security that a bill of rights in the Constitution of the United States would be enforced; namely, the state legislatures will jealously and closely watch the operations of the Federal Government and will resist, with more effect "than any other power on earth can do," every unconstitutional assumption of power; the state legislatures will be "sure guardians of the people's liberty." [10]

From the vantage point of more than a century and a half later we can see that, except for some misplaced emphasis, Madison's mind was uncanny in its perspicacity. As we see the situation today, more emphasis must be placed on the role of the courts in defense of basic freedoms than on the role of state legislatures; but state nullification of federal action, it should be recalled, was in fact a prominent feature of constitutional theory until after the Civil War; [11] and even recently an occasional resuscitation of nullification has been attempted by leaders of the South on racial segregation issues. But the ultimate reliance for the observance of the Bill of Rights must be found today, as Justice Frankfurter has said—echoing the views of Madison—"outside of their vindication in courts of law. Only a persistent positive translation of the faith of a free society into the convictions and habits and actions of a community is the ultimate reliance against unabated temptations to fetter the human spirit." [12]

James Jackson, congressman from Georgia, spoke against Madison's motion. He said that he opposed inserting a declaration of rights in the Constitution. There were urgent calls for attention to "important business," he said, and a bill of rights, if not dangerous or improper, was "at least unnecessary." Why, he asked, should anyone suppose that the people need to safeguard themselves against actions by Congress? Do not members of Congress belong "to the mass of the people? . . . Do we not return at the expiration of two years into private life? and is not this a security against encroachments? Are we not sent here to guard those rights?" Congress may regulate commerce, but where in the Constitution is the grant of power for Congress to regulate the press? A member of the House, said Jackson, has been attacked in the public newspapers. "Have Congress taken any notice of it? Have they ordered the writer before them?" [13] Besides, the country has had no experience of living under the Constitution: "Why will gentlemen press us to propose amendments . . . ? Can they assure themselves that the amendments . . . will not want amendments, as soon as they are adopted?"

Elbridge Gerry, of Massachusetts, said that he would favor amendments "when the proper time arrives," but just now Congress should concern itself with the organization and the operations of the Government. He felt, however, that it was quite important to amend the Constitution, and this for a number of reasons: Rhode Island and North Carolina must not remain outside the Union, as if they were foreign nations, but must be won over by satisfactory adjustments in the organic law of the land. Without the amendments, there will be a fear of the powers of the Government among the people, and a reluctance by Congress to exercise those powers; but the amendments will relieve the people of their fears and will release the energies of the Government.

Samuel Livermore, of New Hampshire, thought a consideration of a revenue measure more exigent, for if Congress "did not sow in seedtime, they would be beggars in harvest." The people, he said, never could imagine that the amendments should be the first work of Congress. Roger Sherman, of Connecticut, spoke briefly and petulantly: "It seems to be the opinion of the gentlemen generally, that this is not the time for entering upon the discussion of amendments: our only question therefore is, how to get rid of the subject." Thomas Sumter, of South Carolina, considered the matter of amendments one of great importance to the Union, but was willing to postpone a consideration of them "when we shall have more leisure." Later the Constitution should, however, be amended, for, unless this were done, there would be lacking harmony and confidence between the people and Congress, and as a consequence of such lack "the measures of Government will prove abortive, and we shall have still to lament that imbecility and weakness which have long marked our public councils." John Vining, of Delaware, "found himself in a delicate situation" because, he said, he came from a small state "and therefore his sentiments would not be considered of so much weight as the sentiments of those gentlemen who spoke the sense of much larger states." Besides, he added, Delaware had approved the Constitution without suggesting any amendments, and he shared "the declared sense of the State of Delaware. . . . Proposing amendments at this time, is suspending the operations of Government, and may be productive of its ruin." Madison's arguments were all answerable, but why take up the time of Congress to do so? He contented himself with saying "that a bill of rights was unnecessary in a Government deriving all its powers from the people."

At the conclusion of the debate on June 8, the matter of amendments was referred to a committee of the whole. It was not until July 21 that Madison, when there appeared to be, "in some degree, a moment of leisure," moved the House of Representatives to go into a committee of the whole for a consideration of the amendments. Fisher Ames, of Massachusetts, objected: the business could best be handled, he said, by a select committee. Ames was supported by Theodore Sedgwick and George Partridge, also of Massachusetts, and by Sherman and Jackson. Madison was supported by Gerry, and by Alexander White and John Page, his colleagues from Virginia, and by Thomas Tudor Tucker, of South Carolina. The question was brought to a vote: 34 voted against consideration of the amendments by a committee of the whole, 15 voted for such consideration. The amendments were then referred to a select committee consisting of Vining, Madison, Sherman; Nicholas Gilman, of New Hampshire; Benjamin Goodhue, of Massachusetts; Elias Boudinot, of New Jersey; George Gale, of Maryland; George Clymer, of Pennsylvania; Egbert Benson, of New York; and Edanus Burke, of South Carolina.[14]

Three weeks later, on August 13, the House of Representatives resolved itself into a committee of the whole to consider the report of the select committee. This was accomplished, however, not without strong objections. William Smith, of Maryland, said that Mr. Page was ill advised in saying that the business could be disposed of in short order because of the "simplicity and self-evidence" possessed by the proposed amendments. "That may be his opinion, but truly, sir, it is not mine"; some of the amendments are neither simple nor self-evident, and some should be rejected; besides, there are supposed to be three branches of government, but thus far there were only two—"the judicial is uncreated," and without courts it is not possible to collect revenue, prevent illicit trade, or punish breaches of the law. Even several members of the select committee spoke for delay. But the arguments of Madison and Page prevailed. Elias Boudinot, of New Jersey, took the chair as the House resolved itself into a committee of the whole.

Madison spoke for incorporating the amendments into the body of the Constitution itself at appropriate places; "it will certainly be more simple," he said, "when the amendments are interwoven into those parts to which they naturally belong, than it will if they consist of separate and distinct parts. . . . If they are placed upon the footing here proposed, they will stand upon as good foundation as the original work." Several Congressmen argued that the original Constitution should be left intact, so that the world would see its perfection; whatever amendments may be made should appear separate from the Constitution. At this point in the debate, when the issue was put to a vote, Madison's proposal as to form won.[15]

The select committee of the House of Representatives recommended the following amendments to the Constitution:

1. No religion shall be established by law, nor shall the equal rights of conscience be infringed.

2. The freedom of speech and of the press, and the right of the people peaceably to assemble and consult for their common good, and to apply to the Government for redress of grievances, shall not be infringed.

3. A well regulated militia, composed of the body of the people, being the best security of a free state, the right of the people to keep and bear arms shall not be infringed; but no person religiously scrupulous shall be compelled to bear arms.

4. No soldier shall, in time of peace, be quartered in any house, without the consent of the owner, nor in time of war, but in a manner to be prescribed by law.

5. No person shall be subject . . . to more than one trial or one punishment for the same offence, nor shall be compelled to be a witness against himself, nor be deprived of life, liberty, or property, without due process of law; nor shall private property be taken for public use without just compensation.

6. Excessive bail shall not be required, nor excessive fines imposed, nor cruel and unusual punishments inflicted.

7. The right of the people to be secure in their persons, houses, papers, and effects, shall not be violated by warrants issuing without probable cause, supported by oath or affirmation, and not particularly describing the place to be searched, and the persons or things to be seized.

8. The enumeration in this constitution of certain rights shall not be construed to deny or disparage others retained by the people.

9. No State shall infringe the equal rights of conscience, nor the

freedom of speech or of the press, nor of the right of trial by jury in criminal cases.

10. In all criminal prosecutions, the accused shall enjoy the right to a speedy and public trial, to be informed of the nature and cause of the accusation, to be confronted with the witnesses against him, to have compulsory process for obtaining witnesses in his favor, and to have the assistance of counsel for his defence.

11. The trial of all crimes (except in cases of impeachment, and in cases arising in the land and naval forces, or in the militia when in actual service in the time of war, or public danger) shall be by an impartial jury of freeholders of the vicinage, with the requisite of unanimity for conviction, the right of challenge, and other accustomed requisites; and no person shall be held to answer for a capital, or otherwise infamous crime, unless on a presentment, or indictment, by a grand jury. . . .

12. In suits at common law, the right of trial by jury shall be preserved.

13. The powers delegated by this constitution to the Government of the United States, shall be exercised as therein appropriated, so that the Legislative shall not exercise the powers vested in the Executive or Judicial; nor the Executive powers vested in the Legislative or Judicial; nor the Judicial the powers vested in the Legislative or Executive.

14. The powers not delegated by the constitution, nor prohibited by it to the States, are reserved to the States respectively.

These propositions were considered and debated by the House for five days in April as it sat as a committee of the whole. All the amendments, with some changes, were approved.[16] On August 19 the House of Representatives took up the amendments to the Constitution as reported by the committee of the whole. The first action it took was to decide by two-thirds vote that the amendments be appended as a supplement to the Constitution rather than distributed throughout the original document.

On the following two days the House of Representatives took up and disposed of all the proposed amendments that were to constitute the Bill of Rights. It affirmed by the required two-thirds vote, except for a few changes, the previous action it took when it sat as a committee of the whole.[17] On August 22 the

House of Representatives referred the adopted amendments to a committee of three—Egbert Benson, Roger Sherman, and Theodore Sedgwick—who were directed "to arrange the said amendments and make report thereof." Two days later this committee reported an arrangement of the articles, and introduced a resolution that the amendments be proposed to the legislatures of the states, and any that are ratified by three-fourths of the legislatures shall be valid as amendments of the Constitution. This resolution was adopted.

On the same day the resolution of the House of Representatives, incorporating articles to be added to the Constitution, was presented to the Senate. Debate on these articles was postponed; they were taken up in the following week. The record of the Senate action is unfortunately extremely meagre; we shall try to state what the Senate Journal reports.[18]

Attempts were made to amend the article on religious freedom: amendments were offered to prohibit the preference or the establishment of one religious sect, denomination, or society, but these efforts failed; a motion to omit the phrase, "nor shall the rights of conscience be infringed," was carried. It was urged that the free press article should be amended so that freedom of the press would be guarantied "in as ample a manner as hath at any time been secured by the common law," but the Senate did not accept this suggestion. It was contended that the freedom of the people to assemble peaceably and consult for their common good should be limited by the phrase "to instruct their representatives." This effort failed, as a similar effort in the House of Representatives had failed. This article as it was first approved by the Senate took the following form: "That Congress shall make no law abridging the freedom of speech, or of the press, or the right of the people peaceably to assemble and consult for their common good, and to petition the Government for a redress of grievances." The Senate dropped the provision regarding the exemption of conscientious objectors from military service; but an attempt to provide that "in all cases the military shall be under strict subordination to, and governed by the civil power," and that there be no standing army or regular troops in peacetime without the consent of two-thirds of the members of Congress, and that standing armies in peacetime be avoided "as far as the circumstances and protection of the community will admit," and that no soldier be enlisted for any term longer than the continuance of the war, failed. The double jeopardy provision was changed so as to provide that no person "be twice put in jeopardy of life or limb by any public prosecution." The provision regarding trial by jury in criminal cases was dropped except the clause that provided that "no person shall be held to answer for a capital, or otherwise infamous crime, unless on a presentment or indictment by a grand jury." The Senate disapproved of the article that "no state shall infringe the right of trial by jury in criminal cases, nor the rights of conscience, nor the freedom of speech, or of the press." It disapproved of the separation of powers article. It approved the other articles. It is doubtful if the Senate devoted to this action more than two normal session days.

A number of amendments were offered in the Senate that are of interest although they failed to pass. It would be worth a great deal to have a record of the debate over them. One proposal was that the Constitution provide:

That there are certain natural rights, of which men, when they form a social compact, cannot deprive or divest their posterity, among which are the enjoyment of life and liberty, with the means of acquiring, possessing, and protecting property, and pursuing and obtaining happiness and safety.

Another proposed amendment read as follows:

That government ought to be instituted for the common benefit, protection, and security of the people; and that the doctrine of non-resistance against arbitrary power and oppression is absurd, slavish, and destructive of the good and happiness of mankind.

A sweeping amendment to secure a remedy for every wrong provided:

That every freeman ought to find a certain remedy by recourse to the laws, for all injuries and wrongs he may receive in his person, property, or character. He ought to obtain right and justice freely without sale, completely and without denial, promptly and without delay, and that all establishments or regulations contravening these rights are oppressive and unjust.

On September 9 the Senate reconsidered some of the amendments on which it had acted only several days before. It combined the amendments relating to religious freedom and freedom of speech and approved an article which read as follows:

Congress shall make no law establishing articles of faith or a mode of worship, or prohibiting the free exercise of religion, or abridging the freedom of speech, or the press, or the right of the people peaceably to assemble, and petition to the government for the redress of grievances.

On September 21 the Senate reported that the House of Representatives had agreed to some of the amendments made by the Senate and had disagreed respecting others, and desired a conference with the Senate concerning the disagreements. The House had named Madison, Sherman, and Vining as its representatives. The Senate named as its representatives Oliver Ellsworth, of Connecticut; Charles Carroll, of Maryland; and William Paterson, of New Jersey. On September 24 a message was read in the Senate to the effect that the House would accept the Senate amendments provided the Senate agreed to go along with the following version of two articles:

1. Congress shall make no law respecting an establishment of religion, or prohibiting the free exercise thereof; or abridging the freedom of speech, or of the press; or the right of the people peaceably to assemble, and petition the government for a redress of grievances.

2. In all criminal prosecutions the accused shall enjoy the right to a speedy and public trial by an impartial jury of the state and district wherein the crime shall have been committed, which district shall have been previously ascertained by law, and to be informed of the nature and cause of the accusation, to be confronted with the witnesses against him, to have compulsory process for obtaining witnesses in his favor, and to have the assistance of counsel for his defence.

On the next day the Senate concurred and so reported to the House of Representatives.

Between August 24, when the House adopted seventeen amendments, and September 25, when the Senate acted approvingly on the final changes recommended by the House, the amendments had been reduced to twelve. The first two amendments, relating to the apportionment of Representatives and the compensation of Senators and Representatives, failed of ratification by the states; the other ten were ratified in the form in which they had been submitted and became our Bill of Rights.

New Jersey ratified the amendments on November 20, 1789, thus becoming the first state to take this action. Virginia was the eleventh state to ratify. This was on December 15, 1791.

The Bill of Rights had been before the Congress of the United States from June 8 to September 25, a period of three and one-half months. While we know little of what went on in the Senate and in committee meetings, it is questionable if a total exceeding seven or eight session days was spent by Congress considering and debating the proposed amendments.

While the House of Representatives and the Senate were trying to reach agreement on the amendments that were to become the Bill of Rights, the Declaration of the Rights of Man and of the Citizen was issued by the Constituent Assembly in Paris on August 26, 1789; and when the new French Constitution came into force in 1791, the Declaration was prefixed to it. In its generalities, the French Declaration was modeled after our Declaration of Independence; in its practical provisions [19] it was modeled after the bills of rights of our colonies and states; [20] and both the Americans and the French had learned from the British models: Magna Carta (1215), the Petition of Right (1627), and the Bill of Rights (1688). While it was James Madison who prepared the first draft of our Bill of Rights, the author was human experience with tyrannical government in Great Britain, France, and the United States. It was written with the blood of men spilled by despots and by revolutions fought in the name of humanity. Everywhere one heard in its phrases "the still, sad music of humanity," and it became the progenitor of constitutional guaranties among nations, old and new, on every continent of the earth.

Reflecting his admiration for the French and his revolutionary zeal against England, Jefferson said: "Every man has two fatherlands, his own and France." Today we can afford to be historically more correct and candid and say that every free man has three fatherlands: England, France, and the United States.

$$
\begin{array}{c}
\text{\ding{73}\ding{73}\ding{73}\ding{73}\ding{73}}
\end{array}
$$

# Notes

## PART I. FREEDOM OF RELIGION

*Chapter 1. The Roots and the Flower*

1. M. Searle Bates, *Religious Liberty: An Inquiry* (New York, 1945). See also surveys of religious freedom in the world in *New York Times,* Dec. 25, 1948, and April 12, 1954.

2. The Universal Declaration was adopted Dec. 10, 1948; 48 nations voted in favor, none against, but the following 8 nations abstained: Byelorussian Soviet Socialist Republic, Czechoslovakia, Poland, Saudi Arabia, Ukrainian Soviet Socialist Republic, Union of South Africa, U.S.S.R., and Yugoslavia (*Yearbook on Human Rights for 1948* [United Nations, 1950], 466). The text submitted by the U.S.S.R. as a substitute read as follows: "Every person shall have the right to freedom of thought and freedom to practise religious observances in accordance with the laws of the country and the dictates of public morality" (*ibid.,* 459).

3. Often religious persecution goes beyond imposing limits on freedom of speech and press. In the *Christian Science Monitor,* Feb. 9, 1953, Robert M. Halle wrote that the organization representing Protestant mission groups in Colombia reported for 1952 the murder of seven Protestants, destruction of 3 churches, bombing of 6 churches and missionary residences, stoning of 12 churches, imprisonment of 40 Protestants, and the closing of 12 schools by the government of Colombia. See also Herbert L. Matthews, in *New York Times,* April 2, 1952.

4. Cecil Northcott, *Religious Liberty* (London, 1948), 43.

5. Luigi Luzzatti, *God in Freedom: Studies in the Relations between Church and State* (New York, 1930), 6.

6. Anson Phelps Stokes, *Church and State in the United States* (New York, 1950), I, 514. This work is the most comprehensive treatment of the

subject and is an indispensable source book. It is in three volumes, consisting of approximately 2,700 pages.

7. That establishment has its price, see Bates, 86–87 for Great Britain, 48 for Italy. See also Cyril Garbett, Archbishop of York, *Church and State in England* (London, 1950), especially ch. v and Epilogue.

8. Alexis de Tocqueville, *Democracy in America,* ed. Phillips Bradley (New York, 1945), I, 308.

9. James Bryce, *The American Commonwealth* (2d ed. rev.; London, 1891), II, 583.

10. *The World Almanac* (1953), 705–706. The figures show that in January 1953 there were an estimated 325,856 churches and a church membership of 81,355,494. See also *New York Times,* March 11, 1952, and April 12, 1954. Cf. William Warren Sweet, *Religion in Colonial America* (New York, 1942); also Stokes, I, 228 ff. and 50 ff. In 1955 the National Council of Churches reported that the total of Americans with church or synagogue membership was 97,482,711—or 60 per cent of the population (*New York Times,* Sept. 6, 1955).

11. Lewis Mumford, *The Condition of Man* (New York, 1944), 198, 256.

12. Cardinal Spellman's statement was published in the *New York Times,* Aug. 6, 1949.

13. F. Ernest Johnson, ed., *American Education and Religion: The Problem of Religion in the Schools* (New York, 1952). The position summarized in the text has the support of the Educational Policies Commission of the National Education Association, the American Association of School Administrators, the American Jewish Committee, the National Community Relations Advisory Council, and other groups.

*Chapter 2. What Is a Church?*

1. The speech as copied in the text appears in J. W. Allen, *English Political Thought, 1603–1660* (London, 1938), I, 217. "This speech might quite possibly have been made in 1620" (*ibid.,* 218). "The authenticity of this noble and characteristic address has been very unworthily questioned by some modern theologians" (Douglas Campbell, *The Puritan in Holland, England, and America* [4th ed. rev.; New York, 1892], II, 249). *Contra:* "The authenticity of Robinson's reputed 'farewell address' is so dubious that it seems advisable not to consider it as part of the writer's thought" (W. K. Jordan, *The Development of Religious Toleration in England, 1603–1640* [Cambridge, Mass., 1936], 247). The earliest known version of the speech is in Edward Winslow, *Hypocrisie Unmasked* (1646), 97 ff. Whether authentic or not, the speech is remarkable as a tract for the times. If it was a deliberate invention, its significance is perhaps increased as an instrument of propaganda.

2. Cf. Paul Tillich, *The Protestant Era* (Chicago and London, 1951).

3. In 1953 there were about 230 religious bodies in the United States, all but few of them Protestant (*The World Almanac* [1953], 705–706). It

is reported that 150 denominations have less than 10,000 members each; only 13 claim a membership of over one million members (*The Americana Annual, 1952* [New York and Chicago, 1952], 140, 608).

4. Quoted in Ralph Barton Perry, *Puritanism and Democracy* (New York, 1944), 108.

5. Of course every faith may define orthodoxy for its own adherents and expel as heretics those who deviate from it—e.g., the heresy trial of Rev. Claude Williams by the Presbyterian Church in 1954, and of Rev. George P. Crist, Jr., by the United Lutheran Church in 1955.

6. Quoted in Jordan, 246.

7. *Ibid.*, 247.

8. See Allen, 219; Jordan, 245.

9. He excluded those who serve a foreign power, giving as an example Moslems, but it is generally understood that he meant in fact Roman Catholics.

10. *Works,* VI, 9.

11. Perry, 356–357.

12. Quoted by Allen, 222.

13. A great deal can be, and has been, written on the relations of Puritanism to democracy. The most important books on the topic are Ralph Barton Perry, *Puritanism and Democracy* (New York, 1944), and Perry Miller, *The New England Mind: The Seventeenth Century* (New York, 1939), and *From Colony to Province* (Cambridge, Mass., 1953). Cf. Herbert W. Schneider, *The Puritan Mind* (New York, 1930); Perry Miller and Thomas H. Johnson, *The Puritans* (New York, 1938); James Hastings Nichols, *Democracy and the Churches* (Philadelphia, 1951); Clinton Rossiter, *Seedtime of the Republic* (New York, 1953); Vernon Louis Parrington, *Main Currents in American Thought* (New York, 1930), I: "The Colonial Mind, 1620–1800." For chief Puritan philosophical writings in America, see list in Herbert W. Schneider, *A History of American Philosophy* (New York, 1946), 28–29.

14. Jefferson placed the phrase upon the seal he used on his letters. The phrase was probably the "invention" of Benjamin Franklin. See, for the source of the motto, *The Papers of Thomas Jefferson,* ed. Julian P. Boyd (Princeton, 1950), I, app. II, 677.

15. Perry, 190.

16. *Ibid.,* 196.

17. *Ibid.,* 197.

18. Reinhold Niebuhr, "Democracy, Secularism, and Christianity," *Christianity and Crisis,* March 2, 1953, 19; cf. his *Christian Realism and Political Problems* (New York, 1953), 95–103.

John Dewey, instead of seeing in the historical events an effort to keep the state from interfering with the religious life of the people, saw an effort to keep the state from subjection to the divisive influence of the religious denominations. "This nation was born under conditions which enabled it to share in and to appropriate the idea that the state life, the vitality of the social whole, is of more importance than the flourishing of any segment or class. So far as church institutions were concerned, the doctrine of popular sovereignty was a reality. . . . The lesson of the two and a half centuries lying between the Protestant revolt and the formation of the nation was well learned as respected the necessity of maintaining the integrity of the state as against all divisive ecclesiastical divisions" (John Dewey, *Intelligence in the Modern World*, ed. Joseph Ratner [New York, 1939], 707). From this point of view the intent of the First Amendment is primarily to prohibit the religious denominations from invading the sanctity of the state, though its language conveys the opposite meaning. Justice Jackson has tried to combine both notions. By the First Amendment it was intended, he says, "not only to keep the states' hands out of religion, but to keep religion's hands off the state, and, above all, to keep bitter religious controversy out of public life by denying to every denomination any advantage from getting control of public policy or the public purse" (Everson v. Bd. of Education, 330 US 1, 26–27 [1947]).

## Chapter 4. The Virginia Experiment

1. Passed Dec. 5, 1776 (Stokes, I, 382, 304). See H. J. Eckenrode, *Separation of Church and State in Virginia* (Richmond, Va., 1910).

2. *Letters and Other Writings of James Madison* (Philadelphia, 1867), I, 162 ff. It should be noted that in 1779 the state finally had discontinued payment of salaries of Episcopal clergymen. Such payments had been suspended from year to year since 1776. Kate M. Rowland, *The Life of George Mason* (New York, 1892), I, 243. Cf. Irving Brant, *James Madison the Nationalist, 1780–1787* (Indianapolis and New York, 1948), the most authoritative biography of Madison. This is the second volume of a comprehensive study; the first volume was published in 1941.

3. Cf. N.L.R.B. v. Denver Bldg. & Constr. Trades Council, 341 US 675, 684–685 (1951).

4. Cf. Wilfrid Parsons, *The First Freedom: Considerations on Church and State in the United States* (New York, 1948), which argues on behalf of a modern assessment plan for the benefit of all denominations, in principle similar to the jurisdictionalism of Patrick Henry or the Virginia assessment measure. Father Parsons argues for distinction but no separation, co-operation but not a wall of separation. See also J. M. O'Neill, *Religion and Education Under the Constitution* (New York, 1949). This question will be considered at a later point.

5. Irwin v. Gavit, 268 US 161, 168 (1924); also Le Roy Fibre Co. v. Chicago, Milwaukee & St. Paul Ry., 232 US 340, 353 (1913).

6. Holmes in Bain Peanut Co. v. Pinson, 282 US 499, 501 (1930).

7. Holmes in Interstate Consolidated St. Ry. Co. v. Mass., 207 US 79 (1907).

8. Holmes in Schlesinger et al. v. Wis. et al., 270 US 230 (1925).

9. Holmes in case cited note 7 *supra*.

10. Rutledge in Thomas v. Collins, 323 US 516, 543 (1945).

11. For documents and notes showing Jefferson's views and efforts with regard to religious freedom in Virginia as early as 1776, see *Papers of Jefferson*, I, 525–558; especially the outline of Jefferson's argument in support of his resolutions, 535 ff. The earliest printed text of Jefferson's Bill for Establishing Religious Freedom is reprinted in *ibid.*, II, 305.

12. Text of Virginia Statute of Religious Liberty in Henry Steele Commager, *Documents of American History* (3d ed.; New York, 1943), I, 125. A slightly different form of the text is in Stokes, I, 392–394.

13. Stokes, I, 334, 394.

14. Jefferson letter of Jan. 1, 1802, to a committee of the Danbury (Conn.) Baptist Association. The letter, with the "wall of separation of Church and State" phrase, was quoted by Chief Justice Waite in Reynolds v. U.S., 98 US 145 (1878). Then the phrase was used by Justice Black in Everson v. Bd. of Education, 330 US 1 (1947). Italics supplied.

15. Letter of Madison to Edw. Everett, 1823, in *Letters and Other Writings of James Madison* (Philadelphia, 1865), III, 307–308; quoted in Stokes, I, 396–397.

16. Sanford H. Cobb, *The Rise of Religious Liberty in America* (New York, 1902). This is one of the best books on the pre-Constitutional period. See also William Warren Sweet, *Religion in Colonial America* (New York, 1942); Evarts B. Greene, *Religion and the State: The Making and Testing of an American Tradition* (New York, 1941); R. F. Butts, *The American Tradition in Religion and Education* (Boston, 1950); Joseph L. Blau, ed., *Cornerstones of Religious Freedom in America* (Boston, 1949); see especially Leo Pfeffer, *Church, State, and Freedom* (Boston, 1953).

17. Paul Tillich, *The Courage to Be* (London, 1952), 108.

18. Quoted in Stokes, I, 527.

## *Chapter 5. The First Amendment*

1. *Ibid.*, 526, 530, 537–538. Apparently the only communication to the Constitutional Convention on the subject of religious freedom was one on behalf of Jews. See letter of Jonas Phillips in *ibid.*, 528–529.

2. *The Writings of James Madison*, ed. Gaillard Hunt (9 vols.; New York, 1900–1910), V, 176.

3. *The Federalist*, No. 84, 1788 (Everyman ed., 1911), 439.

4. *Writings of Madison* (Hunt ed.), V, 271; quoted in Luzzatti, 699; Stokes, I, 534; Saul K. Padover, ed., *The Complete Madison: His Basic Writings* (New York, 1953), 253.

5. Quoted in Stokes, I, 533; Padover, 306.

6. Quoted in Luzzatti, 692; Stokes, I, 540–541.

7. The texts of the proposed amendment are in Butts, 78–91. See also Stokes, I, 538–552.

8. See, e.g., Parsons, and O'Neill, and especially "The Christian in

Action," statement by nine Roman Catholic archbishops and five bishops in *New York Times,* Nov. 21, 1948.

9. Stokes, I, 546.

10. Butts, 90; Brant, 353, 355; cf. Stokes, I, 548.

## Chapter 6. The Fourteenth Amendment

1. "The Constitution makes no provision for protecting the citizens of the respective states in their religious liberties; this is left to the state constitutions and laws: nor is there any inhibition imposed by the Constitution of the United States in this respect on the states" (Permoli v. New Orleans, 3 How. [US] 589 [1845]). See Barron v. Baltimore, 7 Pet. (US) 243 (1833).

2. In his dissenting opinion in the Slaughterhouse cases, 16 Wall. (US) 36 (1873), Justice Bradley said that the "right of free exercise of religious worship" was protected by the Privileges and Immunities Clause against state action. Also protected under this clause were, according to Justice Bradley, freedom of speech, press, and assembly, and other substantial rights. In nearly fifty cases parties before the Supreme Court have tried to get the Court to give some meaning to and put some life into the Privileges and Immunities Clause, but to no avail. The clause has been consistently construed as protecting only those interests that grow out of the relations between the citizen and the National Government, e.g., the right of an American citizen to come to the seat of government. See also O'Neil v. Vt., 144 US 323 (1892), dis. ops. by Field and Harlan. For a discussion of this matter, see M. R. Konvitz, *The Constitution and Civil Rights* (New York, 1947), ch. iii.

3. Gitlow v. N.Y., 268 US 652 (1925).

4. Cantwell v. Conn., 310 US 296 (1940). For some later cases, see Konvitz, 40.

5. Palko v. Conn., 302 US 319 (1937).

6. For a clash of these views see Adamson v. Calif., 322 US 46 (1947), conc. op. by Frankfurter; dis. op. by Murphy, with Rutledge joining; and dis. op. by Black, with Douglas joining. See F. R. Coudert, "The Bill of Rights: The Decision in Adamson v. California," 34 *A.B.A. Jour.* 19 (1948); Chas. Fairman, "Does the Fourteenth Amendment Incorporate the Bill of Rights?" 2 *Stanford L. Rev.* 5 (1949); Wm. W. Crosskey, *Politics and the Constitution in the History of the United States* (Chicago, 1953), 1052, 1056, 1146.

7. Adamson v. Calif., 322 US 46, 89 (1947).

8. Betts v. Brady, 316 US 455 (1942); Wolf v. Colo., 338 US 25 (1949).

9. See his dis. op. in Adamson v. Calif.

10. *Ibid.* Cf. William W. Crosskey, "Charles Fairman, 'Legislative History,' and the Constitutional Limitations on State Authority," 22 *U. of Chi. L. Rev.* 1 (1954); Charles Fairman, "A Reply to Professor Crosskey," 22,

*U. of Chi. L. Rev.* 1 (1954), 144; also note, 67 *Harv. L. Rev.* 1016 (1954); also references in note 6 *supra*.

11. Joint Anti-Fascist Refugee Committee v. McGrath, 341 US 123 (1951).

12. *Ibid.*

13. *Ibid.* This essentially was the position of Justices Murphy and Rutledge—see Murphy's dis. op., in which Rutledge concurred, in Adamson v. Calif.

14. Re Oliver, 333 US 257 (1948).

15. In Twining v. N.J., 211 US 78 (1908).

16. Adamson v. Calif. See also Black's dis. op. in Beauharnais v. Ill., 343 US 250 (1952).

## *Chapter 7. Is Freedom of Religion an Absolute?*

1. We use the term "police power" in its broad meaning, to include, e.g., the power of Congress to wage war, the power of states to protect life and property, etc. Technically, it is questionable if one may speak of the police power with reference to the Federal Government. See the articles by Robert E. Cushman, 3 *Minn. L. Rev.* 289, 381, 452 (1919); 4 *Minn. L. Rev.* 247, 402 (1920). Justice Holmes spoke of the police power as an "apologetic" phrase. The "police power," he said, "often is used in a wide sense to cover and, as I said, to apologize for the general power of the legislature to make a part of the community uncomfortable by a change" (dis. op. in Tyson Bros. v. Banton, 273 US 418, 445 [1927]).

2. Matt. 22:15–21.

3. Stokes, III, 601 ff. In 1865 this action was made lawful (13 Stat. 518).

4. As far as I know only the American Humanist Assn. issued a public protest against this stamp, as well as against the three-cent stamp issued in 1953 commemorating the Gutenberg Bible.

5. Zorach v. Clauson, 343 US 306 (1952).

6. Stokes, I, 457. Act of Sept. 22, 1789. Cf. Pfeffer, 151.

7. Cf. Miss. v. Johnson, 4 Wall. (US) 475 (1867).

8. William George Torpey, *Judicial Doctrines of Religious Rights in America* (Chapel Hill, N.C., 1948), ch. vi; Claude Stimson, "Exemption of Property from Taxation in the United States," 18 *Minn. L. Rev.* 411 (1934); M. G. Paulsen, "Preferment of Religious Institutions in Tax and Labor Legislation," 14 *Law & Contemp. Prob.* 144 (Winter 1949); James F. Morton, *Exempting the Churches* (New York, 1916); note, 64 *Harv. L. Rev.* 288 (1950).

9. McCollum v. Bd. of Education, 333 US 203 (1948), dis. op.

10. Laurel Hill Cemetery v. San Francisco, 216 US 358 (1910).

11. Noble State Bank v. Haskell, 219 US 104 (1910).

12. In this connection we may mention also that unless the Supreme Court concedes that a person has a "standing" to raise the constitutional

question, no "case" or "controversy" is presented upon which the Court will act. It is not always easy for a taxpayer to show such a "standing" (see Doremus v. Hawthorne, 342 US 429 [1952]).

13. Hughes v. Superior Court of Calif., 339 US 460 (1950).

*Chapter 8. The Police Power*

1. Reynolds v. U.S., 98 US 145 (1878). The decision was unanimous; the Court's opinion was by Chief Justice Waite.

2. Selective Training and Service Act of 1940, sec. 5(g); 54 Stat. 889 (1940), 50 USC (Supp. 1941), App. 5 (1940). For exemption of conscientious objectors in World War I, see 40 Stat. 76 (1917), sec. 4, which provided for exemption of conscientious objectors who were members of "well recognized" religious sects "whose existing creed or principles forbid its members to participate in war in any form." For a comprehensive treatment of this subject see M. G. Sibley and Philip E. Jacob, *Conscription of Conscience: The American State and the Conscientious Objector, 1940–1947* (Ithaca, N.Y., 1952). See also Julien Cornell, *The Conscientious Objector and the Law* (New York, 1943). For World War I, see Norman Thomas, *Is Conscience a Crime?* (New York, 1923). For the British experience in World War II, see G. C. Field, *Pacifism and Conscientious Objection* (Cambridge, 1945).

3. New York has such an exemption. In signing the bill, Governor Thomas E. Dewey said: "I believe it to be a simple fundamental [*sic*] of freedom of religion that the state shall compel no child to learn principles clearly contrary to the basic tenets of his religious faith" (*New York Times*, March 15, 1950). Rhode Island has a similar law. *Christian Science Monitor*, May 24, 1949.

4. Arver v. U.S. (Selective Draft Law Cases), 245 US 366 (1918). Cf. U.S. v. Macintosh, 283 US 605 (1931); Sibley and Jacob, 433.

5. In cases in which pupils have sought exemption from laws requiring vaccination, the courts have uniformly, in the absence of express statutory exemption, refused to give them relief. See cases cited in Torpey, 268–269.

6. Soon Hing v. Crowley, 113 US 703 (1885); Hennington v. Ga., 163 US 299 (1896); Petit v. Minn., 177 US 164 (1900); People v. Friedman, 302 NY 75, 96 NE 2d 184 (1950), appeal dismissed, 341 US 907 (1951).

7. Meyer v. Neb. 262 US 390 (1923); Pierce v. Society of Sisters, 268 US 510 (1925).

8. Harden v. State, 216 SW 2d 708 (Tenn., 1948).

9. The U.S. Supreme Court in 1949 refused to review a conviction of a North Carolina resident who had been fined $50 for handling a live copperhead snake in a church service. The fine was imposed under an ordinance of the city of Durham (Bunn v. N.C., 336 US 942 [1949]; reh. den. 336 US 971 [1949]).

10. Prince v. Mass., 321 US 158 (1944).

11. Cases in note 7 *supra*.

12. See Sibley and Jacob, ch. xviii, and M. R. Konvitz, "The Case of the Eight Divinity Students," 1 *Bill of Rights Rev.* 196 (1941).

13. The last instance mentioned was reported in *New York Times,* March 10, 1953; it involved parents who were Jehovah's Witnesses and who contended that blood transfusions were against the Lord's injunction to Moses that the children of Israel shall not eat blood (Lev. 17:10–14). The New York Society for the Prevention of Cruelty to Children took the parents to Children's Court in the City of New York, and the judge issued an order authorizing the physicians to give blood transfusions as may be required. Cf. People v. Pearson, 176 NY 201 (1903).

14. In 1954 the Quebec Superior Court held that Jehovah's Witnesses were unlike Roman Catholics, Protestants, and Jews, "and opposed to all three," and so the sect could not be said to practice a religion or constitute a religious denomination (*New York Times,* Aug. 29, 1954). This decision would be impossible in the United States under Supreme Court precedents discussed in the text.

15. Fowler v. R.I., 345 US 67 (1953).

16. Watson v. Jones, 13 Wall. (US) 679 (1871).

17. U.S. v. Ballard, 322 US 86 (1944).

18. W. Va. State Bd. of Education v. Barnette, 319 US 624 (1943).

19. *Ibid.,* dis. op., at 653.

20. W. Va. State Bd. of Education v. Barnette, 319 US 624 (1943).

21. Cf. Hamilton v. U. of Calif., 293 US 245 (1934). See Russell, "Development of Conscientious Objector Recognition in the United States," 20 *Geo. Wash. L. Rev.* 409 (1952).

22. Jackson in case cited in note 18 *supra.*

23. Lochner v. N.Y., 198 US 45 (1904).

24. Holmes in Southern Pacific Co. v. Jensen, 244 US 205 (1916).

## *Chapter 9. The Principle of Separation of Church and State*

1. Reynolds v. U.S., 98 US 145 (1878).

2. Everson v. Bd. of Education, 330 US 4 (1946). Justices Jackson, Frankfurter, Rutledge, and Burton dissented. Their dissents were directed, however, at the application of the principle of separation of church and state to the specific facts in the case rather than at the principle itself. The majority, as we shall see later, held that the payment of the bus fares of parochial school pupils out of public funds was no violation of the principle of separation; the dissenting Justices said that the principle of separation should ban this public expenditure.

3. Ill. ex rel. McCollum v. Bd. of Education, 333 US 203 (1948). Justice Frankfurter wrote a concurring opinion, joined by Justices Jackson, Rutledge, and Burton—the four Justices who had dissented in the *Everson* case. Justice Reed dissented in the *McCollum* case on the application of the principle of separation to the facts presented in the case. Separation,

he said, does not bar "every friendly gesture between church and state"; the principle is "not an absolute prohibition against every conceivable situation where the two may work together." The constitutional guaranty, Reed said, should not be interpreted in such a way that it would conflict "with accepted habits of our people."

In his concurring opinion Justice Frankfurter accepted the separation doctrine but warned that "agreement, in the abstract, that the First Amendment was designed to erect a 'wall of separation between Church and State,' does not preclude a clash of views as to what the wall separates."

Justice Jackson concurred in the Frankfurter opinion and in the decision of the Court but expressed some reservations respecting interference with local schools.

4. Zorach v. Clauson, 343 US 306 (1952). The opinion for the Court was by Justice Douglas. Justices Black, Jackson, and Frankfurter dissented on the ground that the case was indistinguishable from the *McCollum* case; there was no dissent from the principle of separation of church and state.

5. See statements by Roman Catholic bishops in *New York Times,* Nov. 21, 1948, and Nov. 16, 1952, and Parsons, *The First Freedom;* also statement by Cardinal McIntyre, *New York Times,* Aug. 28, 1955.

6. Parsons, 92, 93.

7. *Ibid.,* 79. For a critique of this position, see M. R. Konvitz, "Separation of Church and State: The First Freedom," 14 *Law and Contemp. Prob.* 44 (Winter 1949).

8. Statement of the Roman Catholic bishops, *New York Times,* Nov. 21, 1948.

9. Cochran v. La. State Bd. of Education, 281 US 370 (1930).

10. Black, dis. op., *Zorach* case.

11. Dis. op., *Zorach* case.

12. 60 Stat. 230, c. 281 (1946), 42 USC 1751.

13. Bradfield v. Roberts, 175 US 291 (1899).

14. Servicemen's Readjustment Act of 1944, 58 Stat. 284, 289, c. 268: 38 USC 693.

15. Church of the Holy Trinity v. U.S., 143 US 457 (1892). The opinion for a unanimous Court was by Justice Brewer.

16. U.S. v. Macintosh, 283 US 625 (1930). The opinion was by Justice Sutherland for a majority of five Justices.

17. The attempt to base American institutions on a belief in a Supreme Being is strange doctrine, especially when expressed by a cosmopolitan person like Justice Douglas. Would he say that the feudalism and dictatorship that one finds in some Middle East countries today, among a people who on the whole are fanatically religious, presuppose a Supreme Being? Not so very long ago Christian Europe was also feudal and despotic, and the people then were no less religious than they are today. Were the slave owners in our Southern States before the Civil War less religious than the

Northern abolitionists? In the Union of South Africa the National Party fights for apartheid, with the support of the Dutch Reformed Church. When one sees how religions are distributed among the peoples of the world, and how people belonging to the same nation and the same church will fight for contrary political, economic, and moral ends, it becomes apparent that it is not possible to say that any one nation's institutions presuppose a Supreme Being. To identify an ideological position or political program with a nation's religious faith may be to degrade religion and to idolize social institutions. Cf. Reinhold Niebuhr in *Christianity and Crisis,* July 21, 1952, 97–98.

18. Speech at Springfield, Ill., June 26, 1857 (Philip Van Doren Stern, ed., *The Life and Writings of Abraham Lincoln* [New York, 1940], 415, 421–422).

19. Cf. Stokes, III, 564; also Stokes, I, 47, where the author speaks of "benevolent separation."

20. Citing as "typical" W. Va. State Bd. of Education v. Barnette, 319 US 624 (1943).

21. Here he cited the *Everson* case as typical—taxpayers' money was used to pay the bus fares of parochial school pupils.

22. Doremus v. Bd. of Education of Borough of Hawthorne, 75 A.2d 880 (1950); appeal dismissed, 342 US 429 (1952). In the United States Supreme Court, Justices Douglas, Reed, and Burton dissented.

23. In his dissenting opinion, Justice Douglas (joined by Justices Reed and Burton) urged that the case deserved a decision on the merits. "There is no group," he said, "more interested in the operation and management of the public schools than the taxpayers who support them and the parents whose children attend them."

24. Alabama, Arkansas, Delaware, Florida, Georgia, Idaho, Kentucky, Maine, Massachusetts, New Jersey, Pennsylvania, and Tennessee.

25. Indiana, Iowa, Kansas, North Dakota, and Oklahoma.

26. The statutes in question, however, go back to enactments of 1903 and 1916, with precedents for them in statutes that go back at least to 1867.

27. Tudor v. Bd. of Education of Rutherford, 14 N.J. 31 (1953); cert. den. 348 US 816 (1954).

28. A. H. Lewis, *Sunday Legislation: Its History to the Present Time and Its Results* (rev. ed.; New York, 1902).

29. Case comment in 64 *Harv. L. Rev.* 1195 (1951).

30. E. F. Czarra, Jr., "Sunday Statutes in a Modern Community," 61 *Yale L. J.* 427 (1952).

31. Ex parte Newman, 9 Calif. 502 (1858).

32. Ex parte Andrews, 18 Calif. 679 (1861).

33. See case comment, 64 *Harv. L. Rev.* 1194, at 1195 (1951). Some cases have, however, held invalid Sunday statutes of restricted application where there seemed to be no reasonable ground for the legislative classification of affected callings. Cf. Ex parte Jentsch, 112 Calif. 468 (1896).

34. Soon Hing v. Crowley, 113 US 703 (1885). Later cases: Hennington v. Ga., 163 US 299 (1896); Petit v. Minn., 177 US 164 (1900).

35. Peo. v. Moses, 140 NY 214 (1893).

36. Peo. v. Friedman, 302 NY 75, 96 NE 2d 184 (1950); app. dism. 341 US 907 (1951).

37. In Peo. v. Dunford, 207 NY 17 (1912) the statutory phrase "any property" was held not to include real property. This decision is typical of the crazy quilt of statutory enactments and court constructions with respect to Sunday employment and business. See Johnson and Yost, 219–255.

38. Leo Pfeffer, letter in *New York Times*, June 19, 1951. See also his articles in *Congress Weekly*, Feb. 13, 1950, and May 25, 1953, and his *Church, State, and Freedom*, 227 ff.

The Joint Legislative Committee proposed the following changes in the New York laws, which do not touch on the problem under discussion: to give grocery stores the same privilege as that enjoyed by delicatessen shops and bakeries (to keep open from 4:00 to 7:30 P.M.); to permit the sale of magazines as well as newspapers; to authorize local law to permit parades and processions after 2:00 P.M.; to restrict the seizure of goods illegally displayed for sale on Sunday to the class of goods actually displayed rather than the whole stock of the merchant; and to prohibit the taking of orders for goods by telephone or telegraph on Sunday (*New York Times*, March 12 and March 29, 1953). These changes would only validate practices that have been common and that have shown up the Sunday laws to be hardly more than pious wishes.

39. Connecticut, Iowa, Kentucky, Maine, Michigan, Wisconsin. Memo. submitted by Joint Com. for a Fair Sabbath Law to Legis. of State of N.Y., Leo Pfeffer, gen. counsel, pp. 15–19.

As was noted in text, Nevada is the only state that has no laws regulating conduct on Sunday. States with the most stringent laws are: Connecticut, Maryland, Massachusetts, and New Jersey (E. F. Czarra, Jr., "Sunday Statutes in a Modern Community," 61 *Yale L. J.* 427 [1952].

40. *Ibid.*, 433–434.

41. *Ibid.*

42. *New York Times*, Feb. 1, 1953.

43. Cf. bill in New York Assembly, introduced by Mr. Calli, Jan. 31, 1955, Bill No. 1507, Int. 1484.

*Chapter 10. The Liberty of Private Schools*

1. H. K. Beale, *Are American Teachers Free?* (New York, 1936), 332.

2. Meyer v. Neb., 262 US 390 (1923); also Bartels v. Iowa, decided same day. These cases involved statutes from Oregon, Nebraska, Iowa, and Ohio. Justices Holmes and Sutherland dissented. The dissenting opinion of Holmes contended that the entire Court agreed that the end aimed at by the statutes was a lawful one; namely, that all citizens should speak a

common tongue. The only question is whether the means are lawful; and
as to this question, he said: "I cannot bring my mind to believe that, in
some circumstances . . . the statute might not be regarded as a reasonable
or even necessary method of reaching the desired end." If there are children
who hear only a foreign language at home, it is not unreasonable to provide, said Holmes, that in their early years children shall hear and speak
only English at school. Since reasonable minds might differ as to the
reasonableness of the statutes, "the experiment" should not be prevented
by the Court from being tried.

3. Beale, 413.

4. Pierce v. Society of the Sisters of the Holy Names, and Pierce v. Hill
Military Academy, 268 US 510 (1925).

5. Farrington v. Tokushige, 273 US 284 (1927). See also Mo Hock Ke
Lok Po v. Stainback, 74 F. Supp. 852 (D.C., Hawaii, 1947); rev. on procedural ground, 336 US 368 (1949). See M. R. Konvitz, "The Constitution
and Foreign Languages," 5 *Common Ground* 94 (1945).

6. *New York Times*, Nov. 20, 1955.

## Chapter 11. The Liberty of Churches

1. See, e.g., R. H. Tawney, *Religion and the Rise of Capitalism* (Lon-
don, 1926); Max Weber, *The Protestant Ethic and the Spirit of Capitalism*
(London, 1930); E. Troeltsch, *Protestantism and Progress* (London, 1912);
Frank Knight and T. W. Merriam, *The Economic Order and Religion*
(New York, 1945); William Scarlett, ed., *The Christian Demand for Social
Justice* (New York, 1949); William Scarlett, ed., *Christianity Takes a Stand*
(New York, 1946); Louis Finkelstein, *The Pharisees: The Sociological
Background of Their Faith* (Philadelphia, 1938); Raymond J. Miller, *Forty
Years After: Pius XI and the Social Order* (St. Paul, Minn., 1947).

2. I do not mean to suggest that the destruction of an institution is
proof of its worthlessness, or that survival alone is proof of the value of an
institution. Cf. Reinhold Niebuhr, *Faith and History* (New York, 1949).

3. A recent instance in the United States was the threat in 1953 of investigations, by a congressional committee, of Communist infiltration into
the churches. Cf. *Review of Methodist Federation for Social Action*, 82d
Cong., 2d sess., Union Calendar No. 523, House Report 1661 (1952).

4. Watson v. Jones, 80 US 679 (1872).

5. In recent years efforts have been made to unite the Presbyterian
Church in the U.S.A., the Presbyterian Church in the U.S. (Southern),
and the United Presbyterian Church. The latter organization was formed
through a merger of the Associate Presbyterian Church and the Associate
Reformed Presbyterian Church in 1885, groups which go back to Presbyterian dissenting movements in the Church of Scotland. The Northern
church has 2,500,000 members, the Southern church 700,000, and the
United church 220,000.

6. The Court decided the case in favor of the faction in the Louisville

church that remained loyal to the Presbyterian Church in the U.S.A. (Northern).

7. Kedroff v. St. Nicholas Cathedral of Russian Orthodox Church, 344 US 94 (1952). Only Justice Jackson dissented. The Court's opinion was by Justice Reed. Justice Frankfurter wrote a concurring opinion, joined by Justices Black and Douglas.

8. From the opinion of the New York Court of Appeals in the case. St. Nicholas Cathedral v. Kedroff, 302 NY 1, 96 NE 2d 56 (1950).

9. Art. 5-C of Religious Corporations Law; 50 McKinney's N.Y. Laws 105; L. 1945, ch. 693, as amended L. 1948, ch. 711.

10. Conc. op. of Justice Frankfurter.

11. The same view was expressed in McGuire v. Trustees of St. Patrick's Cathedral, 54 Hun 207 (N.Y. Sup. Ct., 1889), which was an action to secure interment in a church cemetery. The court said: "For we cannot overlook the fact, which pervades this entire controversy, that it is not the mere right to be buried in two foot by eight of ordinary earth which the plaintiff seeks to enforce, but plainly the right to be so buried in consecrated earth. It is thus the spiritual right which, in substance, he asks us to enforce."

12. Matt. 18:20.

13. See essay by Ahad Ha-am (Asher Ginzberg) on "Sacred and Profane" in *Selected Essays,* translated from the Hebrew by Leon Simon (Philadelphia, 1912); also George Santayana, *The Life of Reason* (New York, 1930) Vol. III, "Reason in Religion"; Ernst Cassirer, *An Essay on Man* (New Haven, 1944), especially ch. "Myth and Religion"; Ernst Cassirer, *The Myth of the State* (New Haven, 1946), pt. I, "What Is Myth?"; and Ernst Cassirer, *Language and Myth* (New York, 1946), especially chs. ii and v.

14. This principle was followed in the *Melish* case. John Howard Melish was rector of Holy Trinity Church in Brooklyn for about 45 years. His son, William Howard Melish, was assistant rector. There were complaints against the son for his outside activities; he was active in the National Council of American-Soviet Friendship, which was on the Attorney General's list of subversive organizations. The vestrymen of Holy Trinity asked the rector to remove his son; this he refused to do; they then asked him to retire on a pension; this he also refused to do; they then appealed to Bishop James P. DeWolfe, Bishop of the Protestant Episcopal Diocese of Long Island. Acting in accordance with the canons of the Protestant Episcopal Church, the bishop requested the standing committee of the diocese to conduct an investigation and a hearing; this resulted in a committee recommendation that the pastoral relation between the rector and the church be severed; the bishop entered a judgment accordingly, and then issued a proclamation which gave canonical effect to the judgment. Then a meeting of the congregation ousted the vestrymen and another meeting was called to elect their successors. At this point the vestrymen went to court and asked for an injunction. The injunction was granted, in

effect confirming the judgment and proclamation of the bishop. Justice Steinbrink, of the New York Supreme Court, Kings County, relied on Watson v. Jones (Holy Trinity v. Melish, 194 Misc. 1006 [1949]; affd. 276 App. Div. 1088; 301 NY 679; cert. den. 340 US 936 [1951]).

## Chapter 12. The Law Knows No Heresy

1. U.S. v. Ballard, 322 US 78 (1944).

2. A majority of the Court, for whom Justice Douglas wrote the opinion, reversed the court of appeals and remanded the case to that court to pass on questions that had been by-passed by that court.

Chief Justice Stone (Justice Frankfurter and Roberts agreeing with him) dissented, saying that the constitutional guaranty of freedom of religion does not afford immunity from criminal prosecution for the fraudulent procurement of money "by false statements as to one's religious experiences" or "by making knowingly fake statements about one's religious experiences." If, e.g., the Ballards claimed that they had cured hundreds of persons in San Francisco, and procured money on the basis of this claim, the Government should be allowed to convict them for fraud if it can prove that they had never been in San Francisco. Furthermore, said Stone, "the state of one's mind is a fact as capable of fraudulent misrepresentation as is one's physical condition or the state of his bodily health." In brief, Stone, Roberts, and Frankfurter held that persons may be guilty of fraudulent use of the mail if they solicit money on the basis of misrepresentations as to events or beliefs.

The dissenting opinion of Justice Jackson is discussed in the text.

When the case came back to the court of appeals, that court affirmed the conviction by a two to one vote (Ballard v. U.S., 152 F. 2d 941 [1945]. The Supreme Court reversed the judgment on the ground that women, though qualified by local law to serve on grand and petit juries, had intentionally been excluded (Ballard v. U.S., 329 US 187 [1946]).

3. Heb. 11:1; John 20:29.

4. *Homilies on St. John*, XL.

5. Jer. 4:19; Ps. 44:21.

## Chapter 13. The Right to Seek Converts

1. Quoted by Joseph G. Harrison in *Christian Science Monitor*, July 8, 1949. Protestant chapels in Spain may not be listed in street directories or telephone books (*ibid.*, Dec. 16, 1948).

2. Quoted by Patrick Crosse in *Christian Science Monitor*, May 20, 1953. The writer also quotes from an article by the assistant director of a Vatican newspaper who wrote that "we cannot admit Protestant proselytism, because Italy, a country of ancient Christianity, is not a mission field for sects of other shapes. . . . Proselytism offends us." Cf. Bates, especially sections on Moslem countries, Spain, and Soviet Russia, 1–20.

3. Jefferson, *Notes on Virginia*, in *The Life and Selected Writings of Thomas Jefferson*, ed. Adrienne Koch and William Peden (New York, 1944), 272–277.

4. Rom. 10:14, 15.

5. Acts 1:8.

6. Roberts in Cantwell v. Conn., 310 US 296 (1940). Cf. H. M. Kallen, *Secularism Is the Will of God* (New York, 1955).

7. Douglas in Murdock v. Pa., 319 US 105 (1943). These remarks were made with respect to the distribution of religious tracts, but their broad application is justified in the light of later decisions.

8. Speech in New York, Sept. 9, 1912.

## PART II. FREEDOM OF SPEECH, PRESS, AND ASSEMBLY

### Chapter *14. The Freedom* Not *to Speak*

1. *World Almanac* (1953), 705. Members of the sect did not claim recognition from draft boards as conscientious objectors but exemption as ministers. See M. G. Sibley and Philip E. Jacob, *Conscription of Conscience: the American State and the Conscientious Objector, 1940–1947* (Ithaca, N.Y., 1952), 69–71. Whatever their employment, their "vocation" was that of ministers, Gospel preachers (*ibid.,* 34).

2. Amer. Civil Liberties Union, *Liberty's National Emergency* (New York, 1941), 27.

3. Quoted in Amer. Civil Liberties Union, *Religious Liberty in the U.S. Today* (New York, 1939), 21.

4. *Ibid.* Cf. Anson Phelps Stokes, *Church and State in the United States* (New York, 1950), II, 603; William G. Fennell, *Compulsory Flag Salute in Schools* (Amer. Civil Liberties Union, New York, 1938), which lists 18 states requiring flag exercises.

5. Fennell, 2, where some of the cases are listed. See also Stokes, II, 604–606. That others besides Jehovah's Witnesses were affected—e.g., Mennonites—was noted by Fennell, p. 3.

6. Quoted in Stokes, II, 605.

7. Minersville School Dist. v. Gobitis, 310 US 586 (1940).

8. W. Va. State Bd. of Education v. Barnette, 319 US 624 (1943); also Taylor v. Miss., 319 US 583 (1943). Cf. Stromberg v. Calif., 283 US 359 (1931).

9. While Justice Frankfurter does not believe that any of the freedoms enumerated in the Bill of Rights has a preferred position, in this statement he in effect does admit religious freedom to the enjoyment of such a position. But later he says that "national unity" is an interest "inferior to none" in the "hierarchy of legal values." Does "national unity," then, enjoy a preferred position? Later in the same opinion he seems to put an emphasis on the freedoms that maintain "open and unobstructed" "the

remedial channels of the democratic process," which would seem to put freedom of speech and press and freedom of suffrage in a position of priority. Then this proposition is tied in to the conviction that "to the legislature no less than to courts is committed the guardianship of deeply-cherished liberties. . . . Where all the effective means of inducing political changes are left free from interference, education in the abandonment of foolish legislation is itself a training in liberty."

10. Cf. Konvitz, "On the Right to Be Different," in Sidney Hook and M. R. Konvitz, eds., *Freedom and Experience: Essays Presented to H. M. Kallen* (Ithaca, N.Y., 1947).

11. In a concurring opinion Justice Murphy said that as a judge he has no loftier duty or responsibility than to uphold religious freedom "to its farthest reaches." This freedom includes both the right to speak freely, and the right to refrain from speaking at all "except in so far as essential operations of government may require it for the preservation of an orderly society,—as in the case of compulsion to give evidence in court." The flag salute is "not essential to the maintenance of effective government and orderly society." He quoted from the Virginia Statute for Establishing Religious Freedom: "All attempts to influence [the mind] by temporal punishments, or burdens, or by civil incapacitations, tend only to beget habits of hypocrisy and meanness."

12. For a strong defense of the Frankfurter thesis see Henry Steele Commager, *Majority Rule and Minority Rights* (New York, 1943).

13. See discussion of this problem in M. R. Konvitz, *The Alien and the Asiatic in American Law* (Ithaca, N.Y., 1946), 177–181.

14. Italics supplied.

## Chapter 15. The Freedom Not to Listen

1. Quoted in Leo Pfeffer, *Church, State, and Freedom* (Boston, 1953), 229.

2. Henry Bettenson, *Documents of the Christian Church* (New York, 1947), 333.

3. Commonwealth v. Beiler, 168 Pa. Super. 462, 79 A. 2d 134 (1951); cf. Commonwealth v. Smoker, 110 A. 2d 740 (1955) (same court).

4. People v. Donner, 199 (NY) Misc. 643 (1950); aff'd. 278 App. Div. 705 (1951); aff'd. 302 NY 857 (1951); app. dism. 342 US 884 (1951). Cf. Commonwealth v. Renfrew, 126 NE 2d 109 (Mass., 1955), which involved Buddhist parents who refused to send their child to school.

5. Charles K. Woltz, "Compulsory Attendance at School," 20 *Law & Contemp. Prob.* 3 (1955).

6. Fogg v. Bd. of Education, 76 NH 296, 82 Atl. 173 (1912).

7. State v. Jackson, 71 NH 552, 53 Atl. 1021 (1902).

8. People v. Turner, 98 NYS 2d 886 (1950).

9. Cf. Pfeffer, 596.

10. Pierce v. Soc. of Sisters, 268 US 510 (1925).

11. Stephens v. Bongart, 15 NJ Misc. 80, 189 Atl. 131 (1937), which involved the question of private tutoring, not a parochial school.

12. Pub. Utilities Comm. v. Pollak, 343 US 451 (1952).

13. Max Picard, *The World of Silence* (London, 1948), 21.

14. *Ibid.*, 40.

15. *Ibid.*, 198, 199. See also Paul Halmos, *Solitude and Privacy* (London, 1952). Shortly before his death in 1951, Harold Wallace Ross, founder and editor of the *New Yorker*, successfully led a campaign to prevent the use of loud-speaker devices for broadcasting programs in Grand Central Station in New York City. It should also be noted that after some years radio broadcasts in Washington buses and streetcars were discontinued, apparently because of insufficient advertising revenue.

16. Art. 18 of the Universal Declaration of Human Rights provides that "everyone has the right to freedom of thought." Art. 19 states that "everyone has the right to freedom of opinion and expression; this right includes freedom to hold opinions without interference."

*Chapter 16. The Right to Be Let Alone*

1. Samuel D. Warren and Louis D. Brandeis, "The Right to Privacy," 4 *Harv. L. Rev.* 193 (1890). The authors quote from an English case of 1820 in which Lord Cottenham spoke of "privacy" as a right that had been invaded; and the phrase, the right "to be let alone," they took from Thomas M. Cooley's text on *Torts* (2d ed.; Chicago, 1879), 29.

2. This phrase is used by the authors, p. 200.

3. William Faulkner, "On Privacy—the American Dream: What Happened to It," 211 *Harper's Magazine* 33 (July 1955). Cf. Anne Lindbergh, *Gift from the Sea* (New York, 1955); Virginia Woolf, *A Room of One's Own* (London, 1917).

4. Louis Nizer "The Right of Privacy," 39 *Mich. L. Rev.* 526 (1941).

5. Note, 62 *Yale L. J.* 1123 (1953). The states with statutes are New York, Utah, and Virginia.

6. Melvin v. Reid, 112 Cal. App. 285, 297 P. 91 (1931). The decision was based on a provision of the California constitution which provided that all men enjoy certain inalienable rights, among them the right to pursue and obtain safety and happiness.

7. Mau v. Rio Grande Oil Co., 28 F. Supp. 845 (1939), a federal case in California in which the court followed Melvin v. Reid, cited in the preceding note.

8. Bunstein v. Natl. Broadcasting Co., 129 F. Supp. 817 (1955).

9. Sidis v. F-R Pub. Corp., 113 F. 2d 806 (1940), cert. den. 311 US 711 (1941).

10. Cf. Lee Jones v. Herald Post Co., 230 Ky. 227, 18 SW 2d 972 (1929); Hillman v. Star Pub. Co., 64 Wash. 691, 117 P. 497 (1911).

11. Louis Nizer, 559, 560. See Howard B. White, "The Right to Privacy," 18 *Social Research* (June 1951).

12. Dis. op. in Olmstead v. U.S., 277 US 438 (1928).

13. Roscoe Pound, "Interests of Personality," 28 *Harv. L. Rev.* 343, 445 (1915).

14. *Ibid.*

15. *Ibid.*

16. Chaplinsky v. N.H., 315 US 568 (1942). The last sentence in the passage is from Cantwell v. Conn., 310 US 296 (1940).

17. Quoted in Frank Thayer, *Legal Control of the Press* (Chicago, 1944), 242.

18. Thayer summarizes the law by jurisdictions at 287–288.

19. Carl Stephenson and F. G. Marcham, *Sources of English Constitutional History* (New York, 1937), 427–429. See also documents on this subject in Zechariah Chafee, Jr., *Documents on Fundamental Human Rights* (preliminary ed., Cambridge, Mass., 1952) 3d pamphlet, 810 ff.

20. Stephenson and Marcham, 601.

21. Henry Steele Commager, *Documents of American History* (3d ed.; New York, 1943), I, 111–112.

22. Kilbourn v. Thompson, 103 US 168 (1881), quoting with approval from an English case of 1839.

23. Kilbourn v. Thompson, quoting with approval from a Massachusetts case of 1808.

24. Tenney v. Brandhove, 341 US 367 (1951), opinion by Justice Frankfurter. Justice Douglas dissented.

25. W. G. Hale and I. Benson, *The Law of the Press* (2d ed.; St. Paul, Minn., 1933), 151.

26. *Ibid.,* 151–152; also Thayer, 310 ff.

27. Cowley v. Pulsifer, 137 Mass. 392 (1884), reprinted in Hale and Benson, 176.

28. Wason v. Walter, L.R. 4 Q.B. 73 (1868), reprinted in Hale and Benson, 164.

29. Letter to Edward Carrington, Jan. 16, 1787, in Adrienne Koch and William Peden, eds., *The Life and Selected Writings of Thomas Jefferson* (New York, 1944), 411.

30. See note 24 *supra.*

31. Thayer, 347.

32. *St. Louis Post-Dispatch Symposium on Freedom of the Press* (1938), 12, quoted in William Ernest Hocking, *Freedom of the Press: A Framework of Principle* (Chicago, 1947), 12, 197.

33. Letter to Washington, 1792, in Saul K. Padover, ed., *Democracy by Thomas Jefferson* (New York, 1939), 143.

34. Letter to John Norvell, June 11, 1807, in Koch and Peden, 581.

35. Letter to Thomas Seymour, 1807, in Padover, *Democracy,* 147.

36. See note 32 *supra.*

37. Hocking, 197.

38. Golden North Airways v. Tanana Publishing Co., 217 F. 2d 612

(1954), opinion by Judge Yankwich, author of *Essays in the Law of Libel* (1924).

39. Noral v. Hearst Publications, 104 P. 2d 860 (Calif. 1940).

40. Note in 98 *U. Pa. L. Rev.* 865 (1950).

41. See James Rorty and Moshe Decter, *McCarthy and the Communists* (Boston, 1954), 84.

42. *Op. cit.* note 40 *supra.*

43. Beauharnais v. Ill., 343 US 250 (1952).

44. See note, 61 *Yale L. J.* 252 (1952). For scholarly survey of the law see Joseph Tanenhaus, Group Libel, 35 *Corn. L.Q.* 261 (1950); also by same author, "Group Libel and Free Speech," 13 *Phylon* 215 (1952). Cf. David Riesman, "Democracy and Defamation: Control of Group Libel," 42 *Col. L. Rev.* 727 (1942); also by same author, "Democracy and Defamation: Fair Game and Fair Comment," 42 *Col. L. Rev.* 1085 (1942). See also Will Maslow, "Group Libel Reconsidered," *Congress Weekly,* Jan. 23, 1948; Phil Baum, "Good—and Bad—Group Libel Bills," *Congress Weekly,* Sept. 19, 1949.

45. Zechariah Chafee, Jr., *Government and Mass Communications* (Chicago: University of Chicago Press, 1947), I, 124–125.

46. *Ibid.,* 126.

47. The act was held unconstitutional in State v. Klapprott, 127 NJL 395 (1941).

48. Chafee, *Government,* 127.

49. *Ibid.,* 128.

50. *Ibid.*

51. Tanenhaus, "Group Libel and Free Speech." Cf. same author's "The Protection of Racial and Religious Groups through the Law of Defamation" (Ph.D. dissertation, Cornell University, 1949).

52. See Note, 61 *Yale L. J.* 252 (1952), at 255, for summary.

53. *Ibid.* The states are Massachusetts, Nevada, New Mexico, Connecticut, West Virginia, Indiana, New Jersey, and Illinois. In 1954 the Province of Quebec enacted a religious group libel law. It is broad enough to punish merely "abusive or insulting attacks" upon a religion or religious beliefs. The statute is 2 Eliz. II, Bill 38, revising the Freedom of Worship Act, Revised Statutes, 1941, ch. 307.

## Chapter 17. Fighting Words

1. Chaplinsky v. N.H., 315 US 568 (1942).

2. Cantwell v. Conn., 310 US 296 (1940).

3. Letter to James Main, Oct. 1808.

4. John W. Wade, "Tort Liability for Abusive and Insulting Language," 4 *Vand. L. Rev.* 63 (1950).

5. Bartow v. Smith, 78 NE 2d 735 (Oh., 1948), cited in Wade.

6. There are exceptions to this general rule: liability has been imposed in cases involving carriers, innkeepers, hotels, theatres, other places of

public amusement, telegraph offices, and elevators in general office buildings; also in collection and claim adjustment cases; also on trespassers who use abusive language. Virginia, Mississippi, and West Virginia have statutes that make abusive language a tort. The modern civil law, based on Roman law principles, gives relief for insult or an attack on dignity; so do the laws of Scotland and South Africa.

7. Wade, 106–109.

8. *Ibid.*, at 112–114.

*Chapter 18. Obscene Literature*

1. Wade.

2. Beauharnais v. Ill., 343 US 250 (1952).

3. Zechariah Chafee, Jr., *Free Speech in the United States* (Cambridge, Mass., 1941), 150. Italics supplied.

4. *Ibid.*, 152.

5. See William B. Lockhart and Robert C. McClure, "Literature, the Law of Obscenity, and the Constitution," 38 *Minn. L. Rev.* 296 (1954).

6. People v. Doubleday & Co., 71 NYS 2d 736 (1947); 297 NY 687, 77 NE 2d 6 (1947). No opinions were written by the courts.

7. Doubleday & Co. v. N.Y., 335 US 848 (1948). Justice Frankfurter did not participate.

8. Lockhart and McClure, 298.

9. Commonwealth v. Gordon, 66(Pa.)D. & C. 101 (1949), aff'd *sub nom.* Commonwealth v. Feigenbaum, 166 Pa. Super. 120, 70 A. 2d 389 (1950). The Pennsylvania Supreme Court, however, while affirming Judge Bok's decision, expressly refused to approve the constitutional test as he had applied it in the case. For Judge Bok's notable opinion see M. R. Konvitz, *Bill of Rights Reader* (Ithaca, N.Y., 1954), 390.

10. Report of the Select Committee on Current Pornographic Materials, Pursuant to H. Res. 596, 82nd Cong. (G.P.O., 1952), 6–7. This report is known as the Gathings Report.

11. *Ibid.*, 123.

12. See Anne Lyon Haight, *Banned Books* (New York, 1955); cf. Alec Craig, *The Banned Books of England* (London, 1937), and *Above All Liberties* (London, 1942). Other relevant books are: Mary Ware Dennett, *Who's Obscene?* (New York, 1930); Geoffrey May, *Social Control of Sex Expression* (New York, 1931); Isabel Drummond, *The Sex Paradox* (New York, 1953); Heywood Broun and Margaret Leech, *Anthony Comstock* (New York, 1927); Morris L. Ernst and Alexander Lindey, *The Censor Marches On* (New York, 1940); Morris L. Ernst and William Seagle, *To the Pure: A Study of Obscenity and the Censor* (New York, 1929); Horace M. Kallen, *Indecency and the Seven Arts* (New York, 1930); *Social Meaning of Legal Concepts*, vol. 5: *Protection of Public Morals through Censorship* (New York University School of Law, 1953); Theodore Schroeder, *A Challenge to Sex Censors* (New York, 1938), and *"Obscene" Literature and Constitutional Law* (New York, 1911); *Obscenity and the Arts*, vol. XX,

no. 4, of *Law and Contemporary Problems* (Duke University School of Law, 1955); Zechariah Chafee, Jr., *Government and Mass Communications* (Chicago, 1947), I, 200–366. See also references in Lockhart and McClure, 324, note 199.

13. Butler v. Michigan, 77 S.Ct. 524 (1957).

14. See 146 Hansard, Parliamentary Debates (3d ser. 1857), 327 ff. For the background of the bill see Leo M. Alpert, "Judicial Censorship of Obscene Literature," 52 *Harv. L. Rev.* 40 (1938). Cf. Ernst and Seagle, ch. vi. Lord Campbell's Act is 20–21 Vict. c. 83 (1857).

15. Queen v. Hicklin, L.R. 3 Q.B. 360 (1868).

16. "Rude Words," leading article, *The Times Literary Supplement*, Sept. 25, 1953.

17. The charge to the jury is reprinted in its entirety at the end of the book: Stanley Kauffmann, *The Philanderer* (London, 1954). The case is Regina v. Warburg. See article by the publisher, Frederic J. Warburg, *New Statesman and Nation*, Nov. 6, 1954, 574.

18. "Police Against the Publishers," editorial in *New Statesman and Nation*, Oct. 2, 1954, 380.

19. Norman St. John-Stevas, "Intent and the Law," *New Statesman and Nation*, Oct. 9, 1954, 428–429.

20. Commonwealth v. Buckley, 200 Mass. 346, 86 NE 910 (1909).

21. Commonwealth v. Friede, 271 Mass. 318, 171 NE 472 (1930). See Sidney S. Grant and S. E. Angoff, "Massachusetts and Censorship," 10 *B.U. L. Rev.* 36 (1930); by same authors, "Recent Developments in Censorship," 10 *B.U. L. Rev.* 488 (1930).

22. People v. Pesky, 254 NY 373, 173 NE 227 (1930). The movie *La Ronde* was based on this book by Schnitzler. Censorship of the movie was reversed in Commercial Pictures Corp. v. Regents, 346 US 587 (1954).

23. See Alpert, 61 ff.

24. 19 USC 1305. See Chafee, *Government* I, 244 ff.

25. 18 USC 1461. See Chafee, *ibid.*, 276 ff. The act was amended in 1955. See *Obscene and Pornographic Literature and Juvenile Delinquency*, Interim Report of Senate Subcommittee, 84th Cong., 2d sess. (1956).

26. Heywood Broun and Margaret Leech, *Anthony Comstock: Roundsman of the Lord* (New York, 1927).

27. U.S. v. Kennerley, 209 Fed. 119 (1913), involving *Hagar Revelly*. Judge Hand overruled a demurrer to the indictment, but in his opinion expressed doubts regarding the obscenity law.

28. U.S. v. One Book Called "Ulysses," 5 F. Supp. 182 (1933), op. by Judge Woolsey; aff'd. 72 F. 2d 705 (1934), op. by Judge Augustus N. Hand, in which Judge Learned Hand concurred and from which Judge Manton dissented.

29. Commonwealth v. Isenstadt, 318 Mass. 543, 62 NE 2d 840 (1945); Attorney General v. "God's Little Acre," 326 Mass. 281, 93 NE 2d 819 (1950).

30. U.S. v. Two Obscene Books, 92 F. Supp. 934, 99 F. Supp. 760 (1951); aff'd *sub nom.* Besig v. U.S., 208 F. 2d 142 (1953).

31. Lockhart and McClure, 332–333, 379–387.

32. *Ibid.*, 356–357.

33. *Ibid.*, 358.

34. Chafee, *Government*, I, 215.

35. Connelly v. General Construction Co., 269 US 385 (1925).

36. U.S. v. Five Gambling Devices, 346 US 441 (1953), dis. op. of Justice Clark.

37. Winters v. N.Y., 333 US 507 (1948).

38. *Ibid.* Three Justices dissented.

39. Burstyn v. Wilson, 343 US 495 (1952).

40. Chafee, *Government*, I, 210.

41. See opinion of Holmes in Nash v. U.S., 229 US 373 (1913).

*Chapter 19. Previous Restraint*

1. See F. S. Siebert, *Freedom of the Press in England, 1476–1776* (Urbana, Ill., 1952), 46, 260.

2. The best editions are those edited by John W. Hales (Oxford, 1894) and by George H. Sabine (New York, 1951).

3. C. A. Duniway, *Development of Freedom of the Press in Massachusetts* (Cambridge, Mass., 1906), 41.

4. *Ibid.*, 100–103. To Blackstone freedom of the press meant only freedom from previous restraint. See *Commentaries*, IV, xi.

5. Quoted in G. J. Patterson, *Free Speech and a Free Press* (Boston, 1939), 111.

6. Near v. Minn., 283 US 697 (1931).

7. Lovell v. Griffin, 303 US 444 (1938).

8. Schneider v. Irvington, 308 US 147 (1939). Regarding the sale of publications on public streets, see Valentine v. Chrestensen, 316 US 52 (1942), and Jamison v. Tex., 318 US 413 (1943).

9. Kunz v. N.Y., 340 US 290 (1951). Cf. Saia v. N.Y., 334 US 558 (1948).

10. Terminiello v. Chicago, 337 US 1 (1949).

11. Chafee, *Free Speech*, 417. See Robert K. Carr, "Should We Have a Hyde Park Too?" *New York Times Magazine*, Aug. 28, 1955.

12. Niemotko v. Md., 340 US 268 (1951).

13. Fowler v. R.I., 345 US 67 (1953). Cf. Poulos v. N.H., 345 US 395 (1953).

14. Ruth A. Inglis, *Freedom of the Movies* (Chicago, 1947), 63, 64, 65.

15. *Ibid.*, 68.

16. Mutual Film Corp. v. Industrial Commission, 236 US 230 (1915).

17. Inglis, 69–70.

18. Chafee, *Free Speech*, 543. But cf. Chafee, *The Inquiring Mind* (New York, 1928), 141.

19. Kansas, Maryland, New York, Ohio, Pennsylvania, and Virginia.

20. Chafee, *Free Speech*, 542.

21. *Ibid.*, 545, 547–548.

22. Burstyn v. Wilson, 343 US 495 (1952).

23. Superior Films v. Dept. of Education, 346 US 587 (1954).

24. Holmby Productions v. Vaughn, 76 S.Ct. 117.

25. Near v. Minn., 283 US 697 (1931).

26. The basic law against espionage is the Espionage Law of 1917; present version, 18 USC 2388; cf. Espionage and Sabotage Act of 1954, 18 USC 794, 2151, 2153–2156.

27. For compilation, see *Internal Security Manual* (G.P.O., rev. 1955), 84th Cong., 1st sess., Sen. Doc. No. 40; also, *Adequacy of United States Laws with Respect to Offenses against National Security* (G.P.O., 1953), 83rd Cong., 1st sess., Comm. on Foreign Relations, Special Subcommittee on Security Affairs; and Report of the Subcommittee to Investigate the Administration of the Internal Security Act and Other Internal Security Laws (G.P.O., 1955), 83rd Cong., 2d sess., Senate Committee on the Judiciary.

28. James R. Mock, *Censorship 1917* (Princeton, 1941), Preface.

29. Part of the subject is considered in Harold L. Cross, *The People's Right to Know: Legal Access to Public Records and Proceedings.* (New York, 1953).

30. *New York Times,* Nov. 11, 1955.

31. *Ibid.,* Nov. 8, 1955.

32. The report was published in the *Christian Science Monitor,* Oct. 3, 1955.

33. The report, mimeographed, is dated Oct. 24, 1955. A summary of the report was published in the *New York Times* of that date. The original report is 70 pages long.

34. Cross, 131–132. While this book is concerned largely with state laws, much of what Cross says is relevant to the Federal Government as well as to the states.

35. As of Sept. 30, 1953, the total of morning and evening newspapers sold was 54,472,286. The number of such newspapers was 1,785. There were 544 Sunday newspapers, with a circulation of 45,948,554 (*Information Please Almanac* [1955], 245).

36. *Writings of James Madison* (New York, 1906), VI, 398, quoted by Cross, 129.

## Chapter 20. Picketing in Labor Disputes

1. Felix Frankfurter, "John Marshall and the Judicial Function," 69 *Harv. L. Rev.* 217, 231 (1955).

2. Senn v. Tile Layers Protective Union, 301 US 468 (1937).

3. The analysis of a labor dispute case in terms of means and ends owes much to the thought of Chief Justice Shaw in Commonwealth v. Hunt, 4 Met. [Mass.] 111 (1847), and Justice Holmes in Vegelahn v. Guntner, 167 Mass. 92 (1896), and Plant v. Woods, 176 Mass. 492 (1900).

4. Thornhill v. Ala., 310 US 88 (1940).

5. Carpenters and Joiners Union v. Ritter's Cafe, 315 US 722 (1942). The decision was 5 to 4, with Justices Black, Douglas, Murphy, and Reed dissenting.

6. Bakery and Pastry Drivers v. Wohl, 315 US 769 (1942). In this case the Court set aside an injunction on picketing as violative of the Constitution.

7. See note 1 *supra*.

8. Giboney v. Empire Storage and Ice Co., 336 US 490 (1948).

9. I.B.T. Local 309 v. Hanke, 339 US 470 (1950).

10. Building Service Employees Intern. Union v. Gazzam, 339 US 532 (1950).

11. Local Union 10 v. Graham, 345 US 192 (1953).

12. Hughes v. Superior Court, 339 US 460 (1950).

13. *Ibid.*

14. *Ibid.*

15. *Ibid.*

16. *Ibid.*

17. *Ibid.* See case cited note 5 *supra*.

18. Atchison etc. Ry. Co. v. Gee, 139 Fed. 582 (1905).

## *Chapter 21. Taxes on Knowledge*

1. Siebert, 301.

2. *Ibid.*, 310.

3. *Ibid.*, 312.

4. *Ibid.*, 321.

5. There were acts in 1776, 1789, 1794, 1804, 1815, and 1836. *Ibid.*, 321–322.

6. The tax on paper was ended in 1861.

7. *Ibid.*, 322.

8. A. Aspinall, *Politics and the Press, 1780–1850* (London, 1949), 17.

9. *Ibid.*, 23.

10. See C. D. Collet, *History of the Taxes on Knowledge* (London, 1933), *passim*.

11. Duniway, 136–137.

12. Chafee, *Free Speech*, 382.

13. Grosjean v. Amer. Press Co., 297 US 233 (1936). For several earlier cases in lower courts, see dis. op. of Murphy in Jones v. Opelika, 316 US 584 (1942), and Chafee, *Free Speech*, 381–382.

14. Jones v. Opelika, 316 US 584 (1942).

15. Jones v. Opelika, 319 US 103 (1943).

16. Murdock v. Pennsylvania, 319 US 105 (1943). Cf. Douglas v. Jeannette, 319 US 157 (1943).

17. Follett v. Town of McCormick, 321 US 573 (1944). The antitrust acts apply to newspapers (Associated Press v. U.S., 326 US 1 [1945]). The

National Labor Relations Act applies to newspapers (Associated Press v. N.L.R.B., 301 US 103, 133 [1937]). The Fair Labor Standards Act applies to newspapers (Okla. Press Pub. Co. v. Walling, 327 US 186 [1946]).

18. This proposition has probably been qualified to a degree by the next case considered in the text, p. 209.

## Chapter 22. Limited Abridgments of Speech and Press

1. Amer. Communications Assn. v. Douds, 339 US 382 (1950).

2. 29 U.S.C. 141.

3. Sec. 9(h), 29 USC 159(h). The Communist Control Act of 1954, 50 USC 841, amends the Taft-Hartley Act by providing that a union that is a Communist-action or a Communist-front or a Communist-infiltrated organization shall be ineligible to act as representative of employees. See especially 50 USC 782 ff.

4. The case was heard by only six Justices; of these, only Justice Black dissented.

5. Italics are in the original.

6. It should be noted that Justices Douglas, Clark, and Minton took no part in the case. Another aspect of the case will be treated in the next section of the text.

7. As we shall see, sec. 9(h) itself is far from precise; it was seriously attacked for vagueness.

8. Sec. 206 ff.

9. Youngstown Sheet & Tube Co. v. Sawyer, 343 US 579 (1952).

10. Cf. John Lord O'Brian, *National Security and Individual Freedom* (Cambridge, Mass., 1955), 24.

## Chapter 23. Test Oaths and the Freedom to Think and Believe

1. See note 1, ch. xxii, *supra*.

2. Those who voted to sustain the constitutionality of the provision were Chief Justice Vinson and Justices Reed and Burton. Those who voted against its constitutionality were Justices Frankfurter, Jackson, and Black. Members of the Court who did not participate were Justices Douglas, Clark, and Minton.

3. The only evidence cited by Vinson was the "aims and tactics of the Socialist Workers Party," referring to Dunne v. U.S., 320 US 790 (1943), cert. den. This was the case that involved certain Trotskyites prosecuted under the Smith Act.

4. The phrase is Justice Holmes's (Panhandle Oil Co. v. Miss., 277 US 218, 223 [1928], dis. op.). Said Holmes: "The power to tax is not the power to destroy while this Court sits."

5. Const., Art. III, Sec. 3. Italics supplied.

6. See, e.g., his opinion in Douglas v. Jeannette, 319 US 157 (1943).

7. Dennis v. U.S., 341 US 494 (1951), dis. op.

8. Re Summers, 325 US 56 (1945).

9. Dis. op. of Black in the case.

10. U.S. v. Schwimmer, 279 US 644 (1929); U.S. v. Macintosh, 283 US 605 (1931).

11. Girouard v. U.S., 328 US 61 (1946). Chief Justice Stone and Justices Reed and Frankfurter dissented. Justice Jackson did not participate.

12. The naturalization cases are discussed in Konvitz, *Alien and Asiatic*, 97 ff. It should be noted that sec. 337 of the Immigration and Nationality Act of 1952 (McCarran-Walter Act) attempts to make the naturalization oath conform, on the whole, to the spirit of the Girouard decision.

13. It will be recalled that only six Justices considered the case, and that the decision regarding the belief requirement was upheld by an evenly divided vote, 3 to 3.

14. The dread of test oaths probably started with the first Test Act, 1673, "An act for preventing dangers which may happen from popish recusants." In this act Parliament provided that all office holders and certain other persons must take an oath of supremacy and allegiance, and also subscribe to a declaration that they "do believe that there is not any transubstantiation in the sacrament of the Lord's Supper, or in the elements of bread and wine, at or after the consecration thereof by any person whatsoever." The second Test Act, 1678, provided that no person shall sit in Parliament unless he "audibly repeat" a declaration to the effect that he believes "that in the sacrament of the Lord's Supper there is not any transubstantiation of the elements of bread and wine into the body and blood of Christ" and that the invocation of the Virgin Mary or any saint is "superstitious and idolatrous" (25 Charles II, c. 2; 30 Charles II, st. 2, c. 1, in Stephenson and Marcham, 555–557). The Toleration Act, 1689, provided that all who will take the oath of allegiance and supremacy and the oath against belief in transubstantiation need not attend an Anglican church but may attend public worship in a dissenting Protestant conventicle; but nonconformist clergy were required to subscribe to belief in thirty-four of the Thirty-Nine Articles in the Anglican Prayer Book and part of two other articles. There were special clauses for the benefit of Quakers and Baptists. Thus the Toleration Act perpetuated the test oaths as a disability for non-Anglicans. The Test Acts were not repealed until 1828 (9 George IV, c. 17, in Stephenson and Marcham, 677). In the settlement of America, some of the English colonies enforced the Test Acts (Sanford H. Cobb, *The Rise of Religious Liberty in America* (New York, 1902), 299, 337, 356, 445, 447–449). It was with this experience in mind that the framers of the Constitution provided in Art. 6 that "no religious test shall ever be required as a qualification to any office or public trust under the United States."

## Chapter 24. Loyalty Oaths and Guilt by Association

1. Cited note 1, ch. xxii *supra*.

2. H. K. Beale, *Are American Teachers Free?* (New York, 1936), 65 ff.

3. The Test Oath of July 1862 (Chafee, 263).

4. Henry R. Linville, *Oaths of Loyalty for Teachers* (pamph. pub. by Amer. Federation of Teachers, New York, 1935); *The Gag on Teaching* (pamph. pub. by Amer. Civil Liberties Union, 3d ed., 1940); "Teachers' Oaths" (mimeog. report of Natl. Education Assn., 1937). See also Beale, and Walter Gellhorn, ed., *The States and Subversion* (Ithaca, N.Y., 1952), and Lawrence H. Chamberlain, *Loyalty and Legislative Action* (Ithaca, N.Y., 1951); Richard Hofstadter and Walter P. Metzger, *Development of Academic Freedom in the United States* (New York, 1955), especially ch. x.

5. *The Gag on Teaching*, 22–26.

6. *Ibid.*, 22.

7. Published in the *Bulletin* of the A.A.U.P., March 1937.

8. *Ibid.*

9. Hofstadter and Metzger, *Development of Academic Freedom*, 496.

10. This was shown by a survey made by the National Education Association (*Christian Science Monitor*, July 20, 1949).

11. *The States and Subversion*, pamph. of Amer. Civil Liberties Union (New York, 1953), 3.

12. See Lawrence H. Chamberlain, "New York: A Generation of Legislative Alarm," in Gellhorn, ed., *States and Subversion*, 231 ff.

13. See *The Bertrand Russell Case*, ed. John Dewey and H. M. Kallen (New York, 1941). For the court's opinion, see pp. 213–225.

14. Chamberlain, "New York," 260–262. The 1939 statute is Sec. 12-a of the Civil Service Law. It applies to personnel in the public schools and in all state educational institutions, who are declared ineligible for employment in such institutions if they are members of any organization that advocates the overthrow of government by force.

15. *Ibid.*, 263, italics in original.

16. While no case reached the courts, one case was reviewed, some years later, by the state commissioner of education, who ordered reinstatement. See *ibid.*, 267–268. Regarding the *Schappes* case, see *ibid.*, 270–271.

17. Sec. 3022 of Art. 61, New York Education Law.

18. The statute was amended in 1953 to cover employees and faculty of institutions of higher learning owned or operated by the state. L. 1953, c. 681; sec. 3022 of Art. 61 of the Education Law.

19. Schneiderman v. U.S., 320 US 118 (1943). The case is discussed in Konvitz, *Alien and Asiatic*, 119 ff.

20. The Workers Party was organized in 1921 as an open and legal organization while the Communist Party remained underground. (The Communist Party was forced underground in 1919, in the days of the Palmer raids, which resulted in wholesale arrests and deportations. See Robert K. Murray, *Red Scare: A Study in National Hysteria, 1919–1920* [Minneapolis, 1955].) The two parties merged in 1923 under the name of the Workers Party. In 1925 the name was changed to Workers (Communist) Party of America. In 1929 this became the Communist Party of the United States (or Communist Party of America). See *Organized Commu-*

*nism in the United States*, 83rd Cong., 2d sess., House Report No. 1694, House Committee on Un-American Activities (1953, 1954).

21. The decision was 5 to 3, with Chief Justice Stone and Justices Roberts and Frankfurter dissenting.

22. Italics supplied.

23. Sec. 313 (a) (2) of the Immigration and Nationality Act of 1952 (McCarran-Walter Act) provides expressly that no person who is a member of or affiliated with the Communist Party shall be naturalized.

24. Knauer v. U.S., 328 US 654 (1946). The decision was 6 to 2 sustaining a decree of denaturalization. Justices Rutledge and Murphy dissented.

25. Amer. Communications Assn. v. Douds, 339 US 382 (1950).

26. Italics supplied.

27. Adler v. Bd. of Education, 342 US 485 (1952). Justice Frankfurter dissented on jurisdictional grounds, and Justices Black and Douglas dissented on the merits.

28. Italics supplied.

29. Italics supplied.

30. Italics supplied.

31. Italics supplied.

32. See M. R. Konvitz, "Are Teachers Afraid?" *New Leader*, Feb. 13, 1956, 17–21, at p. 20.

33. John Lord O'Brian, "Loyalty Tests and Guilt by Association," 61 *Harv. L. Rev.* 592, 598 (1948).

34. Cf. Thornhill v. Ala., 310 US 88 (1940).

35. Wieman v. Updegraff, 344 US 183 (1952). Justice Jackson did not participate.

36. See review by Sidney Hook of Robert M. MacIver, "Academic Freedom in Our Time," *New York Times Book Review*, Oct. 30, 1955, and letter by Sidney Hook *ibid.*, Nov. 27, 1955; also his review of E. Merrill Root, *Collectivism on the Campus, ibid.*, Nov. 6, 1955. See also articles by Konvitz and Hook in *New Leader* (Feb. 13, 1956); and Sidney Hook, *Heresy, Yes—Conspiracy, No* (New York, 1953).

37. A comprehensive treatment of the subject is: Milton Greenberg, "The Loyalty Oath in the American Experience" (Ph.D. dissertation, University of Wisconsin, 1955).

38. Gerende v. Baltimore City Bd. of Supervisors, 341 US 56 (1951).

39. Garner v. Bd. of Public Works, 341 US 716 (1951).

40. With regard to the ex post facto contention, Justice Clark also pointed out that a charter provision barred from public employment persons who advocate or teach overthrow of government, and that this provision had been on the books for more than five years prior to the enactment of the oath requirement.

Also, Justice Clark assumed that scienter was implicit in each clause of the oath, for the city had done nothing to negate this interpretation, and it should be assumed that in the future it will so interpret the oath as to make scienter a requisite.

41. United Public Workers v. Mitchell, 330 US 75 (1947).

42. 12 Stat. 502 and 13 Stat. 424.

43. After the Civil War he was pardoned by President Johnson, but the Congressional legislation referred to in the text made no exemption in favor of pardoned Confederate officeholders. In 1867 he was elected to the U.S. Senate but the Senate refused him his seat. In 1874 he was Governor of Arkansas, in 1877 he was again elected to the Senate, and this time he took his seat. He served as Attorney General in the Cleveland administration and wrote several books on the Supreme Court and on constitutional law.

44. Ex parte Garland, 4 Wall. 333, 18 L. ed. 366 (1867). The decision was 5 to 4.

45. Cummings v. Mo., 4 Wall. 277, 18 L. ed. 356 (1867). The decision here was also 5 to 4.

46. McAuliffe v. New Bedford, 155 Mass. 216, 29 NE 517 (1892).

47. 18 U.S.C. 595.

48. United Public Workers v. Mitchell, 330 US 75 (1947). The decision was 4 to 3, with Justices Murphy and Jackson not participating, and Justices Black, Rutledge, and Douglas dissenting.

49. Justice Black calculated that in 1947 there were some three million federal employees, and almost as many state and local government employees.

50. Justice Douglas pointed out that the British equivalent of the Hatch Act was aimed only at administrative personnel.

51. Wieman v. Updegraff, 344 US 183 (1952).

52. Bailey v. Richardson, 182 F. 2d 46 (1950); affd. by an equally divided Supreme Court, without an opinion, 341 US 918 (1951).

53. Act of Aug. 2, 1939, sec. 9A, 53 Stat. 1148.

54. War Service Reg. 2, Nov. 30, 1941.

55. Exec. Order 9835, March 21, 1947, 12 Fed. Reg. 1935.

56. April 28, 1951, 16 Fed. Reg. 3690.

57. Exec. Order 10450, April 27, 1953, 18 Fed. Reg. 2489.

58. Exec. Order 10491, Oct. 13, 1953, 18 Fed. Reg. 6583.

59. This point was strongly argued in Peters v. Hobby, 349 US 331 (1955), but the decision of the Supreme Court by-passed this question as well as other constitutional issues. The decision in Cole v. Young, US (1956), also avoided constitutional issues.

60. Parker v. Lester, 227 F. 2d 708 (1955). The decision was by a 2-to-1 vote. The Government decided not to appeal the decision. *New York Times,* March 25, 1956.

61. Magnuson Act, 50 USC 191–194; Executive Order 10173, 15 Fed. Reg. 7005.

62. Truax v. Raich, 239 US 33 (1915). The case is discussed in Konvitz, *Alien and Asiatic,* 174–175.

63. See also dis. op. of Black in Feldman v. U.S., 322 US 487 (1944);

Edmond Cahn, "The Firstness of the First Amendment," 65 *Yale L. J.* 464 (1956); dis. op. of Douglas in Ullmann v. U.S., 76 S. Ct. 497 (1956).

64. *New York Times*, April 1, 1956; *ibid.*, April 19, 1954; *ibid.*, May 11, 1953.

65. Michael Marsh, *Government Employment* (Editorial Research Reports; Washington, 1951), 651–652.

66. *The People Take the Lead: A Record of Progress in Civil Rights, 1948 to 1955* (pamph. pub. by Community Relations Service, 1955), 3.

67. John Milton, *Paradise Lost*, XI.

68. R. W. Emerson, *The Conduct of Life*.

## PART III. FREEDOM OF SPEECH, PRESS, AND ASSEMBLY: THE CLEAR AND PRESENT DANGER DOCTRINE

### Chapter 25. *The Original Meaning of the Doctrine*

1. Perhaps the only important exception to this generalization is the application of the clear and present danger doctrine to contempt of court by publication. But the decisions on this point are now of doubtful standing in the light of the *Dennis* case, which will be treated at length in the text. In Bridges v. Calif., 314 US 252 (1941) the Court for the first time held that punishment for contempt of court by publication was subject to the clear and present danger test. See also Pennekamp v. Fla., 328 US 331 (1946); Craig v. Harney, 331 US 367 (1947). See Harold W. Sullivan, *Contempts by Publication: The Law of Trial by Newspaper* (1940); Edwin M. Otterbourg, "Fair Trial and Free Press," 37 *J. Am. Jud. Soc'y* 75 (1953); John M. Harrison, "The Press vs. the Courts," *Sat. Rev.*, Oct. 15, 1955; Jerome H. Spingarn, "Newspapers and the Pursuit of Justice," *Sat. Rev.*, April 3, 1954. The subject is tied in with the question of the possible denial of due process in the trial of a criminal case. See Shepard v. Fla., 341 US 50 (1951). The subject is a highly complex one and cannot be treated adequately in the text in view of the uncertainty as to how the Supreme Court would view the constitutional aspects in post-Dennis cases. Sooner or later a state legislature will, I think, adopt a statute modeled in some way upon English practice that will limit newspapers in reporting criminal trials, and then the Court will need to face the constitutional issues squarely. For Pennsylvania bill, see *New York Times*, May 18, 1956.

2. Whitney v. Calif., 274 US 357 (1927), conc. op.

### Chapter 26. *History of the Doctrine*

1. Dis. op. in Everson v. Bd. of Education, 330 US 1 (1947).

2. Henry Steele Commager, *Documents of American History* (3d ed.; New York, 1943), I, 125.

3. Quoted in Conrad H. Moehlman, *The Wall of Separation between Church and State* (Boston, 1951), 77–78.

4. Quoted in J. M. O'Neill, *Religion and Education under the Constitution* (New York, 1949), 286; quoted by Supreme Court in Reynolds v. U.S., 98 US 145 (1878); see also Everson v. Bd. of Education, 330 US 1 (1947); McCollum v. Bd. of Education, 333 US 203 (1948). The letter was addressed to the Danbury Baptist Association and is dated Jan. 1, 1802.

5. *Notes on Virginia;* see Moehlman.

6. Schenck v. U.S., 249 US 47 (1919).

7. Oliver Wendell Holmes, *The Common Law* (Boston, 1881). The quotations are from Lecture II, 39 ff. Italics supplied.

8. Espionage Act of 1917, present version 18 USC 2388; original 40 Stat. 217, 219.

9. Frohwerk v. U.S., 249 US 208 (1919).

10. Debs v. U.S., 249 US 212 (1919).

11. Abrams v. U.S., 250 US 616 (1919). This case is discussed at length by Zechariah Chafee, Jr., *Free Speech in the United States,* (Cambridge, Mass., 1941) ch. iii, especially p. 136.

12. Both circulars are set out in full in Chafee, 109–111.

13. In Whitney v. Calif., 274 US 357 (1927), Brandeis, too, spoke of speech that produces or is intended to produce a clear and present danger.

14. Regarding severity of sentences as a subject of judicial concern, see Chafee, 396.

15. Felix Frankfurter, *The Commerce Clause under Marshall, Taney and Waite* (Chapel Hill, 1937), 56.

16. See *Holmes-Pollock Letters,* ed. Mark de Wolfe Howe (Cambridge, Mass., 1941), II, 7, quoted in part by Chafee, 84. Cf. *Holmes-Pollock Letters,* II, 32.

17. Herndon v. Lowry, 301 US 242 (1937).

18. Brandeis, however, was still a member of the Court in 1937. He retired in 1939.

19. Fiske v. Kans., 274 US 380 (1927). But perhaps one should mention also Meyer v. Nebr., 262 US 390 (1923), in which the Court held that a state may not prohibit the teaching of foreign languages; cf. Pierce v. Society of Sisters, 268 US 510 (1925).

20. De Jonge v. Ore., 299 US 353 (1937); Herndon v. Lowry, 301 US 242 (1937).

21. The Kansas Criminal Syndicalism Act, the Oregon Criminal Syndicalism Act, and the anti-insurrection statute of Georgia.

22. Henry Steele Commager, *Majority Rule and Minority Rights* (New York, 1943), 47, 55.

23. Schaefer v. U.S., 251 US 468 (1920); Pierce v. U.S., 252 US 239 (1920); Gilbert v. Minn., 254 US 325 (1920).

24. In the *Schaefer* case the dissenting opinion was by Brandeis—his first

formulation of the clear and present danger doctrine. In the *Pierce* case, too, the dissenting opinion was by Brandeis. Holmes concurred in both dissenting opinions.

25. The Court conceded, only for the sake of the argument, that the First Amendment freedoms were protected against state infringement. Even if they are thus protected, said the Court, they were not violated by the act.

Brandeis, however, contended that these freedoms were guarantied by the Constitution against state action. They were privileges or immunities of citizens of the United States, of which he may not be deprived by any state; furthermore, they are protected by the liberty guaranty of the Fourteenth Amendment. His point with respect to the Fourteenth Amendment became the position of the Court in Gitlow v. N.Y., 268 US 652 (1925). Cf. Meyer v. Nebr., 262 US 390 (1923).

Brandeis dissented also because, he argued, Congress by the Espionage Act of 1917 had pre-empted the field, and so state legislation must be excluded. In 1956 the Court in effect adopted his position in Pa. v. Nelson, 76 S. Ct. 477 (1956).

This is not an unimpressive record for any opinion, and especially for a dissenting opinion.

26. Paul A. Freund, *On Understanding the Supreme Court* (Boston, 1949), 27–28.

27. *Ibid.,* 69.

28. Stilson v. U.S., 250 US 583 (1919); Holmes and Brandeis dissented. O'Connell v. U.S., 253 US 142 (1920). More significant was U.S. ex rel. Milwaukee Social Democratic Publ. Co. v. Burleson, 255 US 407 (1921), in which the Court upheld a revocation of second-class mailing privileges of the *Milwaukee Leader* for publishing false reports with intent to interfere with the military operations of the Government, in violation of the Espionage Act of 1917. Brandeis and Holmes dissented. In none of these cases was use made by the dissenters of the clear and present danger doctrine.

29. Gitlow v. N.Y., 268 US 652 (1925).

30. Dennis v. U.S., 341 US 494 (1951).

31. As we have already pointed out, the Gitlow case had one significant positive value; namely, it settled the view that the Fourteenth Amendment guaranty of "liberty" against deprivation by state action includes free speech and freedom of the press. This was foreshadowed by Gilbert v. Minn., 254 US 325 (1920), in dis. op. of Brandeis; Meyer v. Nebr., 262 US 390 (1923); and Pierce v. Society of Sisters, 268 US 510 (1925).

32. Cf. C. Herman Pritchett, *Civil Liberties and the Vinson Court* (Chicago, 1954), 28–29.

In his opinion Justice Holmes differentiated the expression of a theory from incitement, and said that sometimes the speaker's enthusiasm makes the difference. It will be recalled that in his Whitney opinion Justice Brandeis distinguished advocacy from incitement. When does advocacy become incitement? Not many cases have touched on this point.

In Musser v. Utah, 333 US 95 (1948) the defendants, fundamentalist Mormons, zealously maintained their belief in polygamy and were convicted of criminal conspiracy "to commit acts injurious to public morals" by counseling, advising, and urging others to practice polygamy. The Utah statute under which they were convicted made it a crime to conspire "to commit any act injurious to the public morals." A majority of the Supreme Court held that this was a broadly drawn statute, one which may be interpreted in such a way as to fail to provide "some reasonable standards of guilt" and would thus conflict with the Due Process Clause of the Fourteenth Amendment. Since this question had not been presented to the Utah Supreme Court, the United States Supreme Court ordered the case remanded to the state court to pass upon this question.

Justice Rutledge (with whom Justices Douglas and Murphy concurred) wrote a dissenting opinion, in which he contended that "a deeper vice" than the vagueness of the statute infected the convictions. In this significant dissenting opinion a distinction is made between the following situations: (1) a person urges a particular individual to commit polygamy; and (2) advocacy of polygamy in the course of religious meetings where, although pressure may have been applied to individuals, considerable general discussion of the religious duty to enter into plural marriages is carried on. The distinction is between (1) "specific incitations" and (2) "more generalized discussions." The constitutional line is drawn not between advocacy and discussion, but between advocacy or discussion, on the one hand, and incitement, on the other hand.

Even the power to punish incitement, however, must be circumscribed. The power to punish incitement, said Justice Rutledge, depends on various factors, such as (1) the nature of the speech—"whether persuasive or coercive"—(2) the nature of the wrong induced—"whether violent or merely offensive to the mores"—and (3) the degree of probability that the substantive evil actually will result.

Advocacy, if it falls short of incitement, is constitutionally protected. Thus a person or a group of persons may criticize the laws which prohibit polygamy and urge that they be changed. But in order to succeed in an effort to have polygamy legalized, it is necessary to convince a substantial number of people that the practice of polygamy is desirable. The conviction that polygamy is desirable has "a natural tendency" to induce the practice of polygamy. This result does not, said Rutledge, remove from the advocacy the constitutional protection; the state may not punish all conduct which induces people to violate the law or all advocacy of unlawful activity. "At the very least," said Rutledge, "under the clear-and-present-danger rule," the law must permit "advocacy of lawbreaking, but only so long as the advocacy falls short of incitement . . . of particular and immediate violations of the law," or so long as the advocacy falls short of "direct and personalized activity amounting to incitation to commit a crime."

Let us note that, on the one hand, freedom of religion or speech does not throw a mantle of protection over teaching when it becomes "direct and personalized activity amounting to incitation to commit a crime"; on the other hand, the right of free speech cannot be curtailed by a charge of criminal conspiracy "to commit acts injurious to public morals," for this may amount to a blanket prohibition on free speech—or on freedom of religion. But when we move away from these two limits we enter into a field of discussion and dispute in which the problems are extremely complex and require the most minute analysis.

A singular case illustrative of the first limit defined above is Gara v. U.S., 178 F. 2d 38 (1949); affd. 340 US 857 (1950). Gara was dean of men at Bluffton College, a Mennonite institution in Ohio. In World War I he had refused to register for the draft, had served a prison sentence for his refusal, and considered it his religious duty to oppose all forms of co-operation with the war effort. A student at the college, Charles Roy Rickert, refused in September 1948 to register for the draft. He was arrested in November 1948 on the campus in the presence of Gara, who said to him at the time: "Do not let them coerce you into registering," or perhaps he said, "Do not let them coerce you into changing your conscience (or mind)." On the same day Gara and his wife wrote a letter to federal law enforcement officials with regard to Rickert's arrest in which they said that they had openly urged young men to refuse to register for the draft and that they will do all in their power to further civil disobedience to conscription. Earlier in the same year Gara made a speech in Pennsylvania in which he advocated that men of draft age refuse to register, and he signed a pledge to assist and support nonregistrants. Gara was convicted of violation of the Selective Service Act by knowingly counseling, aiding, and abetting Rickert to refuse registration. The conviction was upheld by the United States court of appeals; the Supreme Court sustained the conviction by a 4-to-4 vote.

The fact that Gara "sincerely believed that it was his Christian duty to oppose registration," said the court of appeals, "does not absolve him from his violation of the statute."

Gara contended that Rickert had first refused to register on September 10, 1948, which was ten days before his first meeting with Gara as dean of men at Bluffton College. The court held that it was immaterial whether Gara had in fact influenced the student's conduct. Since the statute penalizes an attempt to obstruct military service, as well as actual obstruction, success is not the test. It also was no defense that Gara had counseled only those who were already "inwardly fixed" in their conscience to refuse to register, for the gist of the statutory crime is "the counseling, aiding or abetting the violation, and not the result." Nor was it necessary to prove that Gara had actually brought about Rickert's violation of the act "if his words were used in such circumstances and were of such a nature that they would have a tendency to cause Rickert to refuse to register."

The court of appeals said that Gara had the constitutional right to express his opinions, in public and in private, of the Selective Service Act. He could freely oppose the act, in peacetime and in wartime, and demand its repeal. Here, however, Gara expressed his opinions as part of his counseling a person to violate the law, and counseling is expressly forbidden by the statute. Counseling might or might not be constitutionally protected when it is enmeshed in the expression or discussion of one's views—this question was not before the court in the *Gara* case. Counseling must be expressed in words; but this does not give counseling constitutional immunity if the legislature by express enactment makes counseling a substantively distinct crime. Said the court: "We do not have a mere attempt on appellant's part to comfort or give moral support to someone who is paying the penalty for his refusal to register. Here appellant admits that he agreed in every way possible to assist and support non-registrants. At an open meeting he advocated refusal to register. His repeated letters state that he counseled men of draft age to refuse registration. Such actions, if carried out extensively, might well nullify the law. Appellant may attack the Selective Service Act of 1948 from every platform in America with impunity, but he cannot, under the guise of free speech, nullify it by disobedience to its express provisions." A similar situation was presented in Warren v. U.S., 177 F. 2d 596 (1949); cert. den. 338 US 947 (1950). In this case a stepfather, Wirt A. Warren, counseled his stepson not to register for the draft and offered to pay his fare to Canada. The boy rejected the advice and registered; the stepfather was nonetheless indicted and convicted for violation of the prohibition upon counseling to violate the Selective Service Act. The judgment of conviction was upheld by the court of appeals, and the Supreme Court refused to review the case. The court of appeals held:

(1) Counseling under the act is a primary and not an accessorial offense; it is not necessary, therefore, that the counsel or advice should be followed in order to show the commission of the offense. Even if as here the boy did not follow the advice of the stepfather, the latter could be convicted. (2) The conviction for counseling was no violation of the defendant's freedom of religion or speech, for these are "qualified freedoms" when they impinge upon acts or utterances that are calculated to interfere with the war powers of Congress. (3) Warren argued that he stood *in loco parentis* toward his stepson and had the right to give him religious instruction and to teach him in good faith that war is a great evil and that the draft law should be disobeyed. "That much we concede," said the court of appeals. But if counseling to refuse to register is a crime, a father has no right to counsel. "It is one thing for a person to entertain religious beliefs,

to express those beliefs, and to teach them to his children. It is another thing to counsel and urge violation of valid penal legislation."

The court of appeals quoted with approval a passage from the opinion of Justice Sutherland in the *Macintosh* case, 283 US 605 (1931), that we are "a Christian people," and that we must assume that the laws of the land were made for war as well as for peace, and that as such they "are not inconsistent with the will of God."

A demonstration of the wrongness of this approach is to be seen in the fact that fifteen years after Sutherland's supererogatory opinion, the Supreme Court expressly overruled the Macintosh decision in Girouard v. U.S., 328 US 61 (1946). In 1931 the will of the Supreme Court, by a 5-to-4 vote, was not inconsistent with the will of God. After the passage of fifteen years the Court, by a 6-to-3 vote, discovered that it had misread the will of Congress, and had, therefore, misread the will of God, and this time handed down a decision that was inconsistent with the Macintosh decision, but not inconsistent with the will of Congress (as reconsidered), which was not inconsistent with the will of God (as reconsidered).

But the courts have not, apparently, learned the lesson of humility from this and similar events. They ought to know that it is not possible to be sure of the will of God. As we nervously and fretfully seek to learn that will, we open our ears and hearts to the voice of conscience when it is uttered by others, in the hope that in a moment of transcendent grace God's will may become revealed to us. The revelation may come from a passage in a book, from an encyclical of the Pope, from a sermon by a minister in an obscure village church, from the advice of a father, from the lecture of a teacher, from a conversation with an unlettered cobbler or carpenter. He who civilly shows the way to one who has missed it, said Cicero, is "as one who has lighted another's lamp from his own lamp." The essence of the First Amendment freedoms is the search to light one's own lamp. Wirt Warren's son had the inherent and inalienable right to bring his lamp close to his father's, or to Gara's, to see whether or not it would light. The fact that it did not light shows that he remained a free agent throughout, that it was the will of God and not the will of his father that the boy was seeking, and that he did not identify one with the other. In both the Gara and Warren cases the speech was persuasive and not coercive; the effort was made not to incite rebellion but to light a lamp. For the pointing up of this distinction, the clear and present danger doctrine remains useful and significant.

33. Whitney v. Calif., 274 US 357 (1927).

34. Herndon v. Ga., 295 US 441 (1935).

35. In the decade following *Gitlow,* the following relevant cases were decided: (1) Burns v. U.S., 274 US 328 (1927), in which the California Criminal Syndicalism Act was upheld. The case involved a delegate of the I.W.W. The organization was shown to have advocated sabotage.

Justice Brandeis dissented but without touching constitutional issues. (2) Whitney v. Calif., 274 US 357 (1927), in which the California Criminal Syndicalism Act was upheld. The case involved a conviction for aiding in the formation of the California branch of the Communist Labor Party, which was charged with advocating resort to violent methods to achieve changes in industrial and political conditions. The Court cited *Gitlow* but not *Schenck* on the free speech issue. Brandeis and Holmes concurred, with Brandeis writing a concurring opinion which has been considered in the text. (3) Fiske v. Kans., 274 US 380 (1927), in which the Court unanimously set aside a conviction under the Kansas Criminal Syndicalism Act. The only evidence that had been relied on for a conviction was the preamble to the constitution of the I.W.W. The Supreme Court held that the language of the preamble could not be interpreted as unambiguously teaching or advocating resort to criminal acts. The opinion was by Sanford. (4) N.Y. ex rel. Bryant v. Zimmerman, 278 US 63 (1928). A New York act required every membership organization with twenty or more members, other than labor unions, or benevolent orders, to file with the secretary of state a copy of its constitution and bylaws, its oath of membership, and a roster of its members and officers. The law was limited to organizations that had a membership oath. A member who knew that his organization had failed to comply was to be guilty of a misdemeanor. The action was against a member of K.K.K. The conviction was sustained. The Court held that the state legislature had before it sufficient facts from which to conclude that the requirement of disclosure by the Klan would be in the public interest. "The requirement is not arbitrary or oppressive, but reasonable and likely to be of real effect." Only McReynolds dissented, and on a jurisdictional ground. The New York act of 1923 may in some way have served as a partial model for the McCarran Internal Security Act of 1950. (5) Herndon v. Ga., 295 US 441 (1935). Defendant was convicted under a Georgia statute which made it a crime to attempt, by persuasion or otherwise, to induce persons to join in any combined resistance to the state. The trial court charged the jury substantially in terms of the clear and present danger test. The Georgia supreme court construed the act as not requiring the limitation imposed by this test—the law may punish the defendant if he intended an insurrection to follow at any time. The Supreme Court affirmed the conviction without passing on the constitutional question. Cardozo dissented, with Brandeis and Stone joining. Cardozo argued that while for the case in its posture before the Court it was not necessary to decide whether the clear and present danger test applied, he said that the doctrine "at least" had "color of support in words uttered from this bench, and uttered with intense conviction." The defendant charged in substance with an attempt to enlarge the membership of the Communist Party in Atlanta, Ga., should, according to Cardozo, have been afforded an opportunity by the Court to argue that under the

*Schenck* decision his conviction was unconstitutional, and then the Court could pass on the constitutional test and questions.

36. Herndon v. Lowry, 301 US 242 (1937).

37. Four dissenting members of the Court in the *Herndon* case thought that the standard of guilt in a speech case could constitutionally be that the speaker intend that "combined *forcible* resistance shall proximately result from his act of inducement. . . . The intended point of time must be within the period during which 'he might reasonably expect' his inducement to remain *directly* operative in causing the combined forcible resistance." (Italics in original opinion of Justice Van Devanter, in which Justices McReynolds, Sutherland, and Butler joined.)

38. Thornhill v. Ala., 310 US 88 (1940).

39. Cantwell v. Conn., 310 US 296 (1940).

40. See Philipp Leonard Sirotkin, "Evolution of the Clear and Present Danger Doctrine" (M.A. thesis, U. of Chicago, 1947); Wallace Mendelson, "Clear and Present Danger—From Schenck to Dennis," 52 *Col. L. Rev.* 313 (1952); articles by Chester J. Antieau, "The Rule of Clear and Present Danger—Its Origin and Application," 13 *U. Det. L. J.* 198 (1950); "The Rule of Clear and Present Danger: Scope and Its Applicability," 48 *Mich. L. Rev.* 811 (1950); "Clear and Present Danger—Its Meaning and Significance," 25 *Notre Dame Lawyer* 603 (1950). Also Anno. in 93 *US L. Ed.* 1156 (1950).

41. Bridges v. Calif., 314 US 252 (1941).

42. W. Va. State Bd. of Education v. Barnette, 319 US 624 (1943).

43. Pennekamp v. Fla., 328 US 331 (1946).

44. Dennis v. U.S., 341 US 494 (1951).

*Chapter 27. The Doctrine Reduced to a Phrase:* Dennis v. United States

1. Smith Act, June 28, 1940, 54 Stat. 670, 18 USC (1952 ed.) sec. 2385.

2. Because of ill health there was a severance as to one defendant, William Z. Foster, who has not been brought to trial.

According to information supplied to the author by the Department of Justice, as of May 2, 1956, the number of persons indicted for conspiracy under the Smith Act was 131. Of these, 98 were convicted. Only 9 defendants were acquitted—6 by juries and 3 by courts. With respect to an additional defendant, the jury could reach no verdict.

3. There are many Federal Government publications that give the essential organizational and historical facts regarding the Communist Party. We name here only a few: *Organized Communism in the United States,* 83rd Cong., 2d sess., House Report 1694 (1953); Subversive Activities Control Board, *Report of the Board, Brownell v. Communist Party* (1953); *The Communist Party of the United States of America: What It Is—How It Works: A Handbook for Americans,* 84th Cong., 1st sess. (1955); *Com-*

*munism in Action,* 79th Cong., 2d sess., House Document 754 (1946); *100 Things You Should Know about Communism,* 82d Cong., 1st sess., House Doc. 136 (1951).

4. See *Organized Communism in the United States,* 119.

5. Dennis v. U.S., 183 F. 2d 201 (1950). Judge Medina's charge is reported at 9 FRD 365 (1949). The sentence was five years imprisonment and $10,000 fine for each defendant except Robert G. Thompson, who was sentenced for a term of three years and fined $10,000.

6. The defendants raised other questions on appeal. They challenged the array of the jury, and raised points as to the conduct of the trial. Since these points do not touch on the First Amendment, they are not considered here.

7. See Brief for the United States in the *Dennis* case, submitted to U.S. court of appeals, especially pp. 224–226, 241. Judge Chase, in his concurring opinion in the court of appeals, substantially adopted the views of the prosecution.

8. See Brief for Appellants in the *Dennis* case, submitted to the U.S. court of appeals, especially pp. 21–22, 25, 57–58, 69, 83.

9. The convictions were affirmed by a 6-to-2 vote. Justice Clark did not participate. Justices Black and Douglas dissented. Justices Frankfurter and Jackson wrote concurring opinions.

10. Frankfurter quoted this passage from Freund, *On Understanding the Supreme Court,* 27, 28.

11. Minersville School Dist. v. Gobitis, 310 US 586 (1940).

12. W. Va. Bd. of Education v. Barnette, 319 US 624 (1943).

13. *Ibid.*

14. See U.S. v. Rabinowitz, 339 US 56 (1950).

15. See Bridges v. Calif., 314 US 252 (1941).

16. Frankfurter's dis. op. in *Barnette* case.

17. Of course I do not mean that the Government could or should have been indifferent to the acts of Communists in the United States. I am not discussing normal procedures against acts of sabotage, espionage, and similar offenses. If existing laws were insufficient, new laws could have been enacted, and some in fact were. See *Internal Security Manual,* 84th Cong., 1st sess., Doc. No. 40, rev. ed. (1955). My discussion here is limited to the problem of the Smith Act conspiracy prosecutions and their relation to the clear and present danger doctrine.

18. See John R. Commons *et al., History of Labour in the United States* (New York, 1918), I, ch. v; Sidney and Beatrice Webb, *The History of Trade Unionism* (new ed.; London, 1920), ch. ii.

19. It should be noted that Jackson was not quite clear on this point. His language is ambiguous, to say the least. He said: "The highest degree of constitutional protection is due to the individual acting without conspiracy. But even an individual cannot claim that the Constitution protects him in advocating or teaching overthrow of government by force or

violence. . . . I think direct incitement by speech or writing can be made a crime, and I think there can be a conviction without also proving that the odds favored its success by 99 to 1, or some other extremely high ratio." This falls far short of precise language. Yet when the opinion is read in its entirety it is clear that Jackson reasoned as follows (see especially 341 US at 575): (1) The Government may punish force or violence. (2) It may punish the teaching or advocacy of the use of force or violence. (3) It may punish conspiracy to teach or advocate use of force or violence. In none of these instances, according to Jackson, is the clear and present danger test relevant.

20. Judge Chase expressly adopted *Gitlow* as binding; Justice Jackson did this only by implication.

## Chapter 28. The Loss of a Constitutional Jewel?

1. Sidney Hook, *Heresy, Yes—Conspiracy, No* (New York, 1953), ch. v. Italics supplied.

2. In 1941 the act was successfully used to convict 18 members of the Socialist Workers Party—a Trotskyist organization that certainly had no relations with Moscow, that could not be suspected of a willingness to commit espionage on behalf of the U.S.S.R., and that had no capacity to harm the United States. The court of appeals, relying on the *Gitlow* case, affirmed the convictions, and the Supreme Court denied certiorari (Dunne v. U.S., 138 F. 2d 137 [1943]; cert. den. 320 US 790 [1943]). See also U.S. v. McWilliams, 163 F. 2d 695 (1947). The prosecution of the Trotskyists, Professor Hook rightly has said, was "not merely foolish, but scandalous." While the Trotskyists, more belligerently than the Communists, taught the necessity and desirability of overthrowing the Government, and so fitted even more literally the proscriptions of the Smith Act, it was only the Communists who were foreign agents, and so fitted much more closely the underlying purpose of the Smith Act. Thus the act was misapplied in each instance but for different reasons!

3. See note 17, ch. xxvii, *supra.*

4. See note 2, ch. xxvii, *supra.* At this rate it would take close to 200 years to convict all party members! See note 5.

5. According to the F.B.I., there were 22,663 party members in the United States in 1955. In 1951 there were 31,608. *The Communist Party of the United States of America—What It Is*, 34–35.

6. The maximum penalty under the Smith Act is imprisonment for ten years or a fine of $10,000, or both (18 USC 2385).

7. Communist Control Act of 1954, Pub. L. No. 637, 83rd Cong., 2d sess.

8. See note 5 *supra.*

9. Internal Security Act of 1950, 50 USC 781 (1952).

10. See note 7 *supra.* See Note, 64 *Yale L. J.* 712 (1955).

11. *The Smith Act and the Supreme Court* (A.C.L.U., 1952), 5.

12. See Alexander Meikeljohn, *Free Speech and Its Relation to Self-Government* (New York, 1948), 52–56.

13. Cf. T. B. Macaulay, essay on Hallam, *Edinburgh Rev.*, Sept. 1828.

14. De Jonge v. Oregon, 299 US 353 (1937).

## Appendix: Adoption of the Bill of Rights

1. The relevant parts of this letter are in Adrienne Koch and William Peden, eds., *The Life and Selected Writings of Thomas Jefferson* (New York, 1944), 436.

2. Letter of Nov. 10, 1787, quoted by Dumas Malone, *Jefferson and the Rights of Man* (Boston, 1951), 165.

3. *Ibid.*, 168–169.

4. Saul K. Padover, *The Complete Madison: His Basic Writings* (New York, 1953), 306.

5. *Ibid.*, 253. See Edmond Cahn, "The Firstness of the First Amendment," 65 *Yale L. J.* 464 (1956).

6. *The Debates and Proceedings in the Congress of the United States . . .*, comp. Joseph Gales (Washington, 1834), I, 257. This work is generally referred to as the *Annals of Congress*. This short title will be used hereafter, and the references will be to Vol. I.

7. On the adoption of the Constitution, see Charles Warren, *The Making of the Constitution* (Boston, 1928); George Bancroft, *History of the Formation of the Constitution of the United States* (New York, 1882); Andrew C. McLaughlin, *A Constitutional History of the United States* (New York, 1935), ch. xv; Carl Brent Swisher, *American Constitutional Development* (Boston, 1943), ch. ii. See also Zechariah Chafee, Jr., *How Human Rights Got into the Constitution* (Boston, 1952). For sources, see Jonathan Elliot, ed., *Debates in the Several State Conventions on the Adoption of the Federal Constitution . . .* (5 vols.; Washington, 1836–1845). For debates in the Constitutional Convention of 1787, the source is Max Farrand, ed., *The Records of the Federal of 1787* (3 vols., New Haven, 1911; rev. ed., 4 vols., 1937). See also Robert Allen Rutland, *The Birth of the Bill of Rights* (Chapel Hill, 1955).

8. H. V. Ames, *Proposed Amendments to the Constitution* (Amer. Historical Assn., Report for 1896, vol. II).

9. See *Annals of Congress*, 451–453, for text of Madison's proposals. Technically he offered nine amendments, but the ninth was of a purely formal nature. Not all amendments proposed by the states related to a bill of rights. We omit from the text Madison's amendments that were not concerned with fundamental freedoms.

North Carolina did not ratify the Constitution until Nov. 21, 1789, and Rhode Island not until May 29, 1790. In urging action on a bill of rights, Madison referred to these two states and said that he had no doubt that if Congress were to act favorably on the amendments, "re-union" would take place (*ibid.*, 449).

10. *Ibid.,* 453–459, for Madison's statement to the House of Representatives on June 8, 1789, of which the text is a summary. In his argument that judges would be vigilant to keep the Constitution from being whittled down by the other branches of government, Madison anticipated Marbury v. Madison, 1 Cr. 187 (1803), and the position of Justices Murphy, Rutledge, Black, and Douglas.

11. See McLaughlin, 272–280, 435, 439, 450–451.

12. Dis. op. in W. Va. State Bd. of Education v. Barnette, 319 US 624 (1943).

13. Cf. the examination of James Wechsler, editor of the New York *Post,* by Senator Joseph R. McCarthy, and the views of the special committee of the American Society of Newspaper Editors regarding this matter (*New York Times,* Aug. 12, 1953). See editorial in *Christian Science Monitor,* Aug. 14, 1953, on this matter.

14. *Annals of Congress,* 685–691. In the list of committee members, the name of Vining appears at the head, but without designation as chairman.

15. It should be noted that the term "Bill of Rights" does not appear in the Constitution or any of its amendments; but in the discussion there were frequent references to a bill of rights or a declaration of rights. The appearance of the amendments together in one place, rather than in scattered provisions throughout the Constitution, made it easy to refer to them as a single document under the designation "Bill of Rights." This came about, as we shall see, despite Madison's wishes. See Cahn.

16. The House, as a committee of the whole, debated the amendments on April 13, 14, 15, 17, and 18. It made the following changes in the proposed amendments as set forth in the text: (a) In no. 1 above, the clause was changed to read as follows: "Congress shall make no laws touching religion, or infringing the rights of conscience." (b) In no. 5 above, the guaranty against self-incrimination was limited to criminal cases. (c) In no. 7 above, the language was changed to read: "the right of the people to be secure in their persons, houses, papers, and effects, against unreasonable seizures and searches." (d) In no. 9 above, the language was changed to read: "the equal rights of conscience, the freedom of speech or of the press, and the right of trial by jury in criminal cases, shall not be infringed by any state." (e) In no. 10 above, the clause was changed so as to secure to the defendant the right to be tried in the state where the offense was committed. (f) In no. 14 above, the powers not delegated by the Constitution nor prohibited by it to the states were reserved to the states respectively "or to the people."

17. The changes were as follows: (a) On the motion of Fisher Ames, the religious freedom amendment—no. 1 above—was changed to read as follows: "Congress shall make no law establishing religion, or to prevent the free exercise thereof, or to infringe the rights of conscience." (b) The clause in no. 3 above respecting the exemption of pacifists was changed to read as follows: "but no person religiously scrupulous shall be compelled

to bear arms in person." The intention of the change was to throw upon the pacifist the burden of supplying or paying for a substitute. (c) The last proposition, no. 14 above, was made to read as follows: "The powers not delegated to the United States by the Constitution, nor prohibited by it to the States, are reserved to the States respectively, or to the people."

18. *Journal of the First Session of the Senate of the United States* (New York, 1789), 103–106, 163–164.

It should be noted that the sources are not always in agreement on the wording of the drafts approved by a committee or by a branch of Congress. Cf. *The Journal of the House of Representatives* (Washington, 1826), I, 85. We have done the best we could to reconstruct in the text and notes the official actions without taking the reader into the scholar's underbrush.

19. For example: Article 7 of the Declaration provided that no one "shall be accused, arrested, or imprisoned, save in the cases determined by law, and according to the forms which it has prescribed." Article 8 provided that "no one ought to be punished but by virtue of a law promulgated before the offence." Article 9 provided that a person shall be "counted innocent until he has been convicted." Articles 10 and 11 guaranteed freedom of opinion, speech, and press.

20. Notably the Virginia Bill of Rights, 1776, drafted mainly by George Mason. Among its provisions were the following: no person can be compelled to give evidence against himself; in all criminal prosecutions, the accused has the right to demand the nature of the accusations and to be confronted with the accusers and witnesses, and to a speedy trial by an impartial jury; that excessive bail ought not to be required, nor excessive fines imposed, nor cruel and unusual punishments inflicted; freedom of the press is not to be restrained; all men are entitled to the free exercise of religion, according to the dictates of conscience. The Massachusetts Bill of Rights, drafted largely by John Adams, was adopted in 1780. The Virginia Statute for Establishing Religious Freedom, drafted by Jefferson, was adopted in 1786. For the texts of these documents, see Henry Steele Commager, *Documents of American History* (New York, 1934), I. See also Rutland.

☆☆☆☆☆

# Table of Cases

☆☆☆☆☆

# Index